RISK
RESILIENCE
&
PREVENTION

This book is printed on recycled paper.

RISK RESILIENCE & PREVENTION

Promoting the *Well-Being* of All Children

edited by

Rune J. Simeonsson, Ph.D., M.S.P.H.

Professor of Education
and
Research Professor of Psychology
University of North Carolina
Chapel Hill
and
Adjunct Professor of Medical Psychology
Duke University Medical Center
Durham, North Carolina

Baltimore • London • Toronto • Sydney

Paul H. Brookes Publishing Co.
P.O. Box 10624
Baltimore, Maryland 21285-0624

Copyright © 1994 by Paul H. Brookes Publishing Co., Inc.
All rights reserved.

Typeset by Brushwood Graphics, Inc., Baltimore, Maryland.
Manufactured in the United States of America by
The Maple Press Company, York, Pennsylvania.

Library of Congress Cataloging-in-Publication Data
Risk, resilience, and prevention: promoting the well-being of all
  children/edited by Rune J. Simeonsson.
    p.   cm.
Includes bibliographical references and index.
ISBN 1-55766-166-9
  1. Child welfare—United States. 2. Children—Services for—
United States. 3. Children—Health and hygiene—United States.
I. Simeonsson, Rune J.
HV741.R58 1994
362.7' 0973—dc20   94-8828
                                                                  CIP

British Library Cataloging-in-Publication data are available from the
British Library.

Contents

Contributors vii
Foreword   *C. Arden Miller, M.D.* ix
Preface xi
Acknowledgments xiii

I   OVERVIEW AND DEFINING ISSUES 1
    1 Promoting Children's Health, Education, and Well-Being
       Rune J. Simeonsson 3
    2 Toward an Epidemiology of Developmental, Educational,
       and Social Problems of Childhood
       Rune J. Simeonsson 13
    3 Primary Prevention: The Missing Piece in Child
       Development Legislation
       Robert W. Chamberlin 33
    4 Maternal and Child Health: A Collaborative Agenda
       for Prevention
       Bonnie Strickland and Merle McPherson 53

II PRIMARY PREVENTION CONCERNS 75
    5 Healthy Children: Primary Prevention of Disease
       Nancy W. Simeonsson and Judith N. Gray 77
    6 Preventing School Failure and Dropout
       Sharon Carnahan 103
    7 Adolescent Pregnancy
       Tina M. Smith 125
    8 Drug Use and Pregnancy
       Rebecca Edmondson 151
    9 Child Abuse: A Prevention Agenda
       *Gail S. Huntington, Lorraine Lima,
       and Irene Nathan Zipper* 169
    10 Preventing Injury in Children and Adolescents
       *Joseph E. Zins, Victor F. Garcia,
       Barbara S. Tuchfarber, Kathryn M. Clark,
       and Susan C. Laurence* 183
    11 Externalizing Behavior Disorders
       Rick Jay Short and Richard Brokaw 203
    12 Internalizing Affective Disorders
       Jayne E. Bucy 219

13 Sexually Transmitted Diseases: A Paradigm for
   Risk Taking Among Teens
   *Susan L. Rosenthal, Sheila S. Cohen,
   and Frank M. Biro* 239
14 Promoting Literacy Development
   Dixie Lee Spiegel. 265

III IMPLICATIONS 297
15 Policy and Practice: Implications of a
   Primary Prevention Agenda
   Rune J. Simeonsson and Melva Covington 299
16 Promoting Children's Well-Being
   Rune J. Simeonsson and Daphne Thomas 321

Index 345

Contributors

Frank M. Biro, M.D., Associate Professor, Pediatrics and Internal Medicine, University of Cincinnati College of Medicine, and Associate Director, Research, Division of Adolescent Medicine, Children's Hospital Medical Center, 3333 Burnet Avenue, Cincinnati, OH 45229-3039

Richard Brokaw, M.Ed., Doctoral Candidate in School Psychology, The Pennsylvania State University, 227 CEDAR Building, University Park, PA 16802

Jayne E. Bucy, M.A., Doctoral Candidate in School of Psychology, Frank Porter Graham Child Development Center, University of North Carolina at Chapel Hill, CB #8180, Chapel Hill, NC 27599-8180

Sharon Carnahan, Ph.D., Assistant Professor of Psychology, and Director, Child Development Center, Rollins College, 1000 Holt Avenue-2760, Winter Park, FL 32789-4499

Robert W. Chamberlin, M.D., M.P.H., Consultant, Maternal and Child Health, Adjunct Professor, School of Health and Human Services, University of New Hampshire, and Adjunct Professor, Dartmouth Medical School, P.O. Box 12, Canterbury, NH 03224

Kathryn M. Clark, B.S., Injury Prevention Program Administrator, University of Cincinnati Children's Hospital Medical Center, 3333 Burnet Avenue, Cincinnati, OH 45229-3039

Sheila S. Cohen, Ph.D., Research Coordinator, Division of Adolescent Medicine, University of Cincinnati Children's Hospital Medical Center, 3333 Burnet Avenue, Cincinnati, OH 45229-3039

Melva Covington, M.P.H., Doctoral Candidate in Special Education, School of Education, University of North Carolina at Chapel Hill, CB #3500, Chapel Hill, NC 27599-3500

Rebecca Edmondson, Ph.D., Assistant Clinical Professor of Psychiatry, Clinical Center for Development and Learning, University of North Carolina at Chapel Hill, CB #7255, BSRC 220H, Chapel Hill, NC 27599-7255

Victor F. Garcia, M.D., Director of Trauma Service, and Associate Professor of Pediatric Surgery, University of Cincinnati Children's Hospital Medical Center, 3333 Burnet Avenue, Cincinnati, OH 45229-3039

Judith N. Gray, R.N., M.S., P.N.P., S.N.P., C.S., Pediatric and School Nurse Practitioner, Coordinator of Medical Health Services, South Metropolitan Association, 800 Governor's Highway, Flossmoor, IL 60422

Gail S. Huntington, Ph.D., Fellow, Frank Porter Graham Child Development Center, University of North Carolina at Chapel Hill, Chapel Hill, NC 27514

Susan C. Laurence, Injury Prevention Coordinator, University of Cincinnati Children's Hospital Medical Center, 3333 Burnet Avenue, Cincinnati, OH 45229-3039

Lorraine Lima, M.S.W., Program Director, Bienvenidos Family Services, 5233 East Beverly Boulevard, Los Angeles, CA 90022

Merle McPherson, M.D., Director, Division for Children with Special Health Care Needs, U.S. Department of Health and Human Services, Maternal and Child Health, Parklawn Building, 5600 Fisher's Lane, Rockville, MD 20857

Susan L. Rosenthal, Ph.D., Associate Professor of Pediatrics, University of Cincinnati College of Medicine, and Director of Psychology, Division of Adolescent Medicine, University of Cincinnati Children's Hospital Medical Center, 3333 Burnet Avenue, Cincinnati, OH 45229-3039

Rick Jay Short, Ph.D., Assistant Executive Director for Education, American Psychological Association, 750 First Street, NE, Washington, DC 20002-4242

Nancy W. Simeonsson, R.N., M.A., P.N.P., S.N.P., C.S., Pediatric and School Nurse Practitioner, Frank Porter Graham Child Development Center, University of North Carolina at Chapel Hill, CB #8180, Chapel Hill, NC 27599-8180

Rune J. Simeonsson, Ph.D., M.S.P.H., Professor of Education, and Research Professor of Psychology, University of North Carolina at Chapel Hill, and Adjunct Professor of Medical Psychology, Duke University Medical Center, Durham, North Carolina, CB #3500, Chapel Hill, NC 27599-3500

Tina M. Smith, Ph.D., Postdoctoral Fellow in Pediatric Psychology, Clinical Center for Development and Learning, University of North Carolina at Chapel Hill, CB #7255, Chapel Hill, NC 27599-7255

Dixie Lee Spiegel, Ph.D., Associate Dean for Students, School of Education, University of North Carolina at Chapel Hill, CB #3500, Chapel Hill, NC 27599-3500

Bonnie Strickland, Ph.D., Public Health Analyst, U.S. Department of Health and Human Services, Maternal and Child Health, Parklawn Building, Room 18A-20, 5600 Fisher's Lane, Rockville, MD 20857

Daphne Thomas, Ph.D., Assistant Professor, Special Education Department, School of Education, University of South Florida, Tampa, FL 33620

Barbara S. Tuchfarber, R.N., B.A., M.S., Epidemiologist, Trauma Service, University of Cincinnati Children's Hospital Medical Center, 3333 Burnet Avenue, Cincinnati, OH 45229-3039

Joseph E. Zins, Ed.D., Professor of Education, University of Cincinnati, 339 Teachers College, Cincinnati, OH 45221-0002

Irene Nathan Zipper, M.S.W., Doctoral Candidate in Special Education, and Instructor, School of Social Work, University of North Carolina at Chapel Hill, CB #3550, Chapel Hill, NC 27599-3550

Foreword

Health policy in the United States seems driven by a system recognizing only health problems that can be resolved by elaborations on medical care. As a consequence, major medical centers and hospitals of all sizes behave like profiteering corporations, while a burgeoning insurance industry regards shareholders rather than policy holders as clients of greatest concern. In this context, the rare child with a serious medical problem is likely to receive expert attention. The many children who would benefit from routine preventive services and health promotional supports of another kind receive uncertain care.

Currently debated health-care reforms address these problems by defining age-specific benefits as entitlements to be fulfilled by managed care plans. The entitlements for children are extensive and well defined, incorporating usual approaches to medically comprehensive care. The provider structures for fulfilling the entitlements are less reassuring. Even the most highly regarded managed care plans admit to substantial failure to assure full participation of enrollees in such basic preventive measures as immunization of young children. It is fair to regard early childhood immunization not only as protection against contagious disease, but also as a proxy measure for participation in other preventive practices for which data are not available. They include developmental assessment, perceptual screenings, and anticipatory guidance on injury prevention. The presumption is defensible that where immunization rates of young children are low, participatory rates in these procedures are also deficient.

Three policy issues are involved: 1) a priority for children, 2) the meaning of comprehensive care, and 3) the realities of access. These issues must be addressed by meaningful proposals to promote children's health.

A currently prevailing policy theme centers on universal care, which implies that if everyone is served, of course children will be served, too. Experience belies that optimism. A separate and identifiable priority is required for children, or they get pushed to the end of the medical queue. Experience with Medicaid is instructive. Available funds became increasingly committed to domiciliary care for the elderly, while only a small proportion of eligible children was reached by a program that mandated early diagnosis and treatment of health problems. Nations with the best records of child health have not only established universal programs of financing and access to medical care, but also have maintained separate identifiable community programs of preventive care for maternal and child health.

The meaning of comprehensive health care deserves new attention. It has come to mean a continuum of all care within the medical domain—from entry into the system to death, from the newborn nursery to the intensive care unit and beyond. The continuum fails to embrace many of the health services required by children. Bierman's longitudinal studies on the health of children on Kauai (Werner, Bierman, & French, 1971) are instructive in this regard. In the first 2 years of life, only 6.3% of children required medical or nursing services beyond routine well-child care. By age 10 years, 21% of children were in need of long-term help, and 18%, of short-term help. More than five times as many children required special educational services (39%) as those who required special medical care. The greatest need was for long-term educational or mental health services or both. Clearly, for these children, comprehensive care, more than providing strong linkage within the medical care system, means strong linkage involving education, mental health, and social support services, most of which exist outside the domain and expertise of medical providers.

The third policy issue has to do with the realities of access. As medical care becomes increasingly corporatized, its provider sites become more daunting. One major children's hospital, a likely candidate for sponsoring managed care, boasts 125 different specialty clinics. They are a welcome recourse for children who need them. Such a site represents an expensive, chaotic, and threatening atmosphere for other children who require routine well-child care linked to a different set of specialty services and supports.

Risk, Resilience, and Prevention by Simeonsson and colleagues addresses these issues in a fresh and constructive way. A prevention agenda is developed in ways that establish a priority for children and their families, utilizing perspectives that are appropriately comprehensive and interdisciplinary. Best of all, the programs are proposed to be school oriented and community based. The services go where the children are, in surroundings and with people familiar to them. The necessary medical components can be maintained by such a system, as has been demonstrated by Head Start and by experience with school-based clinics both here and in other countries. No matter what shape health care reform may take in the immediate future, revisions and improvements will be required for an extended time. *Risk, Resilience, and Prevention* provides models that must be considered in that negotiating process.

REFERENCE

Werner, E.E., Bierman, J.M., & French, F.E. (1971). *The children of Kauai. A longitudinal study from the prenatal period to age 10.* Honolulu: University of Hawaii Press.

C. Arden Miller, M.D.
Professor of Maternal and Child Health
School of Public Health
University of North Carolina at Chapel Hill

Preface

The Decade of the Brain, the Human Genome Project, and the Information Highway symbolize the best intents and achievements of our times and visions for the future. Alienation, mistrust, violence, and unrealized potential symbolize the failures of our times and, particularly for our children, diminished hopes for the future. As we note in Chapter 1, it is the best of times and the worst of times. With an ever-expanding knowledge base and incredible tools of technology at our disposal, the health, education, and well-being of children should be better than ever before. However, for far too many children, statistical trends tell us that this is not true. Overburdened and inadequately coordinated service systems are finding it difficult to address the increasingly complex needs these statistics represent.

The premise of this volume is that there must be a paradigmatic change of emphasis from treatment to prevention to reverse these trends. In such a paradigm, the prevention of children's problems is seen as complementary to promoting their well-being. This is an essential distinction in that the prevailing intervention focus in this society has been to objectify and technicalize children's problems. Illustrative of this focus are national goals for children to acquire competencies, use technology, and gain access to information. While these are not unimportant, they do not adequately recognize the subjective side of well-being. Thus, a prevention agenda for children is needed in which building character is as important as building competence, where developing trust is as important as developing skills with technology, and where learning to communicate is as important as acquiring information. In essence, it would be timely and right for this nation to advance an agenda for Children's Well-Being in a scope and manner equivalent to that of the Information Highway and the Human Genome Project initiatives.

It is the goal of the volume to elaborate this agenda across major problems manifested by children in today's society with the hope that their incidence and prevalence can be reduced in tomorrow's society. The problems, while representative, by no means constitute all aspects of the many pressing issues concerning children's health, education, and well-being. We also cannot claim that the preventive approaches that are advanced are exhaustive, although we can be confident that they encompass exemplary efforts. The focus of this volume is interdisciplinary in nature, as are the complex problems addressed. It is therefore written for interdisciplinary audiences, those engaged in the interface of services for children. In addition to the health field, of particular priority are the disciplines of psychology, education, and clinical therapies for which primary prevention may be a relatively new strategy. To this end, the book is divided into three sections, with the first section providing a framework and overview of prevention issues. In the second section, representative problems of children's health, education, and behavior are defined in separate chapters, and approaches to primary prevention and promotion are described. The two chapters in the last section provide a synthesis of themes and issues and the identification of implications for practice, policy, training, and research.

*Train up a child in the way he should go
and when he is old he will not depart from it.*
Proverbs 22:6

Acknowledgments

The preparation of any book is a joint effort, and this volume is no exception. I am in debt to each of my colleagues who contributed so richly as authors or coauthors to provide depth of coverage. Also of tremendous help were staff in the School of Education and the Frank Porter Graham Child Development Center at the University of North Carolina at Chapel Hill, providing both technical support and encouragement. The enthusiastic support of Melissa Behm and Victoria Thulman of Paul H. Brookes Publishing Co. from the very beginning of this project has been most welcome. I particularly want to express my appreciation to Sue Vaupel for her considerate, patient, and thorough handling of the production of the manuscript. There are, of course, many colleagues and students whose encouragement I have valued as well. Finally, as families have been a central focus of this volume, so has my family been central to the completion of this effort. They know my enduring appreciation and affection.

To the futures of Nicole, Samuel,
Hannah, Daniel, Jordan, and children
of the coming generations everywhere

RISK
RESILIENCE
&
PREVENTION

I

OVERVIEW AND DEFINING ISSUES

P*rimary prevention, risk factors, vulnerability, resilience, protective factors—* these are terms heard with increasing frequency. Their increased use is a testimony to the fact that the major institutions in our society— health, schools, and human services—are unable to meet ever-growing treatment, care, remediation, and rehabilitation demands. Prevention is seen as the logical and necessary strategy to stem the demand of manifested physical, social, and psychological problems. To that end, there are calls for health reform, school reform, welfare reform, and reform of related human services systems at local, state, and national levels.

The urgency of a prevention agenda in general is mirrored for the problems of children. This urgency has been endorsed by the last three occupants of the Surgeon General's office, each of whom has elevated children's concerns as national priorities. The timeliness of a comprehensive prevention agenda is evident for a number of reasons, first and foremost because of the epidemic proportions with which children's problems are manifested. There are also, however, positive reasons for the timeliness of an agenda to prevent such problems. Among these are a recognition of the value of interdisciplinary efforts, the emergence of inclusive conceptual models, and the research methods and analytic tools to test those models. Finally, it is appropriate to recognize the inherent value of promoting children's well-being as a priority in its own right.

Major disciplines, notably public health, have consistently advocated for primary prevention of children's problems. Other social and behavioral disciplines, including education, have not been as proactive in this regard. Recognizing that childhood and youth constitute a defined developmental phase, and that the problems in this period are often interactive, contributing to vicious cycles of cumulative risk, it is essential that a comprehensive prevention agenda builds on an alliance of education, health, and social agencies in our communities.

This book advances such an alliance, documenting the need for primary prevention of representative childhood problems. To that end, we begin with a section defining the issues and developing a rationale for an epidemiological approach to a prevention agenda. In the second section, a review is made of 12 selected high-frequency problem areas encompassing children's health, behavior, education, and physical and psychological fitness. The last section concludes with a synthesis of issues and the identification of implications for professional training, for practice, for policy, and for research.

1

Promoting Children's Health, Education, and Well-Being

Rune J. Simeonsson

It was the best of times, it was the worst of times, it was the age of wisdom, it was the age of foolishness, it was the epoch of belief, it was the age of incredulity, . . . it was the spring of hope, it was the winter of despair, we had everything before us, we had nothing before us. . . .
Dickens, A *Tale of Two Cities*

Three million crimes a year are committed in or near schools.
Ruby, 1993

Every 5 seconds of the school day, a student drops out of public school.

Every year, 2,695,010 children are reported abused or neglected.

Every 4 hours, a child commits suicide.

Every 59 seconds, a baby is born to a teen mother.

Every 7 minutes, a child is arrested for a drug crime.

Every 4 minutes, a child is arrested for an alcohol-related crime.

Every 30 seconds, a baby is born into poverty.

Every 2 hours, a child is murdered.
Children's Defense Fund, 1994

A century later and an ocean away, daily news reports reconfirm the irony of Dickens's paradoxical statement—it is the best of times and the worst of times. As in Dickens's day, children are among those most affected. The resources, opportunities, and individual freedoms found in the United States have often been seen as prototypes for the Western world. It is an exciting time of skyrocketing technology with the prospects of information highways, virtual reality, and interactive systems bringing distant experiences within everyone's reach. Children and adults are exposed as never before to the output of the electronic media in the form of entertainment, music, advertising, and news. Advanced health care and technology, and the provision of universal education and protective and entitling laws in society would support the assumption that all children will grow up enjoying good health, will receive an appropriate education, and will experience well-being.

Sadly, as we know too well, this is not the reality. The statistics cited above seem inconsistent with what should be the best of times. More than one third of children in America do not enjoy good health, one fourth are raised in poverty, and an alarming number are inadequately educated and experience social and psychological distress. In the midst of plenty and progress, children in the United States are being robbed of childhood and its joys: the joy of learning, the joy of trust, and the joy of innocence. For too many, life itself is the victim, with almost 50,000 children and youth dying violent deaths in the decade between 1979 and 1991. These statistics are documented in our scientific literature, with trends indicating that childhood problems, disorders, and maladjustments are increasing at an alarming rate.

Such statistics raise significant questions and challenges for which no immediate answers are evident. What is the scope of childhood problems these statistics imply? What demands do they place on current services for children and youth? What are the projections for services needed in the future? What kinds of approaches are needed to meet the growing demand for services? It is clear that the scope of problems is extensive, spanning the range from mild to extreme expressions and encompassing the acute problems of intentional injury and violence and the endemic problems of school failure and delinquency. It is also clear that current services are unable to address the full extent of the problems and disorders of children and youth. What are the projections for meeting the needs of these children in the future? Each of the major institutions of society serving children—the fields of health, education, and social services—have identified similar projections. These projections indicate that the demand will outstrip available resources by significant ratios in the foreseeable future. If trends continue without interruption, it is not unreasonable to estimate that 25%–50% of children in the United States will require services to address health, educational, and social problems.

Given this scenario, what options should be pursued to prevent the trend of increased physical, educational, social, and behavioral problems of children? More importantly, what programs are needed to promote the development of children and youth? Simply continuing to acknowledge the problems while failing to address them through actions is an unacceptable societal response. Although commendable efforts continue to be made in response to demands for treatment and intervention services, the gap between demand and supply will continue to grow. Furthermore, continued attempts to match services to increasing demands, even if it is seen as an affordable option, perpetuates an inadequate solution. It is inadequate in that it fails to prevent problems in the first place. Not only is such a solution more costly to society, but more to the point, it fails to capitalize on developmental momentum to promote children's health achievement and well-being.

Few would deny the reality of the fact that a significant number of children in the United States today are "in peril" for illness, injury, and compromised development (Martin, 1992). This state of peril is documented by the overall grade of C− on the 1993 Child Health Report Card, which provides a summary of health indicators for children (Wynder, 1994). Few also would deny the value of a preventive approach. However, the recognition of its urgency, the development of a comprehensive plan, and the commitment of resources lack a national mandate. On the positive side, there are many successful individual efforts and model projects with demonstrated efficacy. More importantly, there appears to be a growing awareness of the critical need for prevention programs in the national debate on health and medical care. It also appears promising that such awareness will be followed by consensus and political and social action.

The prevention challenge faced by the major social institutions serving children in this country is to address the increasing number of children and youth at risk for significant physical, developmental, educational, and social problems. At-risk status is not simply a concept that applies to problems of infancy and early childhood. It encompasses all developmental phases from the fetal period (drug exposure) and early childhood (learning problems) to the problems of delinquency, teen pregnancy, and school failure in adolescence. As the research base develops in the health and social sciences, the nature and significance of risk factors are beginning to emerge. It is clear that the contributory role of risk factors is often cumulative as well as synergistic in nature, resulting in "vicious circles" as elaborated by Chamberlin in Chapter 3 of this volume. In these vicious circles or cycles, the status of risk is elevated and repeated within the development of one individual and often perpetuated across generations, resulting in familial patterns of increased risk.

The limited capacity of intervention and treatment services alone to address the growing numbers of children with identified problems as well as those at risk has been recognized in national policy priorities in health, education, and rehabilitation. In the area of health, *Healthy People 2000: National Health Promotion and Disease Prevention Objectives* (1991) has defined a comprehensive preventive framework for the U.S. people, including specific priorities for children and youth. Among these priorities are prescribed goals for preschool child development programs and high-quality in-school health education programs. Reflecting a recognition of the vicious cycle of risk and compromised outcomes, priorities have been set for such representative needs as primary care provision for infants, reduction of drug abuse, and reduction of teenage pregnancy.

Paralleling the objectives for healthy children is *America 2000: An Education Strategy* (1991), a set of national educational goals developed by state governors and the U.S. Department of Education to promote the academic achievement of children. A major goal is the promotion of school readiness, emphasizing that all children should enter school ready to learn and to master academic skills and content. Another goal of a preventive nature pertains to ensuring adequate environments for learning, for example, schools that are free of drugs. Complementary goals seek to prevent school failure and drop out and increasing high school graduation rates. Although the title is *America 2000*, this policy statement could alternately be labeled *Healthy Schools*.

Another policy document with recommendations for the addition of a prevention agenda is that produced by the Institute of Medicine (Institute of Medicine, 1991) on priorities in disability and rehabilitation. In this arena as well, the increasing scope of needs associated with acquired and developmental disabilities has resulted in a call for comprehensive prevention paradigms.

The federally sponsored initiatives of *America 2000* (1991) and *Healthy People 2000* (1991) reflect the theme of setting prevention agendas for the 21st century. This theme is also evident in parallel initiatives undertaken by the American Public Health Association in the *Healthy Communities 2000* and the *Healthy Cities* program advanced by the World Health Organization (Flynn, 1992).

A PRIMARY PREVENTION AGENDA

The recognition of prevention goals and priorities calls for the enactment of a prevention agenda to promote the health, education, and well-being of children and youth. Such a prevention agenda should contribute to the realization of broad societal goals to: 1) promote the development of children; 2) reduce the need for diagnostic, curative, and therapeutic services; and 3) reduce the need for rehabilitative, corrective, remedial, and other intensive programs.

This conceptualization of societal goals is consistent with the formulation of levels of prevention advanced by Caplan and Grunebaum

(1967) differentiating primary, secondary, and tertiary levels of prevention. Within this approach, the focus of primary prevention is to reduce the incidence, that is, the number of new cases, of an identified problem or condition. In a complementary manner, it can be defined as the primary promotion of health, development, and adaptation. In secondary prevention, the focus is on reducing the number of existing cases and lowering the prevalence of the manifested problems or condition in the population. From the standpoint of promotion, emphasis is placed on the acquisition of compensatory skills and behaviors. The premise of tertiary prevention is to reduce the expression of sequelae and complications of the diagnosed or identified condition. Programs and services of this nature are likely to have a rehabilitative and remedial focus.

ASSUMPTIONS FOR PRIMARY PREVENTION AND PROMOTION

What are the assumptions on which to base a primary prevention agenda to address the physical, educational, and social problems of children and youth? Building on the definition presented in the previous paragraph, primary prevention and primary promotion are proposed as complementary processes. As shown in Figure 1.1, any activity or service that promotes a child's development, adaptation, or functioning has the reciprocal benefit of preventing maladaptation, delay, or disorder. This reciprocity of benefits is recognized in the health field where there is growing use of the complementary concepts of disease prevention and health promotion (Stachtchenko & Jenicek, 1990). Furthermore, this recognition has contributed to the growth of wellness programs, a concept encompassing proactive, preventive behaviors

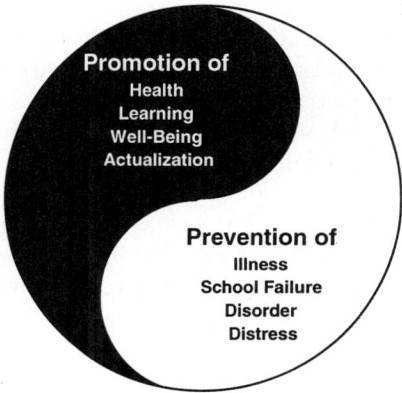

Figure 1.1. Complementary nature of primary promotion and prevention efforts in child development.

conducive to health and well-being (Schaaf & Davis, 1992). A complementary dimension in this regard is the reciprocity of major societal agencies as reflected in a proposal developed by Novello, DeGraw, and Klienman (1992) linking parallel national goals in public health and education.

A second major assumption underlying a primary prevention agenda is that the manifestation of the problem or condition of interest is preventable. In this book, we focus on a number of representative problems of childhood that are preventable in the population at large and in subpopulations at increased risk. Building on the well-established public health model of levels of prevention described above, primary prevention efforts can be delineated further in terms of the relative risk status of populations. Gordon (1983) has proposed that the scope of primary prevention can range from universal efforts designed to benefit everyone, to efforts directed toward increasingly restricted subgroups defined by higher probabilities of risk. Specifically he has proposed successive levels defined in terms of universal, selected, and indicated primary prevention. Each of these levels reflects an increase in relative risk status with a corresponding increase in need for prevention. As shown in Figure 1.2 for the problem of juvenile delinquency and in Figure 1.3 for unintentional injury, primary prevention can be directed toward the general population at average risk and to selected and indicated subpopulations at increased and high risk, respectively.

Thus, primary prevention efforts of a universal nature are designed to promote well-being in the population at large. Examples of universal efforts are population-based immunization programs and mandatory public school attendance. Selected primary prevention programs target groups at increased risk on the basis of group, rather than individual, characteristics. Examples in the health arena are immunization programs directed toward subgroups defined by age, such as very young children or elderly persons, or by other group identifiers such as migrant child status. In the education arena, prevention focused on selected groups could take the form of special classes for children for whom English is a second language. The highest risk group for primary prevention is defined as the indicated group; in the case of health services, subgroup members are identified on the basis of characteristics unique to a given individual (e.g., prematurity, genetic markers, behavioral markers). Again in the educational realm, indicated primary prevention could be targeted toward children whose failing performance in school places them at risk for grade retention.

An assumption crucial to primary prevention efforts is that of the ability to identify causal chains. In the health sciences, this is achieved when it is possible to identify specific agents and vectors of disease. In

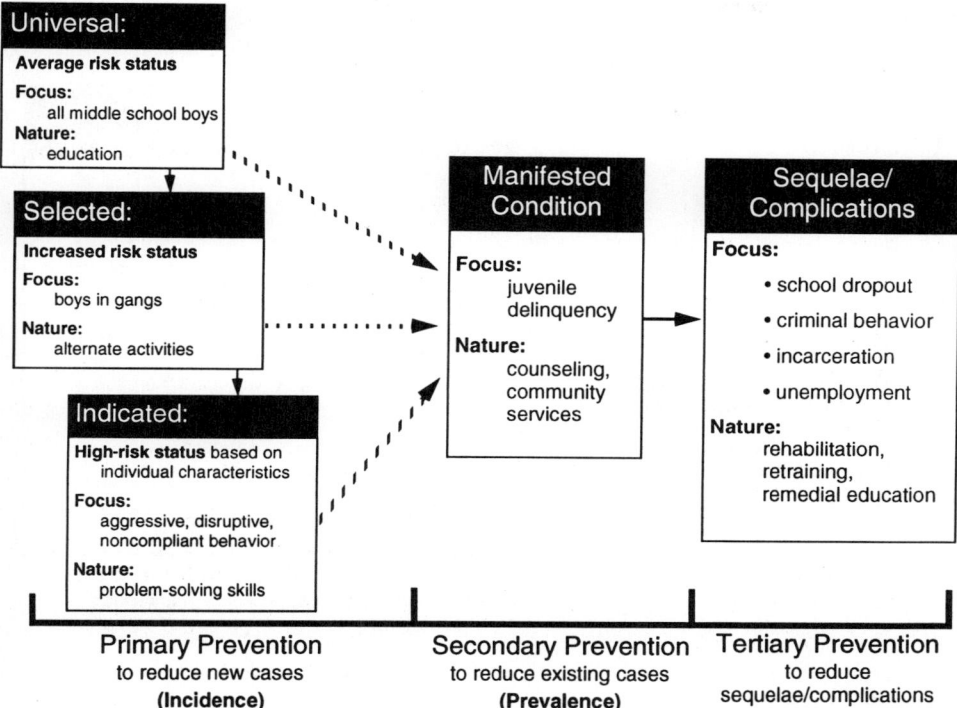

Figure 1.2. Focus and nature of primary, secondary, and tertiary prevention: Juvenile delinquency.

the behavioral and social sciences, such causality may not be inferred as readily. Thus, it may be more appropriate to substitute the concept of *risk chains*, as proposed in Chapter 2 of this volume. In any case, development of primary prevention and primary promotion programs requires that a causal, or at least sequential, chain is proposed in order to establish a logical foundation on which to base the nature and timing of prevention efforts. A final assumption for the success of a primary prevention initiative is the importance of taking advantage of lead time in development, thereby capitalizing on the momentum provided by the developmental forces afforded in childhood.

ELEMENTS DEFINING SUCCESSFUL PRIMARY PREVENTION

With the key assumptions providing the structural basis for primary prevention efforts, what elements define successful prevention programs? There is growing evidence of the efficacy of primary prevention from which we can benefit (Price, Cowen, Lorion, & Ramos-McKoy,

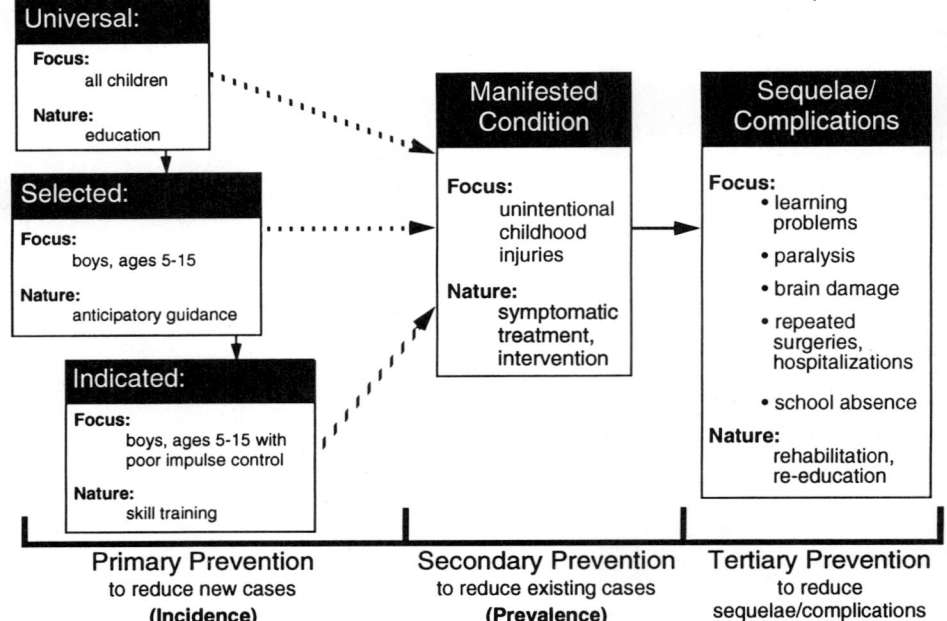

Figure 1.3. Focus and nature of primary, secondary, and tertiary prevention: Unintentional childhood injuries.

1989). On the basis of an extensive review of primary prevention programs, Schorr (1991) identified a number of elements associated with success. Among these is the fact that successful prevention programs are interdisciplinary in nature and minimize bureaucratic boundaries. They are also characterized by a strong family and community orientation, and they ensure convenient and ready access to a wide array of services. Finally, successful prevention programs promote relationships of trust and respect, and they seek to personalize preventive services relative to the extent of risk.

Timeliness of a comprehensive primary prevention and primary promotion agenda for escalating problems and conditions in children is based on the premise that risk status can be approached at different prevention levels. Viewed in this way, any problem or condition can be defined in functional terms to derive relative risk status. Within this framework, prevention efforts can be operationalized at each of the three levels to effect a reduction of the manifestation of problems of childhood. Placing particular focus on primary prevention, the designation of universal, selected, and indicated prevention yields a framework that may be used to differentiate prevention relative to the degree of need and the degree of risk. Many problems and disorders of childhood in contemporary society warrant primary prevention. These include illness and injury, abuse and neglect, adolescent pregnancy, sexually transmitted diseases, drug abuse, internalizing and externalizing disorders, school failure, and limited literacy. Although these problems are often identified as separate conditions, they clearly are the products of complex factors, and they often act in synergistic ways to delay or distort development and adaptation. Recognition of such synergism is evident in the growing awareness of the need for interagency and interdisciplinary solutions. Furthermore, in keeping with an appreciation of the school as the central environment of children, schools are increasingly proposed as the locus for integrated community-based services (Finn-Stevenson, Linkins, & Beacon, 1992; Waxman, Walker deFelix, Anderson, & Baptiste, 1992). This book examines these childhood problems within a primary prevention and primary promotion framework, and it identifies implications for policy, practice, and research.

REFERENCES

America 2000: An education strategy. (1991). Washington, DC: U.S. Department of Education.

Caplan, G., & Grunebaum, H. (1967). Perspectives on primary prevention. *Archives of General Psychiatry, 17,* 331–346.

Children's Defense Fund. (1994). *The state of America's children.* Washington, DC: Author.

Finn-Stevenson, M., Linkins, K., & Beacon, E. (1992). The school of the 21st century: Creating opportunities for school-based health care. *Child and Youth Care Forum, 21*(5), 335–345.

Flynn, B.C. (1992). Healthy cities: A model of community change. *Family and Community Health, 15*(1), 13–23.

Gordon, R.S., Jr. (1983). An operational classification of disease prevention. *Public Health Reports, 98*(2), 107–109.

Healthy People 2000: National health promotion and disease prevention objectives. (1991). Washington, DC: Public Health Service, U.S. Department of Health and Human Services.

Institute of Medicine. (1991). A.N. Pope & A.R. Tarlov (Eds.), *Disability in America: Towards a national agenda for prevention.* Washington, DC: National Academy Press.

Martin, D.A. (1992). Children in peril: A mandate for change in health care policies for low-income children. *Family and Community Health, 15*(1), 75–90.

Novello, A.C., DeGraw, C., & Kleinman, D.V. (1992). Healthy children ready to learn: An essential collaboration between health and education. *Public Health Reports, 107*(1), 3–15.

Price, R.H., Cowen, E.L., Lorion, R.P., & Ramos-McKoy (1989). The search for effective prevention programs: What we have learned along the way. *American Journal of Orthopsychiatry, 59*(1), 49–58.

Schaaf, R.C., & Davis, W.S. (1992). Promoting health and wellness in the pediatric disabled and "at-risk" population. In J. Rothman & R. Lorine (Eds.),

Prevention practice: Strategies for physical therapy and occupational therapy (pp. 270–283). Philadelphia: W.B. Saunders.

Schorr, L.B. (1991). Children, families and the cycle of disadvantage. *Canadian Journal of Psychiatry, 36*(6), 437–441.

Stachtchenko, S., & Jenicek, M. (1990). Conceptual differences between prevention and health promotion: Research implications for community health programs. *Canadian Journal of Public Health, 81*(1), 53–59.

Waxman, H.C., Walker deFelix, J., Anderson, J.E., & Baptiste, H.P., Jr. (Eds.). (1992). *Students at risk in at risk schools.* Newbury Park, CA: Corwin Press.

Wynder, E.L. (1994). Child health day task forces report. Introduction: Toward national comprehensive school health education. *Preventive Medicine, 23*(1), 106–118.

2

Toward an Epidemiology of Developmental, Educational, and Social Problems of Childhood

Rune J. Simeonsson

At first glance prevention of childhood disorders is a most attractive concept. Who would deny that focusing on building skills and competencies is preferable to remediating deficits? Who would argue with the statement that if children can be spared contact with physical and psychological distress, this is superior to attempting to delimit their distress? . . . It may be very surprising then to learn that preventive efforts typically have a small constituency, continue to be underfunded and are underresearched.
Peterson, Zink, and Farmer, 1991, p. 951

Given the obvious logic of promoting development rather than remediating problems, it is surprising that the commitment to preventive priorities and practices has been so limited. The premise of prevention is widely acknowledged and institutionalized in our culture in such popular idioms as "a stitch in time saves nine" and "an ounce of prevention is worth a pound of cure." In most service settings addressing the health, educational, and social needs of children however, treatment rather than prevention, has been the predominant, if not the exclusive, emphasis. A consideration of the current scope of medical care, social services, special education, and rehabilitation programs for children would lead us to agree with Miller's (1990) conclusion that, "Curative care is what the U.S. does best" (p. 1126). In contrast, prevention has not been a priority, and the little that has been done has not been adequately recognized or translated into wider applications. This is reflected by the fact that less than 3% of total expenses for health are accounted for in prevention or public health efforts (McKinlay, 1992).

A number of factors can be proposed for the disproportionate emphasis assigned to curative treatment relative to prevention. A central factor underlying this imbalance is no doubt the primacy assigned to the individual as the focus of intervention by the major helping professions. This primacy is expressed in the identification of the person receiving intervention as patient, student, or client for medical, educational, and social services, respectively. This focus on the individual is a well-established tradition across clinical disciplines, and it clearly defines the nature of intervention efforts. Even in public health, as McKinlay (1992) has noted, "The almost exclusive focus on personal attributes in public health . . . and centering efforts for change at the individual level may not be suited to solve current public health problems at the level of communities and larger social entities" (p. 511). This concern about the limiting nature of focusing on the individual is likely to constrain approaches to the array of health, educational, and social problems of children and youth in contemporary society.

These broader problems call for an alternate approach in which a population-based approach, rather than a focus on individuals, becomes the basis for efforts requiring the adoption of a preventive framework. Although preventive efforts for children do exist, they have been selective in focus and relatively small in scope. However, there is neither a lack of precedence for primary prevention nor a lack of evidence of its benefits. "In some small ways, preventive health care has been around for a long time. We vaccinate our children and fluoridate our drinking water and many of us have regular medical checks . . ."(Koop, 1991, p. 289). Few would question the value of prevention in these areas; in fact, most would take such preventive efforts for granted. A major reason that there is some societal commitment to prevention in these specific areas is no doubt related to the fact that an obvious link is established between prevention and outcome. The extension of a link to preventable developmental, educational, and social problems of children and youth, however, has been less obvious. Thus, commitment to primary prevention programs where the contexts are more complex and the link far less obvious has been severely limited. A number of reasons may account for the difficulty of operationalizing a comprehensive agenda to prevent childhood problems. These are elaborated below.

PROBLEMS IN OPERATIONALIZING PRIMARY PREVENTION

Implicit in the implementation of primary prevention is the identification of the condition to be prevented. Although there is broad agreement that major problems and disorders of children and youth exist, compromising their development and adaptation, agreement on definitions and diagnostic entities is less widespread. There is often a lack of common definitions and conceptual models among the practitioners of the various disciplines that address these conditions. Diagnoses and nomenclature may, in fact, be idiosyncratic to specific disciplines, resulting in lack of consensus and imprecise communication. Illustrative of such disciplinary idiosyncrasies are children identified as having behavioral and emotional disabilities in special education settings but who are assigned *Diagnostic and Statistical Manual of Mental Disorders* (3rd ed., rev.) (DSM-III-R) (American Psychological Association, 1987) diagnoses in mental health service settings. When there is inconsistency in defining children's conditions across disciplines it is likely that there will be corresponding difficulties in operationalizing risk definitions.

A second factor that might mitigate against the adoption of a comprehensive primary prevention agenda for children and youth is the contingency of meeting established eligibility criteria as prerequisite to receiving services. The criteria typically define deficits in quantitative terms, specifying a threshold level. Within this model, at-risk children who fail to trigger the quantitative criteria will not be eligible for services, although their scores may be near those that would qualify them for some form of intervention. On reassessment, the problem characteristics may have escalated to such a level that the criteria for eligibility are met, but valuable time for prevention will have been lost.

A third factor limiting the implementation of a prevention agenda is the fact that the statistical documentation of problem frequency is measured in terms of children who have received or are currently receiving services. Populations defined in these terms would be made up of candidates for secondary or tertiary prevention in which the goals are to reduce the severity and/or duration of the conditions and their possible sequelae and complications. The net result is a statistical database descriptive of *prevalence*; that is, of children *already* served. However, such a database does not provide the basis for estimating incidence or for projecting future service needs. Such estimates and projections are essential to the implementation of a primary prevention approach.

Associated with this statistical problem is the lack of causal modeling and the derivation of risk chains for problems and disorders of children and youth. These factors have resulted in the dominance of an intervention approach defined in terms of secondary and tertiary prevention that has limited the development of primary prevention efforts. The lack of an epidemiology of developmental, educational, and behavioral problems and their complications in children and youth has severely restricted the enactment of a comprehensive prevention approach in society.

EXPANDING PARADIGMS: AN EPIDEMIOLOGICAL APPROACH

If there is to be a substantive move toward prevention of problems of childhood, nothing less than a conceptual paradigm shift is required, paralleling similar agendas in health promotion (Lincoln, 1992). Such a shift would emphasize an investment in preventive services that would parallel that of curative services, or a move from prescribed eligibility for services to presumptive eligibility and expanding the focus from individuals to populations. In general terms, such a shift would reflect the addition of an epidemiological perspective to the clinical approach in order to address the developmental and behavioral problems of children and youth more effectively (Cowen, 1982; Rae-Grant, 1988).

By definition, an epidemiological approach is one that seeks to identify the distribution of a defined condition in the population and identify risk factors. Epidemiology typically has focused on risk and causal chains of disease in biological terms; however, a broader model of risk is needed to establish an epidemiology of developmental and behavioral problems of childhood. Garbarino (1991) has aptly defined this in terms of the human ecology of risk, emphasizing that the "habitat of the child at risk includes family, peers, neighborhood, church, and the school as well as immediate forces that constitute the social geography and climate (e.g., laws, institutions and values, and the physical environment)" (p. 78).

To move toward an epidemiological approach to developmental and behavioral problems of children and youth, several key issues must be considered. Because the number and burden of childhood problems in society are formidable, some basis for prioritizing prevention targets must be considered. Speaking on behalf of the Safe Kids Campaign, Koop (1993) stated that if the number of injuries experienced by children were seen as a biological epidemic, society would demand that immediate and appropriate medical steps be taken. By extension, if childhood disorders and problems are approached in an epidemiological framework, a comprehensive primary prevention approach is implied. The corollaries of such a perspective include an assumption of vicious cycles, additive and synergistic risk, defining risk and its assessment, and identifying indicators for population screening.

The extensive scope of problems of children and youth could be approached in a number of ways. One way that might be productive would be to distinguish between lower frequency/higher intensity problems versus higher frequency/lower intensity problems, as illustrated in Figure 2.1. From this perspective, lower frequency/higher-intensity disorders would be those that are likely to have biological and/or congenital etiologies, that have been identified in early develop-

Developmental, Educational, and Social Problems / 17

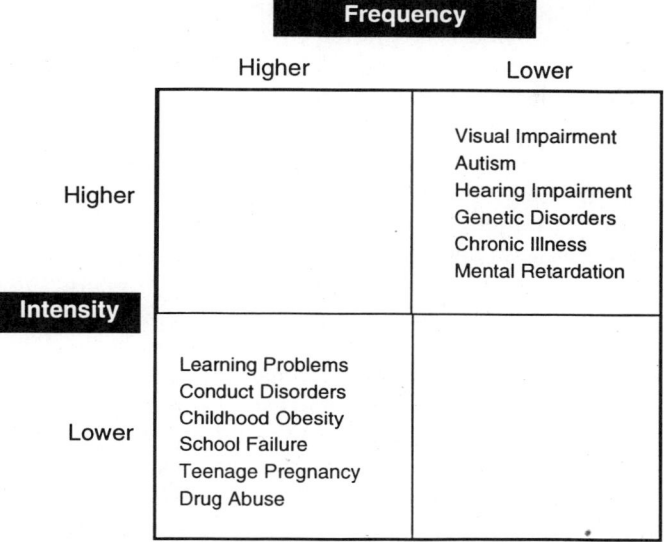

Figure 2.1. Representative childhood conditions and problems as a function of intensity and frequency.

ment, and that require significant treatment and/or rehabilitative services. Typical of these conditions of childhood would be the sensory impairments of blindness and deafness, orthopedic impairments, autism, and other developmental disabilities. Primary prevention of many of these low-incidence conditions is often biomedical in nature and encompasses genetic counseling, prenatal care, and management of high-risk pregnancies and deliveries. It is also clear that primary prevention of childhood disability in terms of lower incidence conditions is a significant priority with developmental interventions provided in infancy and early childhood (Simeonsson, 1991a, 1991b). Specific efforts with these conditions are not be detailed in this volume, although there is likely to be significant overlap in primary prevention priorities with important benefits.

Higher frequency/lower intensity problems would encompass various problems of health, learning, behavior, and socialization that interfere with development, adaptation, and coping in life situations. These populations include what Haggerty, Roghmann, and Pless (1975) referred to as the new morbidity, as distinct from the old morbidity of lower frequency/higher intensity conditions associated with genetic, congenital, and prenatal complications. Furthermore, this distinction is consistent with a prevention perspective in which the old morbidity is more likely to be associated with secondary and tertiary prevention efforts, whereas primary prevention can serve as the major strategy to address the new morbidity. As noted earlier in this book, however, the additive and synergistic risk experienced by many children in contemporary society may well result in the elaboration of vicious circles or cycles both within and across generations (Chamberlin, 1992). Thus, a child whose preschool years are characterized by delayed language and attentional deficits secondary to an inconsistent caregiving environment is at increased jeopardy for a risk chain of school failure, school dropout, and the sequalae of unemployment and criminal activity. It is children with these and other higher frequency/lower intensity problems who are the focus of this volume.

Another important issue is the lack of a comprehensive epidemiological approach to developmental, educational and social problems of childhood. There is growing interest in establishing an epidemiological base for childhood problems and disorders (Kellam et al., 1991). Much of the focus in this regard, however, has been within psychiatric contexts involving children with disruptive disorders (Cohen, Cohen, & Brook, 1993; Costello & Angold, 1993). An epidemiology encompassing a broader spectrum of childhood problems and disorders is required if effective primary prevention programs are to be established. Of related interest is the concept of vicious cycles and the conceptualization of risk and how to assess risk (Lorion, 1991). Clearly, the concept of risk implies a relative vulnerability among children so that some children are at greater risk, whereas others are at lesser risk. In keeping with a transactional model of human development (Sameroff & Chandler, 1975), the conceptualization of risk must consider factors intrinsic to the child, to proximal and distal environmental variables, and to the interaction of child and environment. It would be useful here to extend the epidemiological conceptions of relative risk and attributable risk to childhood problems and disorders.

Although the analogy between risk and disease and risk and childhood developmental and behavioral problems may not be exact, application of the concept of relative risk may be useful in two ways. On one level, it can serve to quantify the degree of jeopardy faced by some children as compared to others in ways in which current conceptualizations do not. At a second and perhaps more important level, relative risk requires a process of narrowing down potential risk factors—in effect, making best guesses about needed preventive strategies. This is important because although transactional models do reflect the complex nature of factors governing developmental and behavioral outcomes, they are often difficult to operationalize, and the implementation of intervention efforts that simultaneously take myriad factors into account is likely to be both unwieldy and overwhelming. Operationalizing relative and attributable risk requires a logical investment in the most probable factors associated with increased risk for unfavorable outcomes, and it yields corresponding implications for the nature of prevention efforts. In some cases, the implication might be to reduce relative risk by removing an identified risk factor; in others, it might be to reduce the child's vulnerability by promoting skill acquisition. In still another case, the approach might be to combine two or more primary prevention strategies.

A final issue relevant to the epidemiological approach is a consideration of indicators for population screening and primary prevention efforts. In this regard, Offord (1982) has identified four key indicators, with the first being that the problem or condition of interest is preventable. A second indicator for primary prevention is that the condition is present in at least 1% of the population. A third indication is that the condition is, or has the likelihood of being, chronic. Finally, feasibility of implementing primary prevention is an important indicator. The problems reviewed in this volume all meet the criteria of these indicators.

STEPS IN DEVELOPING PRIMARY PREVENTION INITIATIVES

If the commitment to primary prevention is made, and the indicators have been met, what are the methodological steps to follow in implementing the primary prevention of problems and disorders of children and youth? At least seven steps can be identified. These are summarized below.

1. Operationalize the target conditions and risk factors.
2. Generate risk models and causal, sequential, or risk chains.
3. Define the nature of risk in child × environment transactions.
4. Differentiate the characteristics of universal, selected, and indicated primary prevention.
5. Propose temporal frames for primary prevention.
6. Prioritize the form and nature of primary prevention efforts.
7. Monitor and evaluate prevention outcomes.

Operationalize Target Conditions and Risk Factors

Central to any primary prevention effort is the operationalization of the target condition; that is, what is the problem or disorder of concern? What is the nature of its manifestation that requires secondary and tertiary prevention? What are the direct and indirect sequelae of the condition for which tertiary prevention is indicated? Although many common disorders of childhood and youth have developmental and behavioral manifestations, the condition itself is often defined in terms of a diagnostic entity, which may be less than clear. A clear and complete description of the problem or target condition, in operational terms, is a necessary prerequisite to any prevention effort and to the second step of identifying probable causal, sequential, or risk chains. This may be approached productively by schematizing the manifested condition or problem of concern in context as shown in Figure 2.2. Once the condition has been operationalized, what are the factors that place the child at increased risk for the condition? In this context, it is important to recognize that "risk to development can come both from direct threats and from the absence of more expectable opportunities" (Garbarino, 1991, p. 79).

Generate Risk Models and Causal, Sequential, or Risk Chains

The identification of causal chains is essential to an epidemiological approach to population-based primary prevention. A common way in which causal chains are derived in the epidemiology of a disease is to identify its probable natural history. As Sackett, Haynes, Guyatt, and Tugwell (1991) have noted, spelling out the natural history of a disease reveals the sequence of its manifestation and the critical points at which intervention is differentially more effective or efficient than at other

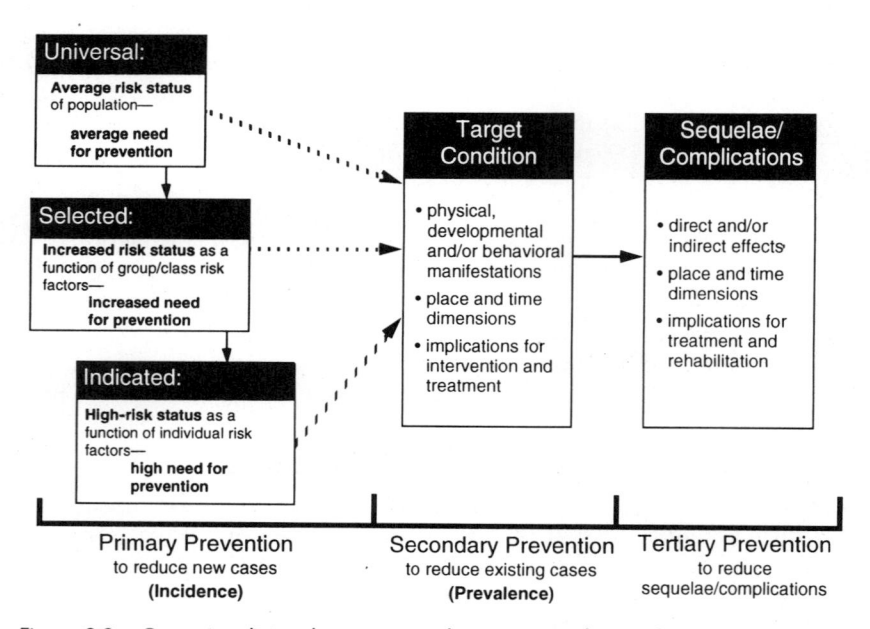

Figure 2.2. Operationalizing the target condition, its sequelae, and groups for primary prevention.

points. In the context of illness and disease, the derivation of causal chains and critical points at which screening and primary prevention are indicated is an activity that often can be accomplished with success.

For problems of development and behavior, the identification of risk mechanisms and derivation of causal chains are likely to be more difficult because the relationships are complex and usually nonlinear. In many instances, attempts to trace causal chains are likely to be contingent upon a number of qualifications, a situation defined as *contextualism* by Garbarino (1991). It is probably more appropriate to think in terms of identifying mechanisms of risk and the derivation of risk chains because the relationships are less likely to be exact. It is, however, important to identify probable risk mechanisms and derive risk chains as the basis for developing primary prevention. As shown in Figure 2.3, a risk chain is predicated on the fact that a childhood condition or problem is defined in operational terms, and probable risk mechanisms and critical points for screening and primary prevention are identified. The generation of risk chains involves both the derivation of logical causal sequences and the identification of the most likely risk factors from relevant research. Thus, the generation of risk chains involves both a commonsense conceptualization of targeted conditions as well as the identification of causal mechanisms derived from research findings. A central basis for such identification is the estimation of relative risk. Causal or risk chains provide the logical frame for identifying probable risk factors. The strength of these factors can be calculated in terms of the likelihood of differential vulnerability or relative risk. Using the statistical tools of epidemiology, the likelihood of risk can be estimated effectively by drawing on retrospective data from case-control studies to derive odds ratios (ORs). Stronger estimates can be derived through prospective cohort studies in which relative risk (RR)

What is the nature / typical history of the target condition?

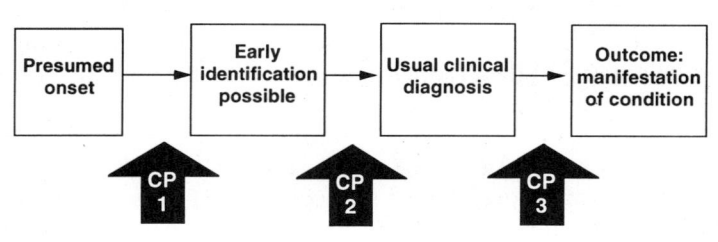

Presumed onset → Early identification possible → Usual clinical diagnosis → Outcome: manifestation of condition

CP 1   CP 2   CP 3

What are the critical points (CP) in the history of the problem or condition?

Figure 2.3. Generating causal, sequential, or risk chains.

indices are calculated on the basis of the ratio of incidence of the condition in an exposed group to the incidence in a nonexposed group. Application of these tools in the estimation of risk for the problem of school dropout is illustrated in Figure 2.4.

In the case of the retrospective study, in which students are identified on the basis of outcome status after the fact, the estimated risk is five times greater (OR = 5.4) for grade-retained students than for those who were not retained. In the example using a prospective cohort, it is possible to calculate risk directly in terms of a risk ratio of students experiencing or not experiencing grade retention. The relative risk for school dropout in this hypothetical cohort is almost six times (RR = 5.87) higher for retained versus nonretained peers. Applying this and the related indices of attributable risk and population attributable risk percentage would support the premise that grade retention constitutes a strong determinant in a risk chain model of school dropout. This is consistent with national follow-up data (U.S. Department of Education, 1993) in which not liking school (42.9%) and failing school (38.7%) were the top two reasons given by students dropping out.

It is clear, however, that grade retention is only one of a number of factors that may place students at increased risk for school dropout. A variety of factors can be identified from research and the clinical literature as well as a consideration of factors that may be unique to a particular school or community. To proceed in a logical and systematic manner, it would be important to compare the relative strength of different risk factors and design and prioritize prevention initiatives accordingly. This can be done either on the basis of retrospective data to yield odds ratios to estimate risk factors, or through prospective studies to derive risk ratios. Such data can then be examined in a summary form as shown in Table 2.1 for a prospective cohort. While the values in the table are hypothetical, they draw on Wagner's (1991) findings on failure to complete school in the general population (24.4%) and among students identified as having learning disabilities (36.1%) and serious emotional disturbance (54.8%). The scope of the dropout problem is also evident in recent data from the National Center for Education Statistics (U.S. Department of Education, 1993) showing an overall dropout rate of 12% for the prospective cohort of 1988 eighth graders. The dropout rate for minority students was higher, with 15% and 18% of African-American and Hispanic students, respectively, dropping out of school. Complementing demographic markers of age, gender, and ethnicity, it would be useful to examine personal, situational, or behavioral factors that would elevate risk for failure to complete school specific to a community or region. Comparing the values in this hypothetical cohort, grade retention, drug use, teenage pregnancy, and serious emotional disturbance are associated with the highest relative risk for

A Secondary School Outcome Status

Exposure/Experience	Dropout	Graduate	
Grade Retention	(a) 111	(b) 199	310
No Retention	(c) 73	(d) 1117	1190
	174	1316	1500

$$Ie = \frac{\text{Incidence}}{\text{Exposure}} = \frac{a}{a+b} = \frac{111}{310} = .358 \qquad Ie = 358 \text{ per } 1000$$

$$Io = \frac{\text{Incidence}}{\text{Nonexposure}} = \frac{c}{c+d} = \frac{73}{1190} = .061 \qquad Io = 61 \text{ per } 1000$$

$$It = \frac{\text{Overall Incidence}}{\text{Total Population}} = \frac{a+c}{a+b+c+d} = \frac{174}{1500} = .116 \qquad It = 116 \text{ per } 1000$$

$$\text{Relative Risk} = \frac{Ie}{Io} = \frac{.358}{.061} = 5.87$$

$$\text{Attributable Risk} = Ie - Io = \frac{358}{1000} - \frac{61}{1000} = \frac{297}{1000}$$

$$\text{Population Attributable Risk Percent} = \frac{It - Io}{It} = \frac{.116 - .061}{.116} = 47.4\%$$

B Secondary School Outcome Status

Exposure/Experience	Dropout	Graduate	
Grade Retention	(a) 70	(b) 30	100
No Retention	(c) 30	(d) 70	100
	100	100	200

$$\text{Odds Ratio} = \frac{a/c}{b/d} = \frac{ad}{cb} = \frac{4900}{900} = 5.4$$

Figure 2.4. A) Relative risk: hypothetical data for association between grade retention and school dropout for prospective cohort of 1,500 seventh graders through high school; B) Odds ratio: hypothetical data for relationship between grade retention and school dropout for high school students.

Table 2.1. Hypothetical illustration of comparative risk factors for school dropout in a prospective cohort of 1,500 students

Risk factor	Prevalence of exposure		Number of dropouts	Number of dropouts per 1,000	Relative risk
	Number of students	Percent of total cohort			
Grade retention	310	20.7	111	358	5.87
Single-parent home	276	18.4	69	250	2.91
Teenage pregnancy	90	6	23	256	2.39
Gang membership	133	8.9	53	398	4.47
Drug use	175	11.7	53	303	3.33
Learning disability	65	4.3	24	369	3.51
Serious emotional disturbance	60	4.0	31	517	5.22

school dropout. It is of course clear that risk factors are often interactive, significantly increasing the relative risk. Such interactions are not simply additive, but are synergistic in nature, and are likely to apply to many of the risk factors in the table. It would be important to carry out additional logical as well as statistical analyses to determine what preventions should be initiated and the critical points at which they would be most effective and efficient.

Define the Nature of Risk in Child × Environment Transactions

Most risk chains are likely to reflect the fact that the conditions manifested are reflective of transactions involving child and environmental risk factors. To increase the efficiency of primary prevention efforts it is important to identify the probable direction and strength of such transactions. For some conditions, the nature of the transaction may be relatively straightforward and easy to define. In others, the nature of the transactions may be more indirect and its effects more subtle, as in school failure. In keeping with the emphasis on operationalizing the target condition and risk chains in primary prevention, it is equally important to spell out the most probable manner in which transactions transpire. A framework developed by Ottman (1991) to define the nature of gene–environment interactions may serve to illustrate this point. Extending this framework, it may be useful to project the different ways in which the nature of transactions may account for developmental and behavioral problems of childhood. As shown in Figure 2.5, the transactions may reflect the exacerbating, synergistic, or independent contribution of child and environmental risk factors. Although the figure portrays the action of two variables, it is likely that most

DEVELOPMENTAL, EDUCATIONAL, AND SOCIAL PROBLEMS / 25

1) The environment increases expression of risk factor.

```
                    Inept parenting &
                    discipline
                         │
                         ↓
   Association                        Child
   with deviant  ─────────────→       aggressive
   peers                              and violent
                                      behavior
```

2) The environment exacerbates the effect of the risk factor.

```
                Minimal physical activity
                         │
                         ↓
   High-fat diet ─────────────→   Childhood
                                  obesity
```

3) The risk factor exacerbates the effect of the environment.

```
                Inadequate
                parenting
                environment
               ↗           ↘
   Parental                  Neglect
   drug                      or abuse
   abuse                     of child
```

4) Both environment and risk factor are required to raise risk.

```
   Unstructured/
   unsupervised
   environment  ╲
                 ─→  Teenage
                     pregnancy
   Risk-taking  ╱
   behaviors
```

5) The environment and the risk factor influence risk independently.

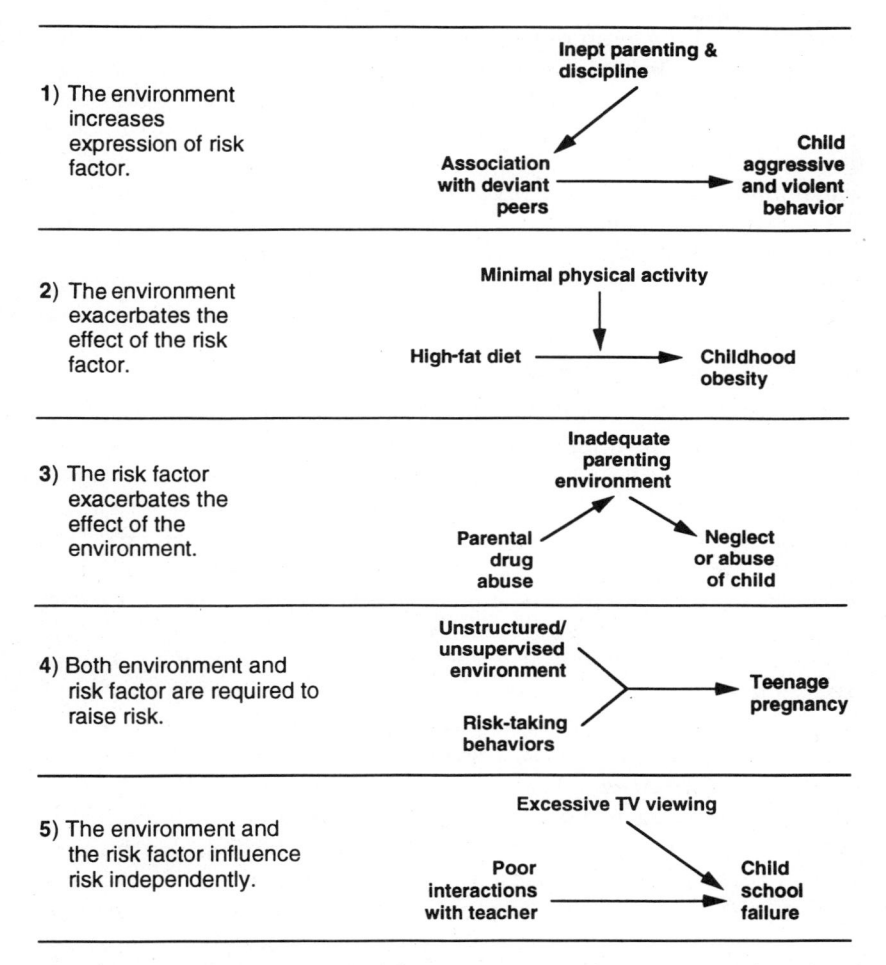

```
              Excessive TV viewing
                         ╲
                          ↘
   Poor                         Child
   interactions ─────────────→  school
   with teacher                 failure
```

Figure 2.5. Defining the nature of risk factors, environmental transactions, and manifested problems: illustrative models (adapted from Ottman, 1991).

problems are more complex. Furthermore, one variable has been defined as environmental and the other as a specific risk factor, when, in fact, both are risk factors. More detailed analyses could serve to categorize the risk factors into predisposing factors and precipitating factors (Rickel & Allen, 1987). The former are pre-existing risk factors that can be further defined as unmodifiable (e.g., gender) or modifiable (e.g., home environment). Precipitating risk factors, however, occur much more closely in time to the manifestation of the condition. Life events such as illness, parental divorce, or stress at school may often serve as precipitating factors for children's problems. Using entry to junior high school as an example of a precipitating factor, Rickel and Allen proposed that children "can be taught survival skills beforehand that will reduce the degree to which school transition is a risk factor" (p. 31). In this context, it is also important to identify the role of potential antecedents of well-being (Kellam & Werthamer-Larsson, 1986), which may take the form of protective factors in the environment and characteristics of resilience in the child. Thus, the value of projecting risk chains is that it seeks to clarify the nature and direction of transactions, thereby providing a basis for prioritizing the form, timing, and manner of primary prevention as well as primary promotion efforts.

Differentiate the Characteristics of Universal, Selected, and Indicated Primary Prevention

A fourth step in the implementation of primary prevention of a childhood problem or disorder is to differentiate the nature of universal, selected, and indicated prevention. As described in the first chapter, Gordon (1983) has proposed that prevention programs can be differentiated in terms of those that are appropriate for all (universal), those designed for subpopulations at increased risk because of their group rather than their individual characteristics (selected), and those designed for subpopulations at highest risk for manifesting a condition based on individual characteristics (indicated). This approach was elaborated earlier in Figure 2.2 in terms of corresponding levels of need for primary prevention represented by average, increased, and high need, respectively. Again, the purpose of this step is to follow a systematic procedure in designing primary prevention to maximize its potential effectiveness. In many instances, it may be desirable or necessary to restrict primary prevention to the selected or the indicated level. The rationale for such restriction may reflect fiscal realities and/or the fact that risk chain modeling suggests that a significant prevention impact can be realized by focusing prevention efforts at the selected or indicated level.

Propose Temporal Frames for Primary Prevention

A closely related step to that of defining the characteristics of the universal, selected, and indicated primary prevention is the projection of temporal frames for implementation. This step builds on the natural history and the risk chain model for the identified problem. Drawing on this information, the critical points at which screening and prevention should be provided can be identified. From a practical standpoint, at what points in children's development should universal, selected, or indicated prevention be provided? Using school dropout in the 10th grade as the problem, what would be the most effective points to implement primary prevention? Depending on the risk chain derived, the nature and timing of primary prevention will vary for specific populations. In one setting, selected prevention may be designed for a group at increased risk in the fifth grade (e.g., migrant children), whereas indicated prevention may be designed for seventh graders who have failed two or more subjects. In another setting, based on another risk model, universal prevention may be geared to improve school readiness skills among all kindergarten children, with selected and indicated prevention provided for second-grade boys and fourth-grade slow learners, respectively. The key issue here is that the timing of universal, selected, and indicated prevention logically reflects the populations and contexts specific to the derived risk model.

Prioritize the Form and Nature of Primary Prevention Efforts

Following the identification of probable risk chains and the generation of temporal frames for universal, selected, and indicated primary prevention, the next step is to specify the manner and means of implementation. Given the fundamental difference between prevention activities and treatment activities, with respective targeting of populations versus individuals, it is essential that the means for implementation be specified in detail. Because prevention is targeted for populations, the nature and intensity of the services are likely to be less distinct than services that target individual children. Furthermore, as seen in the list below, prevention activities must be prioritized in terms of their main focus, namely reducing risk, promoting resilience, or modifying transactions. Therefore, it is crucial that primary prevention programs are spelled out in detail in terms of designated populations, the nature and timing of prevention activities, and the roles and responsibilities of prevention agents.

1. Reduce vulnerability.
   a. Remove risk factors.
   b. Reduce risk factors (intensity, severity, duration).
   c. Change environments.
2. Increase resiliency.
   a. Facilitate development.
   b. Improve/enhance environment.
   c. Add protective factors.
3. Modify transactions.
   a. Introduce catalyst(s).
   b. Alter valence of risk factors.
   c. Promote synergism.

Monitor and Evaluate Prevention Outcomes

As Remington (1990) notes, one of the key liabilities of primary prevention is the anonymity inherent in its population-based focus. Because prevention is directed toward populations rather than individuals—often without prior knowledge about whom it might benefit—it is difficult to document effectiveness, as traditionally done with clinical interventions. Documentation of program implementation, as Rohrbach, Graham, and Hansen (1993) have demonstrated, is a crucial element in the building of a comprehensive prevention agenda. A final step in the design and implementation of primary prevention programs is thus the development of plans to monitor and evaluate prevention outcomes. Steps for such monitoring and evaluation are listed in the questions that follow.

1. Is there an epidemiology of risk factors and the targeted condition in terms of:
   a. incidence (new cases); and
   b. prevalence (existing cases)?
2. Monitoring: Is there a change in risk status of identified populations over time?
3. Evaluation: Is there evidence of change in the incidence and/or prevalence of the targeted condition in the population?

Here, as in previous steps, the epidemiological perspective provides the framework for efforts. Within a broad frame, the effectiveness of primary, secondary, and tertiary prevention can be documented by population trends. In this regard, tertiary prevention is effective if there is evidence that there has been a reduction in the frequency of sequelae or complications of a given disorder. Similarly, secondary prevention can be shown to be effective if there is evidence that the prevalence of a specified problem, or its duration or severity, has been reduced over time. Because the goal of primary prevention is reducing the incidence, that is, the number of new cases manifesting the problem, evidence for a reduction in the population over time becomes the basis for documenting the effectiveness of primary prevention. Within the practice of clinical epidemiology, there are rules of evidence that can be applied to determine if there is a causal relationship between exposure and disease. If primary prevention involves the reduction of exposure to risk or the increase of exposure to protective factors, a similar conclusion of causality is of interest. To that end, it would seem appropriate to apply the same evidentiary rules to broader prevention initiatives. The first rule, according to Hennekens and Buring (1987), is to determine that chance, bias, and confounding do not constitute viable explanations for obtained statistical associations. A conclusion of causality is supported to the extent that an obtained index of association meets the following criteria.

1. The magnitude of the index is substantial.
2. The association has biological credibility.
3. The finding is consistent with other studies.
4. The temporal sequence is plausible.
5. There is a logical dose–response relationship.

Similar guidelines have been proposed by Beaglehole, Bonita, and Kjellstrom (1993), who include the additional criteria of reversibility of effect, strength of study design, and the number of lines of evidence to support a conclusion of causality. Although the fit of each of these rules of evidence to the broader nature of children's problems and associated prevention efforts may not be exact, extensions seem appropriate. For example, the criteria of biological credibility could be expanded to encompass credibility of psychological and social hypotheses. The dose–response relationship could analogously be placed in the context of intensity and scope of prevention efforts relative to observed effects and outcomes. These rules of evidence can serve as useful additions to the more traditional strategies employed to evaluate the outcomes of behavioral and social interventions. Central to all prevention strategies, however, is the priority of longitudinal, prospective studies. Through study of prospective cohorts over time, risk and resilience can be verified as predictors of developmental outcome, and the efficacy of primary prevention and primary promotion for children's well-being can be documented.

REFERENCES

American Psychiatric Association. (1987). *Diagnostic and statistical manual of mental disorders* (3rd ed.—revised). Washington, DC: Author.

Beaglehole, R., Bonita, R., & Kjellstrom, T. (1993). *Basic epidemiology*. Geneva, Switzerland: World Health Organization.

Chamberlin, R. (1992). Preventing low birth weight, child abuse, and school failure: The need for comprehensive, community wide approaches. *Pediatrics in Review, 13*(2), 64–71.

Cohen, P., Cohen, J., & Brook, J. (1993). An epidemiological study of disorders in late childhood and adolescence—II. Persistence of disorders. *Journal of Child Psychology & Psychiatry & Allied Disciplines, 34*(6), 869–877.

Costello, E.J., & Angold, A. (1993). Toward a developmental epidemiology of the disruptive behavior disorders. *Development and Psychopathology, 5*, 91–101.

Cowen, E.L. (1982). Primary prevention research: Barriers, needs and opportunities. *Journal of Primary Prevention, 2*(3), 131–137.

Garbarino, J. (1991). The human ecology of early risk. In S.J. Meisels & J. Shankoff (Eds.), *Handbook of early childhood intervention* (pp. 78–96). New York: Cambridge University Press.

Gordon, R.S. (1983). An operational classification of disease prevention. *Public Health Reports, 98*(2), 107–109.

Haggerty, R.J., Roghmann, K.J., & Pless, I.B. (1975). *Child health and the community.* New York: John Wiley & Sons.

Hennekens, C.H., & Buring, J.E. (1987). *Epidemiology in medicine.* Boston: Little, Brown.

Kellam, S.G., Werthamer-Larsson, L., Dolan, I.J., Brown, C.H., Mayer, L.S., Rebok, G.W., Anthony, J.C., Landolff, J., & Edelsohn, G. (1991). Developmental epidemiologically based preventive trials: Baseline modeling of early target behaviors and depressive symptoms. *American Journal of Community Psychology, 19*(4), 563–584.

Kellam, S.G., & Werthamer-Larsson, L. (1986). Developmental epidemiology: A basis for prevention. In M. Kessler & S.E. Goldston (Eds.), *A decade of progress in primary prevention* (pp. 154–180). Hanover, NH: University Press of New England.

Koop, C.E. (1991). *Koop: The memoirs of America's family doctor.* New York: Random House.

Koop, C.E. (1993, May 19). Safe kids in America. *USA Today.* p. 5A.

Lincoln, Y.S. (1992). Fourth generation evaluation, the paradigm revolution and health prevention. *Canadian Journal of Public Health, 83* (Suppl. 1), S6–S10.

Lorion, R.P. (1991). Targeting preventive interventions: Enhancing risk estimates through theory. *American Journal of Community Psychology, 19*(6), 859–865.

McKinlay, J.B. (1992). Health promotion through healthy public policy: The contribution of complementary research methods. *Canadian Journal of Public Health, 83* (Suppl. 1), S11–S19.

Miller, C.A. (1990). Summation and commentary. *Pediatrics 86*(6)(Suppl.), 1124–1127.

Offord, D.R. (1982). Primary prevention: Aspects of program design and evaluation. *American Academy of Child and Adolescent Psychiatry Journal, 21*(1), 225–230.

Ottman, R. (1991). An epidemiological approach to gene–environment interaction. *Genetic Epidemiology, 7*(3), 177–185.

Peterson, L., Zink, M., & Farmer, J. (1991). Prevention of disorders in children. In C.E. Walker & M. Roberts (Eds.), *Handbook of clinical child psychology* (2nd ed., pp. 951–965). New York: John Wiley & Sons.

Rae-Grant, N. (1988). Primary prevention: Implications for the child psychiatrist. *Canadian Journal of Psychiatry, 33*(6), 433–442.

Remington, R.D. (1990). From preventive policy to preventive practice. *Preventive Medicine, 19*(1), 105–113.

Rickel, A.I., & Allen, L. (1987). *Preventing maladjustment from infancy through adolescence.* Newbury Park, CA: Sage Publications.

Rohrbach, L.A., Graham, J.W., & Hansen, W.B. (1993). Diffusion of a school-based substance abuse prevention program: Predictors of program implementation. *Preventive Medicine, 22*, 237–260.

Sackett, D.L., Haynes, R.B., Guyatt, G.H., & Tugwell, P. (1991). *Clinical epidemiology.* Boston: Little, Brown.

Sameroff, A.J., & Chandler, M.J. (1975). Reproductive risk and the continuum of caretaking casualty. In F.D. Horowitz (Ed.), *Review of child development research* (Vol. 4, pp. 187–244). Chicago: University of Chicago Press.

Simeonsson, R.J. (1991a). Early intervention eligibility: A prevention perspective. *Infants & Young Children, 3*(4), 48–55.

Simeonsson, R.J. (1991b). Primary, secondary, and tertiary prevention in early intervention. *Journal of Early Intervention 15*(2), 124–134.

U.S. Department of Education. (1993). *Dropout rates in the United States 1992.* Washington, DC: National Center for Education Statistics, Office of Education Research and Improvement.

Wagner, M. (1991). *Drop outs with disabilities: What do we know? What can we do?* Menlo Park, NJ: SRI International.

3

Primary Prevention
The Missing Piece in Child Development Legislation

Robert W. Chamberlin

In response to the large number of children entering our school systems with developmental, behavioral, and learning problems, the U.S. Congress has passed remedial legislation targeted toward variously defined *high-risk* groups. Examples are Head Start programs for preschool children from low-income families followed by Chapter 1 remedial programs for those having continuing difficulty after entering the school system. In addition to these, the Education for All Handicapped Children Act of 1975 (PL 94-142), passed in 1977, mandated special education services for children with disabilities from age 5 through age 21. States had the option of extending services down to age 3 and many decided to do this. More recently, PL 99-457 made these services for preschool children mandatory and, with Part H, provided incentives for states to provide early intervention services for children from birth to age 3. The primary objective of Part H of the Individuals with Disabilities Education Act (IDEA) is to develop a statewide, comprehensive, interagency-based service system for special needs and high-risk infants, toddlers, and their families. Although this is a significant step forward, it will still leave the United States behind almost all Western European countries in terms of preventing developmental disabilities and promoting the health and development of families and children.

INTERNATIONAL COMPARISONS

Recent comparisons have found that the United States is behind other developed countries in preventing low birth weight babies and infant deaths and in getting children immunized. In addition, a greater percentage of our children are hospitalized from injuries and exposed to child abuse and neglect. Our adolescents are more likely to become pregnant out of wedlock, be victims of homicide, and drop out of school (American Academy of Pediatrics 1990; Miller, 1987; Williams & Miller, 1991). For example, in the American Academy of Pediatrics Symposium it was noted that the United States was behind 22 other developed nations in lowering its infant mortality rate. It was also noted that "among Western developed nations, injury death rates in the U.S. are constantly among the highest" (American Academy of Pediatrics, 1990, p. 1068) and "the pregnancy rate for U.S. females age 15 to 19 was twice that of Great Britain in 1981, three times that of Sweden, and almost seven times that of the Netherlands" (American Academy of Pediatrics, 1990, p. 1120).

These statistics are particularly disturbing because all these problems tend to perpetuate each other in a vicious circle that adds to the incidence of developmental disabilities (Chamberlin, 1992). For example, pregnant adolescents are more likely to receive inadequate prenatal care, deliver low birth weight babies, and raise children less ready for learning upon school entry. Children coming into school systems poorly prepared are more likely to fall behind and drop out. School dropouts, in turn, are more likely to have problems with substance abuse and to become pregnant out of wedlock (Figure 3.1).

The countries that are ahead of us in preventing these problems all promote child development in a comprehensive way that combines

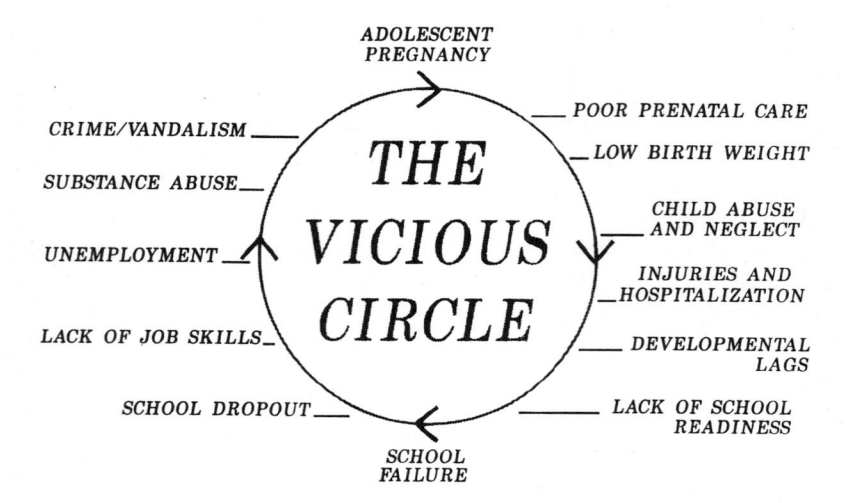

Figure 3.1. The vicious circle. (From Chamberlin, R.W. [1992]. Preventing low birth weight, child abuse, and school failure: The need for comprehensive, community-wide approaches. *Pediatrics in Review, 13*[2], 65; reprinted by permission.)

basic preventive/promotive programs for the population at large with special programs for children with special needs. These preventive programs include universal access to prenatal, well- and sick-child care through national insurance plans, subsidized high-quality child care and early childhood education programs, home visiting, paid family leave for pregnancy and child care, and school health and after-school skill-building and recreation programs for youths and adolescents (Chamberlin, 1988b).

Politicians and some professionals have argued that these differences in child health and developmental outcomes are the result of our country's being larger and more culturally diverse. However, this argument does not hold up when we find similar outcome differences in such small states as Maine and New Hampshire where there are few big cities or large minority groups to complicate service delivery. For example, in 1984 infant mortality rates were below 7 per 1,000 births for Japan, Sweden, and Finland, while at the same time the rate was over 10 in 1,000 in New Hampshire. Only 5% of births were to women younger than 20 in these countries, while 10% of the births in New Hampshire were to teenagers (Chamberlin, 1988b, p. 177).

Additional evidence that these differences are the result of differences in policies and programs rather than of size and diversity comes from recent summaries of demonstration programs in U.S. communities. These show that when basic preventive/promotive programs are made available to all residents in a community, we can reduce low birth weight infants, infant deaths, and adolescent pregnancies, and we can improve the health and developmental status of young children (Chamberlin, 1988a; Dryfoos, 1990; Price, Cowen, Lorion, & Ramos-Mckay, 1988; Schorr, 1988).

THE U.S. APPROACH: WAITING UNTIL CHILDREN ARE "DROWNING"

A more likely explanation for our lagging behind other countries in preventing disabilities is that our system is set up on a deficit model rather on one of health promotion (Bronfenbrenner & Weiss, 1983). Children must demonstrate a developmental lag or families must abuse or neglect children before they become eligible for services. Furthermore, because there is no comprehensive approach to prevention in most communities and schools are now legally mandated to provide services to children with identified disabilities, it is not surprising that some school districts set up rather rigorous exclusionary criteria to keep from becoming overwhelmed. This results in much effort exerted to keep children out of the system and, when they finally become delayed enough to qualify for services, considerable expense in treating problems that might have been prevented.

Another way to describe this approach is to use the river analogy developed by persons working in international health programs (Figure 3.2).

Downstream state agencies and human services providers are trying to rescue "drowning" children by providing neonatal intensive care for low birth weight and sick newborns; family counseling and foster

PARENTING DYSFUNCTION
- Isolated
- Lonely
- Can't cope
- Inexperienced in child care
- Lack of support

PRIMARY PREVENTION

COMMUNITY DYSFUNCTION
- Lack of access to preventive programs
- Inflexible work schedules
- Poor quality child care

EARLY RECOGNITION

SECONDARY PREVENTION
- Pregnant teen
- Child neglect
- Developmental lags

TERTIARY PREVENTION

TREATMENT AND REHABILITATION
- Neonatal intensive care
- Foster care
- Special education
- Reform school
- Welfare

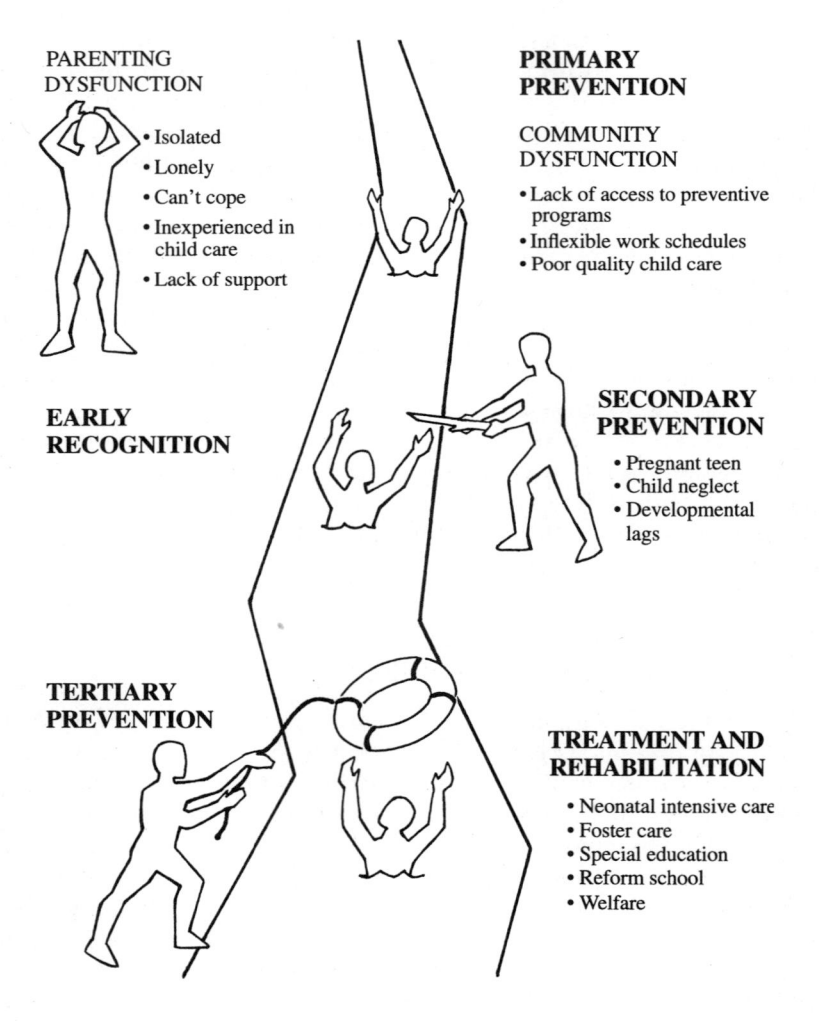

Figure 3.2. The river of risk.

care for children who have been abused or neglected; medical care for those exposed to lead, injured in an accident, or pregnant out of wedlock; special education services for those having trouble learning in school; mental health programs for those with behavioral or emotional problems; and "reform" school for those who have come into contact with the law because of delinquency or crime.

Upstream there is less activity, but people are trying to ascertain whether children swimming in the river are "at risk" for "drowning" and should be rescued. This is the point for early intervention programs.

Still farther upstream children are jumping or falling into the river because of some combination of family and community dysfunction. We see pregnant teens with inadequate prenatal care; isolated and depressed single mothers having difficulty coping with high stress loads; first-time parents inexperienced in child care with no grandparents or other relatives available to help; families where the father has lost his job and has no health insurance; working mothers who are having difficulty getting time off for pregnancy or to care for a sick child; children being neglected in child-care situations with too many children, too few and poorly trained care providers, and unsafe play areas; and adolescents with nothing better to do than hang around on street corners or in malls. We are surprised to find that very little is being done either to teach these children to swim or, more importantly, to keep them from falling into the river.

TWO EXAMPLES OF WORKING IN DEFICIT-ORIENTED CARE SYSTEMS

I have had the opportunity to experience this dilemma in two different care settings. One was as Medical Director of the Child Development Program for the State of New Hampshire and the second was as a developmental pediatrician for the Exceptional Family Member Program of the U.S. Army in Germany. In the New Hampshire program, a multidisciplinary team held monthly statewide clinics to evaluate children under age 6 who had been referred from a variety of sources because of concerns about some aspect of their development. Estimates were that about one third to one half of these children had developmental or behavioral problems that could have been prevented or treated in such basic primary prevention settings as prenatal and well-child programs with home visitors, comprehensive parent–child centers, and high-quality child care, Head Start, or other early childhood education programs. These children often came from highly stressed families that could not afford to pay for high-quality private services. However, in many instances, even when present, these types of preventive programs could not be made available to the family at affordable prices unless it could be shown that the parents had abused or neglected the child. Early intervention programs were often filled with children with more easily recognized disabilities such as cerebral palsy or Down syndrome, leaving those at "environmental risk" on waiting lists. Even when the child was economically eligible, Head Start programs were often filled with 5-year-olds because many communities in New Hampshire do not fund public kindergarten. It was estimated that Head Start programs reached fewer than 20% of eligible 3- and 4-year-old New Hampshire children.

Similar frustrations were encountered in working for the U.S. Army Exceptional Family Member Program in Germany. In 1992 there were thousands of U.S. children of all ages living on military bases in Germany. These bases provided complete school systems from kindergarten through high school to serve the children. However, the Exceptional Family Member Program was mandated to serve only school-age children with disabilities who were dependents of military personnel. Some of the school districts had special education programs for 3- to 5-year-old children with disabilities, but many families lived outside the geographic catchment area for these programs. The only way these families could obtain services for their child was to request a transfer into the school district. This was disruptive to the family, expensive for the military, and often took a number of months to accomplish so that a child could miss from several months to a whole semester of the program. What was especially frustrating was to find families with young children having known disabilities such as Down syndrome referred to bases outside the catchment area of the developmental preschool. This happened because only the health care needs of preschool children were coded and the hospital catchment area was much bigger than that of the developmental preschool. There were no Head Start or other subsidized early childhood education programs for 3- and 4-year-olds. Most bases did provide subsidized child-care centers, but these often had waiting lists and high staff turnover because of low pay for service providers. Also, in 1992, there were no early intervention programs for children under 3 with disabilities. Some services were provided on a space-available basis by dedicated therapists whose primary mission was working in the schools, but this rarely could be done more than once or twice monthly.

The Army program did have some advantages over that of New Hampshire. In addition to having public kindergartens in all the school systems and subsidized child-care programs, financial barriers to prenatal and child health services were not factors, as they were in New Hampshire. What have we learned about how to design care systems so that they are more effective?

EARLY RISK SCORES: INACCURATE PREDICTORS OF FUTURE DEVELOPMENTAL STATUS

As we have seen, efforts to extend coverage in this country, such as Part H of PL 99-457, usually take the form of providing closer surveillance of children identified as being at "high risk" for some kind of disability. For example, tracking systems have been developed to follow low birth weight infants. The problem with this approach is that most children from this risk group develop normally, and those who do have developmental disabilities make up only a small percentage of the total number of children identified as having learning and/or behavior problems in school. An example is the Kauai Study in which all the children born on this Hawaiian island during a 2-year period were followed through adolescence ($N = 1,963$). At age 10, 378 children (19%) either were already in special classes in school or were having academic problems. Only 21 of these (5%) came from a group that had been identified as being at high risk because of perinatal risk scores calculated at birth (Werner, Bierman, & French, 1971).

Almost all investigators tracking birth cohorts have found that as children grow older the best predictors of school problems are various measures of the socioeconomic environment (Chamberlin, 1987). In the large U.S. Perinatal Collaborative Study (Broman, 1984) in which 29,800 children were followed from pregnancy through age 7, it was found that such demographic measures as mothers' level of education, family size, and the number of changes in residence were better predictors of school achievement than were the results of extensive developmental tests carried out when the children were 3 and 4 years of age (Broman, 1984; Nicholas & Chen, 1981).

More recent attempts to predict academic achievement at age 8 from developmental evaluations of symptom-free, low and very low birth weight children at age 5 also showed poor predictability (Blackman, Lindgren, & Bretthauer, 1992; Saigal, Szatmari, & Rosenbaum, 1992).

What seems to be most important in producing disabilities is an accumulation of risk factors, both biological and environmental, over time (Miesele & Wasik, 1990). For example, in a longitudinal study of the development of intelligence in young children by Sameroff, Seifer, Barocas, Zax, and Greenspan (1987), it was found that "different combinations of equal numbers of risk factors produced similar effects on IQ, providing evidence (1) that no single factor identified here uniquely enhances or limits early intellectual achievement and (2) that cumulative effects from multiple risk factors increase the probability that development will be compromised" (p. 343). The authors reported similar relationships for the social/emotional development of the child.

RATIONALE FOR POPULATION-BASED PREVENTIVE STRATEGIES

If we can identify considerable developmental morbidity in the school-age population in the form of learning difficulties and such behavior problems as delinquency; out-of-wedlock pregnancy; sexually transmitted diseases; substance abuse; school failure and dropout; and, more recently, homicide and suicide, but we cannot predict accurately which children will develop these kinds of problems based on their birth histories and early developmental tests, then an alternative, population-based primary prevention strategy seems to be a better approach (Chamberlin, 1988c). With such an approach, we can try to reduce the risk scores for the population as a whole, rather than concentrating only on high-risk groups (Rose, 1992). Examples of this are immunizations for all to prevent infectious disease transmission and recommended lifestyle changes to prevent cardiovascular diseases.

As can be seen in Figure 3.3, when risk scores approximate a bell-shaped distribution, moving the mean risk score for all children in a community to the left significantly reduces the numbers of children falling into the high-risk area. *Primary prevention works by preventing low- and middle-risk families and children from becoming high risk.* How can we do this in the United States?

EXAMPLES OF COMMUNITYWIDE APPROACHES TO PREVENTION

Recently, considerable knowledge and experience have been gained in implementing community wide approaches to health promotion and

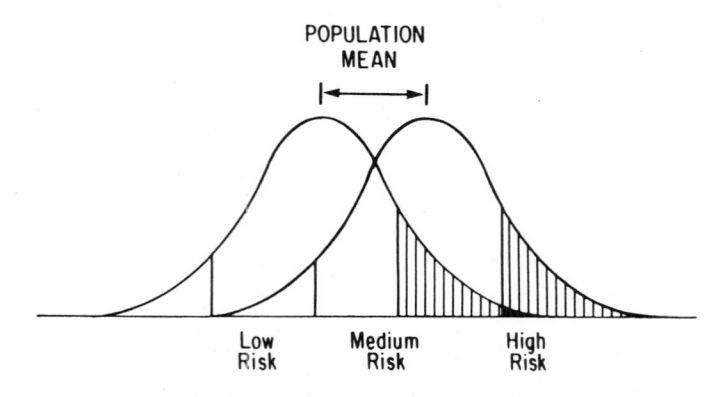

Figure 3.3. Distribution of risk scores for family dysfunction before and after intervention. (From Chamberlin, R.W. [1992]. Preventing low birth weight, child abuse, and school failure: The need for comprehensive, community-wide approaches. *Pediatrics in Review, 13*[2], 67; reprinted by permission.)

disability prevention. Some examples of how this has been done both in the United States and abroad follow.

Addison County, Vermont, Parent–Child Center

This program serves a county with a population of 32,000. It combines a center-based program with extensive outreach into surrounding towns and school systems. The center is located in the largest town with a population of about 7,500. Parents can drop into the center during the day and have someone care for their child while they talk with other adults and/or participate in a variety of activities. There are opportunities to talk with other parents in support groups; to learn such parenting and domestic skills as sewing, cooking, or child care; to receive training in such prevocational skills as preparing a résumé or using a word processor; or to learn how to drive and to maintain and repair a car. The center also serves as a coordination point for a variety of state and local agencies and human services providers. Training in child development for child-care workers is also provided.

Home visitors go out into the community to meet with first-time mothers, teen parents, and families with a child who has a developmental disability or other special needs. Toddler play groups have been established in a number of other towns and meet once weekly throughout the year. Center personnel participate in school-based programs on boy–girl relationships, pregnancy prevention, child development, and parenting. They help towns to stage such community-building events as spaghetti suppers and family fairs. Vans are available to transport parents and children to the center.

After operating for 7 years, an evaluation of program effectiveness was carried out by the University of Vermont. Significant reductions in the incidence of child abuse, teenage pregnancy, low birth weights, school dropout, and welfare dependency were found. For example, teenage pregnancy rates fell from 70 in 1,000 teenage girls during 1979 to 45 in 1,000 during 1986, which is the lowest rate in Vermont. Only 13% of the teenagers served by the center have had repeat pregnancies within 5 years. Fewer than 1% of these teens have delivered low birth weight babies, as compared to 8.9% elsewhere in the state. Among families served by the center from 1983 to 1987, welfare dependency dropped from 40% to 17%, and incidents of child abuse declined from 21% to 2%. The percentage of adolescent parents receiving a high school general education development (GED) or diploma increased from 30% to 71% (Chamberlin, 1992). Because of the success of this center, parent–child centers have now been established in all Vermont counties, and a statewide advocacy group has succeeded in passing legislation to establish a line-item appropriation that provides from about 10%–25% of the operating budgets of these centers.

The Brookline Early Education Program (BEEP)

Another example is the Brookline Early Education Program, developed as a demonstration project in a neighborhood school system in a Boston suburb (Hauser-Cram, Pierson, Walker, & Tivnan, 1991). This project sprang from the school superintendent's concern about the growing number of children requiring special education and his observations that changing family circumstances with an increase in single parents and working mothers were altering the learning environment in many homes. The project was open to any resident of the school district who was expecting a birth over a 1½-year period. The program consisted of four components: 1) a parent drop-in center, 2) home visitation, 3) a center-based early childhood education program, and 4) periodic health and developmental screening. "The home visits and parent groups focused on understanding normal childhood development, on developing networks of people who cared about and assisted each other, and on developing a sense of community—a sense of belongingness into the town" (Chamberlin, 1988a, p. 253). To get some idea of the costs and benefits of different levels of services, three variations in intensity were built into the project, and families were randomly assigned to one of these. The most intense level involved home visits every 3 or 4 weeks, parent group meetings in the center at the same frequency, and unlimited access to the drop-in center. The middle level of services involved home visits and parent group meetings at intervals of 5 or 6 weeks, and the minimum level offered access to the drop-in center with no outreach component. The early childhood education program and developmental screenings were offered to all participants. Children were followed from birth to third grade. Periodic evaluations included interviews with parents and measures of the child's social and academic competence in kindergarten and at the end of second grade.

The interviews revealed that parents felt supported in their parental roles, and they learned to appreciate their children as unique individuals. They felt they had a greater understanding of developmental stages and the wide range of normal development. Parents related that many of their closest friendships had developed through contacts made as program participants.

Children participating in the program were found to be more socially competent at school entry and to have significantly fewer reading problems at the end of second grade. Even children of highly educated parents showed improvement in reading skills, although the children of parents with lower education levels seemed to benefit the most. However, with this group, no benefit was found unless home visiting was included as part of the service package. This led the program director to conclude, "Families with great needs require more than the availability of a drop-in center, even if an early childhood program and health and developmental monitoring are offered" (Pierson, 1988).

Buddle Lane Family Center

Two examples from England provide further information on how to implement communitywide preventive programs. The first illustrates how an isolated child-care center turned itself into a neighborhood-based family center that provided education and support to families with young children (Chamberlin, 1988b). When taken over by the current director, Felicity Thomas, the Buddle Lane Day Nursery in Exeter, England, housed 60 children in two rooms. It was located in a working-class neighborhood of row houses, but it had no defined catchment area. There was little or no staff interaction with the parents and the community, and no contacts with the health-care system, except by referral. The center was run in shifts from 6 A.M. to 2 P.M., 2 A.M. to 5 P.M., and 7 A.M. to 7 P.M., with little pupil–staff continuity. Moreover, it was experiencing vandalism from the surrounding community. The director made a proposal to the education authority to develop a community-based program through collaboration and support by the local Social Welfare, Health, and Education authorities. Social Welfare agreed to pay for maintenance of the facility, transportation costs, and family counseling. Education agreed to furnish educational materials and books and to pay the salaries of two teachers. The Health Authority provided no money, but had a physician visit two afternoons a month to examine children, answer parents' questions, and facilitate interaction with the community health nurses visiting in the area. To reach into the community, a neighborhood catchment area was established for two of the child-care groups, and teachers made home visits to become better acquainted with the families and neighborhood. Toddler play groups were started in several locations around the town. A parents' room was established at the center, which was used as a neighborhood meeting place and sponsored such activities as an exercise program and video club. Relationships were established with five schools in the area in terms of sharing resources and arranging visits for children nearing school age, so that they might become better acquainted with the teachers and the facility. Various community fund-raising activities gave further visibility and opportunities for community participation. Now the center is advised by a panel of representatives from education, social welfare, health, the play groups, and two center parents. Although no formal evaluation of program effectiveness has been made, there has been a striking reduction in the vandalism that plagued the center before it became integrated into the neighborhood.

Lawrence-Weston Community Center

Another example comes from Lawrence-Weston, England (Stewart-Brown, 1989). This is a community of some 8,000 people and consists of a low-income housing development on the urban fringes of the city of Bristol. The initiating factor for the project was a report showing higher rates for infant mortality and child abuse and neglect in this area, as compared to the rest of the city. The report received a lot of publicity and the Health Authority covering the area was pressured to solve the problem. The local chapter of a national advocacy group (the Pre-school Play Group Association) came forward with a proposal that the Health Authority agreed to support. For some time this group had realized that there were few resources in the area to relieve the isolation and loneliness expressed by many of the local young parents. They proposed that a community center be developed in the area to educate and train parents, to provide social support, and to improve access to and coordinate community services. The Health Authority agreed to fund it and a half-time community development worker was hired. She persuaded the City Council to delegate one of the flats in the development for use as a drop-in center, with facilities for both parents and children. A fenced-in outside play area was added later.

The center served as a focal point for meetings of local groups, such recreation and skill-building activities as craft making, and various types of adult education. In addition, the Health and Social Service authorities used it as a meeting place to coordinate services and help families solve problems. Additional play groups were started in other parts of the development. Funding was provided by the Health Authority, the City Council, and through foundation grants.

The center was highly successful in terms of its use by community residents. No figures on rates of infant mortality and child abuse have been provided, but the center had been in operation only a few years at the time of this report, so we would not expect to see dramatic results. Moreover, at the time of this report, the program was in jeopardy because funding cuts had eliminated the paid position of community coordinator. Volunteers had assumed some of these functions; however, the center was surviving on a hand-to-mouth basis. What general principles can be drawn from these and other examples?

IMPLEMENTING COMMUNITYWIDE PROGRAMS

At a recent conference, a number of persons with experience implementing communitywide preventive/promotive programs in the

United States and abroad came together to seek common, successful program components. The following were identified and deemed essential (Chamberlin, 1988a).

Define a Geographic Catchment Area

Although specific numbers were not examined in detail at the conference, the general feeling was that the area should be of sufficient size to provide an adequate population base for effective service delivery, while at the same time small enough to maintain a sense of community and local control. In rural areas this could be a town, a group of towns, or a county. In cities it might be a neighborhood, a political ward, a school district, or a census tract. Based on the experience of others, we estimate that a population base of about 4,000–20,000 would be needed, depending on the geography and population density of the area.

Develop a Broad-Based Coalition

Because no person or agency can achieve this alone, it is necessary to build a coalition of persons who are interested in implementing primary prevention programs and who control enough resources to give implementation a good chance for success. Human services providers; business, education, law enforcement, and religious leaders; community residents with children; and local government officials all must be involved. Although not discussed at this conference, experience from the World Health Organization (WHO) Healthy Cities Project indicates the importance of having political leaders pledge support from the beginning and to ensure that there is enough community commitment to come up with the funds to hire at least a half-time program coordinator (Ashton, 1992; Tsouros, 1991). Coalition building is a time-consuming job, and volunteers will burn out after a period of time unless they are given some support.

Build a Database

This is necessary to establish base rates for the problems you hope to prevent and the risk factors related to them that prevail within the community. In addition, we must know what community resources exist upon which we can build and expand. These measures can then be followed over time to assess progress.

Establish an Overall Framework

When the community profile is complete, we can use these data to identify gaps in services, to set action priorities, and to coordinate existing and newly established programs. The three-column diagram used by the Stanford Heart Disease Prevention Program and others is a practical way to do this (Jackson, 1988). Because of program implications, we have found it useful to adapt it for two different age groups: birth through age 5, and age 6 through 17.

In Tables 3.1 and 3.2 the right columns list the base rates of the various types of problems we hope to reduce. The middle column identifies the risk and protective factors that reside in individuals in terms of the knowledge, attitudes, behaviors, and skills of parents and/or children that influence problem base rates. The left column identifies what needs to happen in families, community organizations, local and state government policies, and the mass media in order to facilitate the individual changes listed in the center column. Using this model, we can identify where the community is now and develop priorities to fill in the missing pieces. Repeated measures over time in these three areas will document whether progress is being made in the desired direction.

Provide an Array of Programs of Proved Value

Experience has shown that there is no one "magic bullet" program or developmental stage wherein we can concentrate all our resources and expect spectacular results. Rather, it is building up an array of programs over time that will meet the needs of different families at different points in time. For new families and those with young children, these can often be organized around a parent–child center as in the previous examples and might include parent support and skill-building activities, home visiting, child care, and early childhood programs.

For families with school-age or adolescent children, programs often can be organized around the school system and might include the

Table 3.1. Overall framework for promoting healthy families and children birth to 6

Environmental factors →	Individual factors →	Status indicators
Family level 　Values and traditions 　Behavioral models	Knowledge about 　Reproduction, child 　development	Rates for 0–5 Low birth weight Child abuse School readiness
Organizational level 　School curricula 　Access to prenatal care 　Paid pregnancy and 　　child-care leave	Attitudes 　Importance of prenatal 　and well-child care Behaviors 　Health habits that influ- 　ence pregnancy 　outcome	
Community level 　Mass media 　Funding of preventive 　　programs	Skills 　Parenting	

Adapted from Jackson (1988).

Table 3.2. Overall framework for promoting healthy families and children 6–18

Environmental factors →	Individual factors →	Status indicators

Family and peer group
  Stability, behavioral
    models, peer pressure
Organizational level
  School curricula
  School health programs
  Life skills training
  Part-time jobs
Community level
  Mass media, youth
    programs
  Opportunities for
    higher learning
    programs
	Knowledge about
	  Reproduction, birth
	    control, hazards of
	    drugs and alcohol
	Attitudes
	  Level of aspiration,
	    self-esteem
	Behaviors
	  Risk taking
	Skills
	  Social, academic, job
		Rates for 6–18
		  School dropout
		  Substance abuse
		  Pregnancy
		  Delinquency

Adapted from Jackson (1988).

following: a health curriculum including reproductive anatomy and physiology and how a mother's health habits affect pregnancy outcome, information on child development and what parents can do to promote healthy development, on-site health services, on-site childcare and parenting programs, peer counseling, life skill-building opportunities, and after-school and evening youth programs.

In addition, family-friendly business benefit packages that include flex time, job sharing, and paid time off for pregnancy and child care, and insurance that covers prenatal and well-child care services can be encouraged among local businesses.

Develop Social Marketing Skills

One point that came up repeatedly in the conference was the need for those who wanted to implement primary prevention programs to become skilled in social marketing techniques. These are necessary to educate the community at large and to turn program need into demand. Many communities in the United States have adopted short-term outlooks and have used such rationales as "prevention doesn't work," "we can't afford it," or "these programs undermine the self-sufficiency of the family" to explain their lack of preventive programs. We must learn how to convince community leaders and residents that prevention does work and that money spent on these programs is an investment in the future that ultimately will benefit all residents in terms of less crime, less child abuse, fewer school dropouts, less adolescent pregnancy, and less welfare dependency. The technology for educating community leaders and residents has been well developed by the Stanford Group and others involved in community-based prevention programs (Bracht, 1990; Brindis, 1991; Farquhar, Maccoby, & Wood, 1985; Manoff, 1985).

Form a Local Advocacy Group

Experience shows that it will be necessary to form a local advocacy group to work at both local community and state levels. This is necessary to facilitate legislative and interagency collaboration at state and local levels to ensure stable, long-term funding and program coordination. Such advocacy groups can also persuade politicians to resist the temptation to cut funding of primary prevention programs at the first sign of a budget squeeze. The loss of funding, as described in the Lawrence-Weston example of Bristol, England, shows what can happen when advocacy is lacking.

COLLABORATION AT THE STATE AND LOCAL LEVELS

These efforts can be facilitated greatly if there is collaboration between the state and local levels of government and between public and private service providers. A resource center that provides technical assistance to local groups is an essential component to help communities undertake these kinds of complicated, long-term projects. One way to coordinate these various components is shown in Figure 3.4.

STATEWIDE PRIMARY PREVENTION INITIATIVES

A number of states are trying to prevent disability and promote the development of the young child in various ways. Missouri and Minnesota have initiated statewide parent education and support programs based in the public school system; however, they have deliberately excluded child-care services as a component because of concern about "undermining the traditional family" (Hauser-Cram et al., 1991; Weiss, 1989). The Missouri program emphasizes sending volunteer home visitors to provide education and support to new parents. The Minnesota program differs from one location to another, but all locations provide such various forms of parent education and support as discussion groups, home visits, developmental activities for children, access to developmental toys and books, and information and referral.

More recently, Zigler and Gilman (1993) developed a school-based model called the "21st-Century School" that combines child care for preschool children 3 and older, an after-school program for those ages 6 to 12, and a family support system geared to coordinate with the

PRIMARY PREVENTION / 49

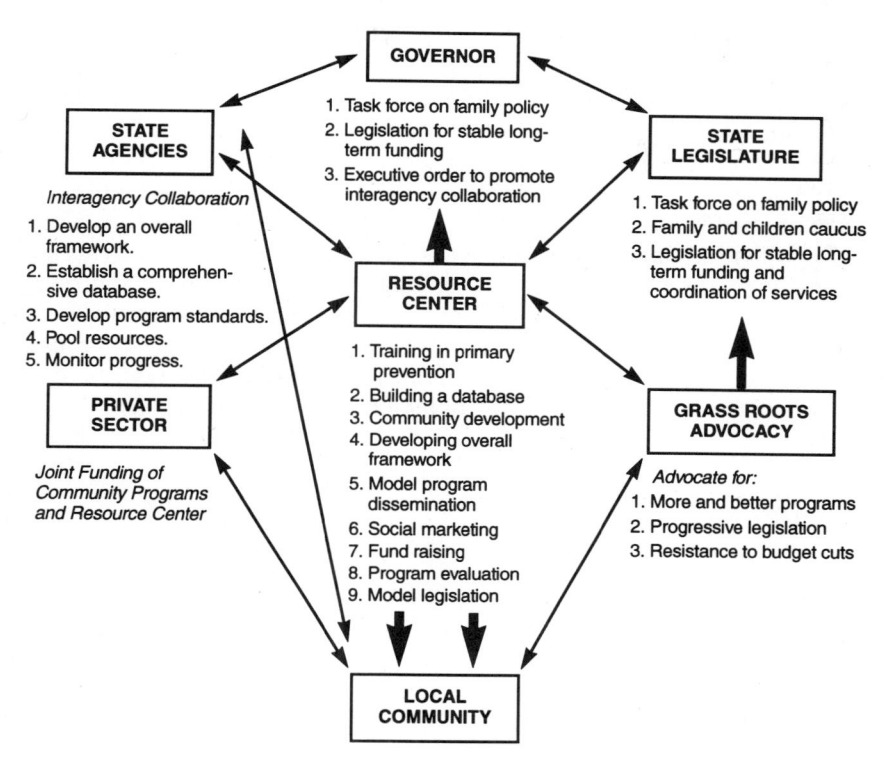

Figure 3.4. Putting it all together. (From Chamberlin, R.W. [1992]. Preventing low birth weight, child abuse, and school failure: The need for comprehensive, community-wide approaches. *Pediatrics in Review, 13*[2], 69; reprinted by permission.)

working day. This includes early childhood education and parent education and support activities in a facility attached to the neighborhood elementary school. These now operate in a number of school districts in several states.

Maryland and Connecticut have developed family support centers in a variety of settings through request for proposal procedures sponsored by the State Department of Children and Youth (Connecticut) and the State Department of Human Resources (Maryland). These may or may not contain child-care components, depending on whether the local communities want such components (Weiss, 1989).

Vermont has established a parent–child center in each county with a set of eight core services. These are child care, parent education, parent support, drop-in services, home-based services, play groups, resource and referral, and community development. These are combined with some individual variations based on local community needs (Mable, 1988).

SUMMARY

Although programs such as Head Start and Part H of IDEA are significant steps toward providing services to children with or at risk for developmental disabilities, they are based on a deficit model. We now have the knowledge needed to prevent a substantial number of developmental disabilities. Considerable experience has been obtained in terms of how to implement communitywide primary prevention programs in the United States. Providing basic primary prevention programs to the population at large, as well as specialized services to those with identified disabilities, seems to be a much more effective strategy than one limited to responding after a problem is identified or trying to predict who will or will not develop a problem at sometime in the future.

REFERENCES

American Academy of Pediatrics. (1990). Child health in 1990: The United States compared to Canada, England and Wales, France, The Netherlands, and Norway. *Pediatrics, 86* (Suppl.), 1025–1127.

Ashton, J. (Ed.). (1992). *Healthy cities.* Philadelphia: Open University Press.

Blackman, J., Lindgren, S., & Bretthauer, J. (1992). The validity of continuing developmental follow-up of high-risk infants to age 5 years. *American Journal of Diseases of Children, 146,* 70–75.

Bracht, N. (Ed.). (1990). *Health promotion at the community level.* Newbury Park, CA: Sage Publications.

Brindis, C. (1991). *Adolescent pregnancy prevention, a guidebook for communities.* Palo Alto, CA: Stanford Center for Research in Disease Prevention.

Broman, S. (1984) The collaborative perinatal project: An overview. In S. Mednick, M. Harway, K. Finelle (Eds.), *Handbook of longitudinal research: Vol. 1. Birth and childhood cohorts* (pp. 185–215). New York: Praeger.

Bronfenbrenner, U., & Weiss, H. (1983). Beyond policies without people: An ecological perspective on child and family policy. In E. Zigler, S. Lynn-Kagan, & E. Klugman (Eds.), *Children, families, and government* (pp. 393–414). New York: Cambridge University Press.

Chamberlin, R.W. (1987). Developmental assessment and early intervention programs for young children: Lessons learned from longitudinal research. *Pediatrics in Review, 8,* 237–247.

Chamberlin, R.W. (Ed.). (1988a). *Beyond individual risk assessment: Community-wide approaches to promoting the health and development of families and children.* Washington, DC: National Center for Education in Maternal and Child Health.

Chamberlin, R.W. (1988b). Community-wide approaches to promoting the health and development of families and children: Examples from Scandinavia and Great Britain. In R. Chamberlin (Ed.), *Beyond individual risk assessment: Community wide approaches to promoting the health and development of families and children* (pp. 176–220). Washington, DC: The National Center for Education in Maternal and Child Health.

Chamberlin, R.W. (1988c). Rationale for a community-wide approach to promote the health and development of families and children. In R.W. Chamberlin (Ed.), *Beyond individual risk assessment: Community-wide approaches to promoting the health and development of families and children* (pp. 3–13). Washington, DC: National Center for Education in Maternal and Child Health.

Chamberlin, R.W. (1992). Preventing low birth weight, child abuse, and school failure: The need for comprehensive, community-wide approaches. *Pediatrics in Review, 13*, 64–71.

Dryfoos, J. (1990). *Adolescents at risk: Prevalence and prevention.* New York: Oxford University Press.

Farquhar, J., Maccoby, N., & Wood, P. (1985). Education and communication studies. In W. Holland, R. Deters, & G. Knox (Eds.), *Oxford textbook of public health* (Vol. 3, chap. 12). Oxford, England: Oxford University Press.

Hauser-Cram, P., Pierson, D., Walker, D., & Tivnan, T. (1991). *Early education in the public schools: Lessons from a comprehensive birth-to-kindergarten program.* San Francisco: Jossey-Bass.

Jackson, C. (1988). A community-based approach to preventing heart disease: The Stanford experience. In R.W. Chamberlin (Ed.), *Beyond individual risk assessment: Community-wide approaches to promoting the health and development of families and children* (pp. 77–97). Washington, DC: National Center for Education in Maternal and Child Health.

Mable, T. (1988). Vermont invests in parent–child centers. *Family Resource Coalition Report No. 3*, p. 9.

Manoff, R. (1985). *Social marketing: New imperative for public health.* New York: Praeger.

Meisele, S., & Wasik, B. (1990). Who should be served? Identifying children in need of early intervention. In J. Shonkoff & S. Meisele (Eds.), *Handbook of early intervention* (chap. 25). New York: Cambridge University Press.

Miller A. (1987). *Maternal health and infant survival.* Arlington, VA: National Center for Clinical Infant Programs.

Nicholas, P., & Chen, T. (1981). *Minimal brain dysfunction: A prospective study.* Hillsdale, NJ: Lawrence Erlbaum Associates.

Pierson, D. (1988). A school system based approach to promoting healthy families and children. In R. Chamberlin (Ed.), *Beyond individual risk assessment: Community wide approaches to promoting the health and development of families and children* (pp. 248–268). Washington, DC. The National Center for Education in Maternal and Child Health.

Price, R., Cowen, E., Lorion, R., & Ramos-Mckay, J. (1988). *14 Ounces of prevention: A casebook for practitioners.* Washington, DC: American Psychological Association.

Rose, G. (1992). *The strategy of preventive medicine*, Oxford, England: Oxford University Press.

Sameroff, A., Seifer, R., Barocas, R., Zax, M., & Greenspan, S. (1987). Intelligence quotient scores of 4-year-old children: Social-emotional risk factors. *Pediatrics, 79*, 343–350.

Saigal, S., Szatmari, P., & Rosenbaum, P. (1992). Can learning disabilities in children who were extremely low birth weight be identified at school entry? *Developmental and Behavioral Pediatrics: Selected Topics, 13*, 356–361.

Schorr, L., with Schorr, D. (1988). *Within our reach: Breaking the cycle of disadvantage.* New York: Doubleday.

Stewart-Brown, S. (1989). Community development in Lawrence-Weston, England. In M. Cordeiro (Ed.), *The child in an urban environment* (pp. 35–48). Lisbon, Portugal: European Society of Social Pediatrics Congress of Portugal.

Tsouros, A. (Ed.). (1991). *World Health Organization Healthy Cities Project: A project becomes a movement. Review of progress 1987 to 1990*. Copenhagen, Denmark: Fadl Publishers.

Weiss, H. (1989). State family support and education program: Lessons from the pioneers. *American Journal of Orthopsychiatry, 59,* 32–48.

Werner, E., Bierman, S., & French, F. (1971). *The children of Kauai*. Honolulu: University of Hawaii Press.

Williams, B., & Miller, A. (1991). *Preventive health care for young children: Findings from a 10-country study and directions for United States policy*. Arlington, VA: National Center for Clinical Infant Programs.

Zigler, E., & Gilman, E. (1993). Day care in America: What is needed. *Pediatrics 91* (Suppl.), 175–178.

4

Maternal and Child Health
A Collaborative Agenda for Prevention

Bonnie Strickland and Merle McPherson

No one would tolerate a fragmented education system in which some children went off to school each morning while others stayed home with no place to go. How then, can we tolerate, year after year, a broken system of health care that denies access to millions of our children? After all, health is a prerequisite to education.
Boyer, 1990

All young children and their families deserve a level and quality of health care to maximize their potentials for life and later achievement. All children and families vary in the levels and extent of care they require over time; however, families of children with special needs continually face the challenge of obtaining not only primary care but also the specialty services they require. Although some issues related to the availability of prevention programs will be resolved through health-care reform, others related to access, use, and coordination will likely remain the responsibility of the community system. In order to address the service needs of children and families adequately we must ensure not only the existence and availability of appropriate services, but also the ability of the community to ensure use of these services. This chapter focuses on the role of maternal and child health as one element of the community providing primary and preventive services to young children at risk for and with special needs.

MATERNAL AND CHILD HEALTH LEGISLATION

Maternal and child health programs have a long tradition of providing primary and preventive health services to mothers and children, particularly those with low incomes or with limited health services availability. Title V of the Social Security Act (1935) provided the original authorization for Maternal and Child Health Services Programs, and recent amendments of the Omnibus Budget Reconciliation Act (OBRA) of 1989 (PL 101-239), have strengthened the commitment of these programs to the preventive aspects of health care. This legislation establishes the leadership role for maternal and child health programs in providing for improvement of the health of all mothers and children by the following measures.

1. Ensuring that mothers and children have access to quality maternal and child health services
2. Reducing infant mortality, the incidence of preventable diseases and disabilities, and the need for hospitalization and long-term care through immunization programs, health assessments, and follow-up diagnostic and treatment services, and preventive and primary care services for low-income infants and children
3. Promoting the health of mothers and infants by providing prenatal, delivery, and postpartum care for low-income, at-risk pregnant women
4. Providing and promoting family-centered, community-based, coordinated care for children with special health-care needs and facilitating the development of community-based systems of services for children and their families

The first three elements of this legislation focus on the recipients and the kinds of services provided through maternal and child health programs. The fourth defines the context in which those services are to be provided and reflects a new paradigm in service delivery for maternal and child health programs; specifically, services must be coordinated and family-centered and must be provided within community-based care systems. Although the legislative language specifically addresses programs for children with special health-care needs, the concept of family-centered, community-based systems of coordinated care has gained wide acceptance as the preferred context of care for all children and families.

Relationship of Maternal and Child Health to Part H of the Individuals with Disabilities Education Act (IDEA)

Significantly, the systems focus of Title V is consistent with the legislative language of other health and education programs serving young children and their families. For example, Part H of IDEA characterizes its systems-building purpose with these words: "to develop and implement a statewide, comprehensive, coordinated multidisciplinary, interagency program of early intervention services for infants and toddlers with disabilities and their families" (*Federal Register,* 1993, p. 40960).

In addition to their systems-oriented purposes, similarities exist in the population of children and families served by early intervention programs and state maternal and child health programs. Maternal and child health programs place a heavy emphasis on ensuring health and related services to poor and minority children and families who would not otherwise have access to health services. Likewise, IDEA is intended to identify, evaluate, and meet the needs of historically underrepresented populations, particularly minority, low-income, inner-city, and rural populations. The majority of children with developmental delays, learning disorders, and behavior disorders requiring special education intervention upon reaching school age come from these groups.

In addition to children at risk, the population served by maternal and child health programs encompasses children with a wide variety of established conditions who also are likely to be eligible for early intervention programs available under Part H of IDEA. This includes children with physical and developmental disabilities, as well as children with chronic health disorders, genetic disorders, and health-related educational and behavioral problems.

In regard to services provided, maternal and child health programs provide many of the health and related services necessary to support early intervention programs. These might include, but are not limited to, health screening, immunization and vaccine programs; nutrition counseling; developmental evaluation; and referral and service coordination. Because many problems of very young children are health related, many state maternal and child health programs serve as the lead agency for Part H early intervention programs.

Maternal and child health programs vary in terms of how services are organized and provided to children and families. In most states, maternal and child health programs, including Children with Special Health Care Needs (CSHCN) programs are located within state health departments. Some states have emphasized establishing a comprehensive system of direct services, whereas others have focused on developing and coordinating access to a variety of public and private community-based services. All states provide core prenatal and perinatal services; however, the nature and extent of these services varies by state depending on identified needs of the state and its communities.

CHARACTERISTICS OF THE MATERNAL AND CHILD HEALTH SERVICE SYSTEM

As we noted earlier, the context in which health care is provided to mothers, children, and their families is an important factor in determining the extent to which families gain access to and use the services offered. Maternal and child health programs nationwide are currently planning and implementing contexts of care in which preventive and intervention services will be provided. This section provides a brief overview of the characteristics of the service system that should be in place to ensure quality services for families and children.

Family-Centered Care

Over the years, providers of services to families and children have come to acknowledge that the quality and utilization of any service is enhanced significantly when families—the consumers of our services—have a significant voice in the design, delivery, and evaluation of those services (Shelton, Jeppson, & Johnson, 1989). As a result, conceptualizations of the design of services and the systems by which they are delivered have changed dramatically. At the policy level, as noted above, this change in paradigm is articulated in the legislation of a number of health and education programs serving children and families. A vivid example is the expansion of Part H of IDEA to include the family as the pivotal decision maker in the design of the individualized family service plan (IFSP), which translates child and family concerns into a comprehensive service program.

Beyond the legislative mandate, principles of family-centered care have been developed for a variety of service settings (Johnson, Jeppson, & Redburn, 1992; McGonigel, Kaufmann, & Johnson, 1991; Shelton et al., 1989), and the changing nature of state and community service systems provides clear evidence that these principles are being implemented by a variety of disciplines in both the public and private sectors in primary, secondary, and tertiary care settings (Federation for Children with Special Needs, 1993). For example, many pediatric hospitals have reconceptualized the design of facilities to incorporate principles of family-centered care by creating environments that are welcoming to and supportive of families. Some facilities have incorporated such family settings as small apartments into their design so families can be together in more natural environments for short periods of time, even when hospitalization for a child may be long term.

Although family-centered care is established as both law and best practice, it is important to recognize that comprehensive implementation of these principles across all service sectors is still developing. Such issues as flexible scheduling of meetings, representativeness of families involved, and sources of and methods for paying families for their service continue to create barriers to full implementation of the principles of family-centered care (Federation for Children with Special Needs, 1993). Because the supportive services that young children and families require are seldom restricted to one discipline alone, it is critical that all health, education, and social service sectors, both public and private, adopt and practice principles of family-centered care. From these principles other essential characteristics of the service system have evolved including such elements as community-based care and cultural competence.

Community-Based Services

One of the greatest barriers to preventive health care is the inaccessibility of services to many families and children with and at risk for disabilities (Koop, 1987). Although location of the service is only one aspect of access to health care, families without transportation, child care, information, and other resources are at a distinct disadvantage when services are located anywhere except in their communities. Because community-based programs are more accessible and are more likely to reflect the specific characteristics of the community, they work better. However, the definition of *community* does not always imply that services must be available in the neighborhood. According to Koop the geographic area covered by a service delivery system depends on a number of factors including population density, political subdivisions, and availability of services. Thus, a service delivery system might cover several counties in a rural area or a single neighborhood in a large urban area.

Although it is desirable that services be provided as near to where the family lives as possible, it is clear that some specialized services are not available in every community, and frequent travel to centralized locations providing secondary and tertiary care may be needed. When such services are provided outside the family's community, mechanisms must be devised to support substantive communication and coordination with those community providers who give ongoing support for families and children.

Coordinated Services

Providing a variety of services is the way various disciplines attempt to address the identified needs of children and families. However, families themselves have indicated that the services provided are often isolated and fragmented, and they fail to interrelate with one another in the best interest of the child and family (U.S. Maternal and Child Health Bureau, 1989). Given the vast array of services for children within any community, coordination is essential. This means that, even when a variety of providers and disciplines may serve a particular family, the intervention program must be consistent and coordinated with both the family and other providers to ensure continuity for the child and family. The issue of coordination is recognized as a major obstacle to the provision of appropriate comprehensive services to families and children.

Culturally Competent System of Care

Access to and use of community-based services go beyond geographic issues to issues of culture and familiarity (Blenden, Aiken, Freeman, & Cory, 1989). Families are more likely to use services identified as important by people they know and that are provided within the context of their own cultural milieu. Thus, the service system must be culturally competent. That is, not only must it be sensitive to diversity, but it must also be competent to organize and provide appropriate services to the culturally diverse groups it is intended to serve. Programs must be designed and implemented to ensure honor and respect for culturally related beliefs, values, interpersonal styles, attitudes, and behaviors of families. The extent to which a program is culturally competent is reflected in the extent to which the culture is reflected in the program staff, the availability of appropriately translated materials and translation services, and the extent to which customs and beliefs of the culture are considered in the delivery of services.

Concepts in the delivery of family-centered, community-based, coordinated, and culturally competent services have evolved directly from the input of families. We know that these factors are critical to ensure that families both have access to and use the services they need. Moreover, we know that it is reasonable to expect communities to create service systems that reflect these principles.

Inclusive Primary Care

In addition to the legislated elements of family-centered, community-based, and coordinated health, services for young, at-risk children and their families should be inclusive. That is, the same quality health care available to most young children and families should be available to all. Establishing separate sources of primary and preventive health care based on income, disability, or other criteria is unacceptable for the same reason that separate education is unacceptable for underachieving and/or children with disabilities in schools. In addition to the ethical questions raised by establishing services based on ability to pay, cost-effectiveness and quality of care issues emerge. For example, the National Health Interview Survey, conducted in 1988, indicated that family income and maternal education has a strong effect on Medicaid coverage for children of all races, but that African-American and Latin-American families were more likely to rely on Medicaid as their primary financing source of health care than were white families (McManus & Newacheck, 1993). If a separate system of health care were established for Medicaid users, that system would consist primarily of poor and minority children and families.

MATERNAL AND CHILD HEALTH ROLE IN PREVENTION AND INTERVENTION

Most health, social services, and education intervention programs recognize the critical role of prevention. Because maternal and child health programs focus specifically on the health and well-being of women and children, prevention programs play a prominent role in the overall maternal and child health picture. This section discusses sources of support for preventive programs for young children and families, maternal and child health prevention programs, and service models with particular relevance to prevention programs in early intervention.

Sources of Support for Maternal and Child Health

Maternal and child health programs contribute to prevention and intervention efforts for children at risk and with disabilities in a number of ways. Three sources provide the primary means of financial support for programs. First a large percentage of Title V Block Grant funds (85%) are awarded to state maternal and child health programs to support the health and well-being of women of reproductive age and their children. At least 30% of these funds must be used to support preventive and primary care services for children, with an additional 30% required to be used in support of programs for children with special health-care needs, including early intervention services.

Second, the federal Maternal and Child Health Bureau supports discretionary grants through Special Projects of Regional and National Significance (SPRANS). These projects are designed to inform national policy through training, research, and the development of new technologies, practices, programs, and service delivery models with the potential for making a positive impact on the lives of children and families. One major SPRANS initiative is the State Systems Development Initiative, designed to encourage the development of state infrastructures that support and facilitate the development of community-based systems of care. These programs currently are being implemented in most state maternal and child health programs to enhance state capacity to support coordinated, community-based, service systems.

Third, OBRA of 1989 (PL 101-239) provided that a percentage of funds appropriated for maternal and child health programs be designated for the Community Integrated Services System (CISS) initiative, a grant program through which specifically designated federal funds are targeted to enhance the development of community-based systems of care through such specific strategies as one-stop shopping, home visiting, private–public partnerships, rural service delivery models, and outpatient and community-based program alternatives to institutional care. This initiative provides the community-based counterpart to the SSDI described above. Taken together, each of these three funding sources is designed to create systems of care that support the comprehensive needs of children and families.

Primary Prevention in Maternal and Child Health Programs

A broad definition of early intervention might include any planned, systematic program of services necessary to prevent and/or minimize the effects of disability on young children with special health-care needs and their families. This broad definition includes the maternal and child health role of developing and implementing programs to: 1) maximize the likelihood of infant survival through prenatal and infant care, 2) prevent the development of delay and disability in children born healthy but whose development is compromised by their environment, and 3) promote the health and development of children who survive but whose health and development are compromised by disability. This section focuses on the first two of these roles. Children with identified special health-care needs are discussed in the next section.

The focus of preventive programs in maternal and child health and other public health programs is provided in *Healthy People 2000* (1990), which articulates the national health objectives to be accomplished in this decade. These ambitious objectives address all areas of health care and all segments of the population, including health objectives for mothers and young children. One of the major goals of *Healthy People 2000* is to reduce infant mortality in the United States. Although infant mortality has declined in recent years, the United States lags behind many countries with nearly 40,000 babies dying each year before their first birthday (Robert Wood Johnson Foundation, 1991). Many more survive but develop a chronic or disabling condition that may have long-term effects on development and school achievement. As might be predicted, infant mortality is highest among at-risk populations with limited access to required services and information. This population is disproportionately represented by African-Americans, Native Americans, and Latin-Americans.

To monitor the achievement of infant mortality reduction and other objectives, state maternal and child health programs are required to conduct a needs assessment every 5 years identifying the need for preventive and primary care services for pregnant women, mothers, infants, and children, including those with identified special health-care needs. From this needs assessment an annual plan is developed that provides a description of how state maternal and child health funds will be used for the provision and coordination of services.

Programs funded through the Title V Block Grant, discussed in the previous section, provide a variety of preventive and primary care services, including health education, prenatal care, and perinatal care for both mothers and infants. To reduce the likelihood of preventable disabilities, intervention must begin before birth and preferably before conception (March of Dimes Birth Defects Foundation, 1993). Because the health and development of an infant is inextricably connected to the health, skills, and knowledge of the mother (Ramey, Bryant, & Wasik, 1992), health care must begin with women of reproductive age and their partners.

Health Education A central component of prevention from a maternal and child health perspective is to increase the likelihood that a child will be born healthy and remain healthy during the critical developmental period prior to entering school. Health education programs, designed to begin in the primary grades and continue through high school, have been identified as a critical mechanism for beginning prevention efforts even before conception. To be effective these programs must begin when children are young and must emphasize such good health habits as regular exercise, adequate nutrition, and avoidance of drugs and alcohol, and must continue with emphasis on reproductive awareness as children approach childbearing age. Self-esteem and self-reliance must be emphasized at all levels. Although most programs are provided through schools, health education can also be provided through community agencies; organizations; churches synagogues, and temples; and civic groups. Regardless of where the program is provided, however, a key element is the linkage with all community health services, to ensure that reproductive awareness messages are reinforced at every health encounter (March of Dimes Birth Defects Foundation, 1993).

Prenatal Care Prenatal care includes regular monitoring of maternal health, nutrition, and pregnancy, and may also include less routine interventions, such as diagnostic ultrasound and management of maternal medical complications for at-risk pregnancy. Ensuring access to prenatal care maximizes the likelihood that a child will not only survive, but will be less vulnerable to developmental delay and disability. Although prenatal care is available in most communities, access to and use of this important preventive service continues to be a problem nationwide. High-risk groups such as adolescents and poor women are among the least likely to receive prenatal care (*Prevention '91–'92*, 1992), and the number of births to adolescents and single mothers has increased dramatically in recent years. Such factors as poverty, having less than a high school education, and being under 20 years old constitute maternal factors that demand provision of sufficient prenatal care.

An expectant mother with no prenatal care is three times more likely to have a low birth weight (LBW) infant (less than 5 pounds, 9 ounces). LBW is linked with approximately three quarters of all infant deaths in the first 3 months, and approximately 60% of all infant deaths occur among low birth weight infants (*Prevention '91–'92*, 1992). In addition, LBW survivors are two to three times more likely to develop chronic physical and learning disabilities that make an impact on later school readiness and achievement (Hack, Horbar, & Malloy, 1991; McCormick, Brooks-Gunn, Workman-Daniels, Turner, & Peckman, 1992; *Prevention '91–'92*, 1992). Maternal and child health programs collaborate with such other community providers as schools, community health centers, and civic organizations to ensure that women of child-bearing age have access to and use community-based sources of information that enhance the likelihood of a healthy birth and subsequent normal development.

A major maternal and child health initiative designed to address the problems of infant mortality and morbidity is the *Healthy Start* initiative. These programs, originally located in 15 communities with extremely high infant mortality rates, are developing collaborative and innovative models for ensuring that the needs of high-risk pregnant women and infants are addressed through community-specific models of intervention and coordination.

Infant and Young Child Care In addition to risk factors related to the health, age, and education of the mother, developmental outcomes for infants and young children are influenced significantly by the environment in which they grow. Even if a child is born healthy, poor nutrition, inadequate shelter, and inadequate caregiving can create compromised development with long-term adverse outcomes (Schorr, 1988). Over one third of infants fall behind schedule in well-child visits and vaccinations. At least a partial explanation for this is lack of access caused by poverty. The poverty rate among children is the highest in the nation, with almost 13 million children living in families whose income is below the federal poverty level. In addition, many young children live in families headed by women, which tend to be poorer because women may receive lower wages and may have less opportunity and fewer sources of support. These circumstances take their toll in school achievement. Developmental delay and learning and behavior disorders, which constitute the vast majority of special education enrollment in schools (*Prevention '91–'92,* 1992), are often the result of compromised health, economic, and social environments during infancy and early childhood, rather than genetic or other physical anomalies.

Maternal and child health programs place significant emphasis on health programs that can influence outcomes during the early developmental years. As increased numbers of children survive compromised births, subsequent health follow-up is essential to promote and maintain development following hospital discharge and during early childhood. Essential preventive health care includes well-child health visits, immunization and vaccine programs, and care for minor common childhood illnesses. For children at risk, coordination with medical, social, and educational services is particularly important. One strategy for increasing access to and facilitating coordination among services for young children and families is one-stop shopping. This model houses an array of health, social, and educational services in a single location. School-based health clinics provide another potential source of community-based preventive care for young children.

Clearly, prevention of disability before it occurs makes sense, and innovative programs are being developed to make prevention services universally available. However, several obstacles present significant challenges to universal access to and use of prevention services. Lack of resources limits accessibility of health care for millions of children (*Prevention '91–'92,* 1992). In many instances, preventive services are not recognized by insurance providers (Davis, Bialik, Parkinson, Smith, & Vellozzi, 1990). Many rural and even some urban communities have extremely limited availability of health care providers. These shortages often exacerbate access problems in already medically underserved communities.

MATERNAL AND CHILD HEALTH ROLE IN EARLY INTERVENTION

Early intervention is a complex and multidimensional experience that spans multiple public and private systems (Shonkoff, Hauser-Cram, Krauss, & Upshur, 1992). The U.S. Maternal and Child Health Bureau (MCHB) early intervention initiative emphasizes the relationship between health and education, and between the public and private service sectors, to ensure the availability of a broad array of early intervention services to young children with special health-care needs and their families. The maternal and child health role in early intervention includes three primary components.

1. Ensuring that the medical–health component of the early intervention system is in place for young children and their families

2. Creating the interdisciplinary/interagency partnerships necessary to ensure continuity of early intervention services
3. Facilitating the development of community-based systems of early intervention services that are comprehensive, family centered, and fully coordinated

Ensuring Access to Health and Medical Services

It is abundantly clear that good health is vital to early development and that good nutrition, immunization, and health education can have significant positive effects on school achievement. However, lack of an ongoing source of health care can significantly compromise the development of young children in both the early years and into the school years. Low birth weight infants for example, require close monitoring after hospital discharge and throughout infancy to minimize the potential for later learning problems in school (McCormick et al., 1992).

Although all would agree that every child needs access to an array of medical and health services necessary for optimum development, 11% of all infants, 18% of those living in poor families, and 20% of African American infants did not have a regular source of preventive care in 1988 (National Center for Health Statistics, 1990). Many more children did have a source of care; however, such care was provided through hospital outpatient departments, walk-in emergency clinics, or health centers, rather than through a private pediatrician's office. Although Part H of IDEA is comprehensive in the services it proposes for most aspects of child growth and development, it does not address the full range of health and medical needs of young children with and at risk for developing disabilities.

The Medical Home The concept of the *medical home* ensures that every child and family has a single, familiar source of health care in the community that also has the capacity to refer to and coordinate with other service providers (Bureau of Maternal and Child Health and American Academy of Pediatrics, 1989). Access to a medical home ensures that the child and family will be maintained within the same community system of health care as other typically developing children. In addition, consistent contact with the same providers increases familiarity between the family and the physician, resulting in reduced child and family anxiety associated with interaction with multiple providers within the health-care system. An additional advantage to the medical home concept is that, through familiarity, the primary care physician can develop a broader understanding of the whole child and family, and thus contribute to the development of a fully integrated program of health services linking secondary and tertiary care with community-based primary care. With more in-depth knowledge of the child and family, the primary care provider will also be better able to assume a key role in ensuring that the health characteristics of a child with or at risk for developing disabilities are considered and integrated into a comprehensive intervention program with nonhealth providers at the community level.

Hawaii provides an example of a medical home model that emphasizes the establishment of linkages and coordination of care between the medical home and early intervention service providers through community forums that include physicians, early intervention providers, and families. In order to implement the medical home model appropriately, primary health-care providers need nonmedical training that includes information related to team participation, family advocacy, strategies for coordination with tertiary and secondary health-care providers, and participation in program and/or IFSP development.

Secondary Prevention Although maternal and child health programs place heavy emphasis on prevention of disability before it occurs, many infants are born with or develop serious health problems that require special interventions and follow-up beyond those required for most infants and young children. Specialty services provide intervention to minimize the effect of the disorder or to prevent additional complications from developing. Examples of specialty providers might include neurologists, respiratory therapists, and disorder-specific specialists. For children requiring these services, the availability of a coordinated system of community-based specialty care is essential to enable the child and family to receive the services they need as close to home as possible and to facilitate maximum coordination with an inclusive program of primary care.

Although specialty services usually are not provided as part of primary care, coordination between these services and the medical home is critical to promote optimal development and benefit from the intervention. Coordinated care plans between specialty and primary care providers is one way in which specialty intervention can be coordinated with the child's ongoing primary health care program, as well as with early intervention and other services provided to the child and family.

Tertiary Prevention There is little doubt that the availability of tertiary care, namely interventions for high-risk pregnancies and neonatal intensive care units for high-risk infants, has dramatically improved the chances of survival and normal development for many children. This level of care, often located within a regional hospital, includes skilled health professionals, inpatient services, and availability of advanced medical technologies to reduce the likelihood of death, low birth weight and/or long-term disability. Tertiary care providers and facilities have flourished in recent years, often in the absence of equal growth in the availability of community-based primary care providers. Although tertiary care services are essential to the survival and development of children with special health needs, this level of care often requires long and frequent hospital stays, often at a location distant from the child's community and family. These factors can compound existing problems for the child and the family.

A significant change in tertiary care occurred when Medicaid, by federal mandate, approved the use of home health care as a cost-effective option to hospitalization for children with chronic illness. As a result, concerted attention has been focused on models for minimizing hospital stays and relocating tertiary care to the community. Although families and providers agree that the best care occurs when children and families receive appropriate care in the community as well as at a hospital or medical center, substantial coordination and training are essential to ensure the success of such programs. One model implemented in Iowa (Nelson & Kisker, 1991) emphasizes close and frequent communication with the community physician during the diagnostic and treatment process, review of the plan of care when the child is ready to return to the community, and 24-hour availability of telephone consultation after the child returns home. Maternal and child health regional nursing staff provide resources to the pediatric center for additional family contact, and ongoing training is routinely available to community providers. Similar to secondary level care, coordination with the medical home not only enables the child to receive care at home, but it can ensure that families receive consistent information from health-care providers involved in the treatment of the child.

Creating Partnerships Among Providers

Collaboration Among Public/Private Health Providers
A truly comprehensive system of services requires full participation by both public and private service providers engaged in providing care to families and young children. There are several reasons why this partnership is critical. First, unlike education provision, children receive health and medical services from a vast array of public and private providers in office settings, hospitals, health clinics, and community health centers. Public/private partnerships are necessary to maintain and improve the array of options available to families and to ensure equal access to quality pediatric services for families, regardless of income level or insurance coverage. Second, public and private programs are dependent upon one another for services and payment. Although the vast majority of health services are provided by private providers, public funds, including maternal and child health funds, pay for about half of all health-care expenditures (Robert Wood Johnson Foundation,

1991). Third, many public programs depend on the availability of private providers to provide the actual services the public program supports. An example is the Medicaid program, which supports health and a number of related services for young children at risk and with disabilities through a system of private and public providers. Being a financing mechanism only, Medicaid depends on the participation of private providers to ensure access to a range of preventive and primary services. Finally, collaboration between public programs and private providers encourages development of and adherence to common goals. For instance, health, education, and social services share a common philosophy regarding the need for community-based services. However, this philosophy can be realized only if each service sector plans, develops, and implements programs in concert with one another.

Family–Professional Collaboration A major goal of *Healthy People 2000* (1990) related to family-centered care (Goal 17.20) creates a new paradigm for health care in terms of how families are considered and represented within the health-care system. This goal recognizes the pivotal role of families in ensuring the health of their children and seeks to restructure services and systems in partnership with them. This means that not only should families have choices in selecting the services they will receive and the source of such services, but that they should have a voice in the design and implementation of programs to ensure that programs are responsive to family needs.

A recent survey of Title V, Children with Special Health Care Needs (CSHCN) programs (Federation for Children with Special Needs, 1993), indicated that the most common form of collaboration was inclusion of family members on advisory committees, with almost every state reporting this type of participation. Approximately half the states responding indicated that family members were hired as paid staff or consultants, and several other states were planning a similar practice.

Although participation in public and private programs in advisory and leadership roles is critical, it is equally important to ensure that families assume leadership roles independent of affiliations with specific agencies around issues of national importance. One such national initiative, "Family Voices," was formed as an organization of families and professionals speaking on behalf of children with special health-care needs, specifically in regard to health-care reform. Still other families prefer to be involved in community-based, family-to-family support activities. Family–professional collaboration initiatives in maternal and child health range from providing education and information programs to facilitate family participation in IFSPs, to sponsorship of national family advocacy initiatives.

Health–Education Collaboration Collaboration between health and education is one of the most often acknowledged needs in regard to prevention of disability. Many would agree that the current system is unable to meet the needs of children and families because of a lack of functional communication among its various public and private agencies (Melaville, Blank, & Asayesh, 1993). At the federal level, the U.S. Maternal and Child Health Bureau has a long-standing collaborative relationship with the Office of Special Education and Rehabilitative Services (OSERS), and Part H of the Individuals with Disabilities Education Act. The MCHB and OSERS have worked closely together both in the enactment and implementation of this legislation.

Facilitating the Development of Community-Based Systems of Care

It is clear that prevention requires a concerted and coordinated effort on the part of all providers of services to young children and families. Maternal and child health programs have the responsibility of providing leadership to create the infrastructure for community-based, comprehensive, family-centered systems of care for children with special health care needs and their families. To do this, it is essential that providers recognize and articulate their relationships to one another. For example, maternal and child health programs must be closely linked with Medicaid and Part H of IDEA because these programs also provide or pay for many of the services provided to the maternal and child health population.

Nationally, maternal and child health programs have an increasing focus on the development of coordinated systems of community-based care. For example, the MCHB provides support for the Community Integrated Services Systems projects, which are designed to support strategies that result in systems development at the community level.

Community-based service systems are becoming a reality nationwide. Because they are based on community-identified needs and resources, each community system is unique. An example of a community-based systems approach to health services is the Child Health Assistance Projects (CHAPS) in Florida. In one of these projects (Siderits, 1991), a needs assessment indicated that: 1) Medicaid was underutilized as a funding source for health care, 2) high-risk obstetrical care was not available at the community level, 3) pediatric services were not available in rural areas, and 4) access to subspecialty acute care and to transportation was inhibited because of lack of funding. Based on these identified needs, a community-based system of care was developed that included the following elements.

1. Comprehensive services with functional linkages between local providers and regional centers
2. A medical home for each enrolled child through private pediatricians' offices
3. Integration of health, human, and education services at the local level through formal and informal agreements
4. Family participation in the development and refinement of the system
5. Maximization of funding sources
6. Expanded local private provider participation
7. Care coordination

This program demonstrated its effectiveness in reducing costs and improving the provision of medical care to children through significant reductions in emergency room visits and the length of hospital stays, and timeliness of immunizations. In addition, families expressed high levels of satisfaction with the program and the services they received from their "private doctor," services that were traditionally received in emergency rooms.

The Community-Based System of Care In addition to providing leadership in facilitating the development of community-based systems of family-centered care for children with special health-care needs and their families, maternal and child health programs play an important role in assuring that children with special health-care needs have access to appropriate quality health and health-related services as health-care reform is implemented at the state and national level. While the primary health and medical benefits provided to children with special needs are similar to those required by all children, access to and coverage for appropriate specialty services is an additional and very important element of health care for children with disabilities. Examples of considerations that are especially important for this population include the following:

1. A comprehensive group of benefits will be made available universally. This means that, regardless of a family's health condition, income, employment, location, or prior use of services, comprehensive health care will be ensured.
2. Primary and preventive health services for children and families with special health-care needs will be provided within the same system as that of children and families without such needs. Specialty services will be provided within the community to the extent possible.

3. The health-care system will be sufficiently flexible to allow families access to services as frequently and intensely as their needs require.
4. The services will be high quality, family centered, culturally competent, comprehensive, and community based.

Maternal and child health programs are working with national and state health-care reform programs to ensure access to and use of community-based systems of services by children with special needs and their families. We know that availability of health care is a major step toward improving the health status of children and families. However, we also know that availability in itself cannot ensure access to and use of services. The community itself and the structure of the local system influence the extent to which services are accessed and used. During the past several years, initiatives in public health, education, and mental health have made a substantial contribution to the development of community-based systems that are responsive to the unique needs of the children and families living in diverse communities. These community systems, each unique, provide the context in which health care and other services are provided to families. Systems-related activities that facilitate access to and use of services will likely remain the responsibility of public programs. For example, one function of maternal and child health programs may focus on the following.

1. Service coordination for families who require assistance gaining access to the services they need
2. Community and state public awareness activities to locate and facilitate access to and use of health benefits and other community services
3. Quality assurance activities
4. Training and community systems development activities
5. Support services, such as respite care and transportation

By making comprehensive health-care benefits universally available and then providing those benefits within multidimensional community-connected systems, optimum access and use can be achieved for children with special needs and their families.

TRAINING PROFESSIONALS FOR NEW ROLES AND RESPONSIBILITIES

Although Part H of IDEA was not intended to create a new cadre of services, it is clear that traditional roles of professional service providers must change in order to fulfill a systems-oriented role in early intervention. Medical, health, social services, and education are all essential to the healthy development of children to ensure that they are ready to begin school.

Interdisciplinary Training

Professional training clearly must change to create a more integrated, community-based system of services. How to produce community leaders responsive to the changing needs of communities is ongoing, but now urgent, as the traditional roles of service providers change in response to the national health agenda. Systems change is not a new topic, and we know that sustainable systems require strong commitment and incentives at every level. We know that simply adding interdisciplinary course requirements to already overcrowded programs does not produce professionals who know how to work within coordinated systems of care. Training programs may have to be redesigned from the ground up, emphasizing what we know is critical to the development of the skills we want professionals to have. Real restructuring is extremely difficult without the full support of university faculty. To develop future leaders who can view educational and social problems from a broader, more interprofessional perspective we must ensure that future leaders:

1. Have extended exposure to real problems related to, but outside, their own specialty area during training and through continuing education
2. Study the community system from inside the community, not from inside the university (Patterson & Blum, 1993)
3. Have sufficient knowledge about the community service system to know what really needs coordinating
4. Gain more than superficial knowledge about related professions

SUMMARY

It is increasingly clear that a comprehensive prevention agenda, beginning with health education and continuing through sustained preventive intervention with at-risk children, is the most effective intervention for minimizing disability and its effects in later years. Prevention can no longer be associated only with the physical health of children. Health, education, and social services have a clear role in creating and sustaining community-based, family-centered systems of care. We must create communities where early intervention is not contingent upon manifestation of a problem, but where prevention means a strong commitment to not only the availability of health, but also to adequate housing, health care, jobs, and education.

REFERENCES

Blenden, R.J., Aiken, L.H., Freeman, H.E., & Cory, C.R. (1989). Access to medical care for black and white Americans: A matter of concern. *JAMA: The Journal of the American Medical Association, 261*, 278–281.

Bloom, B. (1990). Health insurance and medical care. National health interview survey (Advance data, No. 188). Washington, DC: National Center for Health Statistics.

Boyer, E.L. (1990). *Ready to learn: A mandate for the nation*. Princeton, NJ: Carnegie Foundation for the Advancement of Teaching.

Bureau of Maternal and Child Health and American Academy of Pediatrics. (1989). *Establishing a medical home for children served by Part H of Public Law 99-457*. Washington, DC: Georgetown University Child Development Center.

Davis, K., Bialek, R., Parkinson, M., Smith, J., & Vellozzi, C. (1990). Paying for preventive care: Moving the debate forward. *American Journal of Preventive Medicine, 6*(Suppl.), 7–30.

Federal Register. (1993). Early intervention programs for infants and toddlers with disabilities, *58*(145), 40960.

Federation for Children with Special Needs. (1993). *Families in program and policy: A survey of family participation in state Title V programs for children with special health care needs*. Boston: Author.

Hack, M., Horbar, J.D., & Malloy, M.H. (1991). Very low birthweight outcomes of the National Institute of Child Health and Human Development Neonatal Network. *Pediatrics, 87*, 587–597.

Healthy people 2000: National health promotion and disease prevention objectives. (1990). Washington, DC: Public Health Service, U.S. Department of Health and Human Services.

Johnson, B.H., Jeppson, E.S., & Redburn, L. (1992). *Caring for children and families: Guidelines for hospitals*. Bethesda, MD: Association for the Care of Children's Health.

Koop, C.E. (1987). *Surgeon general's report: Children with special health care needs*. Rockville, MD: U.S. Maternal and Child Health Bureau.

March of Dimes Birth Defects Foundation. (1993). *Toward improving the outcome of pregnancy*. White Plains, NY: Author.

McCormick, M.C., Brooks-Gunn, J., Workman-Daniels, K., Turner, J., & Peckman, G.J. (1992). The health and developmental status of very low birth weight children at school age. *JAMA: The Journal of the American Medical Association, 267*, 2204–2208.

McGonigel, M.J., Kaufmann, R.K., & Johnson, B.H. (Eds.). (1991). *Guidelines and recommended practices for the individualized family service plan*. Bethesda, MD: Association for the Care of Children's Health and the National Early Childhood Technical Assistance System.

McManus, M.A., & Newacheck, P. (1993). Health insurance differentials among minority children with chronic conditions and the role of federal agencies and private foundations in improving financial access. *Pediatrics, 91*, 1040–1047.

Melaville, A.I., Blank, M.J., & Asayesh, G. (1993). *Together we can: A guide for crafting a profamily system of education and human services*. Washington, DC: U.S. Government Printing Office.

Nelson, R.P., & Kisker, C.T. (1991, August 24–25). *Coordinating tertiary care and community pediatrics. Hematology/oncology.* Proceedings from the National Conference on Supporting Children and Families through Integrated Services, American Academy of Pediatrics, Philadelphia.

Omnibus Budget Reconciliation Act of 1989, PL 101-239. Title 42, U.S.C. 701–709: *U.S. Statutes at Large,* 105, 2273–2274.

Patterson, J.M., & Blum, R.W. (1993). A conference on culture and chronic illness in childhood: Conference summary. *Pediatrics, 91,* 1028.

Prevention '91–'92: Federal programs and progress. (1992). Washington, DC: Public Health Service, U.S. Department of Health and Human Services.

Ramey, C.T., Bryant, D.M., & Wasik, B.H. (1992). Infant health and development program for low-birthweight, premature infants: Program elements, family participation, and child intelligence. *Pediatrics, 3,* 454–465.

Robert Wood Johnson Foundation. (1991). *Challenges in health care: A chartbook perspective, 1991.* Princeton, NJ: Author.

Schorr, L.B. (1988). *Within our reach: Breaking the cycle of disadvantage.* New York: Doubleday/Anchor Books.

Shelton, T., Jeppson, E., & Johnson, B.H. (1989). *Family-centered care for children with special health care needs* (2nd ed.). Bethesda, MD: Association for the Care of Children's Health.

Shonkoff, J.P., Hauser-Cram, P., Krauss, M.W., & Upshur, C.C. (1992). Development of infants with disabilities and their families: Implications for theory and service delivery. *Monographs in Social Research and Child Development, 57,* 1–153.

Siderits, P. (1991). Florida: Strong private/public partnerships. In American Academy of Pediatrics, *Proceedings from a national conference on supporting children and families through integrated services* (pp. 35–36). Elk Grove, IL: American Academy of Pediatrics.

U.S. Maternal and Child Health Bureau. (1989). *A national goal: Building service delivery systems for children with special health care needs and their families. Family-centered, community-based, coordinated care.* Rockville, MD: Author.

II

PRIMARY PREVENTION CONCERNS

School dropout, delinquency, teen pregnancy, poor health and fitness, underachievement, and problematic behavior are among the high-incidence concerns involving children in contemporary society. The media and the scientific literature confirm their epidemic proportions. While the primary manifestation of each of these problems varies, they all share some common features. One commonality is that they are all developmental in nature, emerging during a life phase of rapid growth and change. A second commonality is that most reflect interactive influences and processes, with the cumulative effect often resulting in what Chamberlin (chap. 3, this volume) describes as viscious cycles, in which one problem exacerbates the manifestation of others. A third commonality, and perhaps the most important one, is that they are all potentially preventable.

The areas of concern reviewed in this section can be seen as representative of the array of problems manifested by children and youth. While clearly not exhaustive, their selection was designed to encompass problems that cut across disciplinary lines and are thus likely to be of common concern to schools and to health and social agencies. In each chapter, a brief vignette introduces the problem, with particular reference to its scope and impact in terms of secondary and tertiary prevention. The epidemiological base and risk factors are identified as the base for a primary prevention approach. Chapters conclude with references to programs that work, illustrating the fact that primary prevention efforts, while not widespread, can be successfully implemented.

5

Healthy Children
Primary Prevention of Disease

Nancy W. Simeonsson and Judith N. Gray

CASE VIGNETTES

Sabrina

Sabrina is a physically well-developed and well-nourished 3-year-old girl. Her developmental milestones were all reached within normal limits, except for walking, which she reached somewhat later than her siblings because Sabrina's brothers and sisters carried her too much and spoiled her. Sabrina is described as "bubbly and easygoing." She has a good temperament and a good appetite. Her mother says that Sabrina eats all foods, if they are well-buttered. Sabrina also likes to salt her food because she sees her father do it. In fact, Sabrina likes all of her father's favorites: creamed soups, fried chicken, cheese, ice cream, whole milk, chips, and dips. Although Sabrina's weight is at the 95th percentile when plotted on growth charts, her parents are not overly concerned about her weight because all the children in the family have been "chubby" babies, which the parents regard as a sign of good health. After all, they reason, Sabrina has had few colds since she was born, so she must be healthy.

Joey

Joey is 6 years old. He is small for his age and appears frail and undernourished. His skin is pale, and he frequently is absent from school. When he does attend, he often seems tired. His teacher has noticed that Joey's breath is foul. He clears his throat frequently, and, at times, he drools. She has noticed that when Joey smiles his teeth are visibly decayed and his gums are swollen. Sometimes Joey does not want to eat his lunch because it hurts when he chews. Joey lives with his parents and six siblings in a rural area where the water is un-fluoridated. Both his parents work part-time in the farm fields, and they have no health-care benefits. Joey's dental health is of concern to his parents, but they feel that these are his "baby teeth," which will fall out anyway.

Marty

Marty is a freckled 10-year-old boy with bright blue eyes and red hair. Marty is overweight, and the other children call him "fatty." He does not like to participate in team sports because he cannot keep pace with the others, and he fears the taunts, critical remarks, and ridicule they usually heap on him. Marty lives with his mother and 16-year-old sister in an apartment on the 10th floor of an inner-city building, and he seldom plays outdoors. Most of his free time is spent indoors watching television and snacking on junk food. Marty's mother, who is also overweight, has high blood pressure and is a diabetic. She works the second shift in a factory across town, leaving home before her children come home from school. Marty and his sister usually must fend for themselves at mealtimes. They usually settle for fast food, or they prepare coldcut sandwiches at home with an occasional bowl of canned soup, although their mother makes an effort to leave more healthy, prepared meals in the refrigerator. Marty's family history, current dietary habits, and limited physical activity put him at high risk for future health problems, including obesity.

CHILDREN'S HEALTH AND THE SCHOOL

Sabrina, Joey, and Marty represent many children in the public education system who come to the educational setting tired, sick, in poor health, or distressed. These children may also suffer from psychological or emotional problems, family violence and abuse, unhealthy lifestyles, poor nutrition, and/or lack of regular health care.

In recent years, children's health has become a growing concern in the United States. Both reflective of and in reaction to this concern, the U.S. Department of Health and Human Services (DHHS) created a national agenda, *Healthy People 2000: National Health Promotion and Disease Prevention Objectives* (1991). Specific national objectives include access to preventive and restorative services through the provision of primary care for children and youth. Although recent federal legislation initiatives enabled individual states to increase their medical assistance to eligible populations, the nation continues to lack a comprehensive program of accessible, affordable, and high-quality health care for all children.

In *Achieving the 1990 Health Objectives for the Nation: Agenda for the Nation's Schools,* the American School Health Association (ASHA) (Allensworth & Wolford, 1988), estimated that approximately one third of the 1990 health objectives pertained directly or indirectly to school-age children. ASHA stressed that America's children not only were at greater risk for certain diseases, accidents, and trauma because of their inherent vulnerability, but that in their formative years, children begin to make choices about behaviors that will have lifelong impacts on their health and well-being.

During the 1980s, a comprehensive approach to school health education became recognized as a national priority by major health and educational organizations (Ellis, Buress, Jones, & Laing, 1992). The emphasis was on curriculum development, availability of health services, health promotion, and disease prevention. The nation's public school systems were perceived to be in a position to make a unique and direct impact on the health of children. Although a decade-long initiative to improve the health of America's children has been launched, progress toward utilizing the public school system as a key setting for meeting the 1990 prevention objectives has been constrained by economic considerations and a number of complex interacting barriers at the national, state, and local levels.

Lack of teacher training on children's health was identified in national surveys as one of the most significant barriers to effective implementation of school health education, particularly at the elementary level (Ellis et al., 1992). It has been suggested that a minimal level of teacher competence would be knowledge about personal health sufficient to model healthy behavior, as well as to teach the generally accepted content areas of a comprehensive school health education curriculum. Another important interactive factor defining effective school health education is the family. Pless (1992) has stated that the family is the most important influence on a child's health care and is a frequently underemphasized but major factor determining the accomplishment of prevention objectives.

Honig (1991) has indicated that since the 1970s, when the concept of comprehensive school health programs began to emerge as an alternative model for delivery of primary health care, only limited and selective growth was achieved. Major emphasis was on the development of health programs for adolescents, leaving a large gap in the availability of health education and primary health care for the majority of today's school-age population.

Honig's (1991) findings are supported by recent reports from the President's Council on Physical Fitness. The council maintains that the fitness of American youth has not improved in the last 10 years, and in some cases, has declined (Brody, 1993; Olsen, 1992). Many children cannot run a mile and are more overweight today than in the 1960s. These authors also report that 40% of children 5–8 years of age have at least one cardiac risk factor, and that only one third of children in grades 5 through 12 participate in daily physical education activities.

Additional sources confirm the scope of constraints that inhibit the primary prevention of disease in children and youth. The Children's Defense Fund (1991) estimated that over 20% of children in the United States were inadequately immunized, incompletely served, and under- or uninsured. Approximately 37 million Americans have no health insurance coverage, and one third of these uninsured citizens are children under 19 years of age, the fastest growing segment of all uninsured populations (Cleveland, 1991). However, insurance coverage does not guarantee adequate health care because most private insurers do not pay for well-child care, developmental examinations, or immunizations (Newacheck, 1990).

Although federal legislation initiatives have enabled local governing agencies to increase their medical assistance–eligible population, the United States continues to lack a systematic program for accessible, affordable, and high-quality health care for all children. Consequently, the devastating impact of the above-mentioned statistics on the nation's children and youth include death, disability, and chronic health impairments, many of which are predictable and preventable.

THE NEW MORBIDITY

Reflective of continuing concerns, the proposed national agenda, *Healthy People 2000* (1991), provides a blueprint for fostering the health and well-being of children in the United States. Included among the many goals and objectives for the nation is the emphasis on health promotion, health protection, and preventive services. Achievement of this ambitious agenda relies heavily on changes in individual behavior, and calls for action at the community level.

The need for preventive health services for children is not a new initiative. About two decades ago Rutstein et al. (1976) stated in the *New England Journal of Medicine*:

> The chain of responsibility to prevent the occurrence of any unnecessary disease, disability, or untimely death may be long and complex. The failure of any single link may precipitate an unnecessary, undesirable health event. Thus, the unnecessary cases of diphtheria, measles, or poliomyelitis may be the responsibility of the state legislature that neglected to appropriate the needed funds, the health officers who did not implement the program, the medical society that opposed community clinics, the physician who did not routinely immunize his patient, the religious views of the family, or the mother who didn't bother to take her baby for immunization. (p. 583)

Their conclusions are consistent with the contemporary argument for adopting community strategies to develop a health-care delivery system that can effectively achieve the goals of health promotion and disease prevention for U.S. children and youth.

The health profile of children in the United States has shifted markedly in the past 40 years. "Public health measures and medical advances, e.g., immunization, sanitation, and antibiotics, have contributed considerably to altering the nature of major health problems. What people do for themselves regarding their health may be more important than what others do for them" (Parcel, 1992, p. 620).

The term *new morbidity* (Haggerty, 1984) has been used to draw attention to this shift in the health profile of children. The term refers to a group of child health problems that are now more prominent than many of the causes of *traditional morbidity*. Thus, in addition to disease and injury, increased attention is given to biological, psychological, and sociological factors that can have a significant impact on the emotional, developmental, and learning potential of America's children. Examples of these "new" factors include poverty, lack of prenatal care, disruptive or dysfunctional home life, child abuse, and neglect (see Table 5.1).

An emphasis on the new morbidity broadens the scope of our considerations for the development and implementation of preventive health-care programs. An associated emerging trend toward delivery of primary health care in schools and community settings, and monitoring the health of children and youth clearly targets the prevention of illness and maintenance of health, with a secondary focus on treatment of disease and disability.

Preventive pediatrics is the core of quality medical care for children. Education and support for children and their parents should be provided during office or clinic visits. In general, however, not much time is spent on such preventive care. Studies have determined that office-based physicians spend 50%–75% of their time doing routine physical examinations during well-child visits. The time spent with each patient averaged 10.3 minutes, while anticipatory guidance constituted only 8.4% of the total visit. Time spent with parents of infants discussing potential problems was 1 minute, 37 seconds, and an average of only 7 seconds was spent talking with adolescents (Adams-Taylor, Fine, & Miller, 1989; Reisinger & Bires, 1980).

The National Commission on Children (1991) identified a number of additional constraints to successful preventive health care, including financial factors, transportation problems, limited or inconvenient office hours, and cultural/social dissimilarities that often interfered with or inhibited effective patient–provider communication. Clearly, these constraints interact in a complex manner influencing the delivery of primary health care services to children and youth. There is a need to

Table 5.1. Child health problems and the new morbidity

- Early adolescents (under 15 years of age) receive the least adequate prenatal care, have the greatest chance of a low birth weight infant, and their offspring have the highest infant mortality rates.
    638 babies a day are born to mothers receiving late or no prenatal care; an expectant mother with no prenatal care is three times more likely to have a low birth weight baby.
- One in 10 infants living in the U.S. has no routine source of health care; approximately 10 of every 1,000 babies born in the U.S. each year die before they reach their first birthday; the mortality rate is higher for black infants who die at twice the rate of white infants.
- 2,685 babies a day are born into poverty; one in 10 infants living in the U.S. has no routine source of health care.
- Nearly one of every eight Americans lives in a family with an income below the poverty level and nearly one fourth of children younger than six are members of such families.
- Several threats to children's health are associated with low socioeconomic status: mental retardation, learning disorders, emotional and behavioral problems, and vision and speech impairments all appear to be more prevalent among children living in poverty.
- Violence toward children has become of increasing concern with rapidly rising rates of reported cases of child deaths due to violence; in 1989, 2.2 million children were reported abused or neglected.
- Risk factors for chronic disease in later years have their roots in youthful behavior: Three fourths of high school seniors who smoke had their first cigarette by ninth grade and one fourth smoked their first cigarette by sixth grade. The average first use of alcohol and marijuana is 13, while 26% of fourth graders and 40% of sixth graders reported their peers had tried alcoholic beverages; an estimated 78% of adolescent girls and 86% of adolescent boys engaged in sexual intercourse by age 20 with approximately 1.1 million girls aged 15 through 19 becoming pregnant each year—84% are unplanned pregnancies.

Source: Children's Defense Fund (1992) and *Healthy People 2000* (1991).

consolidate existing community-based programs by integrating preventive health care into primary practice settings that are affordable and accessible to children and their families. Many communities have taken the initiative to develop such programs and to establish collaborative relationships with a network of medical practitioners who serve children in a variety of health-care settings.

The vignettes presented at the beginning of this chapter are representative of health problems prevalent among today's children and youth. These health conditions reflect cumulative and interactive effects progressing to significant problems that require medical intervention/treatment. Most, if not all of these problems, can be prevented. Recognizing that wellness is more than the absence of disease acknowledges that the health needs of America's children cannot be met by a sole focus on treatment. A preventive approach not only includes immunizations and anticipatory guidance, but, more importantly, also includes teaching children the value and behaviors of being healthy.

Childhood is the opportune period in human development to foster children's attitudes toward health and behavior to help them grow and learn to their fullest potential. School- and community-based health education programs should thus be a significant part of a prevention agenda for children's health and development.

PRIMARY PREVENTION OF CHILDREN'S HEALTH PROBLEMS

As noted in the introductory chapters of this book, any childhood condition or problem can be approached productively in terms of universal, selected, and indicated prevention. Using this framework and defining the concept of physical health as "the prevention of disease and the promotion of wellness," this chapter reviews conditions of the cardiovascular system, oral/dental health, and obesity to illustrate a framework of prevention. The interrelationship of several preventable contributing factors generates a need for early identification and prevention of risk factors associated with these health problems. These objectives can at least reduce the effects and/or major consequences of disease in adulthood.

Cardiovascular Disease

Since risk factors for cardiovascular diseases are related to behavioral practices such as diet and exercise, programs for prevention of these diseases should be started in childhood when these behaviors begin. In his chapter entitled "Physical Fitness in Children," R. Joseph Jopling (1992) identifies cardiovascular disease as a major source of morbidity and mortality. Jopling establishes that cardiovascular diseases are preventable, in part, by changes in lifestyle habits that begin and are learned in the childhood. "It would seem logical that risk factors present in childhood will be present in adulthood . . . therefore the younger the patient, the more likely that changes in lifestyle will help prevent or at least reduce the effects later in life . . ." (p. 246).

deClue and Schocken (1991) identify coronary heart disease as the most prevalent cause of death in the industrialized world. *Healthy People 2000* (1991) reports an estimated 7 million Americans with coronary heart disease and over 500,000 related deaths annually. Contributing factors that directly correlate with increased risk for cardiovascular disease include family history, hypertension, elevated serum cholesterol levels, smoking, obesity, and physical inactivity. To reduce risk, prevention through exercise and diet is emphasized as an objective for the nation by the year 2000.

Certain eating patterns, especially excessive consumption of fats, have been linked to a higher risk of cardiovascular disease. Total dietary fat (including saturated and unsaturated fats) accounts for more than 36% of the total calories consumed in the United States. A fat intake of no more than 30% of calories is recommended by the American Heart Association, the American Cancer Society, and the U.S. Departments of Agriculture and Health and Human Services (*Healthy People 2000,* 1991).

Data obtained from post mortem examination have determined that the onset of atherosclerosis frequently occurs during the first two decades of life. By 22 years of age, 45%–77% of individuals may have evidence of atherosclerosis. Atherosclerotic fatty streaks have been found in children as young as 3 years of age (Jopling, 1992). These findings underscore the importance of early identification of individuals at risk for coronary heart disease associated with elevated serum cholesterol levels. Continually debated, however, is the role of cholesterol in the diet, the relationship between dietary fat content and the development of atherosclerosis, and the need for serum cholesterol screenings. At the 1985 National Institute of Health Consensus Conference on Lowering Blood Cholesterol to Prevent Heart Disease specific recommendations were made for screening children from 2 to 20 years of age (see Table 5.2).

Early identification of heart disease and modification of risk factors could prevent or reduce the atherosclerotic process. With a screening program in place, school and community services could be developed to address the precursors of cardiovascular and other chronic diseases occurring in adulthood.

Attitudes and patterns related to diet, physical activity, and tobacco use may persist from childhood and adolescence into adulthood. Consumer education programs that address preventive measures to ensure cardiovascular health should include all aspects of cardiovascular fitness including exercise, weight control, cessation of smoking, stress management, and nutrition. Many dietary components compromise health maintenance; chief among them is the disproportionate consumption of foods high in fats, especially saturated fats. The 1988 Surgeon General's Report on Nutrition and Health (Public Health Service, 1988) found that eating patterns may shape the long-term health prospects of two out of three Americans who neither smoke nor drink. Considerable evidence continues to associate diets high in fat with increased risk for coronary heart disease.

Hence, a strong focus on nutritional practices is critical to prevention of cardiovascular disease. The guidelines listed in Table 5.3 are consistent with recommendations by the National Cholesterol Education Program (NCEP), the Population Panel, the U.S. Dietary Guidelines, the U.S. Surgeon General, the National Research Council, the

Table 5.2. Summary of National Institutes of Health guidelines for healthy children over two years of age

1. It is desirable to begin prevention in childhood because patterns of lifestyle are developed in childhood. The moderate-fat and moderate-cholesterol diets recommended for the population at large in this report should be suitable for all family members, including healthy children older than 2 years. For children, the diets should provide all nutrients in quantities adequate to growth and development and meet energy requirements. Excessive gain in weight should be avoided.
2. Children at 'high risk' should be identified primarily by carefully obtained family histories rather than routine screening. The history should include parents, grandparents, and all first-degree relatives. A family history of hypercholesterolemia or premature coronary heart disease should alert the physician to obtain at least two blood cholesterol determinations.
3. If the blood cholesterol level in such 'high risk' children is above the 75th percentile (approximately 170 mg/dl for children ages 2–19 years), total and high-density lipoprotein (HDL) cholesterol measurements should be obtained. Those children with blood cholesterol levels between the 75th and 90th percentile (170–185 mg/dl) should be counseled regarding diet and other cardiovascular risk factors and then followed up at 1-year intervals. Those with levels above the 90th percentile (> 185 mg/dl) require special dietary instruction and close supervision with evaluation of other risk factors. A child with a blood cholesterol level above the 95th percentile (> 200 mg/dl) on two occasions is in a special category and may have one of the hereditary hypercholesterolemias. Strict dietary intervention is indicated and will be sufficient for many children. Nonresponders should be considered for treatment with a lipid-lowering agent, a bile-acid sequestrant (such as cholestyramine). All family members should be screened.
4. Dietary management of children with elevated blood cholesterol levels should be part of total management that includes regular exercise programs, maintenance of ideal weight, avoidance of excess salt, and avoidance of cigarette smoking.

From National Institutes of Health Consensus Conference. (1985). Lowering blood cholesterol to prevent heart disease. JAMA: The Journal of the American Medical Association, 253, 2080–2086.

American Heart Association, and the National Cancer Institute. These guidelines can be used by schools and community health providers as a foundation on which to build focused prevention programs to address cardiovascular risk factors in children and their families.

Table 5.3. Nutritional guidelines for school/community health providers

1. Encourage children and parents to adopt recommended eating patterns.
2. Provide nutrition education as a routine part of well-child care.
3. Serve as a resource to communities and schools in developing nutrition education and coronary heart disease reduction programs.
4. Encourage children to exercise and keep fit.
5. Promote health education programs that improve family health skills and establish long-lasting changes in eating patterns.

From National Institutes of Health Consensus Conference. (1985). Lowering blood cholesterol to prevent heart disease. JAMA: The Journal of the American Medical Association, 253, 2080–2086.

Oral Health

Good oral and dental health practices begin long before the child's first visit to the dentist. The process of normal tooth development begins in utero and continues into early adulthood. As with the identification of at-risk status for coronary heart disease, a complete health history and skilled observation provide the means for identification and early intervention of oral and dental disease. Traditionally, the emphasis on promoting oral health begins at about the time a child enters kindergarten or first grade. By this time, however, many children suffer the consequences of poor oral care, such as dental caries, gum disease, and malocclusion. Oral/dental disease ranks among the most common health problems of children today, but much of it is preventable.

Preventive practices should begin as early as the prenatal period when maternal health and nutritional intake can effect the developing dental structure of the fetus. As a newborn, the development of oral muscular patterns can impact on erupting teeth. If an unnatural pattern is formed by atypical tongue and muscle use around the mouth, the subsequent erupting teeth will not be directed into the proper position and may result in a malocclusion. Persistent, forceful thumb sucking and tongue thrusting are additional causes of malocclusion.

Primary teeth begin erupting into the oral cavity at approximately 6 months of age; usually all primary teeth have erupted by 2 years. The most common disturbance in the eruption of teeth is caused by premature loss or extraction of neglected primary or permanent teeth. Early loss impairs mastication and may result in misalignment or impaction of the permanent teeth. Bad oral habits can start early in infancy, often setting the stage for widespread decay and poor oral health. Interceptive practices, such as healthy snacks, toothbrushing, flossing, and fluoridation, can reduce the potential for caries and periodontal disease. While the prevalence of dental caries among children has declined steadily since the 1940s, oral diseases remain a prevalent health problem in the United States (Table 5.4).

Among preventive measures, fluoridation of community water is the single most effective and efficient means of preventing dental caries in children and adults. Yet access to fluoridated water supplies varies considerably across the country. The percentage of fluoridated water supplies across the United States is 23% in the West, 50% in the Northeast, 65% in the South, and 78% in the Midwest. More than one third of individuals with community water systems do not have adequate fluoride and only about one half of those without fluoridated water receive fluoride from other sources (*Healthy People 2000*, 1991). Other potential sources for fluoridation include: 1) school fluoride

Table 5.4. Prevalence of oral disease

Adults over age 65	40% had no natural teeth in 1986
Adults ages 40–44	25% tooth surfaces affected by decay
Adolescents (15 years)	78% have cavities
Children (6–8)	53% have cavities
Oral cancer	30,000 new cases/year, 8,600 deaths/year

Source: Centers for Disease Control (1992).

programs, 2) supplements and/or mouth rinses available for home use, and 3) fluoride toothpaste. The role of state organizations as linking agents is illustrated by the function of many state dental offices (SDOs) in the promotion and adoption of the school-based fluoride mouth rinse program (FMRP) for caries prevention (Monahan & Scheirer, 1988).

Dental caries resulting from poor nutrition habits constitute a significant factor among children from infancy through school age. All sugars and candies (refined carbohydrates) are common contributors to the development of dental caries. During the toddler years the primary contributor to dental caries is "the bottle." *Healthy People 2000* (1991) reports that 53% of children ages 6–8 have dental caries. The possibility of decay occurring at such an early age is increased by such practices as: 1) putting baby to bed with a bottle containing milk, juice, or a sweetened drink; 2) permitting the use of the bottle (containing sweetened liquids) as a pacifier throughout the day, long after the child has learned to drink from a cup; and 3) using sweet snacks between meals as rewards for good behavior.

As children get older their dietary and health habits model those of their parents or caregivers: regular toothbrushing after meals, after snacks, and at bedtime, as well as making intelligent decisions about healthy foods/snacks and tobacco use. If continually reinforced during the school-age years through a comprehensive health education curriculum, such prevention-focused health habits will likely deter the presence of oral disease into adulthood and perhaps for a lifetime.

Pediatricians and other primary health providers can be instrumental in helping families build a strong foundation for establishing preventive oral health practices. However, surveys conducted in 1978 and 1989 determined that many pediatricians (over 75% of those surveyed) felt they were insufficiently trained in preventive pediatric dental care (Nowak, 1993).

A comprehensive school- or community-based health education program should provide children and parents with information on preventive measures and health practices that can reduce the risk for oral/dental disease. Emphasis is needed on such preventive practices as daily toothbrushing, flossing, fluoridation, nutrition counseling, consequences of smoking and use of chewing tobacco, play and sport safety, and the benefits of regular dental checkups.

Obesity

Children who are overweight or obese represent a growing pediatric problem in the United States. In his chapter on obesity in young children, Forbes (1992) comments that obesity is the most common nutritional disorder of Western society today, outranking the classic nutritional deficiency states frequently mentioned in nutrition texts. Obesity is one of the most challenging contemporary health problems for all age groups.

Several authorities in the field concur that a concise definition of obesity is difficult to ascertain. Because there is such variability in height and weight among normal healthy children, it is often difficult to determine the presence or extent of obesity from comparing a set of numbers with a standardized table of weights and heights. Whaley and Wong (1987) point out that the greatest amount of confusion is related to the distinction between the terms *overweight* and *obesity*. Obesity is defined as an increase in body weight resulting from an excessive accumulation of fat or simply the state of being too fat. While the term *overweight* refers to the state of weighing more than average for height and body build, it may or may not include an increased amount of fat. Therefore, it is possible for two children to have the same height and weight and for one to be obese, whereas the other is not. However, aside from the confusion in judging the condition, most studies agree that it is harder to maintain an ideal weight in adulthood if obesity has been established in childhood. Lloyd and Wolff (1981) note that 50% of grossly obese adults were obese as children.

While no definitive statistics are available, conservative estimates report that 10%–20% of American children are obese and that 80%–85% of overweight children will continue to be obese as adults. If one parent is obese, a child has a 40% chance of becoming obese. If both parents are obese, the possibility rises to 80% (Whaley & Wong, 1987; Wilson, 1992). Not only does obesity have serious physical, psychological, and social consequences for the affected child, studies have also shown that obesity predisposes the affected child to serious disease states in adulthood, such as hypertension, cardiovascular disease, diabetes, and elevated serum cholesterol. The proximate cause of obesity is simply the ingestion of calories in excess of need and consequently the caloric excess is stored as fat. Either caloric intake is too high, caloric expenditure is too low, or both.

Other influencing factors believed to play a part in the complex etiology of obesity are genetic influences, environmental factors, activity patterns, psychological factors, socioeconomic factors, cultural influences, and nutritional habits. Dietary patterns are in most instances culturally and socially based, and in some children the food preferences of the family culture may contribute to the development of obesity. Children will eat what their families eat. Hence, instead of encouraging children to eat more (increased fat calories) to meet their energy needs for physical growth and development, greater emphasis should be placed on what children eat (dietary content) to provide the extra energy and decrease risk factors that can lead to obesity (Kimm, Gergen, Malloy, Dresser, & Carroll, 1990).

Experts agree that preventive efforts are essential and must begin in infancy. Recognizing that the family is the constant in a child's life, efforts should be made to help families establish sound nutritional habits early and to encourage a range of physical activities and exercises. Facilitation of parent–professional collaboration could be accomplished through school- and community-developed programs. Programs designed to promote prevention and wellness for children and their families are needed to help them make healthy choices and adopt healthy lifestyle habits. Target objectives could include family-focused workshops on: 1) nutrition, understanding nutrition content on grocery labels, meal planning, cooking strategies, and healthy snack foods; 2) exercise and physical fitness; and 3) behavior modification strategies for weight control. Such family-focused workshops need to recognize family strengths and individuality by considering racial, ethnic, cultural, and socioeconomic diversity.

Comprehensive school health curricula, programs, and campaigns can supplement family efforts to prevent the childhood problems of being overweight and obese. After-school clubs can give children the opportunity to become active participants in making healthy lifestyle choices through activities of: 1) nutrition and dietary counseling, 2) structured physical activity programs, 3) peer support groups, and 4) health consumer awareness. Programs integrating the school and community could be supported by local public health departments, fraternal and professional organizations, and institutions of higher education. A number of initiatives have been developed to teach these concepts to children and adolescents, as listed in Table 5.5.

Current knowledge supports the premise that because obesity is so difficult to modify it would be much better to prevent it in the first place. The *Healthy People 2000* (1991) national objectives give supporting evidence for early identification of children at risk for being overweight or obese, and for reducing potential future risk factors. As previously described, the medical consequences of childhood obesity include orthopedic problems, skin irritation, respiratory compromise, and cardiovascular risk factors. However, most experts emphasize that obese children are also at significant risk for such psychological consequences as rejection by peers, low self-esteem, depression, social isolation, and discrimination. These consequences reinforce the need for the earliest possible prevention initiative.

Table 5.5. Resource list

General Health and Fitness
  Project Health P.A.C.T.
  University of Colorado Health Sciences Center
  School of Nursing
  4200 East 9th Avenue, C-287
  Denver, CO 80262
  (303) 270-7435

  A unique consumer multimedia health education program teaches children from preschool age through high school to participate in their health-care visits and to work collaboratively with health professionals to solve problems and develop appropriate plans of care. Project Health P.A.C.T. (Participatory and Assertive Consumer Training) teaches children to communicate effectively with health professionals and includes a curriculum for Mexican-American children.

  President's Council on Physical Fitness and Sports
  701 Pennsylvania Avenue, NW
  Suite 250
  Washington, DC 20004
  (202) 272-3424

  Works with schools, clubs, and recreation agencies on physical fitness and exercise program design and implementation. Produces informational materials on exercise, school physical education programs, and physical fitness.

  American Alliance for Health, Physical Education, Recreation, and Dance
  1900 Association Drive
  Reston, VA 22091
  (703) 476-3400

  Promotes school health and physical education programs. Distributes materials for professionals.

Dental Caries
  American Dental Association
  Department of Public Information and Education
  211 East Chicago Avenue
  Chicago, IL 60611
  (312) 440-2593

  Offers print and audiovisual educational materials on oral health topics, including fluoridation programs.

(continued)

Table 5.5. (continued)

American Society of Dentistry for Children
211 East Chicago Avenue, Suite 1430
Chicago, IL 60611
(312) 943-1244

Promotes sound dental practices for children and increased awareness of child dental health needs. Offers dental educational materials.

Obesity
U.S. Department of Health and Human Services
Health Resources and Services Administration
National Maternal and Child Health Clearinghouse
8201 Greensboro Drive, Suite 600
McLean, VA 22102
(703) 821-8955

Provides consultation and networking opportunities for consumer groups.

U.S. Department of Agriculture
Food and Nutrition Information Center
National Agricultural Library
Room 304
10301 Baltimore Boulevard
Beltsville, MD 20705
(301) 504-5719

Provides print and audiovisual materials for consumers and professionals on topics in nutrition, food technology, and food service.

Heart Disease and Stroke
American Heart Association
7272 Greenville Avenue
Dallas, TX 75231-4599
(214) 706-1220

Sponsors research, community programs, and professional education on cardiovascular disease. Publishes diet plans and cookbooks focusing on lower dietary fat intake.

U.S. Department of Agriculture
Food and Nutrition Information Center
National Agricultural Library
Room 304
10301 Baltimore Boulevard
Beltsville, MD 20705
(301) 504-5719

Provides bibliographies and resource guides about nutrition and cardiovascular health.

Source: *Healthy People 2000* (1991).

Primacy of Nutrition in Child Health

Prevention of disease and promotion of wellness in a young child cannot be discussed without considering the central role of nutrition. Although the focus of this chapter is on the primary prevention of risk factors associated with cardiovascular disease, oral and dental health, and obesity, a review of the literature clearly establishes the need for adequate intake of essential nutrients for satisfactory growth and development and for maintenance of well-being throughout life. Studies continue to identify increased risk for certain chronic diseases associated with dietary habits. The range of influences that have an impact on a child's nutritional state is extensive and includes family customs, habits, and attitudes toward food; religion and culture; education; media advertising; and environmental and socioeconomic factors. Thus children's nutritional needs are of paramount concern, and should be a primary aspect of health promotion and prevention programs. Primary health care providers must not only identify potential or actual risk factors related to nutritional intake, but should also understand the basic principles of how the body uses food, the links between nutrition and health, and behavioral and educational approaches to encourage children to develop healthy dietary habits.

The science of nutrition continues to expand, and new data continue to emerge relating to nutrients and the amounts considered essential for optimal growth and health. Therefore it is important for primary care providers to remain current on recommended practices about good nutrition if they are to effect changes in the dietary habits of families. Current information and materials about dietary fat content and caloric requirements are available from state and local sources (listed in the telephone directory) as well as from the federal data sources listed in Table 5.6.

SCHOOL/COMMUNITY-ORIENTED FRAMEWORK

Essential to the primary prevention of disease are the availability and accessibility of primary health-care services for children and families through school and community programs and through primary health-care services. Components of school/community health programs vary widely across the nation. Most areas of the country utilize the more established models, which include the basic elements of student-focused health services (first aid, screenings, immunizations), health education (classroom instruction), and healthful environments (physical safety). However, increased recognition of the need for family involvement and family-focused models has placed the emphasis for primary health-care delivery on strong interagency collaboration within the community. Effective programs must be community based and school oriented to: 1) provide adequate access to health care, and 2) foster an environment that encourages a partnership in the delivery of health care.

School/community primary health-care settings allow community providers to mold service availability to meet the specific characteristics

Table 5.6. Federal data sources

Centers for Disease Control 1600 Clifton Road Atlanta, GA 30333 (404) 639-3311	Food and Drug Administration Federal Building 8, Room 1832 200 C Street, SW Washington, DC 20201 (202) 205-4561
National Center for Health Statistics 6525 Belcrest Road Hyattsville, MD 20782 (301) 436-8500	National Institutes of Health Division of Nutrition Research Coordination Building 31, Room 4B63 9000 Rockville Pike Bethesda, MD 20892 (301) 496-9281
Healthy People 2000 Staff 6525 Belcrest Road, Room 630 Hyattsville, MD 20782 (301) 436-3548	
National Center for Chronic Disease Prevention and Health Promotion 160 Clifton Road, NE Atlanta, GA 30333 (404) 639-3942	U.S. Department of Agriculture Food and Nutrition Information Center National Agricultural Library Room 304 10301 Baltimore Boulevard Beltsville, MD 20705 (301) 504-5719

and needs of the targeted consumer group. These services should be sensitive to the cultural norms of the community, and have a small, humanistic organizational structure.

Successful community intervention programs require collaborative relationships between providers and consumers at all levels of involvement. To be an asset to the community, they need to be flexible, intensive, and comprehensive. The Silver Spring Neighborhood Center (SSNC), Milwaukee (Lundeen, 1993), provides an excellent example of a community-based, school-oriented preventive health-care program modeled after the settlement house concept. In 1986, SSNC had no primary health-care services available, but it did have educational, social, recreational, and support services. By introducing a family-oriented case-managed philosophy, nurses were employed to provide community-based nursing services. As case managers, nurses and nurse clinicians were able to provide comprehensive health assessments of child and family needs at the SSNC community-based centers. Additional team members consisted of teachers, police officers, social workers, and various community volunteers. Other professionals and members of the community were included as members of the team on an ad hoc basis as determined by the needs of each individual center. At times, more than 15 different agencies were providing services to individual SSNCs. As knowledge of this widespread collaboration became known, many other organizations were attracted, and satellite programs were developed from the SSNC premise. Multiple sources of funding were identified, and the program was acknowledged as a successful effort by community leaders and consumers.

In keeping with the major theme of this chapter, the public school system increasingly is being considered a prime gateway to health care, accessing the majority of the children in our nation. "Every school day, nearly 47 million students attend elementary and secondary schools in the United States; about six million professional and non-professional workers staff those schools. Thus, schools constitute the center of work activity for nearly one fifth of the U.S. population" (Lavin, Shapiro, & Weill, 1992, p. 217). School-based primary prevention and health promotion programs reflect the growing belief of many authorities in the field that the school system "could do more perhaps than any other single agency in society to help young people, and the adults they will become, to live healthier, and more productive lives" (Allensworth & Kolbe, 1987, p. 409).

Comprehensive school health programs are now recognized as more than just services to prevent communicable disease and the provision of first aid for minor physical ailments of children. Using the public school system as a primary health-care setting is a concept gaining nationwide acceptance. School-based clinics (SBCs) are acknowledged as a cost-efficient method of providing primary care to school-age children. SBCs are also recognized as the link to promoting effective coordination of health-care services between school and community for many uninsured children and youths.

MODELS THAT WORK

The Experience in Baltimore
(Feroli, Hobson, Miola, Scott, & Waterfield, 1992)

An early model of a school-based health clinic movement began in 1970, in Dallas, in response to growing concerns for the psychosocial, medical, and educational risks associated with teen parenting. This model was adopted by the city of Baltimore, which has one of the highest teen pregnancy rates in the nation. Twenty-three percent of all births in Baltimore hospitals are to adolescent mothers. Of the 40,000 patients seen at the city's health department, one third are teenagers. A survey conducted in 1984 showed that 61.9% of Maryland high school students had tried marijuana and 31% were still users. School-based clinics played a very important part in lowering each of these statistics. They allowed teens an avenue for accessible and affordable health care. Because these services were provided in the teens' own setting, they felt more comfortable and were able to communicate more easily.

Approximately 50 students were seen per day and typically were provided with an array of health-care information that would otherwise not be available unless these teens went to a physician's office. Nurse practitioners provided the primary care for students who utilized the SBCs, while also acting as consultants and health educators. Although nurse practitioners function independently in these SBCs, there is frequent communication with community physicians for complex medical problems.

Toward Teen Health: The Ounce of Prevention Fund School-Based Adolescent Health Centers, Chicago (Stone, 1992)

The Ounce of Prevention Fund was established in 1982 as a public/private partnership to promote the well-being of children and adolescents by working with families, communities, and policy makers. In its commitment to improve the quality of life for disadvantaged children and families in Illinois, The Ounce of Prevention program philosophy is based on the conviction that it is more caring and effective to promote healthy child development than to treat problems later in life.

One of the foundation's projects is called the Toward Teen Health Program. It opened the first of three high school–based adolescent health centers at Chicago's DuSable High School in 1985. The DuSable Center was funded by the Illinois Department of Public Aid, private contributions from the Robert Wood Johnson Foundation's Community Care Funding Partners Program, and others. The Rezin Orr Community Academy school-based clinic opened in 1986 and the Crane High School Health Center opened in 1987 with the additional support of the Illinois Department of Public Health.

Today, the Ounce of Prevention Fund supports the operation of these three school/community-based health centers serving more than 3,000 high school students each year in Chicago's toughest and most economically depressed neighborhoods. Since 1985, the Toward Teen Health Program has helped school-age youth find community health services despite the dwindling availability of financial resources. The program has provided comprehensive health-care services to teens growing up in poverty with hypertension, asthma, poor eyesight, heart disease, and/or developmental delays.

The Toward Teen Health Centers are school-based comprehensive health clinics designed to accommodate the special needs of the adolescent. Services address physical and emotional well-being, and help students avoid unhealthy behaviors that put them at risk. Services focus on motivating students to take responsibility for their behaviors. This message is reinforced through implementation of special programs on classroom health education and schoolwide activities, such as health fairs and assemblies.

The centers have physicians available on site at least 3 half-days per week. The physicians are also available for consultation or referral at all times. Each center is also staffed with a full-time nurse practitioner who is the primary care provider and coordinator of all other activities.

Under agreement with the Chicago Board of Education, students using health center services must have consent from a parent or legal guardian on file specifying which service may be provided.

Reaching Youth at the School Site: The School-Based Youth Services Program, New Jersey

In 1987, the New Jersey School-Based Youth Services Program (SBYSP) was enacted. This was the first substantial effort by a state to link schools and social services to help ensure the health and welfare of children and youth. With a focus on adolescents, comprehensive services were placed in or very near high schools. Thirty program sites were developed, at least one in each county, with most in low-income urban or rural areas.

Primary funding for SBYSP is through an annual $6 million state appropriation. Core services include mental health and family counseling, primary and preventive health services (on site or by referral), substance-abuse counseling, employment counseling, summer and part-time job development, academic counseling, and referral to other health and social services not available on site. Recreation programs are offered as a way to attract youngsters. Some sites also offer other services, such as child care services for teen parents, special vocational programs, family planning, transportation, and hotlines. The state does not impose a single statewide design, but it does require each of the sites to offer at least a core set of services and to operate not only during school hours, but also after school, on weekends, and during vacations.

SBYSP is one of the few school-linked service programs that is open to any student in a participating school. There are no limiting eligibility criteria, nor does a student have to have an identified problem. Parental consent is required for all SBYSP services and some family services are available, but generally speaking the target population is the child, not the family (Levy & Shepardson, 1992).

Health and Education Partnership

Former Surgeon General Novello (1992) has stated that good health is a critical partner to education. All children have the right to be healthy.

A child must be healthy in order to learn and must be educated in order to stay healthy.

Today's children and teenagers face more dangerous health risks than have recent generations. Risks such as drug abuse, teen pregnancy, sexually transmitted diseases (STDs), and violence often are exacerbated for those disadvantaged by poverty. In addition to being threatened by a general increase in risky behavior among all young people, these youngsters grow up surrounded by community problems such as unemployment and limited health services.

In poor communities, both rural and urban, even the most concerned parents cannot afford to miss work to take their children to the doctor. In rural communities, lack of transportation can render health care particularly inaccessible. Red tape and waiting lists make it difficult for poor families everywhere to obtain even the basic health services that most take for granted.

In 1987, the Robert Wood Johnson Foundation awarded grants to 18 community institutions around the country to establish school-based health centers. The grantees launched health centers in 24 schools to provide on-site, comprehensive, physical and mental health care for adolescents at risk—ranging from physical exams and lab tests to prescriptions and counseling. While the original focus was on adolescents, the concept of school-based health centers proved effective for younger students as well. Many models now serve various populations.

At that time, this concept was viewed as a controversial experiment. The earliest health centers were mainly in urban high schools; since then, however, the school-based model has expanded. Health centers now thrive in elementary schools, middle schools, and high schools in urban as well as rural communities. It is clearly a model that has successfully delivered comprehensive care to students and earned widespread support (Thornton & Frankenburg, 1983).

> In 1990, the U.S. Public Health Service's *Healthy People 2000* cited school-based health centers as model programs for improving the health of America's youth. In 1991, the Congressional Office of Technology Assessment repeated this recommendation in its report, *Adolescent Health*. From Oregon to Florida, states have launched new, comprehensive school-based health services as a way to meet the needs of underserved children.
>
> The President's Advisory Commission on Social Security recommended that school-based health centers be established in elementary schools and urged the federal govenment to allocate $3 billion to help fund them. The 1993 federal budget requested funds for a program to support these health centers in numerous high-risk communities.
>
> Finally, the model has won the support of the health professionals. The American Medical Association, the American Academy of Pediatrics, the American Nurses Association, the National Association of School Health

Nurses, and other professional organizations have endorsed the establishment of school-based health centers in medically underserved areas. (The School-Based Adolescent Health Care Program, 1993, p. 5)

THE 21ST CENTURY: AN AGENDA FOR CHANGE

In the last few decades several studies have acknowledged the effect of education on health, and conversely the effect of health on education. Yet, little progress has been made toward achieving a more effective and less fragmented system of delivering primary health care, health education, and preventive services to America's children and their families. Since health education involves getting people to change their behavior, we must teach youths to take responsibility for their health and not expect high-tech medicine to prolong their lives. Preventive health measures are simple and cost less (Koop, 1991).

The three health concerns highlighted in this chapter are representative of health problems with risk factors associated with cumulative effects into adulthood: cardiovascular disease, oral/dental problems, and obesity. A tide of evidence confirms the need for an agenda of early recognition of these risk factors and for early implementation of preventive programs. Table 5.7 summarizes the dimensions of this agenda in terms of risk factors and complementary prevention activities and health education activities.

New national health initiatives create important opportunities for the concepts of primary care, prevention, and wellness to be translated into action. Movement toward collaboration and integration of community-based and school-based health-care centers must be expanded to meet both child and family health-care needs. Primary health-care settings must allow for easy access, simplified intake, and provision of flexible, coordinated, and comprehensive responses to the interrelated needs of the family.

Expansion of health provider roles within the school and the community seems timely and appropriate. Nurses and nurse practitioners, in particular, must assume leadership roles in response to the *Healthy People 2000* (1991) national objectives. Such leadership is imperative and central to implementing cost-effective health-care delivery.

The directions we need to pursue are clearly those that America's nurses have long supported. Igoe and Giordano (1992) relate that in 1991 the nation's nursing organizations, through the leadership of the American Nurses Association and the National League of Nursing's Consumer Health Council, endorsed an agenda for health-care reform. The basic concept of the plan is universal access to primary health care, achieved by maximizing the use of consumer-friendly set-

Table 5.7. School health primary promotion/prevention activities

Representative health considerations	Risk factors	Prevention activities	Health education activities
General health and fitness	Poor dietary habits Limited regular exercise/physical activity Lack of primary health care	HM[a] WCC[b] Routine screenings (e.g., vision and hearing) Physical fitness and exercise	Teach children to communicate effectively with health professionals Work with schools to design and implement exercise and fitness programs
Cardiac health	High serum cholesterol Family history Sedentary activity Obesity Smoking Stress	Screening HM WCC Regular exercise Diet to promote cardiac health	Promote nutritional strategies that support cardiovascular health, focusing on lower dietary fat intake
Obesity	Family history Depression and related psychosocial conditions Endocrine disorder Sedentary activity Imbalance of caloric intake vs. caloric needs	Screening HM WCC Regular exercise Diet to promote optimal growth and development	Promote nutritional strategies for appropriate growth and development of children
Dental health	Well water without fluoride No flossing High intake of sweets Poor dental hygiene Chewing tobacco	Screening Sealants Regular dental visits Dental hygiene Fluoride treatment Good nutrition	Promote increased awareness of child dental health needs Promote fluoridation programs in schools

[a]HM, health maintenance.
[b]WCC, well-child check-up.

tings already in existence. The plan calls for: 1) a basic core of essential health care services to be available to everyone; 2) a restructured health care system that fosters consumer participation and responsibility, with services delivered in familiar and convenient sites such as schools, workplaces, and homes; and 3) a shift from the predominant focus on illness and cure to an orientation toward wellness and care (Igoe & Giordano, 1992).

To achieve these goals we must shift the focus of health-care delivery from the traditional restorative approach to that of primary preventive practices. We must reorient, re-educate, and refocus local, state, and national leaders to ensure collaboration and commitment toward improving the health and quality of our nation's children. This chapter has described representative primary promotion/prevention activities that may help us to accomplish this goal. Such opportunities to prevent and/or control the risk for premature onset of disease and disability can only be limited by a lack of vision.

REFERENCES

Adams-Taylor, S., Fine, A., & Miller, C.A. (1989). *Monitoring children's health: Key indicators* (2nd ed.). Washington, DC: American Public Health Association.

Allensworth, D.D., & Kolbe, L.J. (1987). The comprehensive school health program: Exploring an expanded concept. *Journal of School Health, 57,* 409–412.

Allensworth, D.D., & Wolford, C.A. (1988). *Achieving the 1990 health objectives for the nation: Agenda for the nation's schools.* Kent, OH: American School Health Association.

Brody, J.E. (1993, February 24). Unkindest cut of all: Our children's physical fitness. *The Chapel Hill Herald,* B-8, B-9.

Centers for Disease Control. (1992, November 20). *Advance data* (no. 219). Hyattsville, MD: National Center for Health Statistics.

Children's Defense Fund. (1992). *The state of America's children.* Washington, DC: Author.

Cleveland, W.W. (1991). Redoing the health care quilt: Patches or whole cloth? *American Journal of Diseases of Children, 145,* 499–504.

deClue, T.J., & Schocken, D.M. (1991). Cholesterol screening management of Florida's pediatric population. *Clinical Pediatrics, 30*(6), 340–342.

Ellis, J., Buress, C.E., Jones, L.H., & Laing, S.J. (1992). Health instruction responsibilities and competencies for elementary (K-6) classroom teachers. *Journal of Health Education, 23*(6), 352–353.

Feroli, K.L., Hobson, S.K., Miola, E.S., Scott, P.N., & Waterfield, G.D. (1992). School-based clinics: The Baltimore experience. *Journal of Pediatric Health Care, 6,* 127–131.

Forbes, G.B. (1992). Principles of patient care. In S.B. Friedman, R.A. Hoekelman, N.M. Nelson, & H.M. Seidel (Eds.), *Primary pediatrics care* (2nd ed., pp. 194–196). St. Louis: C.V. Mosby.

Haggerty, R.J. (1984). The changing role of the pediatrician in child health care. *American Journal of Diseases of Children, 127,* 545–549.

Healthy people 2000: National health promotion and disease prevention objectives. (1991). Washington, DC: Public Health Service, U.S. Department of Health and Human Services.

Honig, J.D. (1991). A school-based clinic in a preschool. *Journal of Pediatric Health Care, 5*(1), 34–39.

Igoe, J.B., & Giordano, B.P. (1992). *Expanding school health services to serve families in the 21st century.* Washington, DC: American Nurses Publishing.

Jopling, R.J. (1992). Physical fitness in children. In S.B. Friedman, R.A. Hoekelman, N.M. Nelson, & H.M. Seidel (Eds.), *Primary pediatrics care* (2nd ed., pp. 246–256). St. Louis: C.V. Mosby.

Kimm, S.Y.S., Gergen, P.J., Malloy, M., Dresser, C., & Carroll, M. (1990). Dietary patterns of U.S. children: Implications for disease prevention. *Preventive Medicine, 19*(4), 432–442.

Koop, C.E. (Ed.). (1991). *Koop: The memoirs of America's family doctor.* New York: Random House.

Lavin, A.T., Shapiro, G.R., & Weill, K.S. (1992). Creating an agenda for school-based health promotion: A review of 25 selected reports. *Journal of School Health, 62*(6), 212–228.

Levy, J.E., & Shepardson, W. (1992). A look at current school-linked service efforts. In *The future of the children* (Vol. 2, No. 1, pp. 44–55). Los Altos, CA: Center for the Future of Children, The David and Lucile Packard Foundation.

Lloyd, J.K., & Wolff, O.H. (1981). Childhood obesity. *British Medical Journal, 2,* 145–149.

Lundeen, S.P. (1993). Comprehensive, collaborative, coordinated, community-based care: A community nursing center model. *Family & Community Health, 16,* 57–65.

Monahan, J.L., & Scheirer, M.A. (1988, Winter). The role of linking agents in the diffusion of health promotion programs. *Health Education Quarterly, 15*(4), 417–433.

National Commission on Children. (1991). *Beyond rhetoric: A new American agenda for children and families. Final report of the National Commission on Children.* Washington, DC: U.S. Government Printing Office.

National Institutes of Health Concensus Conference. (1985). Lowering blood cholesterol to prevent heart disease. *JAMA: The Journal of the American Medical Association, 253,* 2080–2086.

Newacheck, P.W. (1990). Improving access to health care for children, youth, and pregnant women. *Pediatrics, 86*(4), 626–635.

Novello, A.C. (1992). Healthy children ready to learn: An essential collaboration between health and education. *Public Health Reports, 107*(1), 3–10.

Nowak, A.J. (1993). What pediatricians can do to promote oral health. *Contemporary Pediatrics, 10*(4), 90–106.

Olsen, P.J. (1992). Body mechanics for children. When should prevention start? *Work, 2*(2), 48–52.

Parcel, G.S. (1992). School health education. In S.B. Friedman, R.A. Hoekelman, N.M. Nelson, & H.M. Seidel (Eds.), *Primary pediatrics care* (2nd ed., pp. 620–625). St. Louis: C.V. Mosby.

Pless, I.B. (1992). Morbidity and mortality among the young. In S.B. Friedman, N.M. Nelson, & H.M. Seidel (Eds.), *Primary pediatrics care* (2nd ed., pp. 20–27). St. Louis: C.V. Mosby.

Public Health Service. (1988). *The Surgeon General's report on nutrition and health* (DHHS Publication No. PHS 88-5210). Washington, DC: U.S. Department of Health and Human Services.

Reisinger, K., & Bires, J. (1980). Anticipatory guidance in pediatric practice. *Pediatrics, 66*(6), 889.

Rutstein, D., Berenberg, W., Chalmers, T., Childs, C., Fishman, A., & Perrin, E. (1976). Measuring the quality of medical care. *New England Journal of Medicine, 294*(11), 582–588.

The School-Based Adolescent Health Care Program. (May 1993). *The answer is at school: Bringing health care to our students.* Washington, DC: Robert Wood Johnson Foundation.

Stone, R. (1992). *Toward teen health: The Ounce of Prevention Fund school-based adolescent health centers.* Chicago: Ounce of Prevention Fund.

Whaley, L.F., & Wong, D.L. (1987). *Nursing care of infants and children* (3rd ed., p. 888). St. Louis: C.V. Mosby.

Wilson, M.H. (1992). Obesity. In S.B. Friedman, R.A. Hoekelman, N.M. Nelson, & H.M. Seidel (Eds.), *Primary pediatrics care* (2nd ed., pp. 1392–1395). St. Louis: C.V. Mosby.

6

Preventing School Failure and Dropout

Sharon Carnahan

Most striking about students in programs for potential drop-outs is that they fail to conform to stereotypes. Complex reasons and experiences trigger their disengagement from the process of schooling. It is essential that educators realize that a wide range of students can become at risk of school failure, that students at risk of dropping out are not necessarily those with the least intellectual ability, and that standard labels for student characteristics do not capture the nature of the interaction between at-risk students and the school. It is this interaction between student and school that plays a crucial role in an individual's decision to drop out.
  Wehlage, Rutter, Smith, Lesko, and Fernandez, 1989, p. 73

. . . We are well on the way to creating a soup-kitchen labor force in a postindustrial economy.
  Smith and Lincoln, 1988, p. 2

TWO HIGH SCHOOL DROPOUTS

At 17, Jamal is living with his biological father for the first time. Ten stormy years with his mother and a stepfather ended last year, when the family moved from the East Coast to rural Oklahoma in search of work. Jamal found that he was ahead of his peers in the rural school, although he had been an indifferent student back East. Jamal is a quiet boy, and in the new town, he felt isolated and alone. Even the teachers made fun of his accent and "big city" clothes. Jamal dropped out of school, ran away, and moved in with his father in a Pennsylvania suburb. Now he works for minimum wage at a pinball arcade and spends his money on motorcycle repairs and clothes.

Sarah, 15, has had trouble in school ever since the third grade, when she was retained for her poor reading skills. Neither her mother nor father completed high school, and she is the eldest of five children. Now in high school, Sarah is the one who stays home when any of her brothers or sisters get sick. She feels responsible for helping the family. At school, Sarah is miserable. She seems to fail at everything but getting into trouble. She feels alienated from teachers and school officials, who know little about her life as "assistant mother" at home. However, school will soon come to an end for Sarah when her mother finds out that she is pregnant. Sarah will drop out.

For a generation of youth at risk for high school dropout, the door to the future is locked. Education holds the key, but many children are leaving school too early, with inadequate education for tomorrow's world of work. The origins of school failure and subsequent dropout are deeply buried in our society, as a complex web of interconnecting influences. No single factor predicts this unfortunate outcome. At first glance, the data seem to indicate that the taproot is poverty. It is true that adolescents of low socioeconomic status (SES) are five times more likely to fail to complete high school than are children from middle- and upper-class families (Smith & Lincoln, 1988); however, too many children from all societal strata fail to achieve a level of education to prepare them to become productive, working citizens.

Children who drop out seem to share one characteristic: They lack a vision of the role of education in their present and future lives. Often, like Sarah in our example, they have begun to fail in school as early as the third grade. Certainly, early identification of children at risk for school failure, and prompt, preventive interventions, are crucial. However, effective prevention will require a reconceptualization of the goals of public education, from a triage system in which only the capable survive, to an individualized system where *all* are educated according to their abilities and needs. Communities with low dropout rates have successfully met the challenge to provide an appropriate public education to *every* student. This chapter addresses the problem of school dropout and school failure—the epidemiology, the scope of current prevention efforts, and a rationale for a shift in focus toward appropriate education for all students, rather than re-education of those who have dropped out.

EPIDEMIOLOGY OF SCHOOL DROPOUT

Figures 6.1 and 6.2 show the dropout rates for today's youth. The high value we place on high school graduation in the United States is a comparatively recent phenomenon. For example, in 1900, approximately 4% of young people completed high school; in 1950, the figure was 50% (Larsen & Shertzer, 1987). Today, nearly 75% of young people who enter first grade will graduate (Wehlage et al., 1989). Thus, the high school completion rate in the United States is at an all-time high.

PERCENTAGE OF HIGH SCHOOL DROPOUTS AMONG 16- TO 24-YEAR-OLDS

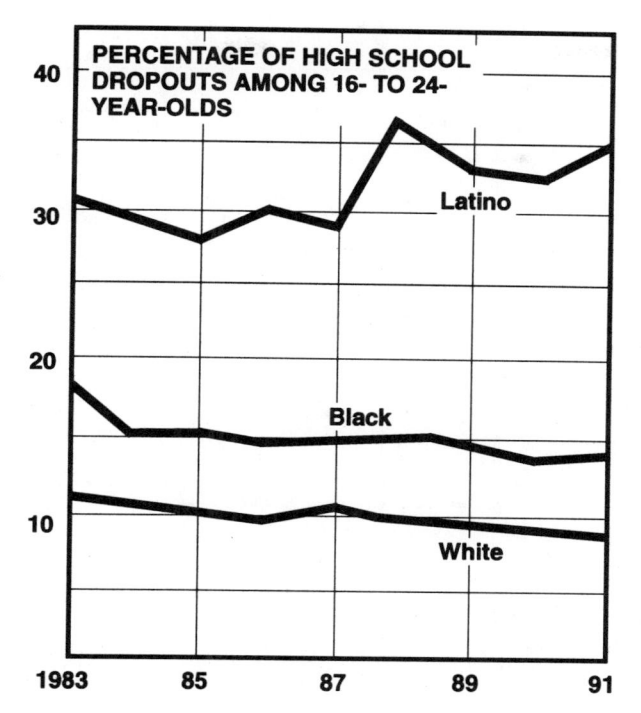

Figure 6.1. Dropout rates. (From U.S. Department of Education, Center for Education Statistics.)

However, it is not enough. Today's job market is unfavorable for dropouts. The percentage of unskilled labor positions has steadily declined, and tomorrow's jobs will require an even better educated workforce (Johnston, 1987). In *Workforce 2000*, the U.S. Department of Labor (1987) estimated that 60% or more of jobs in the 1990s will require the equivalent of 4 years of high school mathematics. Societal losses from school failure are enormous; a dropout is more likely to commit crimes, to rely on public assistance, and not to contribute to the tax base (Johnston, 1987).

Recent data on the frequency of dropping out of school indicate an incidence of about 1 million new cases each year (Smith & Lincoln, 1988). However, school dropout is difficult to define. High school attendance is compulsory in every state, but only until age 14 in five states, age 18 in four states, and age 16 in most of the rest (Toby, 1989). In addition, few studies have differentiated between those who have left school temporarily but will re-enroll and complete school and those who have left the education system permanently. Some states count students as dropouts even if they are enrolled in alternative edu-

High School Completion Rates

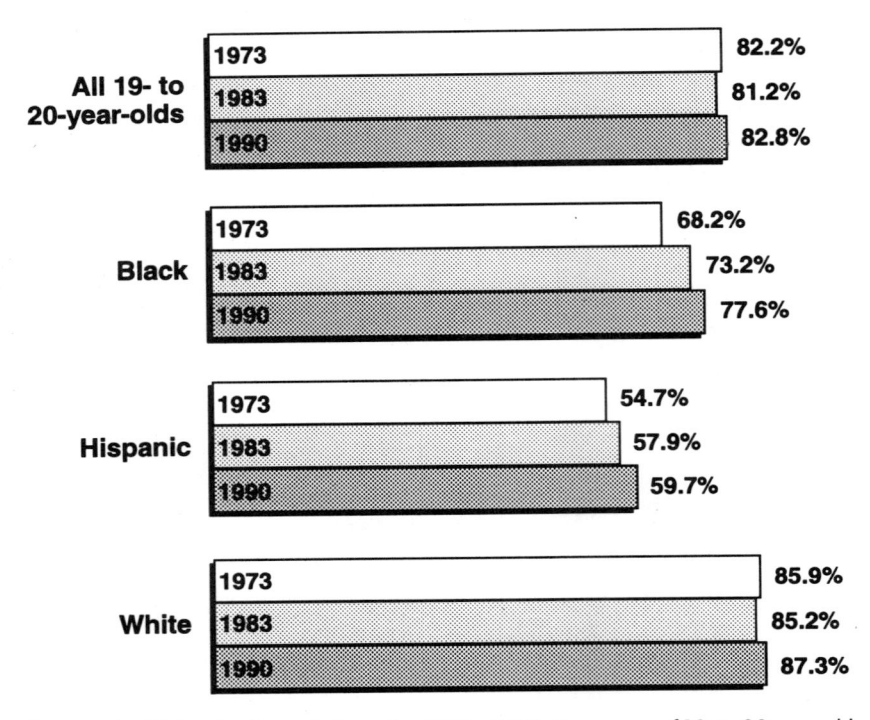

All 19- to 20-year-olds
- 1973: 82.2%
- 1983: 81.2%
- 1990: 82.8%

Black
- 1973: 68.2%
- 1983: 73.2%
- 1990: 77.6%

Hispanic
- 1973: 54.7%
- 1983: 57.9%
- 1990: 59.7%

White
- 1973: 85.9%
- 1983: 85.2%
- 1990: 87.3%

Figure 6.2. High school completion rates, 1973–1990. Percentage of 19- to 20-year-olds completing 12 years of school. (*Source:* U.S. Department of Commerce, Bureau of the Census.)

cation programs (e.g., those for pregnant adolescents), whereas others do not.

The central problem to address is prevention of school failure. The goal of prevention is to identify those who are at varying degrees of risk for failure and dropout, and to intervene appropriately. A child at risk for dropping out or school failure is "one who has left school or who is predictably in danger of leaving school without the skills to be a productive and self-reliant citizen and to succeed in today's workplace and hence, in society" (Smith & Lincoln, 1988, p. 13). Once children are identified, dropout must be prevented through a range of interventions.

WHO IS AT RISK FOR DROPOUT?

Research has indicated that young people who drop out of school differ from those who stay in school in consistent ways, and that the factors most strongly associated with risk can be identified in the elementary school years. These factors contribute to a poor fit between the child's needs and what the school can provide. For example, schools may be forced by economic realities to provide large group instruction, which rests on the assumption that all students share a common culture, language, and a home environment that supports learning. Beck and Muia (1980) raise a cultural congruence hypothesis: Students drop out because they lack the competencies necessary to perform within the educational environment. This discrepancy exists on school entry, and continues to widen, until the fit between child and school is so poor that the child drops out.

Prediction of school dropout is extraordinarily complex. Although some patterns have been discerned, they are not universally applicable. Most published predictive studies access the *High School and Beyond (HSB) Database*. This national longitudinal study of American students, begun in 1980, was based on a random probability sample of 58,000 high school students (36 sophomores and 36 seniors from each of 1,018 schools), and permits an analysis of the salient characteristics of the dropout population (National Center for Education Statistics, Office of Education Research and Improvement, U.S. Department of Education, 1992; Zimiles & Lee, 1991). For example, Ekstrom, Goertz, Pollack, and Rock (1986) found that dropouts are disproportionally from lower socioeconomic status and racial and ethnic minority groups, more likely to be males, and to be from public schools in the urban South or West. In addition, dropouts tended to come from homes lacking in such supports for education as study aids and to have parents who lacked interest or participation in their education (Ekstrom et al., 1986). HSB students from intact families at any income level were less likely to drop out (Zimiles & Lee, 1991). Table 6.1 lists characteristics commonly associated with dropping out. Latino American young people, who are doubly affected by economic hardship and second language learning, have a national dropout rate of nearly 40% (Smith & Lincoln, 1988).

These rates mask the fact that, proportionately, the U.S. dropout population is overwhelmingly white (Wehlage et al., 1989), and that when socioeconomic status is controlled for, African-Americans are less likely to drop out than are whites (Rumberger, 1983). School failure is a problem that crosses cultural lines and affects all communities.

In addition to these macro- and microsystem influences, a variety of variables within the child relate to school dropout. Those who leave school are more likely to have low grades (Ekstrom et al., 1986), or to have been retained in a grade at least once (Bearden, Spencer, & Moracco, 1989). In fact, Smith and Lincoln (1988) point out that low scores on tests of basic skills are characteristic of more dropouts than any other single factor. These children are likely to have behavior problems

Table 6.1. Risk factors for school failure and dropout

Demographic predictors
  Low socioeconomic status
  Minority status, especially African-American or Latino American
  More likely to live in the South
  Urban population greater than rural population
Family predictors
  Single-parent family
  Large family
  Parent dropped out of school
  Parent in jail
Within student factors
  Academic failure
  Grade retention; being 2 or more years behind grade level
  External locus of control for academics
  Delinquency
  Disciplinary problems in school
  Truancy or poor attendance record in elementary school
  Pregnancy

in school, such as truancy, cutting classes, and rebellion (Ekstrom et al., 1986) (see also Short and Brokaw, chap. 11, this volume, for a discussion of psychological problems). However, they are not uniformly of low ability; in one Chicago sample, nearly one third of public school dropouts were reading at or above grade level (Wehlage et al., 1989). It seems likely that there is no single dropout profile, but several.

Although it is known that minority students are more likely to drop out, disagreement exists about the explanation for this. It is clear that these students, who are more likely to be from low SES families and stressful home conditions, are part of the cycle of poverty. In addition, Ekstrom et al. (1986) stress that dropouts have lower school grades and test scores, do less homework, and show deficits in basic academic skills. However, social class is a poor predictor of school success *within* minority groups; higher income minority youths are not necessarily more likely to complete high school (Ogbu, 1989). What other factors could account for these differences? Within each cultural group, individual differences exist in school success and failure. Ogbu attributes some of these differences to a *cultural model of success*. He posits that "voluntary minorities" (recent immigrants, such as Central and South Americans, Koreans, or Punjabis) see a lack of education and cultural differences from middle-class, white standards as barriers to be overcome. These families typically have more of an opportunity to be educated in the United States than in their country of origin, and they compare life in the United States with that of their primary culture. Opportunities are better here, and children are encouraged to practice what Ogbu terms "effort optimism," the belief that hard work will bring rewards.

In contrast, children of "involuntary minorities" (those born in the majority culture, such Native Americans, African-Americans, and the Maoris in New Zealand) get a dual message. Their parents exhort them to do well in school, but the parents' own poor paying jobs, discussions of problems with "the system," and the need for public assistance prove to the children that education has not been a means to success. The involuntary minorities perceive standard English, the high school curriculum, and the practices of the white majority to be detrimental, and a challenge to their minority identity. "Acting white" is a serious violation of cultural norms—even when the "white" behaviors include academic effort. In support of his view, Ogbu (1989) points out that voluntary minorities are more academically successful than involuntary minorities in the United States, the United Kingdom, and Japan, even when the immigrants have less money and greater language barriers to overcome.

In ethnographic evidence, Ogbu (1989) describes some African-American students who adopt successful academic strategies, despite their dissonance in doing so. He lists these types of adaptation: *Emissaries*, who play down their black identities in order to succeed with white teachers in the classroom, but without alienating their peers; *Ivy Leaguers*, who emulate white, middle-class behaviors and dress, and are perceived by their teachers as good students; and *Regulars*, who alternately camouflage their street culture while in school, and their study habits while on the street.

Svec (1987) raises a more controversial hypothesis concerning dropout. He blames the ineptness of educational institutions that guarantee a 50% unemployment rate for African-American teens *with* a high school diploma. He cautions against the dangers of blaming the victims of an unresponsive education system; although dropouts differ from their peers, this may be a byproduct, not a cause, of school failure. He concludes that "retrospective studies that point to personality and depression among the dropout population may in fact be measuring the byproduct of unemployment and not early school leaving" (p. 187). Individual pathology is not efficacious as a causal explanation for widespread dropout.

WHY DO STUDENTS DROP OUT?

Factors such as SES, ethnicity, gender, school performance, and family background allow us to predict *who* will drop out; discriminant function analyses provide nearly 80% accuracy (Catterall, 1987). Similarly, Schorr (1988) points out that adolescent dropout and delinquency can be reliably predicted from family and demographic factors, school performance, and absenteeism from as early as the third grade. Thus, identifying populations eligible for selected or indicated preventive interventions might seem to be a relatively easy task. However, results from a series of interview and questionnaire-based follow-up studies with dropouts give additional insight into the proximal expression of these distal factors. We know *who* drops out, but *why?* Most researchers addressing this issue have employed a retrospective interview- or questionnaire-based methodology in which adolescents are asked to state why they did not finish school. In a review, Pallas (1984) concluded that students cite poor academic performance, social difficulties, and what he terms "accelerated role transitions." These include the assumptions of adult responsibilities in the family, including caring for younger siblings, parenthood, or wage earning. Similarly, in interviews with 82 dropouts, Pittman (1986) found that 48% cited personal problems (with academic and nonacademic origins), not grades or poor achievement, as their chief reason for dropping out. In a survey of 400 dropouts, Bearden et al. (1989) found that problems with teachers and administrators, pregnancy, a desire to work, financial need, and bad grades were the five reasons most frequently cited for discontinuing formal education.

A variety of personal problems are a recurrent theme in the self-reports of students who have dropped out. Students surveyed by Muha and Cole (1991) cited such personal factors as marriage or pregnancy for girls, and economic hardship for boys; however, many also reported feeling alienated from school life. The reasons for this alienation vary. Because of grade retention policies, dropouts may be 1–3 years older than their counterparts at the same grade level (Caliste, 1984). According to an evaluation of the *High School and Beyond Database*, dropouts feel less popular with their peers, and they are more likely to think that others describe them as troublemakers (Ekstrom et al., 1986).

SCHOOL FAILURE OR FAILING SCHOOLS?

Although dropouts may have personal problems and have clearly failed at school, has school also failed them? It is generally accepted that changes in formal public education in the past 20 years have made it harder for the majority of children to succeed and receive a diploma. Downing and Harrison (1990) list a number of barriers to graduation imposed by schools in the interests of rigor: high school graduation requirements that are beyond the capacity of many; teaching approaches that benefit college-bound students only; competency/proficiency exams; propaganda aimed at sending all students to college; restrictive rules; social isolation; and bigotry, especially toward students with other than middle-class values (including the "involuntary minorities" described by Ogbu [1989]).

Were the current education systems designed to graduate 100% of their students? Probably not. In fact, some say that the goal of educating *all* students is too ambitious for our education system to tackle, and not fair to the majority of students. Toby (1989) writes that in order for schools to be safer and more concerned with education, some students should drop out. Striving to retain all students until graduation, schools have tolerated tardiness, truancy, and inattention, effectively creating a class of "drop ins" who are present, but not engaged. Toby argues that schools should give students a clear choice between being educated or dropping out, by making school demands tougher and allowing students to choose whether or not to attend.

Certainly, students have been showing their opinions of curriculum reforms by voting with their feet. Smith and Lincoln (1988) point out that the increasingly rigorous standards encouraged by the Excellence in Education movement of the 1970s had a predictable result: Dropout rates tended to increase as disadvantaged youth fell behind; and budgets for vocational and alternative education programs decreased as funds were used for "get tough" measures.

McDill, Natriello, and Pallas (1986) have reviewed the unexpected consequences of tougher standards for school dropouts and concluded that: 1) the adoption of a restricted core of curriculum requirements (the "back to basics" approach) leads to academic stratification, as low-achieving students have no choice but to pass or drop out, and no alternative routes to success; 2) academic time demands placed on students (homework, longer school days) appear to benefit both high- and low-achieving students; and 3) when required higher levels of achievement seem unobtainable, students are more likely to drop out. When the curriculum is narrowed, those students who cannot meet new standards are separated from the mainstream of their peers into alternative or vocational programs at earlier and earlier ages.

Particular criticism has been aimed at the structures schools use to deal with two signs of trouble: school failure and truancy or frequent absenteeism, markers that predict dropout at the elementary school level. Several strategies have backfired, at least in part. Failing even one grade places a student at high risk for dropping out. Systems that use grade retention when students fail academically may find that they have produced a crop of middle school students who are much older and more physically developed than their academic peers. However, "social passing" graduates functional illiterates and devalues the high school diploma.

These approaches are contrasted with a variation on the regular education initiative (REI), which proposes the merger of regular and special education into a unitary system. Under such a system, all children would be entitled to the same free, appropriate, individualized education now guaranteed to children with developmental disabilities who are eligible for special education services (W.E. Davis, 1989)

PREVENTION EFFORTS FOR YOUTH AT RISK

At present, the United States lacks a coherent national program or policy addressing the problems of youth at risk for school failure or dropout. In any large community in the United States, preventive efforts have a bewildering, kaleidoscopic range of approaches, a variety that reflects the individualized causes of dropping out. Consider the following.

In Arlington Heights, Illinois, students ages 16–26 attend high school classes in the evening. Classes are small and informal, but have rigorous attendance policies. Approximately 65% of those enrolled graduate from high school (S. Davis, 1989).

In Louisiana, eighth and ninth graders who are identified as at risk by school counselors can attend an 8-week summer camp program at a university, designed to "turn them on" to learning (Michael, 1990).

In Virginia, the Passport Literacy Program tests all sixth graders in basic skills to see if they are ready for seventh grade. Those who do not pass will go to summer school (Smith & Lincoln, 1988).

What do these programs have in common? Only that they deal with children at risk, and that each is believed to prevent high school drop out by school administrators. Although some methods have been more successful than others, nearly all approaches reach some of the population served. Preventive efforts must be both comprehensive and individualized to meet the needs of students, reflecting the complex reasons for dropout.

Current efforts are fragmented at best. In a report to the Mott Foundation on youth at risk, Smith and Lincoln (1988) summarized the federal government's contributions. At present, most of these efforts focus on primary prevention of school failure through compensatory or remedial education for children at risk for school failure due to such demographic factors as low SES or minority status. These include Head Start early childhood programs; the Follow Through Program, which disseminates outstanding models of compensatory education for low-income children in the early grades; Chapter 1 of the Elementary and Secondary Education Act, which funds programs for students scoring less than the 50th percentile on standardized tests; and bilingual and vocational education programs. Federally funded secondary prevention efforts include the Job Training Partnership Act (JTPA, 1982), which provides education and training-related services to both youth in school and dropouts, and the Job Corps, which provides work for youth ages 16–24.

Combined, these programs provide an estimated total of $8.7 billion for prevention programs, with the majority spent on Head Start for preschoolers and vocational education for youth and adults. In addition, some funding is available for small demonstration projects from the Departments of Education, Labor, and Health and Human Services.

Despite these efforts, states are serving only a fraction of those identified as at risk. In a survey of JTPA programs in all 50 states that provide education and training for dropouts and other youth at risk, the programs were reaching only 2.1% of the 14- to 15-year-olds and 7.3% of the 16- to 21-year-olds who were eligible for services. Currently, we are serving an estimated 1 in 20 youth in need of job training (Smith & Lincoln, 1988). By far the majority of funds dedicated to adolescents are spent in recapturing the dropout into vocational or alternative high school completion programs.

The economic consequences of this neglect are severe. Today, three of four jobs in the United States require educational or technical training that assumes and goes beyond a high school education (Smith & Lincoln, 1988). Today's at-risk youth are not equipped to enter this workforce; for them, unemployment is the rule. Catterall (1987) estimates that the lifetime lost federal income and other taxes from the dropouts of one national high school graduating class alone are nearly $69 billion.

What are the costs of prevention? The Grant Commission has recommended expenditures of $5 billion per year for the next 10 years, invested in proven models that combine individualized education with job-training programs for at-risk youth (Smith & Lincoln, 1988). The cost of $50 billion would be less than the lost revenue in taxes alone from *one year's* nongraduating class, and this estimate does not consider the additional costs of social services for the unemployable worker. Clearly, we must invest in the future by working to prevent school failure and dropout.

DIMENSIONS OF PREVENTION

Prevention measures are those aimed at decreasing the risk that students will fail to complete their education. Primary prevention of school failure and dropout means ensuring that the initial pattern of failure, disruptive behavior, and disaffection never becomes established in the primary grades. *Universal* measures are those recommended for all children; *selective* measures are for particular population subgroups known to be at increased risk for dropping out; and *indicated* prevention efforts are aimed at those children who, because of their behaviors, show themselves to be in imminent danger of dropping out (Gordon, 1983).

If there are no jobs available to young adults, with or without a high school diploma, then there will be no economic incentives to finish high school. The clearest road to universal prevention of school dropout is an education system that meets the needs of all students for vocational, academic, and life skills education, and prepares them for a productive adulthood. Universal prevention of school dropout consists of having students who are prepared to learn, and a school system prepared to teach them what they must know in order to function in tomorrow's economy. Selected and indicated preventive efforts must be both *customized* to the student at risk, and *systemwide* in nature.

PREVENTION PROGRAMS: GENERAL PRINCIPLES

Successful Programs Are Individualized

Students arrive at the decision to drop out via many different paths, and "generic programs designed to serve all who might be in danger of dropping out are unlikely to be as effective as programs designed with specific students, situations, and aims in mind" (Wehlage et al., 1989, p. 75). Prevention of school failure and dropout can gain valuable lessons from those learned by special educators in implementing PL 94-142, the Education for All Handicapped Children Act of 1975, and PL 99-457, the Education of the Handicapped Act Amendments of 1986, which extended the law to preschoolers and included a focus on interventions involving the family. Under this legislation, each child is guaranteed access to a free, appropriate, public education in the least restrictive (most like other children's) environment possible. The intervention strategies are described in an individualized family service plan (IFSP), which may include goals for change in academic, family, or personal realms.

Such an individualized approach to preventing school dropout is recommended by Downing and Harrison (1990), who note that "the problem is so complex that it seems to exceed the boundaries of our traditional thinking and produces levels of frustration that tend to be dysfunctional" (p. 67). They suggest a paradigmatic shift away from a "one size fits all" approach of broad changes in tougher graduation requirements, core curricula, or school policies. Historically, such an approach has benefited only college-bound students, while exacerbating the poor fit between the school system and students at risk for dropping out. In addition, it ignores what cognitive psychology has told us: that there are a range of intelligences and learning styles.

Downing and Harrison (1990) advocate a "small wins" approach that is analogous to the IFSP method of planning interventions. In this method, school personnel help students set manageable goals, such as getting a high school diploma, rather than long-term goals, such as graduating from college. Then, they identify the barriers to those goals and work for small wins rather than system-level changes. For example, students faced with graduation competency exams might be provided with tutoring aimed specifically at passing the exams. Students who engage in power struggles over minor rules might be provided with tutoring in how to play the "school game" by sitting in the front of the class, asking questions, and so forth. These methods are similar to those used by some minority youth who have succeeded in school (Ogbu, 1989).

A cynical view of this "small wins" approach reveals an attempt to avert widespread depression and career abandonment among school counselors faced with narrowing curricula and student options when a comprehensive approach is needed. School personnel are encouraged to cope with an uncontrollably horrific dropout rate by maintaining their own internal locus of control to effect change in small ways. Viewed in a more hopeful light, the philosophy of "small wins" could lead to an idiographic approach to school dropout, in which each student's risk factors and reasons were taken into account in individualized interventions.

Individual accommodations that are adaptations of existing school structures are within the reach of most schools, according to Baker and Sansone (1990); these may include student contracts, community service opportunities, mentoring, home visits by teachers, and transfers out of problematic classes, offered in response to student need, rather than as a systematic program. An important element of this approach is a staffing committee or multidisciplinary team composed of parents, counselors, teachers, administrators, and other personnel who participate in the individualized plans and broaden the range of intervention options available to schools through pooling contacts and ideas (Baker & Sansone, 1990). Such an individualized approach would require a high degree of communitywide integrated services systems, because at-risk youth need help from mental health, public health, and private industry sources.

Successful Programs Target Subgroups at Risk

The educational needs of academically compliant pregnant adolescents and inner-city male gang members are different; successful school districts build several "niche" programs. A *school within a school* establishes smaller classes and individual attention within the existing school for a subgroup of students who continue to work toward graduation or general equivalency diploma (GED) certificate completion. Programs may have specialized curricula for gifted students at risk of dropout, or they may offer vocational or technical alternatives. The School-Within-A-School program of Madison, Wisconsin, is designed for students who are credit deficient and unlikely to graduate. Students attend regular academic classes plus vocational training in the building trades, child care, health services, and business skills. Juniors volunteer in area agencies, and seniors work in paid jobs in the community. Students' attendance, academic progress, and behavior problems are closely monitored (Wehlage et al., 1989).

Alternative schools serve at-risk students at a separate site, often far from the main public high schools. Birth, Education, Training, and Acceptance, Inc. (BETA) in Orlando, Florida, is a public–private partnership school for approximately 60 pregnant adolescents. The young women live in an on-site dormitory at BETA throughout their pregnancies. In addition to standard high school coursework, each student participates in daily coursework in child development and life skills training. After birth, the newborns are enrolled in an onsite child-care center partially staffed by residents and new parents, who also participate in a parent–infant lab emphasizing adult–child interaction skills.

Vocational-technical schools typically serve students who are unlikely to earn a high school diploma because of their poor academic record. Students receive job training and a GED or vocational certificate. The emphasis is on employability skills. The Croom Vocational High School in Upper Marlboro, Maryland, serves students over age 16 who enroll in a 2-year program. Students spend their first year rotating among vocational "shops" in the morning and academic classes that emphasize basic skills in the afternoon. In their senior year, students choose a primary "shop" and work there every morning.

Successful Programs Focus on Relationships

Each of these successful programs shares a low teacher-to-student ratio (ranging from 5:1 to 11:1), and a "coach" model of teacher–student relationships that is caring, supportive, and encouraging. Wehlage et al. (1989) emphasize that successful schools function as "communities of support," in which students at risk experience a sense of school membership or belonging to a larger effort. This affectional tie seems to give schools more staying power (Baker & Sansone, 1990; Wehlage et al., 1989). Students also cite their pleasure in individual accommodations made to their needs in successful schools, such as extra time with counselors, home visits, student contracts, waivers of past days missed, and work projects as alternatives to detention or suspension for days missed (Baker & Sansone, 1990).

The problem of school failure and dropout appears to be part of a larger issue of intergenerational disadvantage for poor children. On the individual level, risk factors include a poor "fit" between the child and the school environment. Students who drop out also frequently express a sense of individual alienation from school personnel. This alienation can begin early, with school failure in the elementary grades. Improved educational services that address the early and continuing special needs of children at risk are essential, but macrosystems-level changes are important as well. Economic policies that include jobs and job training help make an education worthwhile.

SCHOOL DROPOUT: STEPS TOWARD A PREVENTION AGENDA

A successful prevention agenda will address primary, secondary, and tertiary manifestations of school dropout.

1. *Operationalize the concept of "at risk" for school failure and dropout and develop screening and assessment procedures for use at each level of prevention.* Table 6.1 lists the risk factors most commonly and powerfully predictive of school failure and dropout. Currently, no uniform screening tool is available to identify potential dropouts. Such a tool should include established conditions, such as grade retention, predictive demographic/family background factors, school factors, and student–school interactions, and should be inclusive in nature.

2. *Establish a program of universal primary prevention for school dropout available to all.* Universal prevention of school failure and dropout means having a population of children who are prepared to learn, and a schooling system that can provide them with the education they need to become productive adults. This is a process that takes place throughout the lifespan, from provision of adequate childhood health care to job-training programs for unemployed workers. For example, because school failure is a prime predictor of dropout, programs that address school success in the early years for children at risk can be considered preventive. For this reason, Head Start, the preschool program that coordinates comprehensive educational, medical/dental, and social services to at-risk children and families, is listed among dropout prevention efforts. Programs such as Healthy Start, which provide early identification of children at risk for developmental delay through communitywide screenings and early intervention services, support the child and family economically, socially, and medically, and help the child to arrive at school prepared to learn.

Certain characteristics of schools also make it more likely that children will graduate, and these should be universally available. These include:

A sense of professional accountability from educators toward *all* students
A sense of discipline and order throughout the school system
A redefinition of schoolwork so that a greater number of students can be successful in school (Wehlage & Rutter, 1986)

Schools must also guarantee that the children within their walls are safe from harm; this is a matter of grave concern, especially in increasingly violent urban settings.

3. *Establish a program of selected primary prevention to all who belong to targeted risk groups.* Those most at risk are those with the quietest voices: bilingual learners who lack English proficiency; homeless and migrant children; rural children; and urban African-American males, whose dropout rates exceed 50%. According to Smith and Lincoln (1988), our biggest problem in addressing the needs of these groups of children at risk is "our failure to perceive of them as in need of specific long-term attention" (p. 5). School failure predicts school dropout, and students who are hungry, who do not have a safe place to live, or whose culture is not respected by the school system, are not prepared to learn.

For these targeted, highest risk groups, interventions may include systemwide programs designed to address a particular risk factor; for example, retention programs for adolescent mothers, school-within-a-school programs, mentoring programs, and intensive vocational training. In New Mexico, the Education Reform Act provides help for all limited English proficiency students from first grade to the secondary level (Smith & Lincoln, 1988). For Latino American students, the positive effects on retention in high school can be seen from participation in transitional bilingual elementary school classes; students who receive such instruction are more likely to graduate (Curiel, Rosenthal, & Richek, 1986).

Many caution against the establishment of a vocational education system with a separate diploma; such programs can tend to isolate at-risk youth, and may become de facto ghetto schools attended only by minority children. Catterall (1987) cites the substantial bonding of out-group members to each other, and their increased isolation from the educational mainstream. Some states, such as Alaska, have moved to a school-within-a-school concept in response to these concerns (Smith & Lincoln, 1988).

4. *Establish a program of indicated primary prevention for children at highest risk.* When children show us by their behaviors that they are at increased risk for dropping out, the education system should respond swiftly, with targeted programs. Early behavioral signs of dropout include truancy and grade retention in the elementary school years. Most successful programs "deal with the child as part of a family, and the family as part of a neighborhood and community" (Schorr, 1989, p. 365).

A Comprehensive Dropout Prevention Plan: Orlando, Florida

Orange County, Florida, which includes the city of Orlando, has developed a comprehensive plan for addressing school failure and dropout that includes individual adaptations to students, systematic change, and targeted interventions for high-risk groups. Florida ranks 27th among the 50 states in per pupil expenditures, and 37th in the percentage of students completing high school. In 1980, there were 257,000 16- to 20-year-olds in Florida who either were not in school or were not high school graduates—nearly 18% of the population (Children's Defense Fund, 1990).

Table 6.2 describes elements of the Orange County comprehensive plan for dropout prevention, developed and implemented in response to the state's Dropout Prevention Act of 1986. Florida weights at-risk students at 1.65 full-time equivalents for dropout prevention classes, providing a clear mandate for such services (Smith & Lincoln, 1988). The strengths of the Orange County initiative are that it is heavily weighted toward primary prevention, especially at the level of remediation programs for elementary school students at risk. In addition, it is not "one big program," but many, with individualization and flexibility built in at many levels. Florida allows its school districts to alter the basic curriculum in a variety of ways to help students at risk; for example, standard math courses may include construction measurement or budgeting.

Table 6.2. Orange County school dropout prevention plan, approaches at three levels

	For the dropout	For the unemployed
Universal		
Early identification and screening	Teen parenting and single-parent	Vocational/rehabilitation
Guidance counselors	Retrieval GED programs	Adult literacy programs
School social workers	Project Literacy	Adult and community education
	Alternative high schools	Prison-based programs
Selected		
Hospital/home-based education programs		
Student assistance teams at each school site		
Bilingual/English as a Second Language (ESL) programs		
First Start, Pre-K, Head Start programs for at-risk preschoolers		
Project ALPHA addresses issues of academic self-esteem		
Indicated		
Student alternative education programs		
Vocational and technical high school		
Additional math and reading instruction in grades 1, 2, and 4		
Compensatory education programs in grades 3, 5, 7, and 10		
Educational alternatives classes in regular high schools		
Public/private partnership projects of work + school		
The Challenge Center, Plaza Education Center		
Magnolia Internship Program as tutors for children with disabilities		
Detention center, drug and alcohol rehabilitation programs		
Primary prevention (To reduce new cases—incidence)	Secondary prevention (To reduce existing cases—prevalence)	Tertiary prevention (To reduce sequelae/complications)

GED, general equivalency diploma.

Orange County administrators have also encouraged the development of innovative pilot programs, especially for high school students at risk. In the Magnolia Internship Program, students who are at academic risk attend a school for children who have developmental disabilities. They attend regular high school classes for half of each day, then receive training in special education and serve as a "buddy" to a Magnolia School student. Results indicate a strong influence on retention and future vocational choices.

Public–private partnerships are also encouraged. The Discovery School, located at Walt Disney World, pairs part-time jobs and employability training with a regular high school curriculum. Two programs for adolescent girls, Pace Center for Girls and BETA, are administered by contract with private nonprofit corporations with long-standing ties to the community. Pace has been chosen by the state of Florida for widespread replication; it is one of few national models targeting the needs of nonpregnant adolescent girls, which include issues of poor self-esteem and internalizing problems, such as depression and obesity.

SUMMARY

The problem of school failure and dropout is embedded in the larger cycle of intergenerational disadvantage, and useful solutions must begin with economic opportunity for our youth. However, substantial individual differences exist in rates of school success, even within high-risk groups. Although multiple risks do predict school dropout, single factors (e.g., adolescent pregnancy or grade retention) may trigger failure and school abandonment. Therefore, solutions must be both individualized and systematic. Primary prevention consists of supporting students who are ready to learn and providing an education that prepares them for a productive adulthood. Programs that narrow the curriculum and toughen standards serve to stratify and alienate students already at risk; without remediation, such programs escalate the dropout problem. A complete solution includes both universal screening, remediation, and specialized programs for targeted groups. Both small wins and systematic changes are acceptable solutions to this complex problem.

Future research must address the development of more precise screening and assessment criteria; we can identify students who might drop out, but it is more difficult to identify the most important risk factors for individual students, and assign appropriate educational alternatives. Little research has addressed male–female differences in dropout incidence and reasoning, beyond the obvious issues of consequences of pregnancy. Finally, the majority of evaluations of successful programs remain anecdotal, or process oriented, at best. The few studies that address outcome data seldom record measures other than dropout rates and pupil satisfaction. In order to tell the story of their success, future researchers who describe successful programs must include long-term follow-up data and sufficient detail to enable replication.

REFERENCES

Baker, J., & Sansone, J. (1990). Interventions with students at risk for dropping out of school: A high school responds. *Journal of Educational Research, 83*, 181–186.

Bearden, L.J., Spencer, W.A., & Moracco, J.C. (1989). A study of high school dropouts. *School Counselor, 37*, 113–120.

Beck, L., & Muia, J. (1980). A portrait of a tragedy: Research findings on the dropout. *The High School Journal, 64*, 65–72.

Caliste, E.R. (1984). The effect of a 12-week dropout intervention program. *Adolescence, 19*(75), 649–657.

Catterall, J.S. (1987). An intensive group counseling dropout prevention intervention: Some cautions on isolating at-risk adolescents within high schools. *American Educational Research Journal, 24*(4), 521–540.

Children's Defense Fund. (1990). *S.O.S. America! A children's defense budget*. Washington, DC: Author.
Curiel, H., Rosenthal, J., & Richek, H. (1986). Impacts of bilingual education on secondary school grades, attendance, retentions and drop-out. *Hispanic Journal of the Behavioral Sciences, 8*(4), 357–367.
Davis, S. (1989). Evening classes for at-risk kids cost only a little, but they help a lot. *American School Board Journal, 176*(11), 33.
Davis, W.E. (1989). The regular education initiative debate: Its promises and problems. *Exceptional Children, 55*(5), 440–446.
Downing, J., & Harrison, T.C. (1990). Dropout prevention: A practical approach. *School Counselor, 38*, 67–74.
Education of the Handicapped Act Amendments of 1986, PL 99-457. (October 8, 1986). Title 20, U.S.C. 1400 et seq: *U.S. Statutes at Large, 100,* 1145–1177.
Education for All Handicapped Children Act of 1975, PL 94-142. (August 23, 1977). Title 20, U.S.C. 1401 et seq: *U.S. Statutes at Large, 89,* 773–796.
Ekstrom, R.B., Goertz, M.E., Pollack, J.M., & Rock, D.A. (1986). Who drops out of high school and why? Findings from a national study. *Teachers College Record, 87*(3), 356–373.
Gordon, R.S. (1983). An operational definition of disease classification. *Public Health Reports, 98*(2), 107–109.
Job Training Partnership Act of 1982 (JTPA), PL 97-300. (October 13, 1982). Title 2 A & B: *U.S. Statutes at Large, 96,* 1322.
Johnston, W.B. (1987). *Workforce 2000: Work and workers for the 21st century* (Report No. HI-3796-RR). Indianapolis, IN: Hudson Institute. (ERIC Document Reproduction Service No. ED 290 887)
Larsen, P., & Shertzer, B. (1987). The high school dropout: Everybody's problem? *School Counselor, 34*(3), 163–169.
McDill, E., Natriello, G., & Pallas, A. (1986). A population at risk: Potential consequences of tougher standards for student dropouts. In G. Natriello (Ed.), *School dropouts: Patterns and policies* (pp. 106–147). New York: Teachers College Press.
Michael, N. (1990). Participants' views of a drop-out prevention program: Louisiana State Youth Opportunities Unlimited. *High School Journal, 73,* 200–212.
Muha, D., & Cole, C. (1991). Dropout prevention and group counseling: A review of the literature. *The High School Journal, 74*(2), 76–80.
National Center for Education Statistics, Office of Education Research and Improvement, U.S. Department of Education. (1992). *High school and beyond: 1980 to 1986.* CD-ROM [Computer program]. Washington, DC: Government Printing Office. (S/N 065-000-00470-4)
Ogbu, J. (1989). The individual in collective adaptation: A framework for focusing on academic underperformance and dropping out among involuntary minorities. In L. Weis, E. Farrar, & H. Petrie (Eds.), *Dropouts from school: Issues, dilemmas and solutions* (pp. 181–204). Albany: State University of New York Press.
Pallas, A. (1984). *The determinants of high school dropout*. Unpublished doctoral dissertation, The Johns Hopkins University, Baltimore.
Pittman, R.B. (1986). Importance of personal, social factors as potential means for reducing high school dropout rate. *High School Journal, 70,* 7–13.
Rumberger, R. (1983). Dropping out of high school: The influence of race, sex, and family background. *American Educational Research Journal, 20,* 199–220.

Schorr, L.B. (1989). Early interventions to reduce intergenerational disadvantage: The new policy context. *Teachers College Record, 90*(3), 362–374.
Smith, R.C., & Lincoln, C.A. (1988). *America's shame, America's hope: Twelve million youth at risk.* Chapel Hill, NC: MDC, Inc.
Svec, H. (1987). Youth advocacy and high school dropout. *High School Journal, 70*, 185–192.
Toby, J. (1989). Of dropouts and stay-ins: The Gershwin approach. *Public Interest, 95*, 3–13.
U.S. Department of Commerce, Bureau of the Census. (1900). Washington, DC: U.S. Government Printing Office.
U.S. Department of Education, Center for Education Statistics. (1900). Washington, DC: U.S. Government Printing Office.
U.S. Department of Labor, Bureau of Labor Statistics. (1987). *Workforce 2000.* Washington, DC: U.S. Government Printing Office.
Wehlage, G., & Rutter, R. (1986). Dropping out: How much do schools contribute to the problem? *Teachers College Record, 87*(3), 374–393.
Wehlage, G., Rutter, R., Smith, G., Lesko, N., & Fernandez, R. (1989). *Reducing the risk: Schools as communities of support.* Philadelphia: Falmer Press.
Zimilies, H., & Lee, V. (1991). Adolescent family structure and educational progress. *Developmental Psychology, 27*(2), 314–320.

7

Adolescent Pregnancy

Tina M. Smith

Brittany is a 15-year-old with a 3-week-old infant, Dominique. Brittany has not been to school since well before Dominique was born. Although she does not miss the schoolwork, Brittany misses her friends desperately. None of her friends call any more, but Brittany often thinks to herself that it wouldn't matter if they did because she would have to stay home with her baby. Brittany lives with her mother, whom she had hoped would help with the baby. Lately, however, Brittany and her mother fight all the time about who will care for the baby. Being a mother is not at all what Brittany had expected.

In recent years, adolescent pregnancy and childbearing have been implicated as major contributors to cycles of hopelessness and poverty. Although sexual activity among teenagers is not a new phenomenon—women in their teens have been having babies for centuries—the conditions under which present-day teenagers are bearing and rearing children have changed. Since the 1960s, the average age for marriage has risen, while the age at which individuals begin sexual activity has declined, resulting in more young, single mothers. Single-parent families received national attention in the 1992 presidential campaign with the considerable dialog about "traditional family values." Although the campaign generated discussion of the issues, during the 1980s, most efforts to prevent teenage pregnancy were, at best, reactive (Jorgensen, 1991). At the same time, the trend since the 1960s of earlier sexual activity has created a situation in which younger and younger adolescents are placing themselves at risk for a host of problems, such as unwanted pregnancies and sexually transmitted diseases including acquired immunodeficiency syndrome (AIDS).

The purpose of this chapter is to approach the contemporary problem of adolescent pregnancy within a comprehensive framework of prevention. (For a discussion of prevention of sexually transmitted diseases in adolescence, see Rosenthal et al., chap. 13, this volume.) To this end, the chapter begins with a consideration of the epidemiology of teenage pregnancy within the larger context of adolescent sexual behavior. The consequences of early parenting for the mother, child, and society are described in the context of secondary and tertiary prevention efforts. This is followed by a rationale for primary prevention of unwanted early pregnancy and a description of representative programs.

SCOPE OF THE PROBLEM

Estimates of the number of sexually active teenagers range from 12 million (Hechtman, 1989) to 13 million (Frager, 1991). Of this number, approximately 5 million are females, over 1 million of whom become pregnant every year (Hechtman, 1989). The number of women under 20 who become mothers actually decreased between 1960 and the mid-1980s—teen births dropped in the 1970s and stabilized during the 1980s. However, the number of teenagers who engage in sexual activity outside marriage has increased, from 30% of all 18-year-olds in 1962 to more than 50% in 1984 (Newcomer & Baldwin, 1992). Moreover, the likelihood that a teenager will engage in sexual activity outside marriage increases as a function of other risk behaviors such as alcohol use and low self-esteem (Richter, Valois, McKeown, & Vincent, 1993).

What may be more relevant than the actual number of very young women who become pregnant is that the proportion of young mothers who are most vulnerable to developmental problems (e.g., girls in their early teens, unmarried teens) is increasing (Frager, 1991). Although the underlying causes for the trend of early sexual activity paired with later marriage remain obscure, there is speculation that earlier onset of menarche (Hechtman, 1989) and less adult supervision (Pete & DeSantis, 1990) may account in part for earlier initiation of sexual activity. Several reasons have been postulated for later marriage, including underemployment for adolescent males, particularly in communities characterized by lower socioeconomic status (SES) (Frager, 1991). In addition, young women, particularly African-American adolescents, have expressed the perception that marriage is a more serious commitment than parenthood; as a result of this perception, they do not see a contradiction in becoming a parent before getting married (Finkelstein, Finkelstein, Christie, Roden, & Shelton, 1982; Presser, in Simpkins, 1984; Wise & Grossman, 1980).

Because the trend toward earlier initiation of sexual activity and later marriage seems unlikely to reverse in the near future, teenage sexuality and pregnancy will remain an issue that educators and health-care providers must address. As described in Chapter 1, a prevention framework for less than optimal developmental outcomes for children can be conceptualized as occurring at three levels—primary, secondary, and tertiary. The goal of primary prevention is to reduce the prevalence of the problem; as applied to adolescent pregnancy, primary prevention efforts would seek to reduce the number of adolescent pregnancies. However, as is the case with most social problems, most existing social services reflect secondary and tertiary prevention efforts. In the case of adolescent pregnancy, secondary prevention programs target girls who are already pregnant, with the focus on reducing the likelihood of later problems for the mother and child. Tertiary prevention can be seen as "damage control"—the goal of these programs is the remediation of sequelae and complications (e.g., maternal school dropout and unemployment, infant abandonment or abuse) that may follow teenage childbearing. (See Figure 7.1 for a diagrammatic illustration of prevention levels as they apply to adolescent pregnancy.)

CONSEQUENCES OF ADOLESCENT PREGNANCY

Considerable research investigating the consequences of adolescent childbearing for the young mother and her child suggests that both members of the dyad are at risk for compromised developmental outcome along a number of dimensions. This section begins with a brief discussion of the findings from relevant research and concludes with a description of representative secondary and tertiary prevention programs designed to address the problems associated with adolescent childbearing.

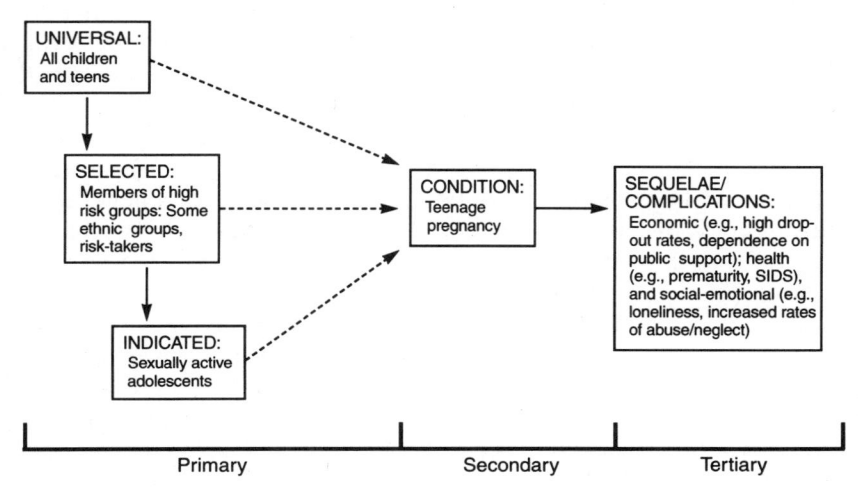

Figure 7.1. The focus and nature of primary prevention. (SIDS, sudden infant death syndrome.)

Consequences for the Mother

Economic Problems The economic ramifications of early pregnancy, particularly if the mother remains unmarried, are staggering. Pregnancy is the most common reason girls drop out of high school (Hechtman, 1989). As a result of their diminished educational opportunities, teenage mothers have a much greater need for public assistance (Finkelstein et al., 1982). The cycle of dependency is often perpetuated by the birth of more children: 50% of all adolescent mothers have another child within 36 months of the first birth (Furstenberg, 1976, cited in Hechtman, 1989).

Physical Problems Partially as a result of the economic problems associated with teenage pregnancy, adolescents are more likely to experience increased physical consequences of pregnancy and childbirth. For example, teenagers are more likely to have poor nutrition, unhealthy personal habits (e.g., alcohol and drug use), inadequate health insurance, and, therefore, poor prenatal care (Finkelstein et al., 1982). Not surprisingly then, teenagers are also more likely to have such pregnancy complications as toxemia and hypertension (Finkelstein et al., 1982). As a result, their infants are more likely to have lower birth weights (Lawrence & Merritt, 1981) and to be stillborn (Black & DeBlassie, 1985).

Social and Emotional Problems In addition to the physical and economic problems associated with adolescent pregnancy, a number of negative social and emotional consequences have been identified, including a considerably higher suicide rate than that of other teenagers (Bayatpour, Wells, & Holford, 1992). Depending on the developmental level of the young women, they may be cognitively and emotionally unprepared for the new role of mother. Adolescence has been described as a period of "intense internal disequilibrium" (Hansom, 1990, p. 629) during which the individual undergoes rapid cognitive and phychosocial developmental changes (Blos, 1967; Elkind, 1967; Erikson, 1959). Likewise, the birth of a child can be a stressful period as the new parent makes the transition to parenthood (Levenson, Atkinson, Hale, & Hollier, 1978). Sadler and Catrone (1983) refer to this combination of stressors as a "dual developmental crisis."

The adolescent's desire for independence and need for peer approval are two aspects of her developmental crisis that are affected by early parenthood. Part of the transition to parenthood requires changes in lifestyle that may lead to alienation from peers (Hechtman, 1989). In addition, economic constraints force many adolescents to become more dependent upon their families at the very stage when their developmental agenda mandates greater independence (Hechtman,

1989). At the same time, many adolescents face disapproval from their families (Dunst, Vance, & Cooper, 1986; Levenson et al., 1978); as a result, they are more likely to express dissatisfaction with all family relationships (Hechtman, 1989).

As parents, adolescents are more likely to show less positive attitudes and less adaptive emotional adjustment to parenting. For example, adolescent parents are characterized by greater external locus of control; they have less empathy (Mercer, 1986) and more resentment of their parenting role (Klein & Cordell, 1987); they experience more anxiety regarding the infant (Klein & Cordell, 1987; Reis & Herz, 1987). Of 48 young mothers in DeLissovoy's study (1975), only 5 expressed deriving any enjoyment from the child. Dissatisfaction with the parenting role may be explained, at least in part, by adolescents' tendency to have unrealistic expectations of their children (de Cubas & Field, 1984; Hansom, 1990; Hart & Hilton, 1988; Mercer, 1986).

Consequences for the Child

Physical Problems Given the problems faced by young mothers, the finding that children of adolescent mothers are at greater risk for a number of problems, including physical, emotional, and cognitive consequences, is not surprising. The tie between the physical consequences for infants and the prenatal characteristics (e.g., age, nutritional status, prenatal care) of their mothers has been demonstrated repeatedly. For example, in addition to lower birth weights, the rate of sudden infant death syndrome (SIDS) is six times higher for babies of adolescents than it is for babies of older mothers (Babsin & Clark, 1983). The physical consequences for children of teenagers do not end with infancy; young maternal age is also associated with higher incidence of childhood illness (Finkelstein et al., 1982). In addition, children of adolescent mothers have been found to be at greater risk for maltreatment and neglect (Fox, Bausch, Goldberg, & Helmuth, 1987; Steir, Leventhal, Berg, Johnson, & Mezger, 1993).

Emotional Problems The emotional consequences of adolescent pregnancy have been well documented as well. Children of young mothers have more trouble adjusting to school, are more resentful of authority, have more problems relating to peers, and are more aggressive and impulsive (Kellam, Ensinger, & Turner, 1977). In general, children of adolescent mothers have more psychiatric problems in childhood (Hechtman, 1989).

Intellectual and School Problems In addition to physical and emotional risks, children of adolescents also have more trouble in school. A study by Hardy, Welcher, and Standly (1987) demonstrated that at ages 7 and 12, children of adolescent mothers had lower IQs and performed less well in school than peers of older mothers. Other characteristic behaviors seem to interfere with their school performance as well, such as increased distractibility (Kellam et al., 1977). They are also more likely to be diagnosed with a learning disability (Hardy et al., 1987; Kellam et al., 1977).

Consequences for the Mother–Child Relationship

The characteristics of adolescent parents described above obviously have implications for the mother–child relationship. A number of studies have found adolescent mothers to be less likely to interact positively with their infants than older mothers (Helm, Comfort, Bailey, & Simeonsson, 1990; Lamb, Hopps, & Elster, 1987; Landy, Cleland, & Schubert, 1984). For example, younger mothers talk less to their infants, use physical forms of communication, including physical punishment, more often (Garcia-Coll, Hoffman, Van Heuten, & Oh, 1987), and are more likely to have children with disrupted attachment relationships (Fraiberg, 1983; Lamb et al., 1987; Landy et al., 1984; Wise & Grossman, 1980). Some authors suggest that the developmental stage of teenage mothers sometimes interferes with their ability to have empathy for the child, making it more difficult for them to recognize the child as an individual (Klein & Cordell, 1987).

Tertiary Prevention

Tertiary prevention differs from secondary prevention programs in that the focus of the former is to address complications and sequelae among children with a defined problem or condition. As such, tertiary efforts may be remedial, corrective, and/or therapeutic. In the context of teenage pregnancy, tertiary prevention efforts are likely to include maternal drug abuse, AIDS in both mother and child, child abuse and abandonment, maternal underemployment, and so forth. Characteristically, tertiary prevention programs are reactive, and in a certain sense, society is obligated to provide them. Given this volume's focus on primary prevention, discussion of tertiary prevention is incorporated with relevant sections of secondary prevention that follow (see Table 7.1).

Secondary Prevention

Secondary prevention is designed to reduce the prevalence of a documented or diagnosed condition. The above review of research on adolescent pregnancy and childbearing provides a basis for defining the condition of being pregnant during adolescence as the criterion for providing secondary prevention services. However, although adolescent pregnancy raises the risk of complications among mothers and

Table 7.1. Common consequences of adolescent childbearing and their remediation

Consequences	Remediation
Economic problems, lower earning potential due to higher dropout rates and child-care responsibilities	Increased reliance on public support (e.g., WIC, AFDC, Medicaid). Job training programs GED
Health risks for expectant mother and child include increased incidence of STDs, toxemia, premature birth and lower birth weights, SIDS, and so forth	Longer perinatal hospitalizations Increased use of health-care system during crises
Social-emotional risks for mother and child	
Mother: loneliness, isolation, poor adaptation to parenting, increased incidence of child abuse	Counseling Protective Services involvement in cases of child abuse
Child: poorer adjustment to school, increased behavioral and emotional problems, poorer school performance	Special education Increased need for psychological interventions
Mother and child at high risk for repeating the cycle	

AFDC, Aid to Families with Dependent Children; GED, general equivalency diploma; SIDS, sudden infant death syndrome; STD, sexually transmitted disease; WIC, Women, Infants, and Children.

infants, negative outcomes are not always realized (Bucholz & Gol, 1986; Dunst et al., 1986). Secondary prevention programs for adolescent mothers, therefore, use strategies that intervene before the maternal and child complications associated with young parenting are manifested. Parenting classes and prenatal support groups for pregnant adolescents are examples of secondary prevention efforts.

For some prevention strategies and programs, the distinction between secondary and tertiary prevention is clear-cut. A support group for pregnant teenagers is an example of secondary prevention, whereas academic remediation for a young mother who has dropped out of school can be considered tertiary prevention. For many programs and strategies, however, the distinction may be less clear-cut, with similar content applied differently depending on the needs of the individuals involved. For example, parenting classes could be considered secondary or tertiary, depending on the target audience. The course content used to prevent parenting problems could also be used to remediate parenting problems. Therefore, while the following discussion describes strategies that, for the most part, are intended to intervene with the documented problem at the secondary level, many of these strategies may also be applied at the tertiary level to address complications of teenage pregnancy.

Obviously, some basic interventions (e.g., social support and access to prenatal care) can be identified as important components of all interventions with pregnant or parenting adolescents. Because there is so much variation in developmental levels and psychosocial needs among adolescents, individualization of intervention is necessary to ensure effective intervention within this diverse group. However, secondary prevention programs can be clustered based on the primary focus. A review of the literature suggests three broad categories: 1) education and training opportunities; 2) parent training, or strategies to improve mother–infant relationships; and 3) counseling support for the young woman. These are summarized in Table 7.2.

Education and Training Opportunities The primary goal of these programs is to increase the skill level of the young mother, thereby increasing her employment options and decreasing the likelihood that she will have to depend on public assistance. These programs often are school based, with the intent of keeping the young mother in school. In addition to regular education programming, effective school-based programs must provide parenting skills training and on-site infant care (Furstenberg, 1980). Because one early pregnancy is a risk factor for additional pregnancies, comprehensive programs also include continued family planning. In addition to the more traditional intervention efforts targeted at the young mother, Furstenberg also recommends vocational training for their male partners to encourage and enable young fathers to support their families.

Table 7.2. Secondary prevention strategies

Educational	High schools with on-site child care
	School or community-based vocational education for expectant mothers and fathers
	Availability of low-cost, high-quality child care for young mothers who work
Parenting	Parent training should begin prior to or soon after the birth and include the following:
	Information on child development to foster realistic expectations for child behavior
	Alternatives to physical discipline
	Ideas for games to play with babies
Counseling	Family therapy for pregnant adolescents or new parents and their families of origin
	Individual psychotherapy or counseling
	Peer-led support groups

Parent Training Other secondary prevention programs focus on the parent–child interaction; Furstenberg (1980) calls this category "Family Life Education." An important component of programs of this type is information about child care and development. The young woman's familiarity with infant and child development are important factors in providing effective information about child care. Fraiburg (1983) describes an adolescent mother who was convinced that her infant preferred hot dogs and potato chips to formula because she herself did. This example points out the need to consider the adolescent's level of cognitive development in addition to her knowledge of basic child care.

Interventions to foster positive attachment between the young mother and her child also fit within this category. Because adolescents are more likely to express dissatisfaction with parenting and with their child, interventions that encourage the young mother in her new role and encourage positive perceptions of her infant could be vitally important to the mother–child relationship. One technique documented as an effective intervention to improve the mother–child relationship is demonstration of infant assessment using the Neonatal Behavioral Assessment Scale (NBAS) (Brazelton, 1984) as intervention. de Cubas and Field (1984), who used the NBAS to foster more positive interactions between adolescent mothers and their newborns, found positive effects throughout the infancy period. Infant mental health programs in which professionals facilitate mother–child attachment by structuring and reinforcing positive interactions fall in this category as well.

Counseling Support Counseling support for pregnant and parenting teens can be an important means of providing social support during the stressful transition to motherhood. For adolescents undergoing this transition, traditional counseling goals (e.g., improving the clients' coping strategies) may not be the most important outcomes. A study by Giblin, Poland, and Sachs (1987) demonstrated the importance of social support by documenting the relationship between the adolescent's feeling supported and her positive feelings about the child. Counseling efforts with adolescent mothers can take the form of one-to-one therapy, group therapy, or peer counseling (Furstenberg, 1980). Older adolescent parents could also function as co-leaders of groups of pregnant adolescents.

Because most adolescent mothers live at home (Finkelstein et al., 1982; Giblin et al., 1987), their families are also appropriate participants in counseling sessions. Although living at home can provide much needed financial support and help in taking care of the baby, depending on the family's dynamics, the arrangement can also contribute additional stress. The new mother may need help adjusting to the dual roles of daughter and mother. She may even find herself competing with her own child as she would with a sibling (Klein & Cordell, 1987; Levenson et al., 1978).

In addition to parenting stress, adolescent mothers may also be dealing with the developmental stress that is a natural part of adolescence and is augmented by the new parenting role. Consequently, counseling efforts should provide support for successful navigation of adolescent development (Sadler & Catrone, 1983). Because peer support is so vital to adolescents, it may also be important to include the girl's friends in intervention efforts to ensure that she has a supportive social network.

PRIMARY PREVENTION

Unlike secondary and tertiary programs that focus on the manifestation of a specified condition or problem, primary prevention programs attempt to prevent problems well before they are manifested, the underlying philosophy being that early intervention pays off in the long run by eliminating the need for costly remediation. In the context of this chapter, primary prevention has as its goal the prevention of new pregnancies among adolescents. Although the nature of the consequences of adolescent pregnancies impedes accurate cost–benefit analyses of primary prevention programs, it is clear that intensive secondary and tertiary programs, although laudable for their effects, are costly to society (Furstenberg, Brooks-Gunn, & Chase-Lansdale, 1989). For example, the Center for Population Options (CPO) estimated that, in 1986, the cost of teenage childbearing (taking into account Aid to Families with Dependent Children, Food Stamps, and direct payments to teenage caregivers) was $18 billion; each birth to a mother younger than 20 cost the American taxpayer $14,852, and births to mothers younger than 15 cost $18,913 (Kobokovich & Bonovich, 1992).

Despite these high costs of early childbearing, there has always been a conspicuous lack of programs designed to reduce the number of new adolescent pregnancies (Furstenberg, 1980). In order to reduce the number of adolescent pregnancies effectively, primary prevention efforts must address either or both of two basic objectives: 1) reduce the rate of sexual activity among teenagers; or 2) increase the likelihood that teenagers engage only in protected sex (Jorgensen & Alexander, 1982).

Targets of Primary Prevention

Primary prevention efforts can be targeted in terms of three levels—universal, selected, and indicated strategies—each reflecting increasing degrees of risk, as shown in Figure 7.2. As the name implies, universal programs are those targeting an entire population; for example, a program for all seventh graders. Individuals in a universal primary prevention program are not singled out as being at greater risk for unwanted pregnancy than any other members of that population. Such programs, although popular and widespread, also tend to generate controversy because of the moral and ethical dilemmas associated with the topic of adolescent sexuality.

Despite the controversy surrounding them, universal primary prevention programs should be considered ideal simply because all children and adolescents are assumed to be at some degree of risk (albeit low), and such programs could generate significant benefits in terms of broad preventive objectives such as high self-esteem and responsible decision making. However, because resources for prevention are scarce, practical realities often require that limited funds be allocated to subsets of the population at increased risk. Selected primary prevention programs are defined as those that narrow the scope of potential participants by identifying subpopulations whose group characteristics place them at increased risk for engaging in unprotected sexual activity. Because selected programs are targeted to an identified subgroup rather than universally, it is possible to provide more intense intervention. Individuals likely to be included in this target group can be adolescents with characteristics, such as certain risk-taking behaviors, highly associated with unprotected sexual activity. The definition

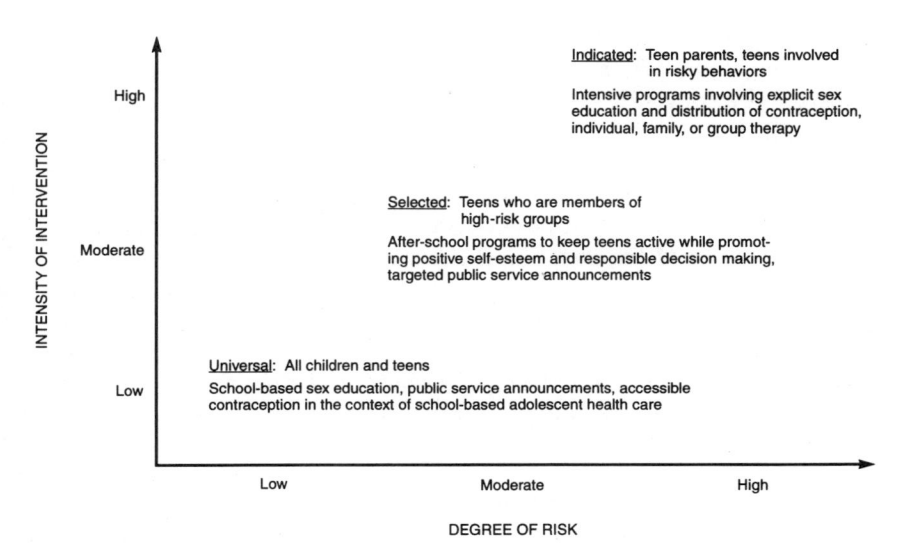

Figure 7.2. Levels of primary prevention.

of primary prevention programs at the indicated level targets adolescents at even greater risk—those identified on the basis of individual characteristics (e.g., being sexually active).

Obviously, the distinction between adolescents who are eligible for selected versus indicated programs is easier to make in theory than in practice, because determining that teenagers are, in fact, engaging in unprotected sex is often impossible. For the purpose of this chapter, selected and indicated levels of risk are considered as a continuum ranging from more generic risk factors (e.g., membership in a low-income, minority population) at the selected end of the continuum, to more specific risk factors (e.g., prior pregnancy, acknowledged sexual activity, diagnosis of sexually transmitted diseases) at the indicated end of the spectrum.

Selected Risk

For many years, researchers have attempted to develop a profile of the sexually active adolescent. Recently, the emphasis has shifted from attempts to develop personality profiles toward identifying risk characteristics of adolescents likely to engage in sexual activity without adequate protection against pregnancy and sexually transmitted diseases. In the course of this research, a number of risk factors have been identified that are associated with sexual risk taking among adolescents.

Developmental Factors Adolescents' ability to make mature decisions regarding birth control and sexual activity is governed to some extent by their level of cognitive maturity. This premise is well supported; several studies have found that adolescents' use of birth control was associated with their levels of cognitive and emotional maturity (Hart & Hilton, 1988; Johnson & Green, 1993; Orr & Langefield, 1993). Clearly, the risks are augmented when physical development outpaces cognitive development. When selecting girls who may be in greater need of pregnancy prevention efforts, the relationships among cognitive, emotional, and physical development must be considered.

Psychosocial Factors A number of psychosocial characteristics can be used to identify adolescents at greater risk for unprotected sexual activity. Low self-esteem is an example of a generic characteristic that places children and youth at relatively mild risk for adolescent pregnancy (Patten, 1981; Santelli & Beilensen, 1992). School problems, however, may reflect greater risk for unprotected sexual activity than low self-esteem. Low academic performance, aggression and acting out, having friends who drop out, and not liking school are all related to the risk of not using contraception (Mills, Dunham, & Alpert, 1988). One of the most salient risk factors is the presence of other risky or unhealthy behaviors, including drug, tobacco, and alcohol use, or even lack of exercise (Orr & Langefield, 1992; Richter et al., 1993). Drug and alcohol abuse are examples of specific risk behaviors that may place students at indicated, rather than selected, risk.

Family Factors The relationships between adolescent sexual behavior and family variables have not been entirely sorted out (Ralph, Lochman, & Thomas 1984). Nevertheless, a number of family factors are believed to be related to sexual risk taking in adolescents. One generic family risk factor is having a mother with a lower educational level (Ralph et al., 1984). The degree of parental control over dating and free time (Hogan & Kitigawa, cited in Santelli & Beilensen, 1992; Pete & DeSantis, 1990), not living with both parents (Mills, Dunham, & Alpert, 1988), and poor communication between parents and children about parental attitudes toward sexuality (Santelli & Beilensen, 1992) have been shown to be related to poor contraceptive use among adolescents. These factors represent more specific, and therefore more serious, risk than the generic factor of having a mother with limited education.

Knowledge and Attitudes Clearly, adolescents' knowledge and attitudes about human reproduction and contraceptives will have an impact on their sexual behavior. Males have been found to weigh the perceived long-term benefits relative to short-term inconvenience in determining whether or not to use condoms (Orr & Langefield, 1993). Also, for adolescents, attitudes are shaped largely by perceptions of peers' attitudes. In developing a prevention program for selected groups of teenagers, an assessment of the adolescents' attitudes toward contraception as well as their knowledge about sexuality would be an important first step in determining which individuals need intervention most.

Demographic Factors A number of demographic factors have been identified as potentially important determinants of sexual behavior. Lower socioeconomic status has received considerable attention as a major risk factor (Hechtman, 1989; Santelli & Beilensen, 1992). Davis (cited in Black & DeBlassie, 1985) wrote that the life situations of low-income youth promote "attitudes of fatalism and alienation which undermine the rational, planned use of contraceptive devices" (p. 283).

In addition to SES factors, cultural differences have been found to influence sexual behavior as well as the reactions of teens and families to early pregnancy. Santelli and Beilensen (1992) reviewed the literature and found differences in the rate of effective contraceptive use and abortions among low-income, minority populations, and more middle-class populations. Felice, Schragg, James, and Hollingsworth (1987) examined cultural differences among Mexican-American, African-American, and white adolescents' sexuality, and a number of differences emerged that were independent of SES. For example, Mexican-American adolescents were more likely to be married, whites were more likely to be from a dysfunctional family, and African-Americans were more likely to stay in school. Different patterns also seem to exist between the precoital behavior of African-Americans and white adolescents as well—African-Americans are more likely to move directly to intercourse from the early stages of kissing (Smith & Udry, 1985). The pattern of coitus early in the courting relationship underscores the need for sex education just prior to the onset of puberty, a need that may be particularly pronounced among African-American adolescents.

In their review of the literature, Yawn and Yawn (1993) found evidence for the importance of a belief system in preventing adolescent pregnancy. Adolescents with strong religious conviction (not merely church attendance) tended to delay sexual activity. Therefore, they suggest that community efforts to reduce teenage pregnancy include religious leaders.

The age at which adolescents start dating and early physical maturation have been identified as important considerations in prevention efforts (Santelli & Beilensen, 1992). There is also evidence that sexual abuse in childhood can lead to sexual promiscuity in adolescence (Santelli & Beilensen, 1992).

Primary Prevention for Selected Groups Efforts at this level seem to be based primarily on such demographic factors as SES. Because the participants in prevention at this level are likely to be from disadvantaged environments, the intensity of the programs should adjust to meet the needs of the target group of students.

A successful prevention program for at-risk, inner-city girls is *El Puente*. Specifically designed to serve Latino American girls, the program focuses on community involvement by using successful program graduates as advisory board members, role models, and contributors. Program content includes traditional sex education, as well as group activities to encourage values clarification and career exploration. One unique aspect of the program requires each participant to work with a counselor to plan a community-service project she can complete in lieu of fees for participation in the program. This activity instills a sense of community involvement, as well as encourages planning for the future, and keeps the girls involved during afternoons when they might otherwise be unsupervised (Paget, 1988).

Indicated Risk

In theory, individuals at the indicated level of risk are those who are engaging in unprotected intercourse. Because a number of problems are inherent in determining which adolescents this might include, broadening the definition to include adolescents with a number of risk factors may provide a more useful conceptualization of indicated risk. One group very likely to demonstrate indicated risk for future pregnancies is teenage girls who have had previous pregnancies and their partners. In addition, educators and health professionals working with adolescents should consider cumulative risk when referring individuals to more intensive programs. For example, a physically precocious 14-year-old with low self-esteem who is alone in the afternoons clearly is at greater risk for early pregnancy than a 14-year-old whose only risk characteristic is low self-esteem.

Primary Prevention for Indicated Groups Once it has been determined that a teenager is sexually active, thus at high risk, the obvious intervention is to ensure that the youth has access to contraceptives and to attempt to convince him or her of the importance of using them. The major focus of such preventive efforts is to promote an active role for the teenager in contraceptive use. School-based clinics that provide contraceptives to sexually active students are an example of prevention for groups at indicated risk.

The development of Norplant, a contraceptive device implanted under the skin that provides protection against pregnancy for 5 years, has tremendous implications for this area of prevention. In contrast with more active forms of contraception (i.e., condoms, oral contraceptives), Norplant requires no effort on the part of the female and lasts for 5 years; thus, the technique seems ideal for use with sexually active adolescents. However, despite its advantages, Norplant is surrounded by controversy because of its drawbacks. Several authors have speculated that young women would dislike it because the patch is sometimes visible, while others voice moral or social arguments regarding the impact it may have on low-income communities. However, the strongest argument against this technique is that, although it does protect against pregnancy, Norplant does not protect against sexually transmitted diseases including the human immunodeficiency virus (HIV). In spite of the controversy, Norplant may be a viable option in certain cases, specifically, for girls who are sexually active and are unlikely or unable to take responsibility for active contraception. Because of the growing risk of AIDS among this population, however, condoms remain the most beneficial contraceptive method for most sexually active teens.

Universal Primary Prevention

Traditionally, universal prevention programs have taken one or some combination of the following three approaches to reduce teen pregnancy: 1) teaching about sexuality and contraception, 2) changing adolescents' attitudes regarding sexuality and contraception, and

3) providing contraception and family-planning services (Jorgensen & Alexander, 1982). Recent and more intensive efforts have added the element of community involvement, such as encouraging young people to become involved in community-service projects or with community-service organizations. Community service as an important component of primary prevention is exemplified by the Teen Outreach Project, wherein adolescents are encouraged to participate with the Junior League in local service projects. Facilitating elements and barriers to universal primary prevention are shown in Table 7.3.

Programs Emphasizing Knowledge The earliest sex education programs limited their scope almost entirely to human reproductive biology. Jorgensen (1981) has been an outspoken proponent of broadening the curriculum to include the emotional and social aspects of sexuality. Jorgensen (1983) also advocates for changes in the philosophy of education programs to incorporate the view of adolescent sexuality as "the total complement of an individual's attitudes, cognitions, . . . experiences, and behaviors which could eventually result in any type of erotic stimulation" (p.142). There is considerable support for more comprehensive approaches—Dunn (1982) suggests that to view sex education as merely a means of preventing pregnancy may be confusing and gives adolescents the wrong impression of healthy sexuality.

Although the trend in prevention has been away from fact-based presentations, effective programs must also provide accurate information to participants. The content of the information varies depending

Table 7.3. Barriers to universal primary prevention

Elements	Facilitating factors	Barriers
Knowledge	Element most easily addressed in school setting	Teens' developmental levels
		Controversies over moral/ethical issues
Activities	Active participation increases integration of information	Administrative and practical considerations
		Controversies over moral/ethical issues
Future orientation	Associated with self-esteem and responsible decision making	Economic factors and life circumstances of many teens
		Lack of exposure to same-sex, same-race role models
Society	Concerted effort from all aspects of society is necessary to effect broad-based change	Different societal segments have different priorities
		Media glorification of irresponsible sexual behavior

upon the age and developmental levels of the participants but over the course of adolescence should include information on reproductive biology, normal sexual development, contraception, pregnancy and birth options (Schinke, Gilchrist, & Small, 1979), as well as an emphasis on the importance of prenatal care (Kingsman & Slap, 1992). A survey of inner-city, at-risk seventh and eighth graders provides evidence supporting the need for accurate information. The study found that while urban adolescents were aware of specific contraceptives, 12- to 14-year-olds could not identify ways to obtain contraceptives or to use them effectively. The study also emphasized a need for basic information: The adolescents lacked basic understanding of the processes of conception and believed a number of myths (e.g., girls can't get pregnant the first time they have sex) (Herz & Reis, 1987).

Attitudes Although traditional, classroom-based sex education increases the participants' level of knowledge about contraception and human reproductive biology, it has not been found to cause appreciable changes in attitudes (Kirby, 1992). Most programs focus on decision making, personal responsibility, and values clarification (Patten, 1981). Because peer support is such an important component in attitude change for adolescents, programs should involve a strong peer component (Paget, 1988). Small group discussions are one way to facilitate personal development and values clarification, as are groups co-led by adults and older adolescents.

Future Orientation Because the ability to project oneself into a successful future is associated with effective contraception (Ralph et al., 1984), programs should encourage a future orientation among participants (Paget, 1988). The lack of future orientation among low-income youths may have implications for many unhealthy behaviors, and the consequences of such risky behaviors as early childbearing are diminished in importance for many teenagers because they fail to look beyond the here and now. This inability to project themselves into a successful future may explain the higher rates of sexual activity among minority adolescents. Yawn and Yawn (1993) suggest that rural adolescents also may be influenced by perceived limitations in future careers because they lack exposure to a wide range of experiences. Therefore, they suggest that increased awareness of educational and vocational options be incorporated into pregnancy prevention programs.

The ability to plan ahead, either for the short term (e.g., completing school assignments on time), or for the long term (e.g., finishing high school), is a skill that developmentally immature students may lack. At the same time, some degree of planning is necessary for contraception to be carried out effectively. Consequently, an important component of pregnancy prevention programs is to focus on helping adolescents look toward the future, even if this only means providing strategies for remembering to take condoms on dates.

Accessibility of Contraception School-based clinics providing contraceptive support to adolescents are perhaps the most controversial of the approaches to pregnancy prevention, despite evidence that the presence of family-planning clinics does not lead to increased sexual behavior among teenagers (Kirby, 1992). The importance of accessible contraception has been demonstrated in research with sexually active male adolescents—"inconvenience" is one of the most frequently cited reasons for not using condoms (Kirby, 1992). Providing condoms in schools may increase their continued use for two reasons: 1) by convincing teens that condoms are socially acceptable; and 2) by reducing the discomfort teens may feel if they have to obtain condoms in a public place, such as a drug store (Kirby, 1992).

Community Involvement Like *El Puente*, other programs incorporate community involvement in addition to more traditional, classroom-based activities. The "Teen Outreach Project" (Allen, Phillber, & Hoggson, 1990) is a nationwide project open to all students in areas where it is implemented. Unlike *El Puente*, Teen Outreach is not limited to one cultural or SES group. Students who participate in Teen Outreach through their high schools are expected to enroll in a class that includes information on sexuality as well as activities to encourage values clarification. The community involvement aspect is facilitated by local Junior League chapters that include the teens in such volunteer activities as hospital visitation, homeless shelters, and so forth. The guiding philosophy of community involvement is to enable young people to enjoy "help-giving" roles rather than exclusively "help-receiving" roles (Allen et al., 1990).

Systems-Level Considerations for Successful Primary Prevention

One of the most frequent criticisms of prevention efforts in this area is that any prevention effort is seen as preferable to none at all, and evaluation efforts are rare. Nevertheless, certain factors have been identified as important components of a successful, comprehensive program.

Age of Participants There is almost universal agreement that sexuality should be addressed early. For prevention efforts to be effective, discussions of issues surrounding sexuality should begin with children long before they are physically ready to become sexually active (Jorgensen & Alexander, 1982; Kirby, 1992; Reichelt, 1986; Yawn & Yawn, 1993; Zabin & Clark, 1983). Self-esteem and responsible decision making do not have their origins in puberty; consequently, interventions to encourage positive self-image and sound judgment should begin in elementary school, long before those skills are needed to make responsible contraceptive decisions.

Context of the Program To the extent possible, messages about responsible sexual behavior should be consistent across all facets of the young person's life. The best school-based programs focus on overall school climate and involve families (Mills et al., 1988; Patten, 1981). This requires the support of all school personnel, including administrators, school boards, and principals. In many school settings, the principal's support is vital, particularly if nontraditional techniques (e.g., homework assignments to visit clinics, obtain birth control) are to be included (Barth, Middleton, & Wagmann, 1988).

Sexuality education need not be limited to health education or home economics classes. Paget (1988) provides several suggestions for incorporating issues of sexuality education into the total curriculum. For example, in literature classes, students can be asked to discuss ways in which the lives of adolescent heroes and heroines would be changed if they had a baby. Similarly, students in math classes can be asked to calculate the costs associated with starting a family. These approaches are likely to extend the students' awareness of teenage pregnancy and childbearing beyond that of a biologic or physical fact, and they can explore the personal and economic consequences.

In addition to consistency in educational settings, community support for programs is vital. Perhaps the best way to accomplish this is by active and creative involvement of community agents such as religious leaders, parents, and the media to produce a more comprehensive and consistent message for adolescents (Kirby, 1992; Mills et al., 1988). Adolescents often get a mixed message when the images and views expressed in the media conflict with the responsible decision-making strategies taught in sexuality education programs. As much as possible, liaisons among the community, school, and parents should be used in sexuality education to provide a consistent program (Paget, 1988). Positive role models from the adolescents' own background could be used as guest speakers to make the information more relevant, particularly for members of ethnic minorities.

A basic but frequently overlooked strategy in primary prevention of pregnancy as well as a host of other adolescent problems is to provide adolescents with structured, supervised activities after school. Because most young adolescents become pregnant between 3 P.M. and 6 P.M. (Compton, Hughes, & Smith, 1987, in Paget, 1988), structured school and community programs that occupy that time, particularly for high-risk youth, could be very worthwhile investments. Schools and communities could profitably consider enabling all students to become involved in sports activities, clubs, and so forth that not only serve to deter sexual activity in the afternoon, but also build self-esteem, social skills, and goal-setting skills.

Adolescents Should Be Active Participants in Primary Prevention Programs Several studies have demonstrated that without an experiential component, programs failed to change adolescents' behaviors (Barth et al., 1988; Kirby, 1992; Schinke et al., 1979). Consequently, traditional educational environments can be limiting if alternatives to the more rigid structure of classroom-based instruction are not possible. Schinke et al. endorse a cognitive–behavioral, experiential approach based on four steps: 1) exposure to information, 2) understanding the information, 3) personalizing information, and 4) development of behavioral skills to implement the new knowledge. Kirby suggests that a role-playing context can be a good way to personalize information and simulate reality without leaving the classroom. Barth et al. go a step further and recommend such homework assignments as locating and visiting the nearest family-planning clinic to ensure that students are able to apply their new knowledge in a real-world setting.

Barriers to Effective Primary Prevention

Barriers to effective primary prevention of adolescent pregnancy can be identified at a number of levels, ranging from the level of the individual adolescent to society at large.

Characteristics of Adolescents Characteristics of the adolescents themselves often serve as barriers. The variability among developmental levels of adolescents and the need to individualize interventions limit the effectiveness of widespread awareness efforts. Jorgensen and Alexander (1982) also point out that many adolescent pregnancies are intentional. Fraiburg (1983) supports this idea and suggests that many adolescent girls become pregnant because of the inadequacy of their relationships with their own families. She suggests that such girls may want a baby to fulfill their needs for love and nurturance. Although such motivations may account for a relatively small number of adolescent pregnancies (Furstenberg et al., 1989), adolescents who become pregnant intentionally may differ from other pregnant adolescents; therefore, they might require differentiated intervention (Matsuhashi & Felice, 1991).

Administrative Barriers Public schools are the most common setting for pregnancy prevention programs. Within this system, a number of administrative barriers prevent effective, continuous sexuality education, including inconsistent support for programs and lack of involvement of such key, powerful people as administrators, school boards, principals, and so forth (Jorgensen & Alexander, 1982). Because public schools are often strapped for money, most programs are not staffed by an expert knowledgeable about human sexuality. Typically, teachers pulled from the physical education and health department or from home economics are given the responsibility of maintaining a pregnancy prevention program with inadequate training or support (Jorgensen & Alexander, 1982). The structure of schools can limit the effectiveness of pregnancy prevention programs as well. If the class is taught during the regular school day, the format of sex education will likely be classroom-based, with few opportunities for such real-world contact as visiting adolescent health clinics or obtaining contraceptives.

Societal Barriers Conger (1988) comments that "most Americans, regardless of their political or ideological persuasion, agree that adolescent pregnancy presents serious problems, both for the individual and the nation" (p. 297). However, people of different ideological or political persuasions tend to disagree over the methods by which pregnancy will be prevented. Scales (1990) and Reichelt (1986) point out that various special interest groups continue to lobby against the provision of comprehensive sex education programs. For one outspoken minority, abstinence is the only acceptable, moral means of preventing pregnancy. They object to education about contraception in the schools or other public forums for fear adolescents will be encouraged to become promiscuous. Conger counters this argument with the observation that, given the percentages of teenagers who are already sexually active, sexuality education is unlikely to be the first time adolescents have considered sex.

The political climate of the 1980s also served as a deterrent to primary prevention of adolescent pregnancies. Despite the potential savings of providing contraceptive services to adolescents, the CPO reports that, after accounting for inflation, the federal government decreased spending on family-planning services for adolescents by more than one third during the 1980s. Thus, at the same time that more and more adolescents were becoming sexually active outside of marriage, fewer and fewer were receiving family-planning services.

Because of the sensitivity of the issues that revolve around sexuality, particularly among unmarried teenagers, the controversy over providing contraceptive information in schools and community organizations continues. To overcome the continual opposition, Scales (1990) suggests that advocates for primary prevention programs must become more effective and active in presenting their own political agenda. Although most educators and health-care professionals agree that abstinence is the safest contraceptive method, pragmatics dictate that we must also recognize that a "just say no" approach will not be effective for all teenagers. The social and economic consequences for sexually active teenagers, their children, and the greater society require the continued implementation of comprehensive and differentiated primary prevention efforts.

SUMMARY

The underlying ideal of primary prevention of adolescent pregnancy is a "wellness model" that seeks to reduce risk taking among adolescents, not only in terms of sexual activity, but in other behaviors such as the abuse of drugs, cars, and weapons. Strategies that make schools more personal, more enjoyable, and more rewarding also encourage better school performance and more positive self-esteem (Mills et al., 1988). Better school performance and higher self-esteem, in turn, contribute to the development of individuals better equipped to make responsible decisions. The ultimate goal of primary prevention efforts in this area should be to create a preventive mindset among all children and adolescents (Paget, 1988). The first task, however, is creating a preventive mindset among all professionals who work with children and adolescents.

REFERENCES

Allen, J.P., Phillber, S., & Hoggson, N. (1990). School-based prevention of teenage pregnancy and school drop-out: Process evaluation of the national replication of the Teen Outreach Program. *American Journal of Community Psychology, 18*(4), 505–524.

Babsin, S.C., & Clark, M.G. (1983). Relationships between infant death and maternal age. *Journal of Pediatrics, 103*, 391–393.

Barth, R.P., Middleton, K., & Wagmann, E. (1988). A skill building approach to preventing teenage pregnancy. *Theory Into Practice, 28*(3), 183–190.

Bayatpour, M., Wells, R.D., & Holford, S. (1992). Physical and sexual abuse as predictors of substance use and suicide among pregnant teenagers. *Journal of Adolescent Health, 13*, 128–132.

Black, C., & DeBlassie, R.R. (1985). Adolescent pregnancy: Contributing factors, consequences, treatment, and plausible solutions. *Adolescence, 20*(78), 281–290.

Blos, P. (1967). The second individuation process of adolescence. *Psychoanalytic Study of the Child, 22*, 162–182.

Brazeton, T.B. (1984). *Neonatal behavioral assessment scale* (2nd ed.). Philadelphia: J.B. Lippincott.

Bucholz, E.S., & Gol, B. (1986). More than playing house: A developmental perspective on the strengths in teenage motherhood. *American Journal of Orthopsychiatry, 56*, 347–359.

Conger, J.J. (1988). Hostages to fortune: Youth, values, and the public interest. *American Psychologist, 43*(4), 291–300.

de Cubas, M., & Field, T.M. (1984). Teaching interactions of black and Cuban teenage mothers and their infants. *Early Child Development and Care, 16*(1–2), 41–56.
DeLissovoy, V. (1975). Child care by adolescent parents. *Child Today, 2,* 22–25.
Dunn, P. (1982). Reduction of teenage pregnancy as a rationale for sex education: A position paper. *Journal of School Health, 52*(5), 611–613.
Dunst, C.J., Vance, S.D., & Cooper, C.S. (1986). A social systems perspective of adolescent pregnancy: Determinants of parent and parent–child behavior. *Infant Mental Health Journal, 7*(1), 34–48.
Elkind, D. (1967). Egocentrism in adolescence. *Child Development, 38,* 1025–1033.
Erikson, E. (1959). Identity and the life cycle. *Psychological Issues, 1,* 1–171.
Felice, M.E., Schragg, P., James, M., & Hollingsworth, D.R. (1987). Psychosocial aspects of Mexican American, white, and black teenage pregnancy. *Journal of Adolescent Health Care, 8,* 330–335.
Finkelstein, A.W., Finkelstein, J.A., Christie, M., Roden, M., & Shelton, C. (1982). Teenage pregnancy and parenthood: Outcomes for mother and child. *Journal of Adolescent Health Care, 3,* 1–7.
Fox, R.A., Bausch, M.J., Goldberg, B.D., & Helmuth, M.C. (1987). Parenting attitudes of pregnant adolescents. *Psychological Reports, 61,* 403–406.
Frager, B. (1991). Teenage childbearing: Part I. The problem has not gone away. *Journal of Pediatric Nursing, 6*(2), 131–133.
Fraiberg, S. (1983). The adolescent mother and her infant. *Adolescent Psychiatry, 10,* 7–23.
Furstenburg, F.F. (1980). Burdens and benefits: The impact of early childbearing on the family. *Journal of Social Issues, 36*(1), 64–87.
Furstenberg, F.F., Brooks-Gunn, J., & Chase-Lansdale, L. (1989). Teenage pregnancy and childbearing. *American Psychologist, 44*(2), 313–320.
Garcia-Coll, C.T., Hoffman, J., Van Heuten, L.J., & Oh, W. (1987). The social context of teenage childbearing: Effects on the infants' caregiving environment. *Journal of Youth and Adolescence, 16*(4), 345–360.
Giblin, P.T., Poland, M.L., & Sachs, B.A. (1987). Effects of social supports on attitudes and health behaviors of pregnant adolescents. *Journal of Adolescent Health, 8,* 273–279.
Hansom, R.A. (1990). Initial parenting attitudes of pregnant adolescents and a comparison with the decision about adoption. *Adolescence, 25*(99), 629–643.
Hardy, J.B., Welcher, D.W., & Standly, J. (1987). Long-range outcome of adolescent pregnancy. *Clinical Obstetrics and Gynecology, 21,* 1215–1232.
Hart, B., & Hilton, I. (1988). Dimensions of personality organization as predictors of teenage pregnancy risk. *Journal of Personality Assessment, 52*(1), 116–132.
Hechtman, L. (1989). Teenage mothers and their children: Risks and problems: A review. *Canadian Journal of Psychiatry, 34,* 569–575.
Helm, J.M., Comfort, M., Bailey, D.B., & Simeonsson, R.J. (1990). Adolescent and adult mothers of handicapped children: Maternal involvement in play. *Family Relations, 39,* 432–437.
Herz, E.J., & Reis, J.S. (1987). Family life education for inner-city teens: Identifying needs. *Journal of Youth and Adolescence, 16*(4), 361–377.
Johnson, S.A., & Green, V. (1993). Female adolescent contraceptive decision making and risk taking. *Adolescence, 28*(109), 81–96.
Jorgensen, S.R. (1981). Sex education and the reduction of adolescent pregnancies: Prospects for the 1980s. *Journal of Early Adolescence, 1*(1), 38–52.

Jorgensen, S.R. (1983). Beyond adolescent pregnancy: Research frontiers for early adolescent sexuality. *Journal of Early Adolescence, 3*(1–2), 141–155.

Jorgensen, S.R. (1991). Project taking charge: An evaluation of an adolescent pregnancy prevention program. *Family Relations, 40*(4), 373–380.

Jorgensen, S.R., & Alexander, S.J. (1982). Research on adolescent pregnancy-risk: Implications for sex education programs. *Theory Into Practice, 22*(2), 125–133.

Kellam, S.G., Ensinger, M.E., & Turner, R.J. (1977). Family structure and the mental health of children. *Archives of General Psychiatry, 34*, 1012–1018.

Kingsman, S.B., & Slap, G.B. (1992). Barriers to adolescent prenatal care. *Journal of Adolescent Health, 13*, 146–154.

Kirby, D. (1992). Research on effectiveness of sex education programs. *Theory Into Practice, 32*(3), 165–171.

Klein, H.A., & Cordell, A.S. (1987). The adolescent as mother: Early risk identification. *Journal of Youth and Adolescence, 16*(1), 47–58.

Kobokovich, L.J., & Bonovich, L.K. (1992). Adolescent pregnancy prevention strategies used by school nurses. *Journal of School Health, 62*(1), 11–14.

Lamb, M.E., Hopps, K., & Elster, A.B. (1987). Strange situation behavior of infants with adolescent mothers. *Infant Behavior and Development, 10*, 39–48.

Landy, S., Cleland, J., & Schubert, J. (1984). The individuality of teenage mothers and its implications for intervention strategy. *Journal of Adolescence, 7*, 171–190.

Lawrence, R.A., & Merritt, T.A., (1981). Infants of adolescent mothers: Prenatal, neonatal, and infancy outcomes. *Seminars in Perinatology, 5*, 19–24.

Levenson, P., Atkinson, B., Hale, J., & Hollier, M. (1978). Adolescent parent education: A maturational model. *Child Psychiatry and Human Development 9*(2), 104–118.

Matsuhashi, Y., & Felice, M.E. (1991). Adolescent body image during pregnancy. *Journal of Adolescent Health, 12*, 313–315.

Mercer, R.T. (1986). The relationship of developmental variables to maternal behavior. *Research in Nursing & Health, 9*, 25–33.

Mills, R.C., Dunham, R.G., & Alpert, G.P. (1988). Working with high-risk youth in prevention and early intervention programs: Toward a comprehensive wellness model. *Adolescence, 23*(91), 643–660.

Newcomer, S., & Baldwin, W. (1992). Demographics of adolescent sexual behavior, contraception, pregnancy, and STDs. *Journal of School Health, 62*(7), 265–270.

Orr, D.P., & Langefield, C.D. (1993). Factors associated with condom use by sexually active male adolescents at risk for sexually transmitted disease. *Pediatrics, 91*(5), 873–879.

Paget, K.D. (1988). Adolescent pregnancy: Implications for prevention strategies in educational settings. *School Psychology Review, 17*(4), 570–580.

Patten, M.A. (1981). Self-concept and self-esteem: Factors in adolescent pregnancy. *Adolescence, 16*(64), 765–778.

Pete, J.M., & DeSantis, L. (1990). Sexual decision making in young black adolescent females. *Adolescence, 25*(97), 145–154.

Presser, H.B. (1989). Some economic complexities of child care provided by grandmothers. *Journal of Marriage and the Family, 51*(3), 581–591.

Ralph, N., Lochman, J., & Thomas, T. (1984). Psychosocial characteristics of pregnant and nulliparous adolescents. *Adolescence, 19*(74), 283–294.

Reichelt, P.A. (1986). Public policy and public opinion toward sex education

and birth control for teenagers. *Journal of Applied Social Psychology, 116*(2), 95–106.
Reis, J.S., & Herz, E.J. (1987). Correlates of adolescent parenting. *Adolescence, 22*(87), 599–609.
Richter, D.L., Valois, R.F., McKeown, R.E., & Vincent, M.L. (1993). Correlates of condom use and number of sexual partners among high school adolescents. *Journal of School Health, 63*(2), 91–99.
Sadler, L.S., & Catrone, C. (1983). The adolescent parent: A dual developmental crisis. *Journal of Adolescent Health Care, 4*(2), 100–105.
Santelli, J.S., & Beilensen, P. (1992). Adolescent sexuality: Pregnancy, sexually transmitted diseases, and prevention. *Journal of School Health, 62*(7), 255–261.
Scales, P. (1990). Overcoming future barriers to sexuality education. *Theory Into Practice, 28*(3), 172–176.
Schinke, S.P., Gilchrist, L.D., & Small, R.W. (1979). Preventing unwanted adolescent pregnancy: A cognitive–behavioral approach. *American Journal of Orthopsychiatry, 49*(1), 81–88.
Simkins, L. (1984). Consequences of teenage pregnancy and motherhood. *Adolescence, 19*(73), 39–47.
Smith, E.A., & Udry, J.R. (1985). Coital and noncoital behaviors of white and black adolescents. *American Journal of Public Health, 75*, 1200–1203.
Steir, D.M., Leventhal, J.M., Berg, A.T., Johnson, L., & Mezger, J. (1993). Are children born to young mothers at increased risk for maltreatment? *Pediatrics, 91*, 642–648.
Wise, S., & Grossman, F.K. (1980). Adolescent mothers and their infants: Psychological factors in early attachment and interaction. *American Journal of Orthopsychiatry, 50*(3), 454–468.
Yawn, B.P., & Yawn, R.A. (1993). Adolescent pregnancies in rural America: A review of the literature and strategies for primary prevention. *Family Community Health, 16*(1), 36–45.
Zabin, L.S., & Clark, S.D. (1983). Why they wait: A study of teenage family planning clinic patients. *Family Planning Perspectives, 13*, 205.

8

Drug Use and Pregnancy

Rebecca Edmondson

Jacqueline is a 26-year-old woman with two children, ages 6 years and 18 months. She is in the 7th month of pregnancy with her third child and during her first two trimesters, she used a variety of drugs: alcohol, tobacco, cocaine, and marijuana. Jacqueline is the oldest of four children and grew up in an impoverished and abusive home with an alcoholic stepfather. She left home at age 17 after her junior year of high school to escape constant physical and emotional abuse. Jacqueline has worked on and off over the past 8 years and has been involved in several unhealthy and abusive relationships. She began partying and using drugs with one of her boyfriends soon after leaving her parents' home. She lived with this man for 1½ years and was beaten frequently. Jacqueline became addicted to crack-cocaine and alcohol, and she remained in this relationship because her boyfriend supported her habit. When Jacqueline found out she was pregnant with her first child, she moved out and tried to go straight. She moved in with two girlfriends and remained clean until her son, Jacquim, was 3 months old. At this time, Jacqueline was struggling financially and felt left out of her social group because her roommates and friends continued to use drugs. Gradually, Jacqueline began to party again, drinking on weekends and occasionally snorting cocaine. Within 6 months, however, she was using a mixture of drugs on a regular basis, and Jacquim was placed in foster care. By the time Jacqueline became pregnant with her second child, Raphael, she was using regularly. Following the delivery, Raphael was removed from her custody and placed in foster care. Since that time, Jacqueline has been quite depressed. She has thought about committing suicide and continues to use drugs. She did not discover she was pregnant with her third child until she began severe cramping and was taken to an emergency room during her second trimester. She was identified as a drug user by hospital staff and was encouraged to seek help for her addiction. At this time, Jacqueline is trying to stop using drugs and is involved in a treatment program. She hopes to retain custody of this child and eventually get her other sons out of the foster care system. Her success remains to be seen.

Prenatal drug exposure of children is a national problem of alarming proportions. As the vignette illustrates, it is a complex biopsychosocial problem reflecting the relationship of maternal, child, and environmental factors. Jacqueline's story is much like those of thousands of other young women across the United States. As drug use among women has spiraled in this country during the past 15 years, so has concern for the safety and development of the children born following in utero drug exposure. As a result of the recent media focus on children exposed to drugs, the public has become acutely aware of the risks involved with prenatal substance abuse. Unfortunately, the women who face such multiple and complex problems as drug addiction, poverty, malnutrition, and abuse are portrayed as criminals all too often and assumed to be unfit for parenthood, rather than seen as mothers struggling with addiction. They frequently are described as a difficult and hard-to-reach population whose problems and needs strain the resources of our service provision systems. The majority of these services are, at this time, reactive rather than proactive, thus they typically have not effectively addressed the risk factors associated with substance abuse in women prior to pregnancy and childbearing.

This chapter focuses on the problem of prenatal drug exposure of children by: 1) addressing the prevalence and characteristics of substance abuse among women in their childbearing years; 2) identifying the complications related to drug abuse during pregnancy, with specific focus on alcohol, marijuana, tobacco, and cocaine; 3) reviewing cost estimates and treatment options for women with addictions; and 4) describing a primary prevention model for this biopsychosocial problem.

SUBSTANCE ABUSE IN WOMEN

Prevalence

Estimates from the National Household Survey on Drug Abuse (National Institute on Drug Abuse [NIDA], 1991) suggest that millions of women may use drugs during their reproductive years. Although substance abuse crosses the boundaries of race, ethnicity, and socioeconomic status, studies reveal a higher incidence of reported use by poor, uninsured, minority women (Castro, Azen, Hobel, & Platt, 1993). In addition, the choice of drug seems to vary among ethnicities—white women were more likely to admit to having used alcohol or marijuana during pregnancy, and African-American women admitted to having used cocaine (Frank et al., 1988; Frank, Zukerman, & Amaro, 1989; Streisguth et al., 1991). However, because of inadequate and inconsistent methods of identifying women who use and abuse drugs, prevalence estimates must be interpreted with caution.

The National Household Survey on Drug Abuse (NIDA, 1991) is a widely used source for prevalence and epidemiologic data on substance abuse among women. From a sample size of 3,522 women, projections were made concerning the 60 million women considered to be of childbearing age, 15–44 years. Figure 8.1 shows estimates for the most commonly used licit and illicit drugs and compares 1990 NIDA statistics with those of 1988 and 1985.

As shown, many women continue to use such legal substances as alcohol and tobacco, although there seems to have been a decline in illicit drug use between 1985 and 1990. Hopefully this represents a true decline in usage rather than a reluctance to report use as a result of media attention and fear of legal repercussions.

Characteristics

Drug addiction is a chronic, relapsing disorder that frequently is accompanied by a host of physical, psychological, and sociological problems. The incidence of addiction-related physical and mental health problems, as well as social and emotional disorders, is especially high in drug-dependent women (as opposed to men), who typically are without family and community support systems or economic resources, and whose own family histories often include abuse and/or addiction (U.S. Department of Health and Human Services [USDHHS], 1992).

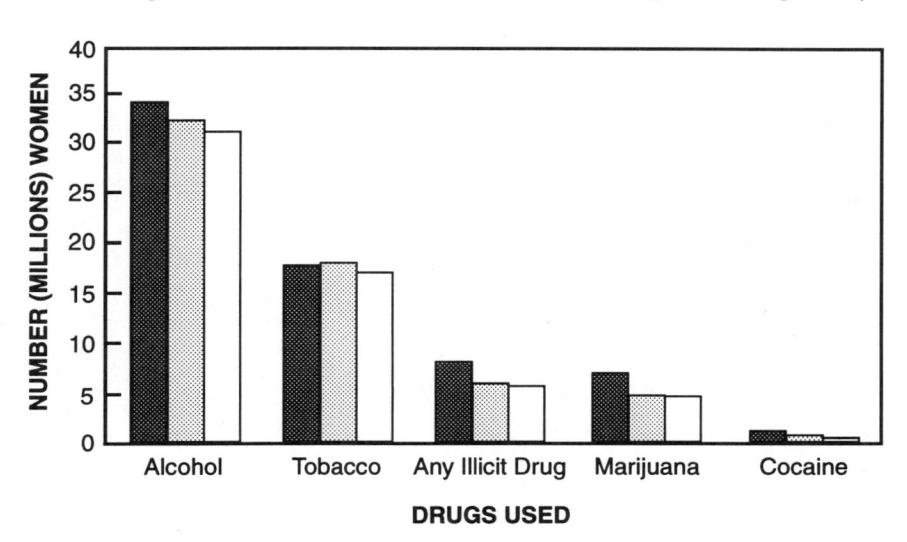

Figure 8.1. Number (millions) of women of childbearing age (15–44 years) who reported the use of licit and illicit drugs during the previous month in 1985 ■, 1988 ▨, and 1990 ☐. (Data from National Household Survey on Drug Abuse, 1985, 1988, 1990.) (From Khalsa, J.H., & Gfroerer, J. [1991]. Epidemiology and health consequences of drug abuse among pregnant women. *Seminars in Perinatology, 15*[4], 266.)

Table 8.1 lists some of the risk factors that may accompany substance abuse by women.

The transgenerational cycle of drug use, physical and sexual abuse, poverty, and poor family relations places many young women at risk for using drugs themselves. This risk chain of intergenerational substance abuse not only affects those currently involved, but it may also have subsequent detrimental effects on future generations. Growing up in such impoverished, chaotic home environments is likely to deprive children of nurturing, supportive models for their own future parenting skills, thus passing on the problem to the next generation. Women who are denied the opportunity to develop such healthy connections—as those among daughters, parents, partners, and friends—may be those who are most vulnerable to substance abuse (USDHHS, 1992).

Substance abuse has a direct impact on both the physical and psychological health of women and can be particularly detrimental during pregnancy to both mother and child. Drug abuse is associated with dysmenorrhea and amenorrhea, which can make birth control and pregnancy detection difficult (Bry, 1983). This, combined with the pervasive effects of poverty, lack of access to services, and fear of legal repercussions, often results in the lack of prenatal care or in delayed care for many women. Of additional concern is the current ineffectiveness associated with delayed or selective screening and early identification efforts to reach women of reproductive age who may be using drugs. By the time many women discover they are pregnant and become involved in the health-care system, the pregnancy may already have been compromised.

COMPLICATIONS OF SUBSTANCE ABUSE DURING PREGNANCY

Recent research efforts have concentrated on the effects of prenatal drug exposure on the subsequent development of the fetus and child. It is beyond the scope of this chapter to provide a comprehensive review of the research related to prenatal drug use; however, brief summaries of complications associated with the use of alcohol, marijuana, tobacco, and cocaine are presented.

Alcohol

Concern about drinking during pregnancy and awareness of its effects on the unborn child have been expressed for centuries. For example, the Bible (Judges 13:4) warns women against taking wine or strong drink lest they injure their unborn children.

Alcohol is the drug most frequently used by women in the United States, and 1 in 6 women in the peak childbearing years of 18–34 years

Table 8.1. Risk factors in a biopsychosocial model of substance abuse

Poverty	Co-morbidity with mental illness
Minority group member	Early use of illicit substances
Homelessness	Family history of drug abuse
Low self-esteem	Poor family relations
Genetic constitution	History of abuse or neglect
Domestic violence	Illiterate/uneducated

may drink enough, either chronically or episodically, to present a hazard to the unborn infant. It is estimated that 73% of pregnant 12- to 13-year-olds may have drunk alcohol sometime during their pregnancies (Gomby & Shiono, 1991) and that approximately 40,000 infants may be born yearly who are affected by prenatal alcohol exposure (National Council on Alcoholism and Drug Dependence, 1990).

A number of detrimental short- and long-term effects have been associated with maternal alcohol use, including low birth weight (LBW) and cognitive, behavioral, and growth delays. A distinct cluster of characteristics has been identified and termed *fetal alcohol syndrome* (FAS). The criteria for diagnosis of FAS include: 1) growth retardation both prenatally and postnatally; 2) central nervous system involvement including microcephaly, mental retardation, or developmental delay; and 3) characteristic facial dysmorphology with short palpebral fissures, flat maxillary area, thin upper lip, and flattened and elongated philtrum. The incidence of FAS is approximately 1 in 750, or about 5,000 babies per year (National Council on Alcoholism and Drug Dependence, 1990). It is estimated that thousands more children may exhibit fetal alcohol effects (FAE), which are described as the presence of one or two of these characteristics but not the entire cluster. Cases of fetal alcohol syndrome have been documented throughout the world population; however, disproportionately higher incidences have been found among Native Americans, lower socioeconomic groups, and children of older mothers (Council Report, 1983).

Fetal alcohol syndrome is now thought to be the leading known cause of mental retardation in the United States (Abel & Sokol, 1987), and it represents the severe end of the disabilities continuum resulting from prenatal alcohol exposure. There does seem to be a dose–response developmental relationship because detrimental effects seem to increase with the amount and frequency of alcohol consumed (Day & Richardson, 1991). At this time, however, it is still unclear what quantity of consumed alcohol leads to problems, when drinking is most risky during pregnancy, and why some children seem more resilient to exposure in utero than others.

Marijuana

Despite its widespread popularity in the 1960s and its continued use, few studies have focused on the developmental issues of maternal marijuana use, and those available present inconsistent findings. The most frequently cited study investigating effects of marijuana exposure in utero is that of Fried, O'Connell, and Watkinson (1992) conducted at Carleton University, Ottawa, Canada. Children prenatally exposed to marijuana were followed at 12, 24, and 36 months of age. Results indicated no negative effect of marijuana exposure on mental, motor, or language development. At 48 months, poor performance on memory and verbal tests was associated with heavy maternal marijuana use during pregnancy. However, at 60 and 72 months, no differences were noted between the exposed and nonexposed children. Currently, it is estimated that 17.4% of pregnant 12- to 34-year-olds may have been exposed to marijuana at some time during their pregnancies (Gomby & Shiono, 1991).

Tobacco

Approximately 1 million babies each year are placed at increased risk for LBW because they are born to women who smoke cigarettes (Floyd, Zahniser, Gunter, & Kendrick, 1991). Estimates are that 37.6% of pregnant 12- to 34-year-olds may have smoked cigarettes at some point during their pregnancies (Gomby & Shiono, 1991).

As with alcohol, a strong dose–response relationship exists; the more a woman smokes, the greater the likelihood of her having a low birth weight infant. Additional risks from smoking during pregnancy include spontaneous abortion, premature delivery, and stillbirth later in pregnancy (Koop, 1986). Passive exposure to parental smoking has been associated with delays in intellectual, academic, and behavioral development (Rush & Callahan, 1989). These children are likely to be at increased risk for such illnesses as pneumonia, bronchitis, laryngitis, and otitis media (Floyd et al., 1991), which may, in turn, negatively influence developmental progress and outcome.

Cocaine

Analysis of NIDA's recent survey (1991) indicates that more than 4.5 million women in the childbearing age group (15–44 years) were estimated to have used illicit drugs in the previous month, and approximately 601,000 women in this age group seemed to be current cocaine users. There are no accurate data on how many of these women are pregnant, although estimates from several prevalence studies suggest percentages ranging from 1% to 36% (Gomby & Shiono, 1991).

Since the mid-1980s, a wealth of studies have focused on the sequelae of prenatal exposure to cocaine. The range of deleterious effects spans a continuum of severity from physical and neurological impairments to very subtle neurobehavioral differences. Early research focused on the physical sequelae associated with exposure in utero, which included such effects as *abruptio placentae,* low birth weight, short gestational periods, respiratory and genitourinary tract abnormalities, and intrauterine growth retardation (Neuspiel & Hamel, 1991; Rosenak, Diamant, Yaffe, & Hornstein, 1990). Infants exposed to cocaine in utero may also be at increased risk for physical problems indirectly related to the effects of the teratogen itself; for example, cocaine usage is often associated with the abuse of other licit and illicit substances during pregnancy, all of which can, individually and collectively, influence the overall health status of mother and child.

The impact of cocaine on neurobehavioral development has been investigated both prenatally and postnatally. Specifically, studies have linked drug exposure in utero to infants' inability to maintain adequate behavioral state control in the neonatal period, depression of interactive behavior, and poor organizational response to environmental stimuli (Chasnoff, Burns, Schnoll, & Burns, 1985). Mild-to-moderate tremulousness and increased startle responses have also been reported (Smith & Deitch, 1987) in addition to tremors, irritability, abnormal sleep patterns, and poor feeding (Oro & Dixon, 1987). In infancy, few differences have been documented using standard developmental tests, although temperamental and behavioral differences are evident at 6 months of age (Edmondson & Smith, in press). Follow-up studies indicate possible attention and behavioral deficits for some children at 3 years of age (Chasnoff, 1992) and differences in play patterns and behaviors (Rodning, Beckwith, & Howard, 1990).

Although cocaine has been shown to produce the effects noted above, it is still too early to know the long-term nature of cocaine exposure during pregnancy on infant and child development. This lack of definitive conclusions reflects the facts that: 1) longitudinal studies are continuing beyond the early years, and 2) publicized results thus far have not yielded consistent findings. Although this has meant that specific causal models of cocaine exposure have been difficult to define, particularly because cocaine rarely is used in isolation from other drugs, it is clear that the effects on child development can be viewed productively in a temporal sequence relative to prenatal drug exposure. To this end, adverse perinatal outcome will be conceptualized as the manifested condition of prenatal exposure and discussed as the basis for secondary prevention, with subsequent child and maternal complications and sequelae viewed as the focus for tertiary activities (Simeonsson, 1991).

In summary, substance abuse during pregnancy continues to be a serious problem in the United States, placing many women and their infants at risk for less-than-optimal developmental outcome. Drug use jeopardizes the health and well-being of the mother and child both prenatally and postnatally, thus a biopsychosocial view of the complex factors associated with drug abuse is necessary to understand and approach this problem in a comprehensive manner.

COST ESTIMATES AND TREATMENT OPTIONS

Estimates of prevalence rates of prenatal exposure cannot begin to identify the total numbers of children affected by parental substance abuse. Drug use not only affects the fetal and subsequent development of the child, but also increases the risk of child abuse. Although it is difficult to confirm a direct causal relationship, child abuse and neglect have been rapidly increasing and, in 1989, an estimated 2.4 million abused children were reported to child protective services (USDHHS, 1992). Chemical dependency is the dominant characteristic in child protective services caseloads in 22 states and the District of Columbia (McCullough, 1991); however, these figures may be low because not all states routinely investigate for the presence of substance abuse at the time a report is filed.

Children of substance abusers are at increased risk for hospitalization and out-of-home placement, straining already overburdened service systems. Estimates are that several hundred thousand children per year may be placed in foster homes as a direct result of parental substance abuse. Communities hardest hit by crack addiction have experienced the most startling increases in foster care placements. Two states, California and New York, together were responsible for 55% of the increase in foster care caseload from 1986 to 1989, with 41% and 95% increases, respectively (Besharov, 1990).

The estimated costs of caring for these children is staggering. There are both short-term (e.g., neonatal intensive care, extended hospitalization) and long-term (e.g., medical, social, educational interventions) economic implications resulting from prenatal substance exposure. To understand fully the costs incurred from drug use in pregnancy, it will be necessary to know both the number of women using drugs during pregnancy and the number of those pregnancies that had adverse outcomes. As stated earlier, accurate information is not available, and only general estimates of the economic effects can be made. Long-term costs of maternal smoking are estimated to range from $351 million to $852 million (in 1986 dollars) per year, and short-term costs range from $332 to $652 million per year. In comparison, the short-term economic costs (in 1989 dollars) for perinatal cocaine exposure have been estimated to range from $33 million to $1 billion per year (Phibbs, 1991). More specifically, in Los Angeles County in 1986, 915 drug-exposed infants incurred $32 million in hospital costs (Gittler & McPherson, 1990). Although most of the infants' care was covered by Medicaid, a substantial amount of the costs were not, and these were absorbed by the hospitals and the health-care system.

Studies have shown that cessation of substance abuse during pregnancy can improve obstetrical and neonatal outcome. For example, if a woman stops smoking by the 16th week of gestation, her risk of having a low birth weight infant is similar to that of a nonsmoker (Floyd et al., 1991). Estimates are that 20%–25% of women smokers quit at some point during pregnancy on their own, and up to 30% more could be helped to quit through intervention programs (Heckler, 1980). Cessation of cocaine use in the first trimester can result in increased birth weight and head circumference (Chasnoff, Griffith, MacGregor, Dirkes, & Burns, 1989). In addition, research has indicated that detrimental effects associated with tobacco and alcohol are related directly to the amount and duration of use during pregnancy. This information stresses not only the importance of reducing and eliminating drug use during pregnancy but also the need for primary prevention of this problem.

For women with addictions who are sexually active or pregnant, identification as early as possible and referral to an appropriate treatment program are crucial. Currently, the health-care system has assumed a primary role in the identification of women who are using drugs; however, there does not seem to be a routine, systematic way of reaching many women at risk. In addition, there has been a major focus on the availability of treatment programs for women who are addicted, especially those who are pregnant or are the primary caregivers for older children. In a survey of 78 New York City drug treatment centers, 54% refused to serve pregnant, addicted women, 67% refused to treat pregnant women on Medicaid, and 87% had no services for pregnant women on Medicaid who were addicted to crack or cocaine (DeBetterncourt, 1990). A survey of the 50 states by the National Center on Child Abuse Prevention Research revealed considerable discrepancies in services offered to pregnant women (Jones & Ackatz, 1992). The total number of available services per state ranged from 2 to 240, with a national total of 2,093; however, of the total number of treatment programs for male and female addicts, only 30% serve pregnant women. The most frequent type of treatment setting for chemically dependent women is outpatient care, with a scarcity of inpatient treatment services offered. Of the 2,093 programs, less than 15% also provided services for children. With respect to barriers to providing services to this population, child care was the most significant barrier, followed by maternal fear of being reported to authorities, and availability of housing and transportation.

PRIMARY PREVENTION MODEL

The fact that substance abuse in general and, more specifically, prenatal exposure to drugs are entirely preventable is a frustrating and challenging societal reality. The multitude of health, psychological, and social consequences of substance abuse on the parents and on the development of the infant and child demands that efforts be directed increasingly toward the prevention of drug abuse and extend beyond current approaches. It is imperative that such abuse be prevented in women who do not use drugs and that treatment be provided for those who are already addicted. As highlighted in Table 8.2, several models for prevention/intervention have been proposed to address the issue of substance abuse in women of childbearing age.

Past efforts have proved that prevention of this biopsychosocial problem is more complicated than "just say no." Furthermore, a unidimensional or single-focus approach may not be comprehensive enough to address the complexity of addiction and human behavior. For example, providing education about the risks involved in drug use may not prevent a young woman from experimenting if she is being pressured by peers or has grown up in a household where substance abuse is rampant. It is becoming increasingly clear that what is needed is a community-based, systemic, and holistic approach aimed at modifying both individuals and their environments. An interactive prevention paradigm of this sort will need to draw from two previously opposing philosophies: 1) the public health model that targets entire population subgroups (e.g., women); and 2) the clinical–developmental approach that is based on individual differences, motivations, and needs. A suc-

Table 8.2. Models for the prevention of substance abuse

Approach	Goals
Information/awareness	Provide clear information on consequences of drug use
Individual deficiencies	Focus on building self-esteem, clarifying values, decision making
Social influences	Recognize and resist social pressures
Legislative influences	Use criminal prosecution as deterrent
Multilevel community development	Modify individual and environmental contexts

cessful prevention program relies on accurately understanding the complex lives of the targeted recipients and considering their values and beliefs. In addition, three factors may strongly influence the acceptance of and adherence to prevention programs: 1) gender and gender-role socialization, 2) culture and ethnicity, and 3) developmental maturity (Gilchrist & Gillmore, 1992).

A recent conceptualization of primary, secondary, and tertiary prevention in early intervention has been proposed by Simeonsson (1991), which emphasizes intervention efforts at the primary level. This model can be applied readily to the biopsychosocial problem of substance abuse in pregnancy. Figure 8.2 indicates possible target populations (recipients) at each level of prevention.

Using this framework, secondary prevention efforts would focus on the manifestation of the problem; that is, emphasis would be on the infant who has been prenatally exposed to drugs and to the mother's perinatal health. The goal of secondary prevention is to reduce the extent of adverse perinatal outcome experienced by infants prenatally exposed to drugs. To this end, medical attention for the infant is a central tenet at the secondary prevention level to address perinatal issues of low birth weight, intrauterine growth retardation, and possible symptoms of drug withdrawal. At this level, efforts would be made to strengthen and maintain the mother–infant dyad by providing options for maternal addiction recovery, teaching the mother to recognize the unique behavioral cues and needs of her infant, and modeling effective parenting skills. Social support that focuses on the context of their reality is crucial; that is, support that deals with such issues as housing,

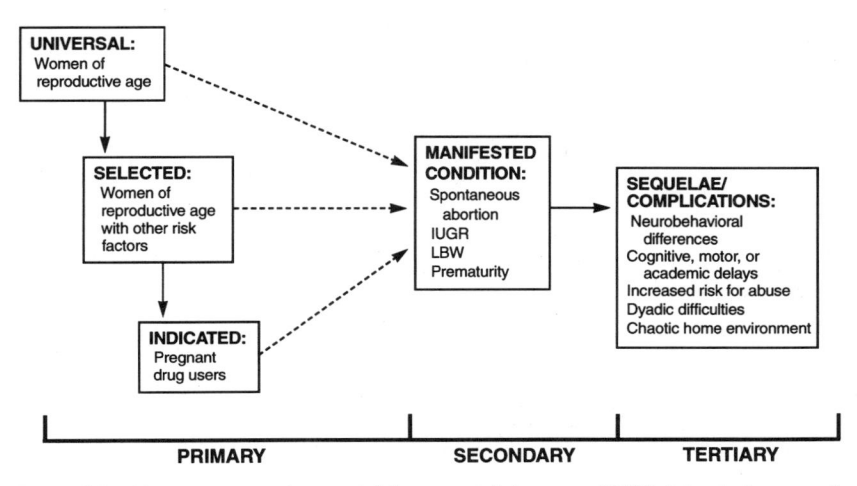

Figure 8.2. Primary prevention model for prenatal drug use. (IUGR, intrauterine growth retardation; LBW, low birth weight.)

transportation, nutrition, and child care. To summarize, service providers must focus on the overall health and well-being of the dyad by embracing a coordinated, multifaceted, interagency approach to address the interrelated medical, psychological, and social issues of the mother–child dyad.

The goal of tertiary prevention is to reduce the complications associated with adverse perinatal outcomes. These activities would focus on the remediation of short- and long-term developmental sequelae of prenatal drug exposure on the child and on the continued drug use by the mother and/or other caregivers in the home. For the child, developmental follow-up is crucial to determine health and educational needs resulting from parental substance abuse. For female substance abusers, assistance must go beyond maintaining abstinence to include job training, social support, and resources that promote drug-free patterns of living. Assessment of the ongoing needs of both partners within their environmental context and adaptation of treatment approaches do add to the complexity of service delivery, but they are crucial to the prevention process.

Given the broad scope of services required and the possible long-term socioeconomic costs accrued at the secondary and tertiary levels, it seems that it may well be more cost effective as well as socially responsible to focus efforts on the primary prevention level.

Within the prevention model described in earlier chapters, primary prevention efforts may be productively considered at three levels of the population: 1) universal (desirable for all), 2) selected (recommended for some), and 3) indicated (targeted recipients). Primary prevention of the drug-related effects on women and children can be implemented at each of these levels. Efforts can be made to reduce or eliminate drug use before, during, and after pregnancy in women of childbearing age; to reduce the incidence of pregnancy in sexually active substance-abusing groups; and to decrease drug use in pregnant users, not only during, but after pregnancy.

Universal Level

The goal of primary prevention is to reduce and, ideally, to eliminate the use of drugs among women in their childbearing years. Therefore, primary prevention efforts at a universal level are directed at all women to minimize the abuse of drugs in general and during pregnancy in particular. Prevention strategies should focus on a better understanding of the etiological determinants of drug use in our society and associated risk factors at a systems, as well as an individual, level. Additionally, public policy makers and the general public must clarify current perceptions of risk and addiction as a disease. It is imperative that we evaluate the cost effectiveness of our current system in dealing with drug abuse and its victims and present alternative primary prevention programs that may subsequently reduce costs at the secondary and tertiary levels.

Because universal primary prevention is by definition for all, the prevention strategies would focus on providing information to dissuade nonusers from drug experimentation as part of a total health awareness and promotion program. Young women must understand the potential impact of substances on their lives, and they must be given options other than drugs when they seek psychological and social support. As summarized in Table 8.3, the methods for universal prevention efforts may effectively use the media and community-based means to raise awareness.

Selected Level

The focus of primary prevention at the selected level is to target subpopulations at increased risk associated with group, rather than individual, characteristics. In the context of substance abuse, there are likely to be various subgroups at increased risk (see Table 8.4). Thus, although chemical dependence certainly is not limited to poor, nonwhite populations, these groups may be reported more often than the middle-class, white population. In addition, the specific needs of poor women may be greater because they have fewer available resources, and they often lack economic and social support. Prevention at the selected level might, therefore, include programs designed for women at increased risk in their reproductive years, as well as men, focusing on the risks involved in drug use, especially during pregnancy. Offering family-planning information and options for birth control to women when they bring older children for well-baby checks might be one route to reach high-risk populations. Communities with high levels of drug use may need to implement additional specialized awareness programs to reach specific subgroups at increased risk. Also, rather than

Table 8.3. Primary prevention at the universal level

Target	Focus	Means/methods
All women of childbearing age	Understand etiology of drug use/addiction	Educational systems
		Mass media
	Dissuade nonusers from experimentation	Communities (houses of worship, grocery stores)
	Provide alternative supports	Health-care system (health departments, hospitals)
		Public policy

Table 8.4. Primary prevention at the selected level

Target	Focus	Means/methods
Women of childbearing age from subgroups with other risk factors	Implement screening programs Improve early identification efforts Provide alternative methods of support	Community-based sites (houses of worship, child-care settings, health departments, clinics, hospitals)

targeting women only, it may be beneficial to expand efforts to include other significant individuals in the immediate environment.

An important consideration in primary prevention is that health services personnel must become more adept at recognizing and identifying high-risk women before pregnancy and providing treatment for them. Comprehensive service systems must be staffed by professionals and paraprofessionals who are trained in the field of addictions and are capable of recognizing signals of potential or ongoing substance abuse.

Indicated Level

Limited services are available for women who seek treatment for drug use, especially if they are pregnant. This situation reflects a significant problem in that primary prevention at the indicated level focuses on those at highest risk because of individual risk factors. In this context, indicated primary prevention would be targeted on pregnant women who are using drugs to prevent the manifestation of adverse perinatal outcomes. Among the difficulties of providing prevention is the fact that agencies may not accept these women because of legal and medical liabilities, and the women may fear legal repercussions as well. In turn, the fear of criminal prosecution may push addicted women to avoid prenatal care and to conceal drug histories, thus jeopardizing their pregnancy outcomes. Currently, substance abuse is one of the most commonly missed of all obstetrical and neonatal diagnoses. The lack of sensitive screening tools to detect women who are at risk and babies who are prenatally exposed to drugs often inhibits early identification. By failing to detect these high-risk groups early, the possibility exists for increased incidence of infants with more complex and costly developmental problems.

There are several reasons why cessation of drug use during pregnancy should be a societal priority. First, research has shown that the teratogenic damage from in utero exposure may be decreased if a woman reduces alcohol, cocaine, or tobacco use throughout the pregnancy. Second, pregnancy may provide a window of opportunity for recovery because a woman's motivation to quit may be heightened, and the pregnancy may serve as the impetus for seeking prenatal care, thus coming to the early attention of health-care providers who can offer treatment options. Third, a woman's improved psychological and physical health would, in turn, enhance her childrearing abilities.

The focus of primary prevention at an indicated level would be to provide treatment for pregnant, addicted women by responding to the multiple medical and social needs that can complicate recovery and favorable outcomes for their children. The emphasis may need to be a continuum of care to reduce drug use; that is, gradual reduction of drug use rather than immediate elimination (see Table 8.5). This method may be difficult for professionals trained in substance abuse treatment for whom immediate abstinence is the primary goal.

A multidimensional problem, such as substance abuse, requires a multidisciplinary approach that includes the following elements: drug abuse treatment, health care, child welfare, early intervention and education, mental health, and social and family support services. This comprehensive approach can enable service providers to confront this societal concern by addressing such practical needs as child care, transportation, food, and social support. Community-based initiatives must be developed to increase the system's capacity for serving low-income and/or minority women in a culturally sensitive and individualized manner. Successful prevention programs must not only help women who are chemically dependent to reduce their drug use; it must also add positive experiences to their lives; that is, it should help them to identify "alternative highs" (Bry, 1983). In addition, programs must be designed to ensure provision of the continued follow-up and support crucial to helping their participants to remain drug free and to become effective parents and members of society.

To date, numerous grants have been awarded for innovative prevention projects, and there seem to be some promising models. How-

Table 8.5. Primary prevention at the indicated level

Target	Focus	Means/methods
Pregnant drug users	Reduce/eliminate current drug use	Community-based treatment programs, hospitals, health departments
	Treat addiction as disease	
	Provide prenatal care and support	One-stop-shopping model
	Child abuse prevention efforts	

ever, few projects have been thoroughly evaluated at this time, and little documentation is available regarding their effectiveness in addressing this challenge. To address this problem, NIDA is supporting 20 treatment reasearch demonstration grants designed to evaluate the effectiveness of various strategies for improving enrollment, retention, and outcome in treating addicted pregnant women and addicted mothers with children. These carefully controlled clinical research demonstration studies will examine both short- and long-term effects in a variety of settings and provide a broad range of social and health care services. When the results of the research demonstration programs have been analyzed, it will be possible to make recommendations regarding model drug treatment strategies and alternatives for drug-abusing pregnant women (USDHHS, 1992).

SUMMARY

Preventing abuse of both licit and illicit substances by women of reproductive age and averting potential harmful consequences for their children are serious and complex biopsychosocial problems that may be very difficult to understand or eliminate completely. However, we must continue to approach these problems rationally and compassionately in efforts to combat the intergenerational cycle of substance abuse, poverty, and poor health.

If progress is to be made, comprehensive primary prevention efforts must be mounted that extend the current focus on secondary and tertiary prevention. Programs are needed that support and build upon one another within a seamless, holistic service delivery system that encompasses and promotes the continuity of primary, secondary, and tertiary prevention.

REFERENCES

Abel, E., & Sokol, R. (1987). Incidence of fetal alcohol syndrome and economic impact of FAS-related anomalies. *Drug and Alcohol Dependency, 19,* 51–70.

Besharov, D.J. (1990). Crack children in foster care: Re-examining the balance between children's rights and parents' rights. *Children Today, 19*(4), 21–25.

Bry, B.H. (1983). Substance abuse in women: Etiology and prevention. *Issues in Mental Health Nursing, 5,* 253–272.

Castro, L.C., Azen, C., Hobel, C.J., & Platt, L.D. (1993). Maternal tobacco use and substance use: Reported prevalence rates and associations with the delivery of small-for-gestational-age neonates. *Obstetrics and Gynecology, 81*(3), 396–401.

Chasnoff, I.J. (1992, June). President's message: Perinatal addiction research and education. *Update,* p. 2.

Chasnoff, I.J., Burns, W.J., Schnoll, S.H., & Burns, K.A. (1985). Cocaine use in pregnancy. *New England Journal of Medicine, 313*(11), 666–669.

Chasnoff, I.J., Griffith, D.R., MacGregor, S., Dirkes, K., & Burns, K.A. (1989). Temporal patterns of cocaine use in pregnancy: Perinatal outcome. *JAMA: The Journal of the American Medical Association, 261*:1741–1744.

Council Report. (1983). Fetal effects of maternal alcohol use. Council on Scientific Affairs. *JAMA: The Journal of the American Medical Association, 249*, 2517–2521.

Day, N.L., & Richardson, G.A. (1991). Prenatal alcohol exposure: A continuum of effects. *Seminars in Perinatology, 15*(4), 271–279.

DeBetterncourt, K. (1990). The wisdom of Solomon: Cutting the cord that harms. *Children Today, 19,* July–August, 17–20.

Edmondson, R., & Smith, T.M. (in press). Temperament and behavior of drug-exposed infants: Implications for the mother–infant dyad. *The Infant Mental Health Journal.*

Floyd, R.L., Zahniser, C., Gunter, E.P., & Kendrick, J.S. (1991). Smoking during pregnancy: Prevalence, effects, and intervention strategies. *Birth, 18*(1), 48–53.

Frank, D.A., Zuckerman, B.S., Amaro, H., Aboagye, K., Bauchner, H., Cabral, H., Fried, L., & Hingson, R. (1988). Cocaine use during pregnancy: Prevalence and correlates. *Pediatrics, 82,* 888–895.

Fried, P.A., O'Connell, C.M., & Watkinson, B. (1992). 60- and 72-month follow-up of children prenatally exposed to marijuana, cigarettes, and alcohol: Cognitive and language assessment. *Journal of Developmental and Behavioral Pediatrics, 13*(6), 383–391.

Gilchrist, L.D., & Gillmore, M.R. (1992). Methodological issues in prevention research on drug use and pregnancy. In M.M. Kilbey & K. Asghar (Eds.), Methodological issues in epidemiological, prevention, and treatment research on drug-exposed women and their children. *National Institute on Drug Abuse Research Monograph Series, 117,* 1–17.

Gittler, J., & McPherson, M. (1990). Prenatal substance abuse: An overview of the problem. *Children Today, 19*(4), 3–7.

Gomby, D.S., & Shiono, P.H. (1991). Estimating the number of substance-exposed infants. *The Future of Children, Drug Exposed Infants, 1*(1), 17–25.

Heckler, M.M. (1980). Public health reports. Public Health Service, 85–50193.

Jones, E.D., & Ackatz, L. (1992). *Availability of substance abuse treatment programs for pregnant women: Results from three national surveys.* (Working Paper No. 855). Chicago, IL: The National Center on Child Abuse Prevention Research, a Program of the National Committee for Prevention of Child Abuse.

Khalsa, J.H., & Gfroerer, J. (1991). Epidemiology and health consequences of drug abuse among pregnant women. *Seminars in Perinatology, 15*(4), 265–270.

Koop, C.E. (1986). Smoking and pregnancy. *American Pharmacy, 26*(7), 34–35.

McCullough, C.B. (1991). The child welfare response. *The Future of Children, Drug Exposed Infants, 1*(1), 61–71.

National Council on Alcoholism and Drug Dependence. (1990). *NCADD fact sheet: Alcohol-related birth defects.* New York: Author.

National Institute on Drug Abuse. (1991). *National household survey on drug use: Population estimates of 1990* (DHHS Publication No. ADM 91-1732). Washington, DC: U.S. Government Printing Office.

Neuspiel, D.R., & Hamel, S.C. (1991). Cocaine and infant behavior. *Developmental and Behavioral Pediatrics: Selected Topics, 12*(1), 55–64.

Oro, A.S., & Dixon, S.D. (1987). Perinatal cocaine and methamphetamine exposure: Maternal and neonatal correlates. *Journal of Pediatrics, 111,* 571–578.

Phibbs, C.S. (1991). The economic implications of prenatal substance exposure. *The Future of Children, Drug Exposed Infants, 1*(1), 113–120.

Rodning, C., Beckwith, L., & Howard, J. (1990). Attachment in play in prenatal drug exposure. *Development and Psychopathology, 1,* 277–289.

Rosenak, D., Diamant, A., Yaffe, H., & Hornstein, E. (1990). Cocaine: Maternal use during pregnancy and its effect on the mother, the fetus, and the infant. *Obstetrical & Gynecological Survey, 45*(6), 348–359.

Rush, D., & Callahan, K.R. (1989). Exposure to passive cigarette smoking and child development. *Annals of New York Academy of Sciences, 562,* 74–100.

Simeonsson, R.J. (1991). Primary, secondary, and tertiary prevention in early intervention. *Journal of Early Intervention, 15*(2), 124–134.

Smith, J.E., & Deitch, K.V. (1987). Cocaine: A maternal, fetal, and neonatal risk. *Journal of Pediatric Health Care, 1,* 120–124.

Streissguth, A.P., Grant, T.M., Barr, H.M., Brown, Z.A., Martin, J.C., Mayock, D.E., Ramey, S.L., & Moore, L. (1991). Cocaine and the use of alcohol and other drugs during pregnancy. *American Journal of Obstetrics and Gynecology, 164,* 1239–1243.

U.S. Department of Health and Human Services (USDHHS). (1992). *Maternal drug abuse and drug exposed children: Understanding the problem.* Washington, DC: U.S. Government Printing Office.

9

Child Abuse
A Prevention Agenda

Gail S. Huntington, Lorraine Lima, and Irene Nathan Zipper

Child abuse and neglect are issues of growing concern. The extent of these problems is indicated by these national statistics: every 13 seconds, a child is reported abused or neglected; every 53 minutes, a child dies from poverty; every 3 hours a child is murdered (Children's Defense Fund, 1992). The results of an annual survey of child protective service agencies in the United States conducted by the National Committee for the Prevention of Child Abuse (NCPCA) indicate that the total number of reports of child abuse rose to over 2.9 million in 1992 (American Humane Society, 1993; McCurdy & Daro, 1993). This number, based on reports from 40 states, is almost 8% higher than that of 1991, and represents a 132% rise over the past decade. Four primary reasons are cited for the increases over the past 4 years. They are: 1) economic stress caused by poverty, 2) unemployment and related work concerns, 3) substance abuse, and 4) improvements or changes in reporting. Although child abuse occurs at all socioeconomic levels, children born or raised in poverty are much more likely to be maltreated than are children raised in homes above the poverty level. Nationally, 40% of child abuse reports are substantiated following an investigation. This leads to estimates that 1,160,400 children were substantiated victims of abuse and neglect during 1992 (McCurdy & Daro, 1993). Of those confirmed cases, fewer than two thirds of the children involved received services from child protective services, leaving almost half a million confirmed cases in which no therapeutic or supportive interventions were provided during 1992 (McCurdy & Daro, 1993).

ONE FAMILY'S STORY

As disheartening as these statistics may be, they do not convey the effects on individuals as forcibly as does a real situation. The following is the story of a young mother and her family who were fortunate enough to become involved with services to prevent the abuse of the children.

> Twenty-nine-year-old Sonia lived in fear that she would be killed by her husband and that there would be no one to care for her three children. The final breakup of the marriage and the effects of 10 years of domestic violence had left Sonia with little energy, unable to care for her own needs, and with almost no resources to meet the challenges of her children's special needs. Child Protective Services had concerns about Sonia's ability to care adequately for and nurture her 7-year-old daughter, Monica, who was blind from birth, and her 2-year-old twins, John and Mark. John was withdrawn and had significant developmental delays. He was so small that he frequently was mistaken for his twin's younger brother. Mark was extremely aggressive toward John, and Sonia could not seem to manage his behavior or meet John's special care needs. Until her contact with Child Protective Services, Sonia didn't know how to get help. She wanted to do a better job of parenting, but she was overwhelmed by the circumstances of her life. Because being viewed as a neglectful parent was almost too much for Sonia, she further isolated herself from the community and from the help she needed. Sonia and her children were referred to Bienvenidos Family Services in a state of extreme crisis. Sonia and her children were provided the "safety net" they needed to begin the healing process. For Sonia, the safety net took the form of parent support groups, service coordination, and child care. These services allowed the family to begin nurturing itself. The situation is much different for Sonia now. By attending parenting support groups and working closely with her service coordinator and family support worker, who provides home-based service, Sonia has been able to regain a sense of control over her life. The twins are enrolled in an early intervention program. She is consistently obtaining appropriate medical care for the children and feels hopeful about her future. She helps facilitate the parenting classes and has been available to share her story in the hope that it will encourage other parents to ask for help when they need it. Sonia has become, in the truest sense of the word, an advocate.

This story might have had a different ending without preventive intervention. Too often, the lack of attention to child abuse prevention results in further contributions to the alarming increase in the incidence of child abuse and neglect.

UNDERSTANDING CHILD ABUSE

Over the years, a variety of explanations for the abuse of children have been advanced. Among these are explanations derived from psychodynamic theory, learning theory, sociologic theory, and environmental theories (Daro, 1988; Gelardo & Sanford, 1987). A currently accepted theory is an ecological theory simultaneously implicating both interpersonal and societal factors (Belsky, 1980). The premise of ecological theory is that abuse is complex and multidetermined. Thus, for any specific act of abuse, it is rare that a single factor can be identified as the sole contributing cause; rather, it is likely that several factors, in interaction, have brought about the incident. A variety of specific factors, both intrinsic and extrinsic to the child and family, have been proposed as causal. Among these are physical and behavioral characteristics of the child, inadequate or inappropriate parenting, substance abuse, stress related to living in conditions of poverty, and unemployment (Cohen & Warren, 1990; Garbarino, Brookhouser, & Authier, 1987; Gelardo & Sanford, 1987; Holden, Willis, & Corcoran, 1992; Krugman, Lenherr, Betz, & Fryer, 1986; Sherman, 1989). These factors imply a need for a prevention approach to address the neglect and abuse of children.

NEED FOR A PREVENTION PERSPECTIVE

Basic to our understanding of child abuse is the recognition that it is a preventable phenomenon (Finkelhor & Korbin, 1988). A public health perspective, in which approaches are conceptualized in terms of their primary, secondary, or tertiary prevention aims, provides a framework for the conceptualization of services (Simeonsson, 1991). A comprehensive prevention model must include primary, secondary, and tertiary approaches to effectively address the complex issues involved. Preventive and supportive services should be provided early (Brown, 1992). An effective, comprehensive prevention program, therefore, must focus on primary prevention, by targeting those who have not abused their children in order to reduce the probability of their doing so at some time in the future. Such primary preventive approaches, aimed at reducing the incidence of new cases of child abuse, are advocated and discussed in this chapter. Secondary approaches, aimed at reducing the prevalence of child abuse, have been the main focus of intervention and treatment efforts. Because such programs reduce the likelihood that individuals in groups who are at greatest risk—those who have abused their children in the past—will continue to do so, they are a key aspect of an effective prevention program. The need for tertiary prevention, focused on reducing the sequelae of child abuse, has become increasingly apparent. Family preservation approaches, aimed at supporting the family so the child can remain in the home, constitute a major effort to prevent the devastating consequences for the child of removal from the home following abusive behavior (Nelson, 1990). Programs such as Homebuilders, providing intensive in-home family support services, are an important means of supporting families (Kinney, Haapala, Booth, & Leavitt, 1990; Schorr, 1988). They can be conceptualized as both secondary and tertiary prevention approaches, because their goal is to prevent both the recurrence of abuse and/or neglect (secondary prevention), and the consequences inherent in the child's removal from the home (tertiary prevention).

HISTORY OF PREVENTION EFFORTS

Concern with child abuse prevention has developed only relatively recently. Because children were viewed as the property of their parents, there was no clear national policy related to the welfare of children until this century. The Societies for the Prevention of Cruelty to Children were established in the late 1800s; by 1900 there were more than 250 such agencies in the United States. Their establishment indicated the recognition that society was responsible for the protection of children, when necessary (McGowan, 1990).

The first White House Conference on Children was held in 1909 to consider issues in the care of dependent children. With the establishment of the Children's Bureau in 1912, the country demonstrated its commitment to children. Since the 1960s, when articles about the problem of child abuse began to appear in the literature (Kempe, Silverman, Steele, Droegemueller, & Silver, 1962; Steele & Pollock, 1968), the federal government has focused on the problem, beginning with the passage of the model state reporting statutes. By the late 1960s, every state had enacted a child abuse and neglect reporting law (Willis, Holden, & Rosenberg, 1992). The National Center on Child Abuse and Neglect was established in the early 1970s. Its authority was expanded with the passage of the Child Abuse Prevention, Adoption, and Family Services Act of 1988 (PL 100-294). Although considerable progress has been made in enacting laws to protect children, little progress has been made in the area of prevention. Over the next few years, the U.S. Advisory Board on Child Abuse and Neglect plans to develop ideas for legislation to improve prevention efforts and to increase research into the causes and consequences of child abuse (Willis et al., 1992).

Research and intervention efforts before the 1980s focused on the causes of child abuse and neglect. During the 1980s, the focus was on services, advocacy, public education, and public involvement, supplemented by various research and demonstration projects. Comprehensive approaches to child abuse prevention included support and education for parents, opportunities for child care, programs for abused children, life skills training for children, self-help and family support groups, community organization activities, and public education to prevent child abuse (Cohn, 1988). The growing interest in an ecological perspective on the child (Bronfenbrenner, 1979), coupled with the growing recognition of the effectiveness of service models geared to the specific needs of the child and family, led to a renewed interest in prevention on a variety of fronts. Prevention efforts then included attention to services, advocacy, public education, and public involvement (Donnelly, 1991).

CHALLENGES TO A PREVENTION APPROACH

Some of our societal practices may be unintentionally conducive to the abuse of children. The regular depiction of violence in the media serves to anesthetize us to its horror, increasing the likelihood that some of us will engage in violent behavior. Approval of the use of physical punishment in the public schools constitutes tacit approval of violence against children. A basic primary prevention approach must address the ways in which we condone violence in our society, specifically violence directed against children.

Primary prevention is impeded further by the many barriers to effective interagency coordination and collaboration. These include inconsistencies among agencies in terms of their policies and procedures for determining eligibility for services and establishing fees; for making referrals, facilitating transitions, and following up with families; and for record keeping and evaluation of service provision. It is essential that these barriers be removed in order to address child abuse effectively (Sherman, 1989). Concerted primary prevention efforts require the collaboration of all elements of the child-serving system. Through such collaboration, complementary policies and procedures may be established that can support communitywide prevention efforts.

PAST EFFORTS AT SECONDARY PREVENTION

The lack of a coherent strategy to address the complex issues has been coupled with difficulty in evaluating the effectiveness of prevention programs and the reality of funding constraints in most communities. These factors have resulted in a piecemeal approach to eradicating child abuse focused on secondary prevention. In 1991, 61% of all elementary schools reported offering some kind of prevention education (Donnelly, 1991). Such programs constitute secondary prevention efforts by alerting children to the realities of child abuse. Concern about the isolation typical of mothers who engage in child abuse has led to the formation of parent groups (Wayne, 1979). Programs that provide education, counseling, and respite care for family members can all be conceptualized as secondary prevention approaches.

NEED FOR PRIMARY PREVENTION

A new approach to prevention of child abuse and neglect is needed. The incidence of child abuse will be reduced only if a focus on primary prevention is added to our secondary and tertiary prevention efforts.

It is increasingly obvious that child abuse cannot be prevented without attention to modifying the environment (Belsky, 1980; Donnelly, 1991; Schorr, 1988). Because child abuse results, ultimately, from extrinsic and theoretically preventable societal stressors and is not necessarily intrinsic to the child or family, it is clear that we need to address the economic conditions that result in so many young children living in conditions of poverty and its resultant stresses. The most essential form of primary prevention we can provide in this regard is to alleviate the conditions that cause stress in our society; that is, we must work to promote the actualization of potential among families and children.

Ecological perspectives on the child and family emphasize the importance of family and community in the life of the child. Recent efforts at conceptualizing the interaction of child, family, and community have led to the view that the nurturing of children is the joint and interdependent responsibility of the family, the state, the volunteer community, and the private economic sector (Weiss, 1990). A primary prevention approach grounded in an ecological perspective should, therefore, involve all these elements. The African proverb "It takes a community to raise a child" implies that we are all responsible for supporting the development of children in the context of their families and communities. A broad array of primary prevention approaches, grounded in collaborative community-based efforts, is needed. In the past, a number of factors have conspired to make such collaboration difficult. Institutional barriers, resource limitations, "turf" issues, and other factors may make the implementation of such a comprehensive primary prevention effort difficult. Nevertheless, effective primary prevention must involve the entire community. Primary prevention efforts may take many different forms. Some programs should target the general public. Information about prevention programs should be provided to parents through radio and television programs, public service announcements, and newspaper articles and advertisements. Through direct telephone call-in services, parents could get immediate support and be provided with information about available programs. Public service announcements on radio and television; posters in buses and subway cars; and literature in public health offices, public housing, and child-care centers could provide information about the dangers of child abuse and neglect. Campaigns such as this, focused on a specific issue, can be conducted at relatively low cost and can reach a large percentage of the population.

Targeting new parents may be a particularly effective primary preventive strategy. Such programs could be aimed at parents during the perinatal period, when they constitute a "captive audience" (Helfer, 1987) and during the postnatal period when parents are "getting to know" their baby. Teaching new parents the skill of communicating with their infant has the potential to enhance this special interpersonal relationship, leading to prevention of a serious breakdown in parent–child interaction and, in turn, lessening of abuse and neglect (Helfer, 1987). Home-visiting programs are being re-established in some communities. Through such programs, mothers with new babies receive home visits from lay community members, therapists, or foster grandparents (Anisfeld & Pincus, 1987; Hardy-Brown, Miller, Dean, Carrasco, & Thompson, 1987; Larner & Halpern, 1987). The visitors may provide new parents with information, role modeling, emotional support, and help in arranging for various community-based services. Where such programs exist, they typically are available broadly, rather than being restricted to families who specifically request them. In many European countries such services are routinely and universally provided to all families (Miller, 1988). The home health visitor program that has been established in England, for example, has been shown to be effective (Daro, 1988). Such programs have been advocated in the United States as well, as a means of both universal and selected prevention (Cohen & Warren, 1990; Sherman, 1989). The challenges and tensions inherent in such programs have been considered (Larner & Halpern, 1987). They constitute an important form of primary prevention, frequently targeting those families at increased risk for child abuse because of the stresses resulting from poverty. Further research regarding the efficacy of these and other pre- and perinatal preventive interventions is needed (Sherman, 1989).

Model prevention programs are being conceptualized. For example, in Hawaii, Early Start is a primary prevention program that began as a small effort in one community. Following an evaluation of the services that showed it was effective in preventing abuse and neglect, the program was adopted by the state and is now available across the islands. In addition, comprehensive prevention programs of the same sort have been established in California in response to the growing concern about the needs of children. It was felt that by the time families came to the attention of the service system, their service needs were so complex and their abilities to meet the developmental and other needs of their children were so compromised that "prevention" was more accurately defined in terms of the interventions needed to form the most minimal temporary safety net for children. At the same time that a comprehensive prevention perspective is needed, those involved in the delivery of services are faced with increasing caseloads and shrinking resources. The California Child Welfare Strategic Planning Commission (1991) in its final report, *The Vision For the Children of California*, concluded that in order to build a "wellness model" for all children and families in California, a continuum of services involving two major elements must be established. The nurturing and developmental component was identified as *prevention*, and an authoritative intervention component was identified as *protection*. The commission envisioned a continuum of services that went beyond the current definition of child welfare services. The continuum places prevention on one end and protection, for those children who require government or systems intervention to ensure their safety, on the other. Because each family is unique in its ability to benefit from different interventions, the preferable approach is one of prevention to promote wellness, rather than remediating the effect of damage and trauma. The prevention-to-protection continuum is connected and allows for the provision of services needed at any point along it. However, according to the report, prevention must become more than a concept: It should be a community effort that focuses on wellness; parents should be viewed as the first line of fundamental support to their children; and families require support and encouragement from their extended families and communities to be successful in carrying out this responsibility.

BIENVENIDOS FAMILY SERVICES: A PROGRAM FOCUSED ON PRIMARY PREVENTION

Bienvenidos Family Services, in East Los Angeles, demonstrates a wellness model. It is a family-centered, child-focused, culturally sensitive, comprehensive program designed to support families with many needs and few resources to meet the needs of their children.

Overview of Community

East Los Angeles is primarily Latino, where most residents are bilingual/bicultural. In half of all households, Spanish is the preferred spoken language. Birth rates in the East Los Angeles area are among the highest in the nation. In 1990, the Los Angeles County/University of Southern California Medical Center (LAC/USC Medical Center) delivered 20,000 babies. An estimated 5,000 babies are delivered annually in the East Los Angeles community without the benefit of prenatal care. Few of the children receive well-baby care. Many families in this community experience multiple challenges. Included may be:

1. Diverse ethnic/linguistic/cultural pressures
2. Severely limited affordable housing options
3. Pervasive, chronic effects of the addictive disease process
4. Insecurities related to immigration status
5. Extremely low self-esteem
6. Critical shortage of most basic resources

Bienvenidos offers services for families whose needs fall at any point along the prevention-to-protection continuum.

There are several fundamental beliefs regarding families. Families that can consistently meet the developmental and care needs of each member are families that have the following qualities.

They are *nurturing* as they provide for all primary needs.
They are *supportive* of the development of each member.
They are *respectful* of all members and appreciate their uniqueness.
They are *communicative* in healthy and safe ways.
They have a *familial and "collective identity,"* with cultural and ethnic pride based on individual and collective family members' visions and hopes for the future.
They are *able to experience joy* together.

There are times when *any* family may need support to develop or strengthen these characteristics. Bienvenidos Family Services strives to assist and support families to realize *their* dreams and to be able to support fully all aspects of their children's development. Families reach Bienvenidos through referrals from other social services, hospital neonatal intensive care units, self-referral, and other sources. Each family is assisted in developing, prioritizing, and evaluating their *own* family plans including, but not limited to, the following.

1. Providing a safe and healthy environment throughout a crisis
2. Assessing appropriate services, training, or education
3. Decreasing the probability of violence or other disruptive circumstances
4. Improving each family member's sense of lovability, worthiness, capability, and responsibility
5. Gaining coping skills and problem-solving strategies

Bienvenidos Family Services' wellness model of intervention has three program components. The first identifies families that have not yet experienced child protective services intervention or out-of-home placement; these are provided services within the *prevention* component. The second identifies families whose children have been placed in out-of-home care and/or are in the reunification process; these are served within the *aftercare/reunification* component. Additional support services are offered within the third component of the model, *program support services*. All families are eligible for the full array of comprehensive in-home and center-based support activities, and all benefit from a team-staffing model of support.

Because Bienvenidos Family Services believes that family-centered services must be provided within the *context of the family*, in-home services are essential for providing the foundation for developing a trusting family–program staff relationship. Home-based services are provided by family support workers who address primary needs, family dynamics, homemaking, and any relevant barriers to stability, health, and safety. The family support worker may spend from 5 to 20 hours weekly in the home, as needed; flexibility is essential to meet the needs of the families. Each family support worker is teamed with two other family support workers and guided by a case manager. Sonia and her children experienced the effectiveness of the Bienvenidos program, with the positive outcome discussed earlier.

Home-based services are augmented by the community-based Family Services Center. The Center, located two blocks from a major freeway and one block from public transportation, offers families many activities and services, including a family drop-in center, kitchen facilities, a food pantry, showers, washer and dryer, crisis and planned respite child care, parenting education, peer support groups, individual and family counseling, an early intervention "Baby and Me" program, tutoring, "Off Track" summer programs for children, and special family recreational events.

Strong Features of the Model

Model and Program Design There are two major areas of strength in the model. The first is the program's design, which uses intervention teams and small caseloads that allow for the flexibility of serving families initially, with between 15 and 30 hours of services per week.

The intervention teams are designed to provide intense services along the prevention-to-protection continuum. Family support workers carry caseloads of three to five families each. Three families may be receiving intensive services, while two may be moving through the maintenance phase, receiving less intensive in-home services, yet participating in center-based activities. Families in this phase may spend from 5 to 10 hours per week in the center, and they are provided contact with a family support worker who has expertise in accessing community resources.

Many families in the maintenance phase provide peer support for other families who have just entered the program, as in Sonia's situation. Families are encouraged to design their own program and to assist other families by facilitating the parenting class, offering to be available to other families by telephone, acting as hosts when the center has visitors, participating in community outreach activities, and assisting in program planning. Many accompany staff to community networking meetings and conference presentations.

Family Support The second strength of the wellness model comes from the strong connections staff and families develop. It has been our experience that by providing intensive in-home services that are linguistically and culturally comfortable for a period of 3–6 months, families feel nurtured and supported. They can then begin to risk negotiating the social services system on their own. When transitioned to the maintenance phase, families can practice their newly gained advocacy and parenting skills, while remaining connected to the program. Once families have graduated, they are encouraged to continue using the drop-in center, to remain part of the center's activities, and to provide peer support to other families.

Challenges of the Model

Serving a limited number of families may be viewed as a program limitation. However, given the complex developmental and care needs of families in the East Los Angeles community and because the model offers such a comprehensive array of services and activities, it is our belief that this is what true "family support" is about. Families may benefit to such an extent that little future involvement with the service system is necessary.

Families and staff make powerful humanistic connections in the course of the work. The challenge for supervisors is to provide adequate support and appropriate clinical supervision for staff, which is an ongoing issue. It has been our experience that this wellness model of intervention requires intensive supervision. At least 20% of a work week is set aside for providing this support. Support is provided weekly through staff inservice training opportunities, team meetings, individual supervision/case conferencing, and clinical group supervision. The management team, made up of coordinators, the program director, and the agency's executive director, also meets weekly.

SUMMARY

We must ask, how many families are there like Sonia's—identified as neglectful or abusive; unable to reach out for help; or asking for help but unable to gain access to it because of limited resources, lack of transportation, and other factors? Many out-of-home placements could be prevented if more communities developed supportive programs to help meet the needs of families like Sonia's. The cost in human suffering of child abuse and neglect has been documented repeatedly. We must develop and implement models for primary prevention of child abuse and neglect that are family centered, community based, comprehensive, and collaborative. No single model will meet the needs of all families and all communities. Each paradigm, however, must draw on available resources, must be culturally sensitive and nonjudgmental, and must allow for the flexibility to address each unique situation.

A primary prevention approach should: 1) address such precipitating factors as unemployment, inadequate housing and health care, and lack of social support; 2) target the population at large with information about the nature and dangers of child abuse; and 3) include specific community-based programs that are supportive of families. Policies that facilitate the development of comprehensive approaches to the prevention of child abuse and neglect are needed.

The prevention of child abuse requires attention to the societal problems and difficulties that cause pain and frustration for parents. Primary prevention of child abuse requires, therefore, a broad societal commitment to improving conditions for all. Inequality, discriminatory practices, financial hardship, and other factors must be addressed if the frustrations that may give rise to child abuse are to be reduced. The entire community must be involved in supporting its children. We must reduce all forms of violence in our society if efforts to reduce the incidence of violence toward children are to succeed. Information should be generally available—through the media, through leaflets and brochures, and through telephone call-in services—to ensure that parents know where to turn for support. Specific community-based programs, developed and implemented through collaborative efforts among service providers, policy makers, and families, should be available with no stigma attached to their use. Such programs should include universal access to respite settings, home visiting, and parenting information.

Comprehensive, community-based prevention programs that include primary, secondary, and tertiary prevention approaches are needed. Despite the fact that most maltreated children do not become abusive parents, the research indicates that children who have been abused by their parents are more likely to become abusive parents themselves than are children who have not been abused (Kaufman & Zigler, 1987). Through primary prevention programs that ensure that children never experience the pain of abuse or neglect, we can decrease the likelihood of abuse for subsequent generations of children.

REFERENCES

American Humane Society. (1993). *America's children: How are they doing?* (Fact sheet #8). Inglewood, CA: American Humane Society.

Anisfeld, E., & Pincus, M. (1987). The postpartum support project: Serving young mothers and older women through home visiting. *Zero to Three, 8*(1), 13–15.

Belsky, J. (1980). Child maltreatment: An ecological integration. *American Psychologist, 35,* 320–335.

Bronfenbrenner, U. (1979). *The ecology of human development: Experiments by nature and design.* Cambridge, MA: Harvard University Press.

Brown, J. (1992). Family-centered services: Planning, policies, and professional standards. In J. Brown & M. Weil (Eds.), *Family practice: A curriculum plan for social services* (pp. 23–42). Washington, DC: Child Welfare League of America.

California Child Welfare Strategic Planning Commission. (1991, November). *The vision for the children of California.* Sacramento, CA: State Department of Social Services.

Child Abuse Prevention, Adoption and Family Services Act of 1988, PL 100-294. Title 42, U.S.C. 5101 et seq: *U.S. Statutes at Large, 102,* 102–126.

Children's Defense Fund. (1992). *The state of America's children 1992.* Washington, DC: Author.

Cohen, S., & Warren, R.D. (1990). The intersection of disability and child abuse in England and the United States. *Child Welfare, 69*(3), 235–262.

Cohn, A. (1988). *An approach to preventing child abuse.* Chicago: National Committee for Prevention of Child Abuse.

Cohn, A.H., & Daro. D. (1987). Is treatment too late?: What ten years of evaluative research tell us. *Child Abuse & Neglect, 11,* 433–442.

Daro, D. (1988). *Confronting child abuse.* New York: Free Press.

Donnelly, A.H.C. (1991). What we have learned about prevention: What we should do about it. *Child Abuse & Neglect, 15,* 99–106.

Finklehor, D., & Korbin, J. (1988). Child abuse as an international issue. *Child Abuse & Neglect, 12,* 3–23.

Garbarino, J., Brookhouser, P.E., & Authier, K.J. (1987). *Special children—special risks: The maltreatment of children with disabilities.* Hawthorne, NY: Aldine de Gruyter.

Gelardo, M.S., & Sanford, E.E. (1987). Child abuse and neglect: A review of the literature. *School Psychology Review, 16,*(2), 137–155.

Hardy-Brown, K., Miller, B., Dean, J., Carrasco, C., & Thompson, S. (1987). Home-based intervention: Catalyst and challenge to the therapeutic relationship. *Zero to Three, 8*(1), 8–12.

Helfer, R.E. (1987). The perinatal period, a window of opportunity for enhancing parent–infant communication: An approach to prevention. *Child Abuse & Neglect, 11,* 556–579.

Holden, E.W., Willis, D.J., & Corcoran, M.M. (1992). Preventing child maltreatment during the prenatal/perinatal period. In D.J. Willis, E.W. Holden, & M. Rosenberg (Eds.), *Prevention of child maltreatment: Developmental perspectives* (pp. 17–46). New York: John Wiley & Sons.

Kaufman, J., & Zigler, E. (1987). Do abused children become abusive parents? *American Journal of Orthopsychiatry, 57*(2), 186–192.

Kempe, C.H., Silverman, F.N., Steele, B.F., Droegemueller, W., & Silver, H.R. (1962). The battered child syndrome. *JAMA: The Journal of the American Medical Association, 181,* 17–24.

Kinney, J., Haapala, D., Booth, C., & Leavitt, S. (1990). The Homebuilders model. In J.K. Whittaker, J. Kinney, E.M. Tracy, & C. Booth (Eds.), *Reaching high-risk families: Intensive family preservation in human services* (pp. 31–64). Hawthorne, NY: Aldine de Gruyter.

Krugman, R.D., Lenherr, M., Betz, L., & Fryer, G.E. (1986). The relationship between unemployment and physical abuse of children. *Child Abuse & Neglect, 10,* 415–418.

Larner, M., & Halpern, R. (1987). Lay home visiting programs: Strengths, tensions, and challenges. *Zero to Three, 8*(1), 1–7.

McCurdy, K., & Daro, D. (1993). *Current trends in child abuse reporting and fatalities: The result of the 1992 annual fifty state survey.* Chicago: National Committee for Prevention of Child Abuse.

McGowan, B.G. (1990). Family-based services and public policy: Context and implications. In J.K. Whittaker, J. Kinney, E.M. Tracy, & C. Booth (Eds.), *Reaching high-risk families: Intensive family preservation in human services* (pp. 65–87). Hawthorne, NY: Aldine DeGruyter.

Miller, A. (1988). *Preventive health care for young children: Findings of a 10-country study.* Washington, DC: National Center for Clinical Infant Programs.

Nelson, D. (1990). Recognizing and realizing the potential of "family preservation." In J.K. Whittaker, J. Kinney, E.M. Tracy, & C. Booth (Eds.), *Reaching high-risk families: Intensive family preservation in human services* (pp. 13–30). Hawthorne, NY: Aldine de Gruyter.

Schorr, L.B. (1988). *Within our reach: Breaking the cycle of disadvantage.* New York: Doubleday.

Sherman, B.R. (1989). Confronting child abuse and neglect in New York State. *New York State Journal of Medicine, 89*(3), 163–165.

Simeonsson, R.J. (1991). Primary, secondary, and tertiary prevention in early intervention. *Journal of Early Intervention, 15*(2), 124–134.

Steele, B.F., & Pollock, C.B. (1968). A psychiatric study of parents who abuse infants and small children. In R.E. Helfer & C.H. Kempe (Eds.), *The battered child.* Chicago: University of Chicago Press.

Wayne, J.L. (1979). A group work model to reach isolated mothers: Preventing child abuse. *Social Work with Groups, 2*(1), 7–18.

Weiss, H. (1990). Beyond *parens patriae*: Building policies and programs to care for our own and others' children. *Children and Youth Services Review, 12,* 269–284.

Willis, D.J., Holden, E.W., & Rosenberg, M. (1992). Child maltreatment prevention: Introduction and historical overview. In D.J. Willis, E.W. Holden, & M. Rosenberg (Eds.), *Prevention of child maltreatment: Development and ecological perspectives* (pp. 1–16). New York: John Wiley & Sons.

10

Preventing Injury in Children and Adolescents

Joseph E. Zins, Victor F. Garcia, Barbara S. Tuchfarber, Kathryn M. Clark, and Susan C. Laurence

> *If a disease were killing our children in the proportions that accidents are, people would be outraged and demand that this killer be stopped.*
>
> C. Everett Koop, M.D.
> former U.S. Surgeon General

Eight-month-old Jamie was a very special baby. Karen and Jerry had tried for 9 years to conceive, and were thrilled when the obstetrician's office had called with the news that Karen was finally pregnant. They had spent every spare moment arranging and decorating the nursery so that their baby would have stimulating colors and bright patterns to enjoy.

It took only a moment. When Jamie became fussy, Jerry stopped the car so that Karen could get into the back seat with the baby. Karen had just taken her out of the car seat to nurse when the driver coming the opposite direction swerved into their lane. Jamie was thrown through the front windshield, striking first the hood of the car, then the pavement. She suffered severe head injuries. The broken ribs, perforated right lung, lacerated liver, and broken bones in her arms and legs would eventually heal. Her doctors were less optimistic about her brain injuries.

The environment of the intensive care unit stood in stark contrast to the color and warmth of Jamie's nursery. The constantly beeping monitors were perverse counterparts to the cheerful jingle of the mobiles hanging over her crib at home. Perhaps it was a blessing that Jamie's eyes did not see these strange sights and that the bandages around her head kept her from hearing the alien sounds. Tragically, Jamie's brain injury was irreversible. She died 2 days after the crash.

Appreciation is extended to Sharon Goskoski and Connie Reyes for their assistance with this chapter.

The eastbound school bus driver, momentarily blinded by the sun, made a wide turn onto the parkway, hitting the right front side of the station wagon. On approaching the smashed and twisted wreckage, passersby assumed the obvious—no survivors. In actuality, the three child passengers were treated on the scene and transported by ambulance to the pediatric hospital. The father, protected by a safety belt and an air bag, was uninjured, and accompanied his children in the ambulance. Four-year-old Jason and 8-year-old Justin, who had been riding in the back seat restrained with safety belts, were treated in the hospital emergency room and released. Nine-year-old Katie, who had been restrained in the front seat, was admitted for overnight hospitalization and released the following morning. When the picture of the destroyed car appeared in the newspapers, neighbors were amazed that the family had not been seriously injured or killed in the crash.

OVERVIEW

Childhood injury is a major public health crisis in the United States. During this century, injuries have replaced infectious diseases as the leading cause of childhood death in the United States (Baker & Waller, 1989). Annually, trauma results in nearly 600,000 hospitalizations, and as many as 30,000 children have disabilities and disfigurement (Rodriguez, 1990). Indeed, more children die from injuries than from all diseases combined. The magnitude of the problem is demonstrated by the number of goals related to injury prevention in the U.S. Surgeon General's report, *Healthy People 2000: National Health Promotion and Disease Prevention Objectives* (1991).

A number of effective and promising advances in the prevention and control of injuries among children have been made in recent years, and this chapter provides an overview of these efforts. We begin with a review of relevant epidemiological data, information helpful in identifying risk factors associated with injuries. It is apparent that many injuries are not random, but rather they are predictable occurrences amenable to primary prevention. Next, we review essential components and the scope of effective injury prevention efforts. The chapter concludes with a description of a community-based prevention program.

Throughout the chapter, the term *unintentional injury* is used rather than *accident*. The word *accident* implies that traumas are twists of fate; thus, they are considered by many—even some physicians—to be unavoidable and not preventable (Berger, 1981; Peterson, Farmer, & Kashani, 1990). Also, injuries can be conceptualized from both *medical* and *behavioral* viewpoints. Health professionals often conceptualize preventive efforts from a disease perspective and view injury prevention methodology as similar to that used with other diseases (e.g., immunization to prevent smallpox, hand washing to prevent puerperal fever). However, behavioral scientists typically view injuries as involving behavioral excesses (e.g., playing with matches, running into the street without looking) and deficiencies (e.g., failure to install and maintain smoke detectors, inadequate supervision at the swimming pool), and they view prevention as involving modification of individual and environmental antecedents, consequences, and setting events that maintain problematic behaviors. Both views are incorporated in our discussion. Furthermore, as we document later, there are differences between injuries that occur most frequently and others that, although less common, are more lethal. Our emphasis is on the latter. Finally, because our primary focus is unintentional injuries, we consider interpersonal violence and suicide only briefly.

EPIDEMIOLOGY OF PEDIATRIC INJURY

More than 22,000 children under the age of 19 die in the United States each year as a result of injuries. Although the number of fatal injuries among children has decreased 26% in the past 10 years (National Safety Council, 1992), the United States retains the dubious distinction of being the country with the highest pediatric injury mortality rate in the Western industrialized world (Williams & Kotch, 1990). Motor vehicle–related injuries and intentional injuries account for the excess mortality, and they are disproportionately distributed among 15- to 19-year-olds, especially males.

The number of children dying each year from injuries represents only the tip of the iceberg. As noted previously, hundreds of thousands of additional children require hospitalization, and tens of thousands have permanent disabilities, exacting considerable physical and emotional tolls on each child and family. The cost of childhood injury is staggering, accounting for approximately $4,684,000,000 for direct medical care for children under the age of 14 (Rice et al., 1989). Associated costs and related human suffering are even greater.

Common Mechanisms of Injury

Fortunately, the two most common mechanisms of injury, falls and sports, are not the most lethal. Of the estimated 3.7 million children seeking medical attention for falls in 1985, 97% were treated and released from emergency departments. The second most common cause of childhood injury is sports. More than 2.7 million children were treated for sports-related injuries in 1985, with 4% requiring hospitalization (Guyer & Ellers, 1990).

Motor Vehicle–Related Injuries Motor vehicle–related injuries are both common and deadly (see Table 10.1). They are the leading cause of death during childhood, accounting for 31% of all injury deaths in 1985. More than 6,500 children died in car crashes, and an additional 24,000 required hospitalization (Guyer & Ellers, 1990).

Motor vehicle occupant deaths are disproportionately high among the youngest age groups and among teenagers. In 1990, 624 children under the age of 5 years died; 70% of these were reported to have been unrestrained at the time of the crash (Centers for Disease Control and Prevention, 1991). Teenagers have the lowest rate of safety belt use and the highest rate of fatal crashes (National Highway Traffic Safety Administration, U.S. Department of Transportation, 1991). Furthermore, alcohol is an important contributing factor in adolescent car crashes, and teen drivers in fatal crashes frequently are found to have very high blood alcohol concentrations (Insurance Institute for Highway Safety, 1991).

Homicide and Suicide Disturbingly, the second most frequent cause of death for U.S. children is homicide, with firearms implicated in many of these violent deaths. Many children also are unintentionally shot while playing with firearms or are involved as innocent bystanders in gun-related incidents. In one study, over one half of the families who brought their child to the emergency room for a gunshot wound kept a loaded firearm in the house at all times, and one half of this group did not lock away their guns (Patterson & Smith, 1987). Moreover, suicide is the third leading cause of injury death among children, and the U.S. youth suicide rate has doubled over the past 30 years, largely due to use of firearms (Koop & Lundberg, 1992).

Pedestrian Injuries Pedestrian injuries are also a major mechanism of fatal injury. During 1990, 1,188 children under the age of 19

Table 10.1. Deaths resulting from motor vehicle–related injuries, birth to 19 years of age—1990

Mechanism of injury	Age	Deaths
Motor vehicle–related (total)	< 13 years	2,331
	13–19	6,354
Occupants	< 13 years	1,265
	13–19	5,160
Pedestrians	< 13 years	770
	13–19	418
Bicyclists	< 13 years	183
	13–19	190
Other/unknown motor vehicle–related causes	< 13 years	113
	13–19	150

Adapted from Insurance Institute for Highway Safety (1991).

were struck and killed by motor vehicles. Young school-age children are at the greatest risk, and a gender risk factor is evident because boys are twice as likely to die from pedestrian injuries than are girls (Rivara, 1990). The 1990 mortality rate for pedestrian injuries was highest for 6-year-olds (2.6 per 100,000) (Insurance Institute for Highway Safety, 1991). Between 50% and 60% of the pedestrian deaths among school-age children are the result of the child darting suddenly into the roadway between intersections or failing to search adequately for oncoming vehicles (Rivara, 1990).

Bicycle-Related Injuries Each year, between 400 and 600 children die from bicycle-related injuries (Cote, Sacks, & Lambert-Huber, 1992; Rivara, 1990). The highest mortality rates are among children between the ages of 8 and 15 years. An additional 40,000 children are injured each year while riding their bikes. About 90% of bicycle deaths are motor vehicle–related (Kraus, Fife, & Conroy, 1977), and the vast majority (62%–90%) of these deaths are caused by head injuries (Fife et al., 1983; Sacks, Holmgreen, Smith, & Sosin, 1991). Wearing a bicycle helmet is estimated to reduce a child's risk of serious head and brain injury by about 85% (Thompson, Rivara, & Thompson, 1989).

Drowning As shown in Table 10.2, other non-motor vehicle–related injury mechanisms are particularly lethal to children. Drowning is responsible for 9.2% of pediatric injury mortalities (Centers for Disease Control and Prevention, 1990). Children under 5 and males

Table 10.2. Non-motor vehicle–related causes of unintentional injury deaths, birth to 14 years of age—1989

Mechanism of injury	Age	Deaths
Drowning	< 5 years	683
	5–14	515
Fires/burns	< 5 years	716
	5–14	467
Ingestions (food, objects)	< 5 years	267
	5–14	47
Falls	< 5 years	86
	5–14	54
Poisoning (liquid, solid)	< 5 years	55
	5–14	19
Firearms	< 5 years	42
	5–14	231
Poisoning (toxic gases)	< 5 years	22
	5–14	25
Total	< 5 years	3,770
	5–14	4,090

Adapted from National Safety Council (1992).

between 15 and 19 years of age are at highest risk (Wintemute, 1990). Regional variations are pronounced. Drowning has been the leading cause of death in children under the age of 5 in California, Arizona, and Florida in the 1990s (Hazinski, Francescutti, Lapidus, Micik, & Rivara, 1993). Mortality is about twice as high among African-American children as it is for white children, except in the 1- to 3-year-old age group, in which the opposite is true.

Fires and Burns Fires and burns account for 7.2% of pediatric injury deaths (Centers for Disease Control and Prevention, 1990), and deaths due to burns disproportionately affect the youngest children. In several states, burns are now the leading cause of death in children younger than 5 years (Children's Safety Network, 1991). African-American, Native American, and poor children are at the highest risk for death in a fire. Because of the higher rate of house fires in the South, particularly in the Southeast, children living in these regions are at greater risk than children who live elsewhere.

COMPONENTS OF INJURY PREVENTION

Peterson and Mori (1985) described a useful framework for analyzing injury prevention efforts that incorporates important advantages from the public health and health psychology fields. The framework identifies *targets* to receive the intervention, *methods* of providing it, and *tactics* for delivering the intervention to the target. Moreover, it contrasts with the traditional public health model, which considers the host (the victim), the agent (the injury-causing stimulus), and the environment (the physical and interpersonal setting) (Gratz, 1979). The targets × methods × tactics matrix serves as a conceptual model for describing potential interventions in the following discussion.

Targets

Targets to receive injury prevention efforts are often identified through epidemiological data and include caregivers, policy makers, children and youth, and the injury vector itself (e.g., manufacturers of child-related products) (Peterson & Mori, 1985). For example, parents and others responsible for children can be informed of such important health-related behaviors as providing constant supervision when children are in the bathtub, conducting periodic drills and establishing escape plans in the event of a fire, not bringing infants into bed with them (they can be smothered by an adult or by slipping between the mattress and the wall), or ensuring that children always wear safety belts or use car safety seats.

Policy makers can be provided with information regarding bicycle-related head trauma, with the expectation that they will establish laws making universal helmet use mandatory. Many health professionals also stress the need to enact strict gun control laws because children increasingly have become victims of firearms with an alarming morbidity rate (Ordog et al., 1988). With respect to harmful environmental agents, manufacturers have been required to alter the manner in which baby cribs are made to protect children from strangulation; many communities now require apartment landlords to install smoke detectors and automatic sprinklers; playground equipment and surfaces increasingly are being improved to reduce the chance of injury; and there is mounting pressure on television networks to decrease the violence in children's programming.

Most injury prevention efforts have focused on caregivers, although more recently there has been interest in environmental modifications (Rivara, 1992). The reasons for such an emphasis are that adults have the primary responsibility for protecting children from harm. However, environmental modifications and passive approaches to unintentional injury prevention that require no effort tend to be more successful than those that necessitate ongoing actions.

In addition to caregiving and environmental efforts, targeting children themselves is *also* important for the following reasons. First, injuries frequently occur in the absence of parents or other caregivers, and many parents overestimate their children's self-care skills (Peterson, 1988; Peterson, Mori, & Scissors, 1986). Second, many interventions require significant and consistent adult effort if they are to succeed; even when frequent cooperation or action on the part of caregivers or children is not required (e.g., window guards in high-rise buildings), the potential of these applications has not been fully utilized by our society (Baker & Waller, 1988). Third, not all causes of injury are amenable to environmental or caregiver interventions, and the effectiveness of preventive efforts can be enhanced if children are also targeted so that they learn to engage in safe behaviors and avoid those that potentially are health damaging. Finally, more long-term effects and positive lifestyle changes can occur as a result of influencing behavioral changes in children (Roberts, Elkins, & Royal, 1984). Indeed, there is evidence that programs directed toward children that use intensive modeling, role playing, behavioral rehearsal, performance feedback, clear consequences including positive reinforcement for generalization, and booster sessions can be effective in teaching relevant skills that are maintained over at least several months (Bandura, 1973; Peterson & Roberts, 1992; Zins, Goskoski, & Reyes, 1991). However, although far fewer child-targeted versus environmental- or caregiver-focused approaches have been reported, children as targets can be taught to "stop, drop, and roll" if their clothing catches fire, to cross the street only at intersections while using the left–right–left search approach (Race, 1988), and always to check the depth of water before diving.

Methods

Injury prevention programs also vary along two dimensions according to their method of intervention. They can be mandated (legislated) or educational (persuasive), and passive (environmental) or active. The most common intervention methods are legislative and educational (Peterson & Roberts, 1992).

Mandated Methods Mandated methods attempt to change behavior by encouraging adherence to laws or regulations, such as requiring infants and toddlers to ride in child safety seats.

Educational Methods Educational methods motivate change by providing information about safety issues (percentage of head injuries resulting from bicycle falls when not wearing a helmet), using fear appeals (school displays of a car demolished in a crash when the teenage driver was intoxicated), or providing prompts and reinforcement to achieve change (providing free soft drinks at fast-food restaurant drive-through windows if car occupants are wearing safety belts). Schools can provide academic instruction on injury prevention and control as part of a comprehensive health curriculum. Increased knowledge and awareness alone, however, do not necessarily result in behavioral change (Cataldo et al., 1983); educational methods are most effective when they are part of a comprehensive prevention program.

Passive versus Active Interventions Interventions that achieve the most success tend to be passive (or environmental); that is, they work automatically and require very little or no behavioral change by the target group (airbags in cars, flame-retardant children's sleepwear, window guards) (Rivara, 1992). However, achieving adherence to those regimes that require frequent, repeated, or increasing amounts of behavioral change (i.e., *active* interventions) is more difficult (Cataldo et al., 1983). Success may be inversely correlated to the amount of change required, which can range from changing the battery in smoke detectors yearly, to monitoring the temperature on the hot water heater periodically, to using car safety belts daily.

Tactics

Tactics describe how preventive interventions are introduced to target groups so that the incidence (number of new cases) of injuries is reduced. Chapters in this book address tactics that are universal, selected, and indicated.

Universal Tactics Because of their desirability for all children, *universal* or populationwide tactics are directed to large targets through federal legislation, mass media campaigns, or districtwide school programs. Specific examples include legislated changes requiring that infant clothing be manufactured with fire-resistant materials or reminding everyone in a community to check their smoke detector batteries when daylight savings time changes. Usually, however, universal strategies rely on educational methods, and because they lack the intensity required to modify the complex factors associated with injury, they do not produce sustained behavioral change (Muehrer & Koretz, 1992).

Selected Tactics Selected tactics include efforts directed toward specific segments or subgroups of the population believed to be at increased risk for injury. Examples include teenage drivers, swimming pool owners, children living in high-rise buildings (falls from windows), owners of wood frame houses in the East and South (increased risk for fires), and new parents (use of infant safety seats). The anticipatory guidance provided in many pediatricians' offices regarding the temperature of hot water heaters, use of bicycle safety helmets, and accessibility of loaded firearms is another example. These tactics may require fewer resources than universal tactics, as long as there is a cost-effective means of identifying the specific target groups. In addition, targeting specific populations minimizes the potential of exposing persons not at risk to an intervention with possible negative consequences (Muehrer & Koretz, 1992).

Indicated Tactics Indicated tactics, or efforts aimed at individuals with identifiable risk factors for injury (e.g., the "accident-prone" child whose innate characteristics result in more injuries), have not been very successful. Although such socioeconomic factors as living in a single-parent home, young maternal age and low education level, and high household stress have been associated with increased risk of injury (McCormick, Shapiro, & Starfield, 1981), it is more productive to focus on factors that can be modified more easily (Rivara, 1992). Thus, the majority of injury prevention efforts have used universal and selected tactics.

CONSIDERATIONS IN SELECTING INJURY PREVENTION STRATEGIES

Injury prevention is not a luxury—it is a necessity of singular proportions for this nation. The prevalence of injury-related illnesses and the associated morbidity and mortality alone are compelling arguments for the strategic implementation of effective prevention strategies. However, neither every recognized cause of injury nor every available prevention strategy should be the substance of an injury prevention program.

Three characteristics serve as practical touchstones to determine the direction of prevention efforts: 1) frequency of the injury mechanism, 2) severity of the injury mechanism, and 3) known effectiveness of interventions in preventing or reducing that injury incidence/mechanism (Grossman & Rivara, 1992). The frequency and severity of a particular injury mechanism establishes the significance and priority of the problem and the urgency of the need for a solution. Data, both national and local, should be gathered to assess the frequency and severity of injuries associated with a particular injury mechanism. Motor vehicle occupant injuries are both frequent and severe, with a high risk of serious injury and death. Falls, however, are by far the most common mechanism of childhood injury; however, the types of injuries associated with falls are rarely severe.

In addition, because of the multiple nature and circumstances of falls, there is no effective preventive intervention (e.g., safety belt use for motor vehicle–related injuries or helmet use for bicycle-related injuries) for falls. The selection of a target for which an effective intervention is already known is critical for an initial prevention program (Muehrer & Koretz, 1992). It might be argued that to devote limited resources, on a large scale, to the prevention of falls is not an efficient use of resources.

The target population of the prevention effort should be well defined by age, socioeconomic status, and so forth. The more knowledge and data available on the target population, the better the prevention strategies and approaches can focus on the issues influencing the desired change in behavior.

It is vital that each program have an evaluation component specifically intended to measure to what extent the goals and objectives of the program are met. The ultimate objective of any injury prevention initiative is to increase the number of lives saved. However, to measure the success of the program solely by a reduced mortality rate is unrealistic for a community-based program with a limited study population. The evaluation components should be designed to measure short- and long-term goals and objectives (National Committee for Injury Prevention and Control, 1989). With that in mind, the success of injury prevention programs may be measured better by increased awareness, changed attitudes, and increase in the purchase of injury prevention technology such as safety seats, bicycle helmets, and smoke detectors, and by direct observation of the desired changes in safety-related behaviors.

Only relevant dimensions of the short- and long-term goals need to be measured. For example, based on studies demonstrating that child safety seats are estimated to reduce the risk of death by as much as 69% (Centers for Disease Control and Prevention, 1991), there is no need to invest resources in reevaluating the effectiveness of safety seats themselves. However, it may be desirable to incorporate measurements of the target audience's knowledge of proper safety seat use and their attitudes toward child occupant restraint. Direct observations of the use of child safety seats, however, is essential to determine baseline rates and to evaluate the effectiveness of the injury prevention program.

Demonstration and documentation of efficacy are vital for garnering the needed political, grassroots, and corporate financial support. Success in this regard provides a valuable foundation for future initiative. In addition, this type of documentation can be used with local media to generate awareness. The general public is poorly educated regarding the scope and magnitude of the problem of injury.

Most injury-producing events are far too complex to be resolved successfully through simple, one-dimensional interventions. It is becoming increasingly clear that a multifaceted approach must be directed toward the relevant environmental, behavioral, societal, and educational factors contributing to the risk of injuries. Thus, no individual effort, program, or institution has the capability of reducing the incidence of childhood injury. Interventions involving the collaboration of a variety of professions and organizations are essential.

In addition to targeting parents, teachers, and other caregivers, successful approaches involve strategic efforts in the realms of legislation, law enforcement, education, health care, behavioral sciences, business and community groups, and the media. The comprehensive plans and combined synergy culminating from well-timed efforts in each area should enable the specific injury prevention message to penetrate the target population. In addition, this type of approach stimulates collaboration among experts in each area, bringing diverse perspectives and insights into the development of comprehensive strategies. This multifaceted approach promotes networking and unique partnerships among community groups, fostering a sense of ownership and commitment toward mutual programs for the safety and protection of children.

A common bond of ownership and commitment is essential for the longevity and support of injury prevention efforts. The sense of mutual ownership also frees any organization from the overwhelming and virtually impossible challenge to finance, develop, implement, evaluate, and maintain every aspect of a multidisciplinary prevention program. Additionally, this type of community collaboration avoids the duplication of individual efforts and strengthens already existing programs and plans addressing similar issues. Although facilitation of such a multidisciplinary program requires a significant amount of communication and coordination, the added benefits, advantages, and empowerment of a zealous communitywide effort provides almost limitless opportunities for creative, effective, and sustained changes toward enhancing the safety of our children and our future.

COMPREHENSIVE INJURY PREVENTION: CINCINNATI CHILDREN'S HOSPITAL MEDICAL CENTER CHILD OCCUPANT SAFETY PROGRAM

Identification of the Problem

The initial step in problem identification requires knowledge of the frequency, severity, and characteristics of an injury in the affected community. Regional hospital-based computerized databases, medical examiners' data, police accident reports, and death certificates are important sources of injury information.

The Cincinnati Children's Hospital Medical Center (CHMC) trauma registry indicated that in 78% of the motor vehicle occupant deaths in 1992, the child was not restrained at the time of the crash. Unrestrained children were more likely to be seriously injured, and they required longer hospitalizations, more intensive care unit treatment, and more surgical procedures than restrained children. Only 31% of the children injured seriously enough in car crashes to require hospitalization at CHMC had been restrained.

In response to these facts, injury prevention staff in Trauma Service conducted telephone surveys and observations of car safety seat usage rates for children under the age of 4 years in the Greater Cincinnati area. A 1992 telephone survey of a random sample of county residents found that 76% "always" restrained their children, 11% used safety seats or safety belts "most of the time," and 2% "sometimes" restrained their children. Only 1.1% reported that they never used safety seats or safety belts for their children.

Because self-reported restraint usage rates are known to be higher than observed rates, direct assessment of safety seat usage rates was also conducted. Observers stood in the parking lots of a local grocery store chain to survey cars of shoppers with children under the age of 4. Restraint usage observations were made for 1,556 children. Safety seats were also evaluated for gross misuse, such as an infant seat positioned facing forward or a convertible seat not properly secured with a safety belt. This surveillance indicated that 10% of the children were not restrained in any way. Eighteen percent were wearing safety belts only, despite an Ohio state law mandating car safety seats until the child's 4th birthday or until the child weighs 40 pounds. An additional 19% were riding in safety seats that were grossly misused, which adversely affects or completely negates the protection offered by the seat. Only 53% of the children observed were safely—and legally—restrained.

Use of child safety seats is estimated to reduce the risk of death from a crash by 69% for infants and 47% for toddlers, while use of adult safety belts with toddlers reduces risk of death by 36% (Centers for Disease Control and Prevention, 1991). The Centers for Disease Control and Prevention projected that use of restraints for child passengers, both safety seats and belts, saved the lives of approximately 1,546 children from 1982 to 1990.

The large number of children at risk for potentially serious or fatal injuries despite the availability of effective protective devices presented a public health challenge to the Greater Cincinnati community. An ongoing, multidimensional, community-based injury prevention program was developed to address the suboptimal child safety seat usage rates and the most frequently observed forms of unsafe installation and use. Community groups and resources were identified and collaborative efforts initiated. Civic and charitable organizations, the educational community, pediatric and family practice physicians, obstetric and gynecology practices, law enforcement officials, childbirth education groups, the business community, advertising agencies, and the local media contributed to the injury prevention campaign. This program, launched in 1993, is expected to continue for several years in an ever-expanding form.

Intervention and Preliminary Outcomes

The multicomponent intervention developed to address the issue of proper use of child safety seats is outlined in Table 10.3. Local Kiwanis clubs, who adopted the program as a component of their "Young Children: Priority One" initiative, were a primary source of support and funding. A 4-year commitment was made to donate funds raised through their service projects to the program.

To enhance community education efforts, a local television station produced and donated a videotape graphically demonstrating the importance of child safety seats. Kiwanis clubs underwrote the reproduction costs for approximately 700 of these videotapes for distribution to schools, childbirth education classes, hospitals, fire departments, and physicians' offices.

Table 10.3. Cincinnati CHMC comprehensive communitywide child safety seat campaign

Name of program	Target	Method	Tactic
Kiwanis videotape presentations	Parents of infants through preschoolers	Educational	Selected
GRADS program	Pregnant high school students	Educational	Selected
Childbirth education classes	Expectant parents	Educational	Selected
Law enforcement—child safety seat exchange program	Drivers with unrestrained children under the age of 4	Mandated	Selected
Hospital patient child safety seat program	Parents of hospitalized children under the age of 4	Educational	Selected
Pediatric physicians' office program	Parents of children under the age of 4 treated by pediatricians	Educational	Selected
Obstetricians' office program	Prenatal patients	Educational	Selected
Media campaign	All residents within the broadcast and print media area	Educational	Universal
Preschool car safety program	Preschoolers and parents	Educational	Selected

CHMC = Children's Hospital Medical Center.
GRADS = Graduation, Reality, and Dual-Role Skills.

Recognizing the need for child safety education among teen parents, the videotape was also distributed to the Graduation, Reality, and Dual-Role Skills (GRADS) program, a high school-based intervention for pregnant teens and/or young parents. In response to requests from GRADS teachers for additional safety seat information for their students, injury prevention personnel developed a classroom presentation detailing the importance and proper use of child safety seats.

Another vehicle for reaching expectant parents is through obstetrical offices and childbirth education classes. Members of the local society of obstetricians provide literature and safety seat coupons for their patients. The Cincinnati Childbirth Education Association (CEA) has incorporated a child safety seat module into each series of prenatal classes. Presented by representatives from the CHMC injury prevention speakers' bureau, this program includes the videotape, informational materials, instruction regarding the need for child safety seats, and demonstration of the proper use of safety seats and the correct positioning of infants. Emphasis is placed on the importance of always restraining the child. Community resources that provide infant seats on a loaner basis are identified, and discount coupons for the purchase of safety seats are distributed at both the GRADS and CEA classes. An average of 15 programs are presented to childbirth education classes per month.

The business community plays an integral role in the educational campaign. Many local enterprises, including professional sports teams, provide support through financial donations, in-kind services, discount coupons for purchase of safety seats, or grant funding for program development and evaluation.

One of the most effective tools in injury prevention is law enforcement. Several area law enforcement agencies are participating in a program designed to increase compliance with child occupant restraint laws. Police officers are educated in the proper use and installation of safety seats. When officers issue a citation for failure to properly restrain a child, they install a safety seat in the vehicle so that the child is immediately protected, reinforcing both the urgency and the positive nature of their action. At the court appearance, proof of safety seat possession and return of the seat issued by the officer results in a waiver of the fine. Communities participating in this program have amended their local child passenger safety ordinance to require the maximum fine permitted by state law for failure to restrain a child.

CHMC also initiated distribution of safety seats on a sliding fee scale to families of children admitted to the hospital. This program is funded by Kiwanis clubs, private donations, and through matching grant funds from the Ohio Bureau of Maternal and Child Health. A comprehensive child occupant safety education program is presented to nursing personnel who, in turn, instruct parents in proper safety seat installation and use prior to discharge.

A source of information highly trusted by parents is their child's doctor. A 1992 survey of area pediatric health-care providers showed that only 46% instruct their patients' families about child occupant safety on a regular basis, and that the physicians themselves required additional education before they could effectively address specific issues of child occupant safety with their patients' families. An education program subsequently was held at the hospital to teach community physicians the basics of child occupant safety, provide educational materials for distribution to their patients' families, and enlist their participation in the campaign. All in attendance expressed their willingness to play an active role in educating the children and parents treated in their practices. Several additional child occupant safety outreach programs have been presented at pediatric medical meetings.

The disparate programs and participating agencies were united and energized by the media component of the campaign. Billboards, posters, print advertisements, and radio and television public service announcements were developed by a local advertising agency. The electronic media participated through airing the public service audio- and videotapes; the print media contributed to the campaign through editorial support and print advertisement space.

In addition to the interventions intended for adults, the child occupant safety program also directly targets preschool children. With funding from a local insurance company, a committee composed of preschool administrators, preschool and university faculty, and pediatric health-care personnel developed a curriculum designed to teach parents and children the importance of proper restraint use. Car safety-oriented materials and activities were developed to present the message through a variety of educational media, and monthly newsletters addressing specific child occupant safety issues were sent home to parents. Programs providing parents with additional information and demonstrations of proper use of child safety and booster seats were also offered to participating schools. At the beginning of the school year, the percentage of children observed to be restrained was about 68% in both intervention and control schools. By April, the percentage observed to be restrained at the intervention schools had risen to 82.3%, in contrast to 72% observed at control schools.

This multimedia, multidimensional campaign exposes the community to the child passenger safety message through a variety of diverse and influential sources. Such methodology corresponds to current educational theories advocating an integrated, multifaceted approach when raising awareness and attempting to change behaviors (Elias et al., in press). Although still in its infancy, the results of the preschool car safety program demonstrate that the intervention has already affected the way many young children ride as automobile occupants.

SUMMARY

There are no simple solutions for ameliorating the complex array of environmental, behavioral, societal, and educational factors associated with unintentional injury, although progress has been made in many areas since the mid-1980s. Multifaceted, cooperative efforts that involve a variety of disciplines, institutions, and community members, and include mandated as well as persuasive methods have the greatest potential for initiating and sustaining the long-term change necessary to prevent the negative outcomes of injury. Furthermore, both active and passive interventions are needed to maximize our effectiveness. Finally, we must recognize that the burden for prevention cannot be placed solely on children or their caregivers; it must also involve many child-related institutions and modification of various environmental agents.

Society's limited resolution in addressing these factors is not related to an absence of knowledge about how to effect change—we have the techniques to modify many injury-related risk factors (Robertson, 1983). However, this available technology is often ignored. What is needed is more widespread recognition of the long-term human benefits and cost-effectiveness associated with primary prevention. Furthermore, more cooperative efforts among various disciplines, institutions, and governmental agencies, along with community members, are needed to develop creative, long-lasting solutions to meet this challenge.

REFERENCES

Baker, S.G., & Waller, A. (1988). *Childhood injury: State-by-state mortality facts.* Washington, DC: National Maternal and Child Health Clearinghouse.

Bandura, A. (1973). *Aggression: A social learning analysis.* Englewood Cliffs, NJ: Prentice-Hall.

Berger, L. (1981). Childhood injuries: Recognition and prevention. *Current Problems in Pediatrics, 12,* 1–59.

Cataldo, M.F., Derschewitz, R., Wilson, M., Christopherson, E., Finney, J., Fawcett, S., & Seekins, T. (1983). Childhood injury control. In N.A. Krasnegor, J.D. Araseth, & M.F. Cataldo (Eds.), *Child health behaviors: A behavioral pediatrics approach* (pp. 217–253). New York: John Wiley & Sons.

Centers for Disease Control and Prevention. (1990). Childhood injuries in the United States. *American Journal of Diseases of Children, 144*(6), 627–646.

Centers for Disease Control and Prevention. (1991). Child passenger restraint use and motor-vehicle-related fatalities among children—United States, 1982–1990. *Morbidity and Mortality Weekly Report, 40*(34), 600–602.

Children's Safety Network. (1991). *A databook of child and adolescent injury.* Washington, DC: National Center for Education in Maternal and Child Health.

Cote, T.R., Sacks, J.J., & Lambert-Huber, D.A. (1992). Bicycle helmet use among Maryland children: Effect of legislation and education. *Pediatrics, 89*(6), 1216–1220.

Elias, M.J., Weissberg, R.P., Hawkins, J.D., Perry, C.L., Zins, J.E., Dodge, K.A., Kendall, P.C., Gottfredson, D.C., Rotheram-Borus, M.J., Jason, L.A., & Wilson-Brewer, R. (in press). The school-based promotion of social competence: Theory, research, practice, and policy. In R.J. Haggerty, N. Garmezy, M. Rutter, & L. Sherrod (Eds.), *Risk and resilience in children.* Cambridge, England: Cambridge University Press.

Fife, D., Davis, J., Tate, L., Wells, J.K., Mohan, D., & Williams, A. (1983). Fatal injuries to bicyclists: The experience of Dade County, Florida. *Journal of Trauma, 23,* 745–755.

Gratz, R.R. (1979). Accidental injury in childhood: A literature review on pediatric trauma. *Journal of Trauma, 19,* 551–555.

Grossman, D.C., & Rivara, F.P. (1992). Injury control in childhood. *Pediatric Clinics of North America, 39*(3), 471–485.

Guyer, B., & Ellers, B. (1990). Childhood injuries in the United States. *American Journal of Diseases of Children, 144,* 649–652.

Hazinski, M.F., Francescutti, L.H., Lapidus, G.D., Micik, S., & Rivara, F.P. (1993). Pediatric injury prevention. *Annals of Emergency Medicine, 22*(2), 456–467.

Healthy people 2000: National health promotion and disease prevention objectives. (1991). Washington, DC: Public Health Service, U.S. Department of Health and Human Services.

Insurance Institute for Highway Safety. (1991). *Fatality facts, 1991 edition.* Arlington, VA: Author.

Koop, C.E., & Lundberg, G.D. (1992). Violence in America: A public health emergency: Time to bite the bullet back. *Journal of the American Medical Association, 267*(22), 3075–3076.

Kraus, J., Fife, D., & Conroy, C. (1977). Incidence, severity, and outcomes of brain injuries involving bicycles. *American Journal of Public Health, 67,* 76–78.

McCormick, M.C., Shapiro, S., & Starfield, B. (1981). Injury and its correlates among 1-year-old children. *American Journal of Diseases of Children, 135,* 159–163.

Muehrer, P., & Koretz, D.S. (1992). Issues in preventive intervention research. *Current Directions in Psychological Science, 1*(3), 109–112.

National Committee for Injury Prevention and Control. (1989). *Injury prevention: Meeting the challenge.* New York: Oxford University Press.

National Highway Traffic Safety Administration, U.S. Department of Transportation. (1991). *Occupant protection trends in 19 cities.* Washington, DC: Author.

National Safety Council. (1992). *Accident facts: 1992 edition.* Itasca, IL: Author.

Ordog, G.J., Wasserberger, J., Schlater, I., Owens-Collins, D., English, K., Balasubramanian, S., & Schlater, T. (1988). Gunshot wounds in children under ten years of age: A new epidemic. *American Journal of Diseases of Children, 142*(3), 618–622.

Patterson, P.J., & Smith, L.R. (1987). Firearms in the home and child safety. *American Journal of Diseases of Children, 141*(3), 618–622.

Peterson, L. (1988). Preventing the leading killer of children: The role of the school psychologist in injury prevention. *School Psychology Review, 17,* 593–600.

Peterson, L., Farmer, J., & Kashani, J.H. (1990). Parental injury prevention endeavors: A function of health beliefs? *Health Psychology, 9,* 177–191.

Peterson, L., & Mori, L. (1985). Prevention of child injury: An overview of targets, methods, and tactics for psychologists. *Journal of Consulting and Clinical Psychology, 53*(5), 586–595.

Peterson, L., Mori, L., & Scissors, C. (1986). Mom or dad says I shouldn't: Supervised and unsupervised children's knowledge of their parents' rules for home safety. *Journal of Pediatric Psychology, 11,* 177–188.

Peterson, L., & Roberts, M.C. (1992). Complacency, misdirection, and effective prevention of children's injuries. *American Psychologist, 47*(8), 1040–1044.

Race, K. (1988). Evaluating pedestrian safety education materials for children ages five to nine. *Journal of School Health, 58,* 277–281.

Rice, D.P., MacKenzie, E.L., Jones, A.S., Kaufman, S.R., deLissovoy, G.V., Max, W., McLoughlin, E., Miller, T.R., Robertson, L.S., Salkever, D.S., & Smith, G.S. (1989). *Cost of injury in the United States: A report to Congress.* San Francisco: Institute for Health and Aging, University of California and Injury Prevention Center, The Johns Hopkins University.

Rivara, F.P. (1990). Child pedestrian injuries in the United States. *American Journal of Diseases of Children, 144*(6), 692–696.

Rivara, F.P. (1992). Prevention of injuries to children and adolescents. In H.M. Wallace, K. Patrick, G.S. Parcel, & J.B. Igoe (Eds.), *Principles and practices of student health: Vol. 1. Foundations* (pp. 89–102). Oakland, CA: Third Party Publishing.

Roberts, M.C., Elkins, P., & Royal, G. (1984). Psychological applications in the prevention of accidents and illnesses. In M.C. Roberts & L. Peterson (Eds.), *Prevention of problems in childhood* (pp. 173–199). New York: John Wiley & Sons.

Robertson, L.S. (1983). Injury. In B. Edelstein & L. Michelson (Eds.), *Handbook of prevention* (pp. 343–360). New York: Plenum Press.

Rodriguez, J.G. (1990). Childhood injuries in the United States: A priority issue. *American Journal of Diseases of Children, 144*(6), 625–626.

Sacks, J.J., Holmgreen, P., Smith, S.M., & Sosin, D.M. (1991). Bicycle-associated head injuries and deaths in the United States from 1984 through 1988. *Journal of the American Medical Association, 266*, 3016–3018.

Thompson, R.S., Rivara, F.P., & Thompson, D.C. (1989). A case control study of the effectiveness of bicycle safety helmets. *New England Journal of Medicine, 320*, 1361–1367.

Williams, B.C., & Kotch, J.B. (1990). Excess injury mortality among children in the United States: Comparison of recent international statistics. *Pediatrics, 86*, 1067–1073.

Wintemute, G.J. (1990). Childhood drowning and near-drowning in the United States. *American Journal of Diseases of Children, 144*(6), 663–669.

Zins, J.E., Goskoski, S., & Reyes, C. (1991, June). *Injury prevention: Contributions to social competence promotion programs.* Paper presented at the Hartman Conference on Children and Their Families, New London, CT.

11

Externalizing Behavior Disorders

Rick Jay Short
and Richard Brokaw

Bernard is a 16-year-old resident in a training school in the Southeast. He entered the juvenile justice system at age 14 as a result of a series of breaking-and-entering convictions. However, his behavior problems had been obvious for many years prior to his arrest and placement in the training school. In fact, Bernard's first-grade teacher referred him for an evaluation for special education services because he frequently physically abused his peers and was very unpopular in his school.

Bernard's father left the family when Bernard was 2, leaving his mother alone to raise him and his six siblings. Because his mother worked afternoons and evenings, Bernard was unsupervised throughout most of his childhood. His father would occasionally visit the family, but he was almost always drunk and often abused Bernard verbally and physically during the visits. Young Bernard was remote and angry, teasing and hitting his siblings incessantly. Sometimes he methodically injured cats and other small animals.

The family lived in a poor neighborhood that lacked any form of family or community supports. However, the neighborhood did not lack sources of excitement. These were provided in abundance for youngsters in the forms of the drug trade, bullying, and crimes. Bernard became attracted to these and soon joined a gang of likeminded youths who dominated and terrorized its turf; however, the gang members found him untrustworthy and unpredictable. Bernard began to avoid the gang for his own safety.

Bernard was considerably less enthusiastic about his school performance than his gang activities. In class, he was disruptive and inattentive, and sometimes threatened his peers and teachers. Perhaps as a consequence of these behaviors, Bernard's achievement was low and his grades were consistently failing. He skipped classes whenever he could and spent much of his school time in in-school suspension. He was placed in the district's alternative school, but he was expelled in junior high school for continuous fighting.

Bernard's situation and behaviors are relatively common and much too visible in U.S. society. Although prevalence estimates of childhood psychopathology range from 14% to 22% of children and adolescents

(Brandenburg, Friedman, & Silver, 1990; Costello, 1989), children and adolescents such as Bernard who exhibit the symptoms of their disorders externally typically are the most noticed. Externally directed behavior, whether defined as oppositional, antisocial, or conduct disordered, is among the most pressing concerns facing U.S. society today (Gabel & Shindledecker, 1991). The consequences of these externalized behaviors can prove devastating for the child, those individuals with whom the child comes in contact, and society at large. Therefore, youths who display externally directed behaviors are among the most urgent referrals in children's services (Stewart, Myers, Burket, & Lyles, 1990). In fact, the diagnoses most associated with referrals for treatment are conduct and oppositional/defiant disorder, two of the three syndromes that constitute the disruptive behavioral disorders (Cohen, Kasen, Brook, & Struening, 1991).

CLASSIFICATION AND EPIDEMIOLOGY OF EXTERNALIZING PROBLEMS

The *Diagnostic and Statistical Manual of Mental Disorders* (3rd ed., rev.) (DSM-III-R) (American Psychiatric Association [APA], 1987) identifies three specific behavior disorders that constitute the disruptive behavior disorders. This triad includes attention deficit hyperactivity disorder (ADHD), conduct disorder (CD), and oppositional defiant disorder (ODD). Because the DSM-III-R is the most widely cited index of disorders used in the United States, we give particular attention throughout this chapter to the disorders defined within that system.

Attention Deficit Hyperactivity Disorder

Barkley (1990) suggests three essential features of ADHD. These include inattention, impulsivity, and overactivity. In order to diagnose ADHD, the degree to which referred children display these symptoms must be above what is considered appropriate for their peers. A relatively new component to the definition of ADHD reflected in current research (e.g., Barkley, 1990; DuPaul, Guevremont, & Barkley, 1991) is the existence of cognitive deficits in the regulation of their own behavior; that is, children with ADHD seem to have more difficulty than their peers in using cognitive mediation strategies to regulate their behaviors.

The DSM-III-R (APA, 1987) estimates that up to 3% of children in the United States may have this disorder. Estimates of the prevalence of ADHD typically range from 3% to 6% of the school-age population (Barkley, 1990; DuPaul et al., 1991), although some authors (Costello, 1989) cite a larger range, 2% to 10%, with a median of 6%. Boys are three to four and one half times more likely to be diagnosed with ADHD than are girls (Barkley, 1990; Reeves, Werry, Elkind, & Zametkin, 1987), and some suggest that current DSM-III-R criteria underestimate the prevalence of ADHD and CD in adolescence (Barkley, Fischer, Edelbrock, & Smallish, 1990).

The onset of ADHD occurs before age 4 in approximately half the reported cases. The disorder often goes unrecognized until the child enters school (APA, 1987). The mean age of onset has been identified as between the ages of 3 and 4 with the range encompassing birth to 7-years of age (Barkley et al., 1990).

Conduct Disorder

Conduct disorder is differentiated from other disorders primarily by the severity of the symptoms, which usually result in the violation of another's rights (e.g., fighting, stealing) and/or the destruction of property (e.g., setting fires). It has been suggested that these symptoms appear early, the mean age of onset for CD being estimated at 6 years of age (Barkley et al., 1990). Prevalence estimates of CD vary widely. Costello (1989) reports a prevalence rate of 1.5 to 5.5, with a median of 3.4. The DSM-III-R (APA, 1987) reports rates of 9% for males and 2% for females, whereas Kazdin (1989) cites figures of 4%–10% for the disorder.

Oppositional Defiant Disorder

Oppositional defiant disorder is characterized by a pattern of defiant, negativistic, and noncompliant behavior. Criteria for a diagnosis of ODD include the presence of at least five of the following symptoms: loses temper, argues with adults, actively defies or refuses adult requests, places blame on others, deliberately annoys others, is often angry and resentful, swears, and is spiteful or vindictive. To meet the diagnostic criteria, these symptoms must be exhibited more frequently than same-age peers and over the relatively stable time period of at least 6 months (APA, 1987). Oppositional behavior is contrasted to conduct disordered behaviors in that symptomatology associated with ODD typically does not violate the rights of others. However, some individuals receive dual diagnoses of CD and/or ADHD and ODD. In fact, 65% of children diagnosed as ADHD are likely to exhibit symptoms of ODD at sufficient levels to receive a co-morbid diagnosis (Barkley et al., 1990). Although prevalence estimates for ODD are difficult to construct, Costello (1989) states that the prevalence of ODD is between 5% and 10%, with a median of 6.6%. Barkley et al. (1990) found that the mean age of onset for ODD was 6.7 years.

Co-morbidity

These three disruptive behavior disorders have a high degree of overlap (Reeves et al., 1987; Barkley et al., 1990), which complicates assessment, prevalence, prediction, and treatment issues. Barkley et al. found that of those individuals in their sample who met the criteria for a diagnosis of ADHD, 59% also met the criteria for a diagnosis of ODD, and 43% also met the criteria for a diagnosis of CD. Other studies reflect similar findings. Szatmari, Boyle, and Offord (1989) found that roughly 40% of children with a primary diagnosis of ADHD had an additional diagnosis of CD. Likewise, the symptoms of children who were diagnosed as CD reflected a significant overlap with diagnosis of ADHD; roughly 57% in the 4- to 11-year-old range displayed this co-morbidity.

The severity, frequency, and complexity of these externalizing symptoms, coupled with co-morbidity issues, pose great challenges to interventionists attempting to develop prevention programs for children and adolescents who will manifest these disorders. For this reason, understanding of the risk factors and correlates of the externalizing disorders may be an important tool toward developing such programs.

PSYCHOSOCIAL FRAMEWORK FOR UNDERSTANDING EXTERNALIZING DISORDERS

Externalizing disorders constitute a complex problem with multiple facets, covariates, and determinants. However, a number of characteristics seem to cluster within and around these syndromes in a systematic way, encompassing personal, familial, school, and peer factors. Jessor (1991) and Short and Shapiro (1993) have proposed that these dimensions provide a useful framework for understanding and preventing childhood psychopathology, including externalizing disorders. Personal, familial, school, and peer variables associated with externalizing disorders, along with interactions among them, may provide a powerful explanatory and planning mechanism for providing comprehensive prevention services to children with these disorders. Given the resistance of the disorders to most intervention strategies, a comprehensive, integrated intervention approach that addresses these dimensions and their interactions may be necessary to have a significant preventive or remedial effect on the disorder.

Personal Characteristics

Children and youths with externalizing disorders often exhibit relatively stable personal characteristics that may be particularly important because their onset frequently appears quite early in the child's developmental history. These features may serve as markers for subsequent severe externalizing behaviors. Personal characteristics associated with subsequent externalizing disorders may appear in preschool years, sometimes as early as age 2. These may include resistance to discipline and irritability (Bates & Bayles, 1988), developmental cognitive and language difficulties (Hogan & Quay, 1984), and early aggressive behaviors (Griffin, 1987; Mitchell & Rosa, 1981). Although less clearly substantiated in the literature, other areas such as social cognitive development (Campagna & Harter, 1975; Jurkovic & Prentice, 1977; Short & Simeonsson, 1986), sensation-seeking (Newcomb & McGee, 1991), temperament (Webster-Stratton & Eyberg, 1982), and neurological functioning (Lewis, Shanok, Pincus, & Glaser, 1979; Shapiro & Hynd, 1993) may be associated with the development and display of behavior disorders. Finally, Kauffman (1993) points to the possibility that certain genetic factors may predispose some youths to inadequate impulse control and attention problems that can, when combined with other environmental factors, result in ADHD.

Cognitive factors play an important and well-documented role in externalizing behaviors (Dodge, 1993). Externalizing children often exhibit a cognitive response bias in which they interpret ambiguous interpersonal stimuli as being hostile (Dodge, Price, Bachorowski, & Newman, 1990). This cognitive bias may result in and justify aggressive responses to the misperceived hostile stimulus. Children with externalizing disorders also may be deficient in problem-solving skills, particularly in generating multiple and/or prosocial problem solutions. These children tend to be limited and inflexible in solution generation, resulting in a narrow repertoire for responding to conflict situations (Spivack, Platt, & Shure, 1976).

Three points are important to note in examining these factors. First, most children who exhibit these early markers do not grow up to exhibit externalizing disorders; however, most adolescents with externalizing disorders appear to have exhibited them in their early development (Robins, 1978). Second, earlier onset of these characteristics typically is associated with increased potential for subsequent negative behaviors (Kazdin, 1987). Third, these characteristics probably interact with parent and teacher aspects to exacerbate and intensify problem behaviors (Patterson, 1982); that is, parent and teacher responses to difficult behaviors may shape subsequent responses by the child toward even more difficult behaviors. For this reason, it is critical to look beyond personal characteristics of the child to understand the ecology within which the child develops and interacts in order to develop effective intervention options.

Parental and Familial Factors

Among the most well-demonstrated precursors and covariates of externalizing disorders are parental and familial characteristics and behaviors. Children with externalizing disorders often come from families that are experiencing considerable stress (McGee, Williams, & Silva, 1984; Offord, Alder, & Boyle, 1986; Patterson, 1982), from families in which members are alcoholics or who engage in criminal activities (West, 1982), or from families in which other members exhibit psychopathology (Frick, Lahey, Christ, Loeber, & Green, 1991; Lahey, Russo, Walker, & Piacentini, 1989).

Perhaps the most significant familial factors in relation to externalizing disorders are parent–child interactions and parent management practices (Dumas, 1989; Loeber & Dishion, 1983; Patterson & Stouthamer-Loeber, 1984). Characteristics of discipline practices of parents of children with externalizing disorders typically consist of a combination of inconsistent and highly punitive behaviors, which may increase both deviant behaviors and alienation in their children. Parent interactions in these families often are predominantly negative, particularly in response to negative child behaviors. Positive child behaviors either are not reinforced or are responded to aversively. However, these responses also are unpredictable in that they are implemented inconsistently. Negative child behaviors often gain parent responses that are both aversive and inconsistent, resulting in increased, but unpredictable, attention for antisocial conduct versus prosocial behavior (Dumas & Wahler, 1985). This combination of parent discipline tactics appears to be highly predictive of externalizing behavior in children (Loeber & Dishion, 1983; Pettit, Bates, & Dodge, 1993; Webster-Stratton, 1993). Because parent management practices constitute a relatively malleable factor in externalizing disorders in children, they are promising targets for prevention programs.

School Factors

School variables long have been associated with delinquency and conduct problems (McGee, Share, Moffitt, Williams, & Silva, 1988), and recently they have received attention in theoretical models of the development of antisocial behavior, delinquency, and externalizing disorders (Hawkins & Weis, 1985). Typically, children who exhibit externalizing behaviors in school also are poor readers (Bale, 1981). Antisocial and delinquent behavior has been related to poor academic performance (Frick et al., 1991; Hinshaw, 1992; Tremblay et al., 1992), as well as to low school participation and disruptive behavior in the classroom (Finn, 1988; Rincker, 1990; Walker, Stieber, & Ramsey, 1990, 1991). Increased rates of truancy also have been associated with externalizing disorders (Herbert, 1987), as has dropping out of school (Cairns, Cairns, & Neckerman, 1989; Robins, 1991).

Whereas such variables as poor academic achievement consistently have been shown to relate to deliquency and antisocial behavior, causal relationships between the two variables remain unclear. Hinshaw (1992) has suggested that both academic underachievement and behavior problems may be related to similar antecedent variables, including low socioeconomic status, family problems, and intellectual, neurological, and language deficits. However, a recent study by Tremblay et al. (1992) found poor academic achievement to be a significant variable in a causal path between early disruptive behavior and later delinquent personality. Regardless of the nature of causal relationships associated with achievement and externalizing disorders, their connection is well demonstrated and may have important implications for prevention programs.

Peer Factors

In addition to personal, familial, and school factors, peer variables have been associated with externalizing disorders. Children who exhibit externalizing behaviors often are rejected by their peers (Dodge, Coie, & Brakke, 1982; Ladd, Hart, & Price, 1990; Patterson, DeBaryshe, & Ramsey, 1989), frequently as a response to their negative behaviors (Asarnow, 1983; Shantz, 1986). Early peer rejection and aggression has been shown to predict later externalizing problems (Hymel, Rubin, & Rowden, 1990; Kupersmidt & Coie, 1990), as well as later membership in deviant peer groups (Dishion, Patterson, & Stoolmiller, 1991). These peer groups may consist of several highly aggressive children, all of whom exhibit similar characteristics (Cairns, Cairns, Neckerman, Gest, & Gariepy, 1988). Frequently formed during early adolescence, these deviant groups become involved in serious delinquent and antisocial behaviors (Dishion & Loeber, 1985).

Early peer rejection of antisocial children appears to be a complex phenomenon. There may be at least two groups of rejected students (French, 1988), the more aggressive of whom exhibit more hostile withdrawl behaviors than the other (Waas, 1987). Although more research on these phenomena is needed, these groups may correspond to the diagnostic subcategories of conduct disorder.

PREVENTION OF EXTERNALIZING PROBLEMS

Primary Prevention

Although outcomes for children with externalizing disorders evidently often are more negative than those for many other childhood disorders, considerable effort currently is being given to identifying primary prevention interventions that may mitigate these negative effects. Recent work has noted that parent training (Dumas, 1989; Kazdin, 1989), family interventions (Miller & Prinz, 1990; Webster-Stratton, Hollinsworth, & Kolpacoff, 1989), problem-solving training (Kazdin, 1987; Kazdin, Esveldt-Dawson, French, & Unis, 1987; Lochman, Burch, Curry, & Lampron, 1984), and community-based prevention efforts (Kazdin, 1987) may have some effectiveness in remediating behaviors associated with the disorder.

As noted above, externalizing disorders have shown considerable stability over time, and have proved resistant to a variety of interventions. This may be particularly true when interventions are not implemented until such behaviors as severe physical aggression or criminal behavior occur. Such a combination of serious behaviors, resistance to intervention, and late intervention increases the probability of costly and negative outcomes for children, schools, communities, and society. To counteract this cycle, several writers have suggested that effective interventions for externalizing disorders must occur at this level (Boyle & Offord, 1990; Hawkins & Weis, 1985; Short & Shapiro, 1993). Examples of primary prevention goals for the risk dimensions reported above are provided in Table 11.1.

Secondary Prevention

Secondary prevention of conduct disorders has focused on interventions with children and youth who exhibit characteristics of the disorder. Although diverse interventions targeting the syndrome at the secondary prevention level have been reported, reviews of outcome reports of these interventions have suggested that most secondary prevention efforts have been minimally effective in long-term remediation (Dumas, 1989; Kazdin, 1989). Particularly when externalizing behaviors have an early onset, are pervasive, and are diverse, long-term problems in almost all areas of functioning prevail (Kazdin, 1989). These areas include education, occupation, interpersonal relations, health, relations with legal authorities, and mental health (Kazdin, 1989). Because the syndrome may be an enduring condition that requires continuous monitoring and maintenance to gain and sustain treatment progress, the prognosis for children diagnosed as having externalizing disorders remains guarded (Loeber, 1990; Robins, 1966, 1978). Examples of secondary prevention goals for the risk dimensions reported above are presented in Table 11.1.

Tertiary Prevention

The goal of tertiary prevention is intervention and remediation of already existing problems with the intention of reducing the occurrence

Table 11.1. Levels and goals of prevention of externalizing behavior problems

Level of prevention	General goal of prevention	Prevention goals for children[a]	Prevention goals for families[a]	Prevention goals for schools[a]	Prevention goals for communities[a]
Primary prevention of externalizing disorders	Prevent condition by reducing number of new cases	Reduce new cases through reduction of risk factors	Promotion of parenting skills and parent involvement	Promote positive school climate and involve all students	Develop participatory, connected community
Secondary prevention of externalizing disorders	Prevent condition by reducing number of existing cases	Reduce duration and/or severity of behaviors by maintaining, restoring, or developing new skills	Help family deal with demands of child's behavior	Institute comprehensive fair discipline procedures Develop decision-making process and improve expertise	Cultivate communication and avenues for involvement among families and community resources
Tertiary prevention of externalizing disorders	Prevent condition by reducing direct and indirect effects	Reduce direct and indirect effects through corrective or compensatory intervention	Facilitate adjustment in terms of dynamics, relationships, and/or values	Provide mechanisms to accommodate "difficult" students	Develop coordinated interagency and interdisciplinary services

Adapted from Simeonsson (1991).
[a] Interventions may be additive across levels.

of complications and further difficulties resulting from the problem. Tertiary prevention presupposes the full manifestation and consequences of the identified problem. In the case of externalizing disorders, tertiary prevention would occur in response to chronic or severe manifestations of antisocial behaviors and their sequelae. Tertiary interventions might target children who have experienced personal, school, family, or legal problems resulting from antisocial and severe disruptive behavior. Examples of tertiary prevention goals for the risk dimensions reported above are provided in Table 11.1.

Broad tertiary interventions might include hospitalization, placement in juvenile justice facilities, and supportive vocational skills training programs. These programs often seek to rehabilitate problem children through supportive and compensatory interventions. Although tertiary strategies may be important components of comprehensive prevention programs, their effectiveness with severe externalizing disorders has been relatively minimal (Dumas, 1989; Kazdin, 1989). Particularly because of the characteristics and developmental path of externalizing disorders, primary prevention strategies may be more effective in dealing with the problem.

Rationale for Primary Prevention

Externalizing disorders often have an early onset and may pursue a lifelong course, developing in later years into serious delinquency in adolescence and antisocial personality disorder and criminal behavior in adults (Wolf, Braukmann, & Ramp, 1987). Longitudinal studies also have provided consistent findings regarding the stability of aggressive behavior, sometimes being compared to that found for intelligence (Olweus, 1979). Moreover, Wolf et al. (1987) compare the durability, resistance to short-term treatment, and disabling effects of externalizing behaviors to those of mental retardation, autism, and blindness.

Whereas other disorders of childhood (e.g., internalizing disorders) may respond to treatment or ameliorate spontaneously over time, some aspects of externalizing disorders may persist in a relatively constant form throughout the developmental path (Herbert, 1987). Indeed, a common belief that children who exhibit externalizing behaviors will "outgrow" problem behaviors seems unfounded (Robins, 1966); individuals who exhibit these serious behaviors in adolescence and adulthood typically engaged in similar behaviors when they were very young (Herbert, 1987). Given these findings, the prognosis for intervening with children with the disorder remains poor (Loeber, 1990; Robins, 1966, 1978).

The goal of primary prevention of externalizing disorders is to lower their incidence, rather than to treat occurring cases of the problem (secondary prevention) or its sequelae (tertiary prevention). Primary prevention strategies most often focus either on protective factors or risk factors that have been identified as correlates of the problem. Interventions then seek to modify these variables, either by increasing factors that protect against externalizing disorders or by decreasing factors such as those outlined above that appear to be precursors or covariates of externalizing disorders. Thus, the objective of primary prevention of externalizing disorders is to affect correlates of the problem that may predict the syndrome, rather than to intervene with children with externalizing disorders. Although a primary prevention approach may be costly in terms of finances and requirements for organizational change, these costs may be offset by increased effectiveness in remediating an expensive and intractable societal problem.

SUMMARY

Externalizing disorders constitute a difficult and multidimensional class of behaviors that has been resistant to diverse intervention strategies. The characteristics and stability of the disorders have been well documented, as have personal, family, school, peer, and other correlates. Successful prevention of these disorders must take into account the complexities of the syndrome, which will require collaboration and coordination across a number of settings and among the numerous community agencies and service delivery sites that serve these children. Particularly given the lack of effective, lasting interventions for chronic, severe externalizing problems, primary prevention strategies may be the best hope for resolving this difficult dilemma.

REFERENCES

American Psychiatric Association. (1987). *Diagnostic and statistical manual of mental disorders* (3rd ed., rev.). Washington, DC: Author.

Asarnow, J.R. (1983). Children with peer adjustment problems: Sequential and nonsequential analyses of school behaviors. *Journal of Consulting and Clinical Psychology, 51*(5), 709–717.

Bale, P. (1981). Behaviour problems and their relationship to reading difficulty. *Journal of Research in Reading, 4*(2), 123–135.

Barkley, R.A. (1990). *Attention deficit hyperactivity disorder.* New York: Guilford Press.

Barkley, R.A., Fischer, M., Edelbrock, C.S., & Smallish, L. (1990). The adolescent outcome of hyperactive children diagnosed by research criteria: I. An 8-year prospective follow-up study. *Journal of the American Academy of Child and Adolescent Psychiatry, 29*(4), 546–557.

Bates, J., & Bayles, K. (1988). Attachment and the development of behavior problems. In J. Belsky & T. Nezworski (Eds.), *Clinical implications of attachment* (pp. 253–299). Hillsdale, NJ: Lawrence Erlbaum Associates.

Boyle, M.H., & Offord, D.R. (1990). Primary prevention of conduct disorder: Issues and prospects. *Journal of the American Academy of Child and Adolescent Psychiatry, 29*(2), 227–233.

Brandenburg, N.A., Friedman, R.M., & Silver, S.E. (1990). The epidemiology of childhood psychiatric disorders: Prevalence findings from recent studies. *Journal of the American Academy of Child and Adolescent Psychiatry, 29*(1), 76–83.

Cairns, R.B., Cairns, B.D., & Neckerman, H.J. (1989). Early school dropout: Configurations and determinants. *Child Development, 60*, 1437–1452.

Cairns, R.B., Cairns, B.D., Neckerman, H.J., Gest, S.D., & Gariepy, J.L. (1988). Social networks and aggressive behavior: Peer support or peer rejection? *Developmental Psychology, 24*(6), 815–823.

Campagna, A.F., & Harter, S. (1975). Moral judgment in sociopathic and normal children. *Journal of Personality and Social Psychology, 31*(2), 199–205.

Cohen, P., Kasen, S.K., Brook, J.S., & Struening, E.L. (1991). Diagnostic predictors of treatment patterns in a cohort of adolescents. *Journal of the American Academy of Child and Adolescent Psychiatry, 30*(6), 989–993.

Costello, E.J. (1989). Developments in child psychiatric epidemiology. *Journal of the American Academy of Child and Adolescent Psychiatry, 28*(4), 836–841.

Dishion, T.J., & Loeber, R. (1985). Adolescent marijuana and alcohol use: The role of parents and peers revisited. *American Journal of Drug and Alcohol Abuse, 11*(1–2), 11–15.

Dishion, T.J., Patterson, G.R., & Stoolmiller, M. (1991). Family, school, and behavioral antecedents to early adolescent involvement with antisocial peers. *Developmental Psychology, 27*(1), 172–180.

Dodge, K.A. (1993). Social–cognitive mechanisms in the development of conduct disorder and depression. In L.W. Porter & M.R. Rosenzweig (Eds.), *Annual review of psychology* (pp. 559–584). Palo Alto, CA: Annual Reviews, Inc.

Dodge, K.A., Coie, J.D., & Brakke, N.P. (1982). Behavior patterns of socially rejected and neglected preadolescents: The roles of social approach and aggression. *Journal of Abnormal Child Psychology, 10*(3), 389–410.

Dodge, K.A., Price, J.M., Bachorowski, J., & Newman, J.P. (1990). Hostile attributional biases in severely aggressive adolescents. *Journal of Abnormal Psychology, 99*, 385–392.

Dumas, J.E. (1989). Treating antisocial behavior in children: Child and family approaches. *Clinical Psychology Review, 9*(2), 197–222.

Dumas, J.E., & Wahler, R.G. (1985). Indiscriminate mothering as a contextual factor in aggressive-oppositional child behavior: "Damned if you do, damned if you don't." *Journal of Abnormal Child Psychology, 13*(1), 1–17.

DuPaul, G.J., Guevremont, D.C., & Barkley, R.A. (1991). Attention deficit hyperactivity disorder. In T.R. Kratochwill & R.J. Morris (Eds.), *The practice of child therapy* (2nd ed., pp. 115–144). New York: Pergamon Press.

Finn, J.D. (1988). School performance of adolescents in juvenile court. *Urban Education, 23*(2), 150–161.

French, D.C. (1988). Heterogeneity of peer-rejected boys: Aggressive and nonaggressive subtypes. *Child Development, 59*(4), 976–985.

Frick, P.J., Lahey, B.B., Christ, M.A.G., Loeber, R., & Green, S. (1991). History of childhood behavior problems in biological relatives of boys with attention deficit hyperactivity disorder and conduct disorder. *Journal of Clinical Child Psychology, 20*(4), 445–451.

Gabel, S., & Shindledecker, R. (1991). Aggressive behavior in youth: Characteristics, outcome, and psychiatric diagnoses. *Journal of the American Academy of Child and Adolescent Psychiatry, 30*(6), 982–988.

Griffin, G.W. (1987). Childhood predictive characteristics of aggressive adolescents. *Exceptional Children, 54,* 246–252.

Hawkins, J.D., & Weis, J.G. (1985). The social development model: An integrated approach to delinquency prevention. *Journal of Primary Prevention, 6*(2), 73–95.

Herbert, M. (1987). *Conduct disorders of childhood and adolescence: A social learning perspective.* Chichester, UK: John Wiley & Sons.

Hinshaw, S.P. (1992). Externalizing behavior problems and academic underachievement in childhood and adolescence: Causal relationships and underlying mechanisms. *Psychological Bulletin, 111*(1), 127–155.

Hogan, A.E., & Quay, H.C. (1984). Cognition in child and adolescent behavior disorders. In B.B. Lahey & A.E. Kazdin (Eds.), *Advances in clinical child psychology* (pp. 1–34). New York: Plenum Press.

Hymel, S., Rubin, K.H., & Rowden, L. (1990). Children's peer relationships: Longitudinal prediction of internalizing and externalizing problems from middle to late childhood. *Child Development, 61,* 2004–2021.

Jessor, R. (1991). Risk behavior in adolescence: A psychosocial framework for understanding and action. *Journal of Adolescent Health, 12*(4), 597–605.

Jurkovic, G.J., & Prentice, N.M. (1977). Relation of moral and cognitive development to dimensions of juvenile delinquency. *Journal of Abnormal Psychology, 86*(4), 414–420.

Kauffman, J.M. (1993). *Characteristics of emotional and behavioral disorders of children and youth* (5th ed.). New York: Merrill.

Kazdin, A.E. (1987). *Conduct disorders in childhood and adolescence.* Newbury Park, CA: Sage Publications.

Kazdin, A.E. (1989). Conduct and oppositional disorders. In C.G. Last & M. Hersen (Eds.), *Handbook of psychiatric diagnoses* (pp. 129–155). New York: John Wiley & Sons.

Kazdin, A.E., Esveldt-Dawson, K., French, N.H., & Unis, A.S. (1987). Problem-solving skills training and relationship therapy in the treatment of antisocial child behavior. *Journal of Consulting and Clinical Psychology, 55*(1), 76–85.

Kupersmidt, J.B., & Coie, J.D. (1990). Preadolescent peer status, aggression, and school adjustment as predictors of externalizing problems in adolescence. *Child Development, 61,* 1350–1362.

Ladd, G.S., Hart, C.H., & Price, J.M. (1990). Preschoolers' behavioral orientations and patterns of peer control: Predictive of peer status? In S.R. Asher & J.D. Coie (Eds.), *Peer rejection in childhood* (pp. 90–115). Cambridge, UK: Cambridge University Press.

Lahey, B.B., Russo, M.F., Walker, J.L., & Piacentini, J.C. (1989). Personality characteristics of the mothers of children with disruptive behavior disorders. *Journal of Consulting and Clinical Psychology, 57*(4), 512–515.

Lewis, D.O., Shanok, S.S., Pincus, J.H., & Glaser, G.H. (1979). Violent juvenile delinquents: Psychiatric, neurological, psychological, and abuse factors. *Journal of the American Academy of Child Psychiatry, 18*(5), 307–319.

Lochman, J.E., Burch, P.R., Curry, J.F., & Lampron, L.B. (1984). Treatment and generalization effects of cognitive-behavioral and goal-setting interventions with aggressive boys. *Journal of Consulting and Clinical Psychology, 52*(5), 915–916.

Loeber, R. (1990). Development and risk factors of juvenile antisocial behavior and delinquency. *Clinical Psychology Review, 10*(1), 1–42.

Loeber, R., & Dishion, T.J. (1983). Early predictors of male delinquency: A review. *Psychological Bulletin, 94*(1), 68–99.

McGee, R., Share, D., Moffitt, T.E., Williams, S., & Silva, P.A. (1988). Reading disability, behaviour problems, and juvenile delinquency. In D.H. Saklofske & S.B.G. Eysenck (Eds.), *Individual differences in children and adolescents: International perspectives* (pp. 158–172). London: Hodder & Stoughton.

McGee, R., Williams, S., & Silva, P.A. (1984). Behavioral and developmental characteristics of aggressive, hyperactive, and hyperactive-aggressive boys. *Journal of the American Academy of Child Psychiatry, 23*(3), 270–290.

Miller, G.E., & Prinz, R.J. (1990). Enhancement of social learning family interventions for childhood conduct disorder. *Psychological Bulletin, 108*(2), 291–307.

Mitchell, S., & Rosa, P. (1981). Boyhood behaviour problems as precursors of criminality: A 15-year follow-up study. *Journal of Child Psychology and Psychiatry & Allied Disciplines, 22*(1), 19–23.

Newcomb, M.D., & McGee, L. (1991). Influence of sensation seeking on general deviance and specific problem behaviors from adolescence to young adulthood. *Journal of Personality and Social Psychology, 61*(4), 614.

Offord, D.R., Alder, R.J., & Boyle, M.H. (1986). Prevalence and sociodemographic correlates of conduct disorder. *American Journal of Social Psychiatry, 6*(4), 272–278.

Olweus, D. (1979). Stability of aggressive reactive patterns in males: A review. *Psychological Bulletin, 86*(4), 852–875.

Patterson, G.R. (1982). *Coercive family process.* Eugene, OR: Castalia Publishing.

Patterson, G.R., DeBaryshe, B.D., & Ramsey, E. (1989). A developmental perspective on antisocial behavior. *American Psychologist, 44*(2), 329–335.

Patterson, G.R., & Stouthamer-Loeber, M. (1984). The correlation of family management practices and delinquency. *Child Development, 55,* 1299–1307.

Pettit, G.S., Bates, J.E., & Dodge, K.A. (1993). Family interaction patterns and children's conduct problems at home and school: A longitudinal perspective. *School Psychology Review, 22*(3), 403–420.

Reeves, J.C., Werry, J.S., Elkind, G.S., & Zametkin, A. (1987). Attention deficit, conduct, oppositional, and anxiety disorders in children: II. Clinical characteristics. *Journal of the American Academy of Child and Adolescent Psychiatry, 26*(2), 144–155.

Rincker, J.L. (1990). Academic and intellectual characteristics of adolescent juvenile offenders. *Journal of Correctional Education, 41*(3), 124–131.

Robins, L.N. (1966). *Deviant children grown up.* Baltimore: Williams & Wilkins.

Robins, L.N. (1978). Sturdy childhood predictors of adult antisocial behavior. Replications from longitudinal studies. *Psychological Medicine, 8*(4), 611–622.

Robins, L.N. (1991). Conduct disorder. *Journal of the American Academy of Child Psychiatry, 20*(4), 556–580.

Shantz, D.W. (1986). Conflict, aggression, and peer status: An observational study. *Child Development, 57,* 1322–1332.

Shapiro, S.K., & Hynd, G.W. (1993). Psychobiological basis of conduct disorder. *School Psychology Review, 22*(3), 386–402.

Short, R.J., & Shapiro, S.K. (1993). Conduct disorders: A framework for understanding and intervention in schools and communities. *School Psychology Review, 22*(3), 362–375.

Short, R.J., & Simeonsson, R.J. (1986). Social cognition and aggression in delinquent adolescent males. *Adolescence, 21*(81), 159–176.

Simeonsson, R.J. (1991). Primary, secondary, and tertiary prevention in early intervention. *Journal of Early Intervention, 15*(2), 124–134.

Spivack, G., Platt, J.J., & Shure, M.B. (1976). *The problem-solving approach to adjustment.* San Francisco: Jossey-Bass.

Stewart, J.T., Myers, W.C., Burket, R.C., & Lyles, W.D. (1990). A review of the pharmacotherapy of aggression in children and adolescents. *Journal of the American Academy of Child and Adolescent Psychiatry, 29*(2), 269–277.

Szatmari, P., Boyle, M., & Offord, D.R. (1989). ADDH and conduct disorder: Degree of diagnostic overlap and differences among correlates. *Journal of the American Academy of Child and Adolescent Psychiatry, 28*(6), 865–872.

Tremblay, R.E., Masse, B., Perron, D., Leblanc, M., Schwartzman, A.E., & Ledingham, J.E. (1992). Early disruptive behavior, poor school achievement, delinquent behavior, and delinquent personality: Longitudinal analyses. *Journal of Consulting and Clinical Psychology, 60*(1), 1–10.

Waas, G.A. (1987). Aggressive rejected children: Implications for school psychologists. *Journal of School Psychology, 25*(4), 383–388.

Walker, H.M., Stieber, S., & Ramsey, E. (1990). Middle school behavioral profiles of antisocial and at-risk control boys: Descriptive and predictive outcomes. *Exceptionality, A Research Journal, 1*(1), 61–77.

Walker, H.M., Stieber, S., & Ramsey, E. (1991). Longitudinal prediction of the school achievement, adjustment, and delinquency of antisocial versus at-risk boys. *RASE: Remedial and Special Education, 12*(4), 43–51.

Webster-Stratton, C. (1993). Strategies for helping early school-aged children with oppositional defiant and conduct disorders. *School Psychology Review, 22*(3), 421–457.

Webster-Stratton, C., & Eyberg, S.M. (1982). Child temperament: Relationship with child behavior problems and parent–child interactions. *Journal of Clinical Child Psychology, 11*(2), 123–129.

Webster-Stratton, C., Hollinsworth, T., & Kolpacoff, M. (1989). The long-term effectiveness and clinical significance of three cost-effective training programs for families with conduct-problem children. *Journal of Consulting and Clinical Psychology, 57*(4), 550–553.

West, D.J. (1982). *Delinquency: Its roots, careers, and prospects.* Oxford, UK: Heinemann.

Wolf, M.M., Braukmann, C.J., & Ramp, K.A. (1987). Serious delinquent behavior as part of a significantly handicapping condition: Cures and supportive environments. *Journal of Applied Behavior Analysis, 20*(4), 347–359.

12

Internalizing Affective Disorders

Jayne E. Bucy

On Long Island, a 10-year-old girl is rescued from an underground cell where she had been held captive for 16 days by her nextdoor neighbor. Katie was a thin, neglected child who had few friends. Neighbors described her as a painfully lonely child who sat on the front porch, hoping to befriend anyone walking by. In her loneliness, Katie became a target for the disturbed neighbor who befriended her with a Slurpee and a video movie before imprisoning her in the coffin-like cell.

Schemo, 1993

In a Washington, D.C., suburb, a high school senior makes a fateful decision. Jerry had a history of depression and at least one suicide attempt. He was described as a young man with few friends who felt abandoned by his family. One morning in early May, Jerry decided not to go to class. Instead, he put a note and his helmet on the sidewalk and deliberately crashed his motorcycle at full speed into the brick wall of his high school.

Baker, 1990

These stories reflect the tragedies associated with behavior and emotional problems experienced by many children and youth in contemporary society. Not all outcomes are as tragic, but the human toll of these problems is often underestimated. Witness the experience of children in schools across America, where they are learning much more than the three Rs. They are learning about themselves, about each other, and about the reciprocal nature of friendship. But for those children who are rejected by their classmates, for those who lack the social competence to make and keep friends, for the shy, withdrawn child who is anxious and quiet around his or her peers, the lessons are painful and the penalty for failure to develop social competence is harsh. Friendship provides a source of emotional strength for children, and the absence of friendship can foretell a lifelong risk for social isolation, depression, and anxiety.

Epidemiological estimates of behavior disorders in school-age children vary from 7% to 20% with most studies citing a 15%–18% rate (Cicchetti & Toth, 1988). These disorders, commonly differentiated as *internalizing* or *externalizing* are a frequent focus of research attention (Achenbach & Edelbrock, 1978). Internalizing or overcontrolling behaviors is typified by turning emotions inward, which results in feelings of loneliness, social withdrawal, depression, and anxiety. Conversely, externalizing problems is characterized by undercontrolling behavior typified by such disruptive, acting-out actions as aggression, hyperactivity, and conduct disorders (see Short and Brokaw, chap. 11, this volume).

This chapter describes the prevalence, course, and complications associated with internalizing problems in children and youth. The author examines current intervention approaches to children with these behaviors and describes a preventive framework in which to address these issues.

Researchers and mental health professionals have found it difficult to agree on a conceptualization of internalizing disorders. Diagnostic systems such as the American Psychiatric Association's (APA) *Diagnostic and Statistical Manual of Mental Disorders* (third ed., rev.) (DSM-III-R, 1987) or eligibility procedures for special education placement under the Individuals with Disabilities Education Act (IDEA) offer means of classifying individuals with internalizing disorders in order to provide treatment services. Behavior rating scales such as the Child Behavior Checklist (Achenbach, 1991) operationalize a definition of internalizing behaviors. As a result of these and other definitional attempts, a wide range of behaviors and psychological disturbances have been identified as internalizing (Reynolds, 1990b). The focus of this chapter is limited to two internalizing problems, loneliness and social withdrawal, and to the psychiatric disorders of depression and anxiety. Certainly there is substantial overlap among these problems and the children who display these symptoms. Although it can also be argued that these problems represent a continuum of behavior, this author enforces a somewhat artificial separation by discussing them as distinct entities in an effort to facilitate consideration of their features and implications for intervention and prevention.

RISK CHAINS OF INTERNALIZING PROBLEMS

Let us begin by examining the nature of internalizing problems as they are manifested by tracing the risk chain presented in Figure 12.1. Although childhood internalizing problems have many etiologies, a

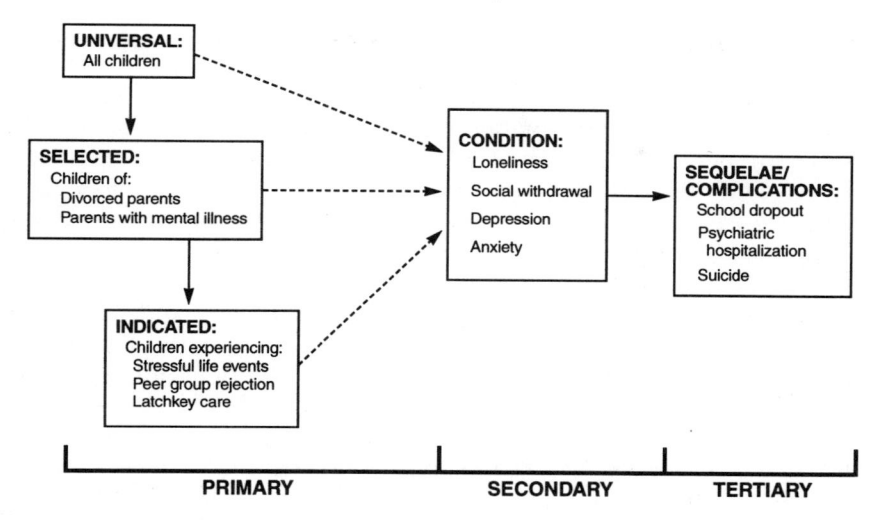

Figure 12.1. Risk chains of internalizing problems.

general risk chain can be proposed to examine the relationship of primary, secondary, and tertiary prevention. In this model, the manifestation of a given internalizing problem is defined in terms of secondary prevention; that is, to reduce the existing number of cases of these problems through a curative approach. We begin with an examination of the problem at this level.

Secondary Level

How common are internalizing problems among our children and youth? An examination of each internalizing behavior can help provide answers.

Loneliness The *American Heritage Dictionary* (Davies, 1976) has defined *lonely* as "without companions or companionship . . . dejected by the awareness of being alone" (p. 415). This defines the daily experience of many children. In a study of 522 third- through sixth graders, almost 14% agreed that the statement, "I feel alone," was true for them most of the time (Asher, Hymel, & Renshaw, 1984). Other statements such as, "I have nobody to talk to" and "I don't have anyone to play with," were endorsed by 12% and 11% of the children, respectively. Asher et al. found an inverse relationship between the number of "best friends" a child has and his or her level of self-reported loneliness. Furthermore, the loneliest children report significant levels of social dissatisfaction and receive the lowest sociometric ratings by their peers (Asher et al.). Feelings of loneliness may not be overcome easily. Research has shown that loneliness in middle childhood is relatively stable across time, particularly for those children who report the highest levels of loneliness (Renshaw & Brown, 1993).

Social Withdrawal The importance of peer relationships in childhood is almost indisputable, and the penalty for failure to develop social competence may be later psychological maladjustment (Parker & Asher, 1987). Social withdrawal has been identified as a relatively stable characteristic associated with both childhood depression and isolation (Rubin & Mills, 1988). Most children will be timid among their peers at one time or another. Among preschoolers, shyness, trouble working and playing with others, fearfulness in daily situations, and speaking more softly than peers are behaviors that most children display at one time or another. For some children, however, these behaviors become dysfunctional. Among 5-year-olds, for example, 7% of both boys and girls may avoid contact with others almost all the time (Crowther, Bond, & Rolf, 1981). Nearly 1 child in 13 is identified by teachers as socially withdrawn in Grades 2–5 (Strauss, Forehand, Smith, & Frame, 1986). Social withdrawal seems to be a stable trait, and socially withdrawn children tend to become more withdrawn over time. Approximately one in three socially withdrawn children in Grades 4 and above will continue to demonstrate extremely withdrawn behavior 3 years later (Moskowitz, Schwartzman, & Ledingham, 1985).

As in the case of loneliness, the concept of risk chains is supported by research showing that social withdrawal in second grade is associated with loneliness in the fourth grade and with teacher-rated anxiety and depression in the fifth grade (Rubin & Mills, 1988). Furthermore, social withdrawal in kindergarten and elementary grades predicts such internalizing problems as loneliness, negative self-perception of social competence, and limited social support in the ninth grade (Rubin & Mills, 1988).

In addition to loneliness and social withdrawal, there are two internalizing behaviors that, in extreme cases, are recognized as psychiatric conditions by the American Psychiatric Association. Although these conditions are diagnosed using clearly defined criteria, individuals who do not manifest all the clinical symptoms may still warrant and receive treatment from mental health professionals. This chapter first discusses disorders of depression, and then anxiety disorders, and finally, those individuals who manifest two or more disorders in tandem.

Depressive Disorders The DSM-III-R (APA, 1987) describes two depressive disorders that can be identified in childhood and adolescence: *major depression* and *dysthymia*.[1] Major depression is a severe

---

[1]The fourth edition of *Diagnostic and Statistical Manual of Mental Disorders* (DSM-IV-R) changes in definition did not affect this author's discussion of major depression and dysthymia.

form of depression characterized by sadness, hopelessness, and loss of pleasure in previously satisfying pastimes. Symptoms may include changes in appetite; significant weight loss or gain; insomnia or excessive sleeping; changes in psychomotor activity; loss of energy and feelings of fatigue; sense of worthlessness or guilt; loss of concentration; and, sometimes, recurrent thoughts of death or suicide. A diagnosis of major depressive episode requires that the symptoms be present for a duration of at least 2 weeks. Dysthymia is a chronic form of depression that shares many of the same features as major depression, but at a somewhat less severe level. Although the severity is less, individuals with dysthymia often manifest the disorder for years at a time (Reynolds, 1990a).

Prevalence In nonclinical samples, major depression is unusual among prepubertal children. An epidemiological study found the prevalence rates of past depressive disorders among 9-year-olds to be 1.1% for severe cases and 9.7% for mild cases (Kashani et al., 1983). By adolescence, however, depression becomes more common. An assessment of 3,283 12- to 14-year-olds in the southeastern United States found a prevalence rate in both males and females of approximately 9%. Rates of dysthymia were somewhat lower, at almost 8% for males and 5% for females (Garrison, Addy, Jackson, McKeown, & Waller, 1992).

Course Depression in childhood often follows a devastating course. The social behavior of depressed children in elementary school has been found to be characterized by more solitary, less interactive play. Depressed children frequently have more negative self-perceptions and lower self-worth than their peers (Altmann & Gotlib, 1988).

Depression is not easily remedied. Kovacs, Feinberg, Crouse-Novak, Paulauskas, and Finkelstein (1984) found the mean length of a major depressive episode among children ages 8–13 years to be 32 weeks. The rate of recovery was unaffected by treatment, with 92% of the children showing maximum recovery 18 months after onset. In a sample of nonreferred adolescents, Keller et al. (1988) found that in the first year following onset of the disorder, approximately one in five children had still not recovered. Dysthymic disorder was more prolonged, with a mean episode of 3 years and a maximum recovery rate of 89% after 6 years. Although gender was not a factor in recovery, age at first onset was. Younger children at the time of onset of major depression or dysthymia take longer to recover than older children (Kovacs et al., 1984).

Anxiety Disorders The DSM-III-R (APA, 1987) distinguishes three anxiety disorders of childhood and adolescence: *separation anxiety disorder, overanxious disorder,* and *avoidant disorder.* All these disorders are characterized by excessive fear, anxiety, and distress, although each disorder has a unique source for the anxiety. Separation anxiety disorder is marked by excessive fear of separation from parents (or other major attachment figure) or from home. Overanxious disorder involves nonspecific, yet excessive, worry or fear. Individuals with avoidant disorder are fearful of strangers; therefore, they avoid social situations and peer interactions.

Prevalence In a nonclinical sample of adolescents, rates of 3.6% for overanxious disorder and 2.4% for separation anxiety were cited (Beitchman, Inglis, & Schachter, 1992a). Anxiety is common in clinical samples, with separation anxiety disorders at an estimated rate of 47% (Last, 1989).

Course The course of anxiety disorders is often protracted and frequently disrupts normal family interactions and activities (Last, 1992). Children with anxiety disorders are challenging to family members who find it difficult to understand and cope with their fears. These children typically worry excessively and need constant reassurance. They have frequent nightmares and often refuse to go to school or to participate in other age-appropriate activities such as scouting or team sports. Somatic complaints of headache and stomachache are common.

Avoidant disorder may be precipitated by a stressful event such as moving to a new home or the illness or death of a family member. It is often seen at such times of childhood transition as moving from elementary to middle school. Although separation anxiety disorder may be either acute or chronic, avoidant and overanxious disorders tend to be chronic, longlasting, and exacerbated at times of stress. Social impairment is characteristic of all of these disorders.

Co-morbidity Often individuals will be diagnosed with depression as well as anxiety or another psychiatric disturbance. Co-morbidity, or the simultaneous occurrence of two or more disorders in an individual, is often indicative of a more serious illness and, especially among depressed individuals, co-morbidity is associated with an extended recovery period (Keller et al., 1988).

Prevalence Reynolds (1992) reported that 63% of a sample of 486 adolescents seen in a clinical setting presented with two or more psychiatric disorders. Among a community sample of 12- to 14-year-olds, Garrison et al. (1992) reported co-morbidity in almost three fourths of children exhibiting internalizing disorders, with separation anxiety frequently overlapping with depression. At least one study found panic disorders co-morbid with major depression in children, despite conventional wisdom that panic disorders are not experienced in childhood (Moreau, Weissman, & Warner, 1989). Children with overanxious disorders frequently exhibit an additional anxiety disorder, usually simple phobia (Last, Hersen, Kazdin, Finkelstein, &

Strauss, 1987). The prevalence of co-morbidity is so great, it led Garrison et al. (1992) to conclude that " 'pure' depression in adolescents is a rare entity" (p. 800).

Parenthetically, depression has also been found to co-occur with such externalizing problems as conduct disorder at a rate ranging from 8% to 37% (Garber, Quiggle, Panak, & Dodge, 1988). This group of depressed, acting-out children generally has a greater rate of long-term problems (Kovacs, Paulauskas, Gatsonis, & Richards, 1988) as well as increased risk for suicide (Hoberman & Garfinkle, 1988; Shafii, Steltz-Lenarsky, Derrick, Beckner, & Whittinghill, 1988). In many cases, despite the conviction that the conduct disorder was a complication of depression, it continued even after the depression remitted (Kovacs et al., 1988). Externalizing disorders have also been shown to co-occur with anxiety. Last, Hersen, Kazdin, Finkelstein, et al. (1987) found attention or oppositional disorders in almost one third of their sample of 69 anxious children.

These internalizing behaviors of loneliness, social withdrawal, depression, and anxiety are frequently long lasting and problematic to both individual children and their families. They are clearly likely to be of concern to school personnel as well. Once identified, these problematic behaviors should become the focus of treatment efforts to reduce the number of children manifesting such problems and to minimize the potential development of associated complications.

However, how many of the children who manifest these conditions actually receive treatment? Studies of children with depression indicate that only a minority are provided with necessary treatment. Some estimates are that one child in five with a psychiatric disorder is treated, whereas others cite treatment rates of about 50% of affected children (Kashani et al., 1983; Offord, 1985).

Treatment, when it is sought, may take the form of individual therapy for the child or family therapy. Medication may be prescribed for children with depression or anxiety in conjunction with therapy. Children may be identified and placed in special education programs if their internalizing behaviors have a negative impact upon their school performance, although placement is more common for internalizing children with disruptive behaviors. Loneliness and social withdrawal are often left untreated, although parents and teachers may express concern for children they identify with these behaviors.

Tertiary Level

Continuing along the risk chain (Figure 12.1), some complications or major sequelae associated with internalizing problems can be identified. Three complications particularly devastating to both the individual and society are addressed below.

School Dropout It is estimated that as many as 4% of 10th through 12th graders drop out of school in any single year (U.S. Bureau of the Census, 1992). Students may leave school prematurely for a number of reasons, but the overriding reason is their sense of isolation and loneliness. In a review of the literature regarding school dropout and peer relationships, Parker and Asher (1987) concluded that:

> These studies indicate a link between drop-out status and barometers of earlier peer-relationship difficulties of every type (peer and teacher measures of acceptance, aggressiveness or shyness/withdrawal). . . . Children who were poorly accepted by their peers were found to be more likely to drop out of school than children who were better accepted. (p. 366)

Other dropouts have developed school phobia as a complication of depression or an anxiety disorder. Among a group of 26 early adolescents referred to an outpatient clinic for school phobia, 69% were diagnosed with depressive disorder, 62% with anxiety disorder, and 50% had both disorders (Bernstein & Garfinkle, 1986). Although not all school dropouts have school phobia, there appears to be an association between these problems.

Psychiatric Hospitalization For those children whose depression is so severe that it requires hospitalization, there is evidence that they will not recover soon. Most are hospitalized because they have become suicidal, uncontrollable, or psychotic. Rehospitalization rates of 35% in the first year and 45% in the second year after discharge illustrate the continued expense and human toll that childhood depression causes (Asarnow et al., 1988).

Suicide According to the U.S. Bureau of the Census (1992), suicide was the third leading cause of death in the United States for 15- to 24-year-olds in 1989. Death rates increase dramatically at adolescence. A rate of 1.4 per 100,000 for children between the ages of 10 and 14 years swells to 11.3 per 100,000 for young people ages 15–24 years.

Interviewing a community sample of 12- to 14-year-olds with high levels of self-reported depression, Garrison, Jackson, Addy, McKeown, and Waller (1991) found that 8.7% of females and 4.0% of males reported suicidal ideation within a 12-month period. Suicidal attempts were reported by 1.9% of males and 1.5% of females. Sexual abuse, social isolation, academic failure, loneliness, and loss of self-esteem are associated risk factors of adolescent suicide. Many researchers point to the roles of alcohol and drug abuse and their association with depression as risk factors for suicidal behavior (Smith, 1992).

However, suicide rates do not tell the complete story of human suffering. It is estimated that for every completed suicide, there are 50–200 attempted suicides (Committee on Adolescence of the American Academy of Pediatrics, 1980). Ryan et al. (1987) reported that 25% of preadolescents and 34% of adolescents made at least one suicide attempt during a major depressive episode, with adolescent attempts rated as significantly more lethal. For those who attempt suicide, it is estimated that between 10% and 14% will make a second attempt within a year (Brooksbank, 1985).

These events—school dropout, psychiatric hospitalization, and suicidal behavior—are common sequelae of internalizing problems. They make evident the enormously complicated issues related to the treatment of internalizing disorders, the often exacerbated and prolonged course of the illness, and greatly increase the financial expense of treatment to restore the affected child to well-being.

In 1985 in the United States, we lost 1,319 children under the age of 15 to mental illness mortality (Rice, Kelman, Miller, & Dunmeyer, 1990). This represents an estimated loss of 95,000 person years and $305 million in lost productivity. Other related direct and indirect costs associated with mental illness not included in these estimates are public expenditures for law enforcement, criminal justice proceedings, legal defenses, motor vehicle accidents, social welfare, and the value of time spent by family members in caring for the child with a mental illness. The pain and suffering experienced by the individual during childhood and often into adulthood, impaired school achievement, diminished self-esteem, lost social and familial relationships, inability to find pleasure and fulfillment in life, as well as a decreased capacity to live independently as an adult are some of the immeasurable costs associated with internalizing problems at the secondary and tertiary levels.

Secondary prevention efforts to reduce internalizing disorders are costly and, as pointed out, many children do not receive the services they need to return to well-being. At the tertiary level, interventions are increasingly expensive, both in terms of time and effort. Most importantly, in both secondary and tertiary prevention the focus is reactive, treating existing conditions and their sequelae. There is an urgent need to take a proactive approach and to promote the development of adaptive skills and behaviors. To this end, both cost-effective and humanistic goals can be addressed by mental health professionals and school and community resources through a comprehensive investment in primary prevention efforts.

RISK FACTORS OF INTERNALIZING PROBLEMS

A number of variables have been implicated as risk factors for the development of internalizing problems. Drawing on a primary prevention framework, Table 12.1 lists some risk factors and associated problems at selected and indicated levels.

Table 12.1. Risk factors of internalizing problems of children and youth

Risk factor	Associated problems	Reference
	Selected	
Ethnicity (African-American)	Increased risk for separation anxiety	Velez, Johnson, & Cohen, 1989
Low socioeconomic status	Increased risk for separation anxiety, depression, and loneliness	Velez, Johnson, & Cohen, 1989; Kaplan, Hong, & Weinhold, 1984
High socioeconomic status	Increased risk for affective disorders	Asher, Hymel, & Renshaw, 1984; Lavori, Keller, Beardslee, & Dorer, 1988
Caregiver with depression and panic disorder	42% of offspring with DSM-III-R diagnosis	Weissman, Leckman, Merikangas, Gammon, & Prusoff, 1984
Caregiver with depression and agoraphobia	28% of offspring with DSM diagnosis	
Caregiver with depression only	26% of offspring with DSM diagnosis	
Caregiver with depression and anxiety disorder	15% of offspring with DSM diagnosis	
Depressed parent	Earlier onset of depression in offspring as compared with normal parents (12 years vs. 16.8 years)	Weissman, Gammon, John, Merikangas, Warner, Prusoff, & Sholomskas, 1987
Onset of parental depression before age 20	Increased risk for major depression; Increased risk for prepubescent onset of depression	Weissman, Warner, Wickramaratne, & Prusoff, 1988
Maternal/paternal affective illness	Increased risk for child affective disorder	Lavori, Keller, Beardslee, & Dorer, 1988; Welner & Rice, 1988
Mother with anxiety disorder	Associated with anxiety disorder in offspring	Last, Hersen, Kazdin, Francis, & Grubb, 1987
Parental divorce	Increased risk for internalizing problems	Kalter, Kloner, Schreier, & Okla, 1989
Maternal pregnancy problems	Increased risk for overanxious disorder	Velez, Johnson, & Cohen, 1989
	Indicated	
Not living with natural parents	Significantly correlated with major depression and dysthymia	Garrison, Addy, Jackson, McKeown, & Waller, 1992

(continued)

Table 12.1. (continued)

Risk factor	Associated problems	Reference
	Indicated	
Stressful life events	Significantly correlated with major depression	Garrison, Addy, Jackson, McKeown, & Waller, 1992
Peer group rejection	Teacher-rated anxiety	Rubin & Mills, 1988
Insecurely attached (males)	Increased psychopathology	Lewis, Feiring, McGoffog, & Jaskir, 1984
Latchkey child	Increased social isolation	Berman, Winkleby, Chesterman, & Boyce, 1992
Behavior inhibition	High risk for anxiety disorders	Biederman, Rosenbaum, Bolduc-Murphy, Faraone, Chaloff, Hirshfeld, & Kagan, 1993

DSM-III-R = Diagnostic and statistical manual of mental disorders (3rd ed., rev.) (American Psychiatric Association, 1987).

TOWARD A TRANSACTIONAL MODEL OF PREVENTION

It is misleading to assume that any one child, family, or environmental characteristic creates a cause–effect action in the development of childhood dysfunction. Instead, outcomes are more likely to be the product of multiple dynamic interactions of a number of variables during the developmental period (Rubin, Hymel, Mills, & Rose-Krasnor, 1988; Sameroff & Chandler, 1975). Research of the risk factors is a means of conceptualizing the development of internalizing problems within a transactional framework.

Rubin and Mills (1991) describe a scenario in which a child's dispositional characteristics interact with caregiver attitudes and beliefs in an environment that contributes its own stressors. This so-called "Temple of Doom" scenario (Rubin & Mills, 1991, p. 304) produces a child who is insecurely attached, socially inhibited, and unprepared for the social interaction of childhood. This retarded development of social competence, according to Rubin and Mills (1991):

> when combined with "wariness" and felt insecurity may lead to the development of negative self-appraisals of competence, which in turn exacerbates withdrawal from peers. These factors *taken together* are hypothesized to predict difficulties of an internalizing nature, such as loneliness and depression. (p. 306)

Peer reactions begin to solidify a child's negative self-perception. We know that children are likely to view aggression in peers as a sign of maladjustment (Coie & Pennington, 1976), but unlike aggression, children are generally forgiving of socially withdrawn behavior at young ages because they have not yet developed the social schema with which to form a social perception of the behavior. But as they grow older, children become more sensitive to social withdrawal in their peers and are more likely to view that behavior as negative and reject the child (Rubin & Mills, 1988; Younger & Boyko, 1987).

A disruption in the family, as the result of divorce, for example, may set into motion a variety of stressful events that interact in such a way as to place some children at increased risk for the development of internalizing disorders. Loss of economic status, parental hostility, and possible parental depression or anxiety may exacerbate the adverse effects of the divorce upon the child (Kalter, Kloner, Schreier, & Okla, 1989).

Much of family experience is constructed in the form of family rituals. Families celebrate anniversaries and holidays. Such rituals mark rites of passage and reward accomplishments. Families also come together to mourn, to pray, to feast, and to fast. These rituals are a powerful aspect of family life that provide a receptacle for affective interactions between family members. Disruption of family rituals, whether through divorce or such parental disturbances as psychopathology or drug or alcohol abuse may put children at risk for later dysfunction (Wolin & Bennett, 1984).

In addition to those factors that exacerbate the development of psychopathology, there are also factors that act to facilitate good outcomes. These "compensatory factors" (Cicchetti & Aber, 1986, p. 115) increase an individual's resilience to the effect of negative or stressful life events. In a primary prevention framework, efforts that increase a child's resiliency may also increase the likelihood of good outcomes.

PRIMARY PREVENTION

In light of the extent of human suffering and the burden to society from childhood internalizing disorders and their associated complications, it is evident that internalizing disorders represent an important public health concern. In order to enhance the psychological well-being of children and reduce the incidence of internalizing problems, we must provide primary prevention services. In the context of the model elaborated earlier in this volume, primary prevention can take the form of *universal, selected,* or *indicated* efforts.

Primary prevention efforts that promote psychological well-being often begin in grade school or within community settings. Primary prevention efforts identified as selected are those that describe a subgroup, or more specifically, situational variables that place children at risk as a group by virtue of group membership. Indicated primary prevention efforts are those targeted for children characterized by individual risk factors.

Many currently offered programs address the goals of primary prevention, and they are likely to have a preventive impact on children who would otherwise develop internalizing disorders (Weissberg, Caplan, & Harwood, 1991). Examples of programs that seem consistent within this conceptual framework are described below.

Universal Primary Prevention

Universal primary prevention can be defined in terms of programs and activities designed for all children. Teachers and guidance counselors have been providing universal primary prevention services since the 1970s, although they may not have identified these programs within the prevention framework. Affective education programs such as Developing Understanding of Self and Others (DUSO, Dinkmeyer, 1970; DUSO-R, Dinkmeyer & Dinkmeyer, 1982) are widely offered to groups of children by guidance counselors and classroom teachers. Through the use of stories, pictures, role playing, creative activities, and puppet play, DUSO attempts to improve self-awareness, increase positive self-images, and facilitate relationships between self and others. The positive impact of these programs upon self-esteem and social adjustment in young children argues for the value of affective education in the classroom (Bockoven & Morse, 1986; Morse, Bockoven & Bettesworth, 1988).

Another universal primary prevention program was proposed by Glasser (1969), who called for a reconstruction of the public school system. His approach, referred to as Reality Therapy, challenged schools to break with the tradition of common practices that led many children to experience continuous failure, and resulting loneliness and withdrawal. In *Schools Without Failure,* Glasser outlines the design for schools that can become places where all children succeed, develop problem-solving skills, and acquire social understanding and tolerance for others. He identifies the importance of heterogeneous classes, abolishing traditional grading systems, and improving teacher training. Many of Glasser's strategies have been incorporated into classrooms throughout the nation. By improving the psychological climate of the school environment, these practices may increase the well-being and resiliency of children, thereby decreasing the development of internalizing problems.

Selected Primary Prevention

Children at selected risk for internalizing disorders can receive primary prevention services through programs that target children identified by group membership. The *Children of Divorce Intervention Pro-*

gram (CODIP) (Alpert-Gillis, Pedro-Carroll, & Cowen, 1989), offered to elementary-age children whose parents have divorced, increases social support and improves coping skills. This program, offered to small groups of children, attempts to facilitate a mutually supportive group experience and to assist children in identifying and expressing their feelings related to the divorce, in gaining an accurate and realistic understanding of the divorce, in increasing problem-solving skills, and in highlighting positive qualities of themselves and their families.

When children who have participated in CODIP were compared with children who received no prevention program, Alpert-Gillis et al. (1989) found that the participating children reported greater adjustment to the divorce and improved ability to cope. Parents and teachers also reported significant improvements in social skills and the children's ability to cope with their feelings.

Indicated Primary Prevention

Unlike children at selected risk, children at indicated risk have individual characteristics that increase their likelihood of developing an internalizing problem; that is, they are at risk on an individual basis. Although more research is needed to differentiate clearly those factors that increase an individual's risk, some already are linked clearly with the internalizing condition or disorders. Problems in social interaction is one such factor. Intervention techniques for children who have difficulty interacting successfully with others typically take the form of social skills training. These interventions generally include modeling and coaching of appropriate social behavior by teachers and peers, increasing skill performance by rehearsal and reinforcement, removing barriers to successful performance, and increasing the generalization of the newly acquired behavior (Gresham, 1990). Although efficacy research of social skills training has been methodologically questioned, the programs seem to offer some improvement of social interaction skills in young people (Conger & Keane, 1981).

What can we conclude about primary prevention of internalizing behaviors? Often, efforts do not identify themselves as programs to prevent internalizing disorders. The fact that a program influences the course of the development of these disorders may go unrecognized because outcome research fails to assess directly their impact on the development of internalizing disorders. We can, however, identify characteristics of these and other programs that are likely to contribute to the prevention of internalizing problems.

All these programs are offered to children at elementary school ages or younger. Although we have not yet identified a temporal "window of opportunity" (if one exists) to tell us when best to provide prevention, it seems likely that sooner, rather than later should be the goal, given the increased complications and prolonged course of illness associated with early onset of internalizing disorders. Moreover, these programs provide strategies to improve social problem-solving skills among the participants. Having the skills to initiate and maintain positive social interactions in childhood provides a means of coping with stress and increases a child's resiliency at times of crisis. Finally, these programs are offered within the child's social arena—the school. In this setting, where children spend a large portion of their day, every opportunity exists to learn and practice new skills in a natural environment with the aid of caring and attentive adults. School personnel are well advised to attend to the prevention of internalizing problems because the benefits to child well-being, classroom management, attendance, and academic achievement will become unquestionably apparent.

FOCUS OF FUTURE EFFORTS

Although some progress has been made toward identifying the risk factors associated with internalizing disorders, there is still much we do not know about the developmental pathways that lead to these disorders (Beitchman et al., 1992b). Why has more progress not been made toward identifying these factors? In general, internalizing problems have been neglected by researchers in favor of studies of externalizing disorders. Some explanations for this research bias include the following.

1. Internalizing problems are frequently difficult to detect, particularly for those who are not mental health professionals (Reynolds, 1990a).
2. Internalizing behaviors may not be viewed as problematic because these children are characteristically quiet, well behaved, and easily managed (Renken, Egeland, Marvinney, Mangelsdorf, & Sroufe, 1989).
3. Children with internalizing problems are generally more competent, are rated as more intelligent, are less egocentric, and are better readers, and they display more adaptive coping styles than those who externalize (Cohen, Gotlieb, Kershner, & Wehrspann, 1985).
4. Internalizing behaviors are generally recognized as being less stable over time, which leads to questions regarding their clinical signficance longitudinally (Cicchetti & Toth, 1988; Fischer, Rolf, Hasazi, & Cummings 1984).
5. Unlike those who internalize, children with externalizing behaviors generally make a greater impact on society by creating both personal and property damage (Beitchman et al., 1992a).

Research efforts are beginning to focus on clearly defining behaviors that are internalizing and identifying the associated risk factors. These efforts may increase the reliability with which children and youth who are at risk for developing internalizing problems can be identified in order to focus our energies on the prevention of these potentially devastating and debilitating disorders of children and youth.

SUMMARY

Internalizing problems of loneliness, social withdrawal, depression, and anxiety are experienced by many children and adolescents, and they exact substantial personal and financial tolls on individuals, families, and society. These behaviors are often longlasting, and they are frequently predictive of adult psychopathology. Treatment is expensive, and the complications of school dropout, hospitalization, and suicide are devastating to human and societal potential. Primary prevention efforts have the potential to reduce the incidence of internalizing behaviors significantly and to improve greatly the quality of life and the well-being of thousands of young people.

REFERENCES

Achenbach, T.M. (1991). *Manual for the Child Behavior Checklist/4–18 and 1991 profile*. Burlington: University of Vermont Department of Psychiatry.

Achenbach, T.M., & Edelbrock, C.S. (1978). The classification of child psychopathology: A review and analysis of empirical efforts. *Psychological Bulletin, 85*, 1275–1301.

Alpert-Gillis, L.J., Pedro-Carroll, J.L., & Cowen, E.L. (1989). The Children of Divorce Intervention Program: Development, implementation and evaluation of a program for young urban youth. *Journal of Consulting and Clinical Psychology, 57*(5), 583–589.

Altmann, E.O., & Gotlib, I.H. (1988). The social behavior of depressed children: An observational study. *Journal of Abnormal Child Psychology, 16*(1), 29–44.

American Psychiatric Association. (1987). *Diagnostic and statistical manual of mental disorders* (3rd ed., rev.). Washington, DC: Author.

Asarnow, J.R., Goldstein, M.J., Carlson, G.A., Perdue, S., Bates, S., & Keller, J. (1988). Childhood-onset depressive disorders. A follow-up study of rates of rehospitalization and out-of-home placements among child psychiatric inpatients. *Journal of Affective Disorders, 15*(3), 245–253.

Asher, S.R., Hymel, S., & Renshaw, P.D. (1984). Loneliness in children. *Child Development, 55*, 1456–1464.

Baker, P. (1990, May 4). Teen's suicide "the ultimate act of revenge against the world." *The Washington Post*, p. C1.

Beardslee, W.R., Keller, M.B., Lavori, P.W., Klerman, G.K., Dorer, D.J., & Samuelson, H. (1988). Psychiatric disorder in adolescent offspring of parents with affective disorders in a nonreferred sample. *Journal of Affective Disorders, 15*, 313–322.

Beitchman, J.H., Inglis, A., & Schachter, D. (1992a). Child psychiatry and early intervention: I. The aggregate burden of suffering. *Canadian Journal of Psychiatry, 37*, 230–233.

Beitchman, J.H., Inglis, A., & Schachter, D. (1992b). Child psychiatry and early intervention: II. The internalizing disorders. *Canadian Journal of Psychiatry, 37*, 234–239.

Berman, B.D., Winkleby, M., Chesterman, E., & Boyce, W.T. (1992). After-school child care and self-esteem in school-age children. *Pediatrics, 89*(4), 654–659.

Bernstein, G.A., & Garfinkle, B.D. (1986). School phobia: The overlap of affective and anxiety disorders. *Journal of the American Academy of Child Psychiatry, 25*(2), 235–241.

Biederman, J., Rosenbaum, J.F., Bolduc-Murphy, E.A., Faraone, S.V., Chaloff, J., Hirshfeld, D.R., & Kagan, J. (1993). A 3-year follow-up of children with and without behavioral inhibition. *Journal of the American Academy of Child and Adolescent Psychiatry, 32*(4), 814–821.

Bockoven, J., & Morse, C.L. (1986). A comparative study of the efficacy of the DUSO and DUSO-R on children's social skills and self-esteem. *Elementary School Guidance and Counseling, 20*(4), 291–296.

Brooksbank, D.J. (1985). Suicide and parasuicide in childhood and early adolescence. *British Journal of Psychiatry, 146*, 459–463.

Cicchetti, D., & Aber, J.L. (1986). Early precursors of later depression: An organizational perspective. In L.P. Lipsitt & C. Rovee-Collier (Eds.), *Advances in infancy research* (Vol. 14, pp. 87–137). Norwood, NJ: Ablex.

Cicchetti, D., & Toth, S.L. (1988). A developmental perspective on internalizing and externalizing disorders. In D. Cicchetti & S.L. Toth (Eds.), *Internalizing and externalizing expressions of dysfunction* (pp. 1–20). Hillsdale, NJ: Lawrence Erlbaum Associates.

Cohen, N.J., Gotlieb, H., Kershner, J., & Wehrspann, W. (1985). Concurrent validity of the internalizing and externalizing profile patterns of the Achenbach Child Behavior Checklist. *Journal of Consulting and Clinical Psychology, 53*(5), 724–728.

Coie, J.D., & Pennington, B.F. (1976). Children's perceptions of deviance and disorder. *Child Development, 47*(2), 407–413.

Committee on Adolescence of the American Academy of Pediatrics. (1980). Teenage suicide. *Pediatrics, 66*, 144–146.

Conger, J.C., & Keane, S.P. (1981). Social skills intervention in the treatment of isolated or withdrawn children. *Psychological Bulletin, 90*(3), 478–495.

Crowther, J.H., Bond, L.A., & Rolf, J.E. (1981). The incidence, prevalence, and severity of behavior disorders among preschool-aged children in day care. *Journal of Abnormal Child Psychology, 9*(1), 23–42.

Davies, P. (Ed.). (1976). *American heritage dictionary*. Boston: Houghton Mifflin.

Dinkmeyer, D. (1970). *Developing understanding of self and others*. Circle Pines, MN: American Guidance Service.

Dinkmeyer, D., & Dinkmeyer, D., Jr. (1982). *Developing understanding of self and others* (rev. ed.). Circle Pines, MN: American Guidance Service.

Fischer, M., Rolf, J.E., Hasazi, J.E., & Cummings, L. (1984). Follow-up of a preschool epidemiological sample: Cross-age continuities and predictions of later adjustment with internalizing and externalizing dimensions of behavior. *Child Development, 55*, 137–150.

Garber, J., Quiggle, N.L., Panak, W., & Dodge, K.A. (1988). Aggression and depression in children: Comorbidity, specificity, and social cognitive processing. In D. Cicchetti & S.L. Toth (Eds.), *Internalizing and externalizing expressions of dysfunction* (pp. 225–264). Hillsdale, NJ: Lawrence Erlbaum Associates.

Garrison, C.Z., Addy, C.L., Jackson, K.L., McKeown, R.E., & Waller, J.L. (1992). Major depressive disorder and dysthymia in young adolescents. *American Journal of Epidemiology, 135*(7), 792–802.

Garrison, C.Z., Jackson, K.L., Addy, C.L., McKeown, R.E., & Waller, J.L. (1991). Suicidal behaviors in young adolescents. *American Journal of Epidemiology, 133*(10), 1005–1014.

Glasser, W. (1969). *Schools without failure.* New York: Harper & Row.

Gresham, F.M. (1990). Best practices in social skills training. In A. Thomas & J. Grimes (Eds.), *Best practices in school psychology–II* (pp. 695–709). Washington, DC: National Association of School Psychologists.

Hoberman, H.M., & Garfinkle, B.D. (1988). Completed suicide in children and adolescents. *Journal of the American Association of Child and Adolescent Psychiatry, 27*(6), 689–695.

Individuals with Disabilities Education Act of 1990 (IDEA), PL 101–476. (October 30, 1990). Title 20, U.S.C. 1400 et seq: *U.S. Statutes at Large, 104,* 1103–1151.

Individuals with Disabilities Education Act Amendments of 1991, PL 102–119. (October 7, 1991). Title 20, U.S.C. 1400 et seq: *U.S. Statutes at Large, 105,* 587–608.

Kalter, N., Kloner, A., Schreier, S., & Okla, K. (1989). Predictors of children's postdivorce adjustment. *American Journal of Orthopsychiatry, 59*(4), 605–618.

Kaplan, S.L., Hong, G.K., & Weinhold, C. (1984). Epidemiology of depressive symptomatology in adolescents. *Journal of the American Academy of Child Psychiatry, 23*(1), 91–98.

Kashani, J.H., McGee, R.O., Clarkson, S.E., Anderson, J.C., Walton, L.A., Williams, S., Silva, P.A., Robins, A.J., Cytryn, L., & McKnew, D.H. (1983). Depression in a sample of 9-year-old children. *Archives of General Psychiatry, 40,* 1217–1223.

Keller, M.B., Beardslee, W., Lavori, P.W., Wunder, J., Drs, D.L., & Samuelson, H. (1988). Course of major depression in nonreferred adolescents: A retrospective study. *Journal of Affective Disorders, 15*(3), 235–243.

Kovacs, M., Feinberg, T.L., Crouse-Novak, M.A., Paulauskas, S.L., & Finkelstein, R. (1984). Depressive disorders in childhood: I. A longitudinal prospective study of characteristics and recovery. *Archives of General Psychiatry, 41*(3), 229–237.

Kovacs, M., Paulauskas, S., Gatsonis, C., & Richards, C. (1988). Depressive disorders in childhood: III. A longitudinal study of comorbidity with and risk for conduct disorder. *Journal of Affective Disorders, 15*(3), 205–207.

Last, C.G. (1989). Anxiety disorders. In T. Ollendick & M. Hersen (Eds.), *Handbook of child psychopathology* (2nd ed., pp. 219–227). New York: Plenum Press.

Last, C.G. (1992). Anxiety disorders in childhood and adolescence. In W.M. Reynolds (Ed.), *Internalizing disorders in children and adolescents* (pp. 61–106). New York: John Wiley & Sons.

Last, C.G., Hersen, M., Kazdin, A.E., Finkelstein, R., & Strauss, C.C. (1987). Comparison of *DSM-III* separation anxiety and overanxious disorders: Demographic characteristics and patterns of comorbidity. *Journal of the American Academy of Child and Adolescent Psychiatry, 26*(4), 527–531.

Last, C.G., Hersen, M., Kazdin, A.E., Francis, G., & Grubb, H.J. (1987). Psychiatric illness in the mothers of anxious children. *American Journal of Psychiatry, 144*(12), 1580–1583.

Lavori, P.W., Keller, M.B., Beardslee, W.R., & Dorer, D.J. (1988). Affective disorder in childhood: Separating the familial component of risk from individual characteristics of children. *Journal of Affective Disorders, 15*(3), 303–311.

Lewis, M., Feiring, C., McGuffog, C., & Jaskir, J. (1984). Predicting psychopathology in six-year-old from early social relation. *Child Development, 55*(1), 123–136.

Moreau, D.L., Weissman, M., & Warner, V. (1989). Panic disorder in children at high risk for depression. *American Journal of Psychiatry, 146*, 1059–1060.

Morse, C.L., Bockoven, J., & Bettesworth, A. (1988). Effects of DUSO-2 and DUSO-2-Revised on children's social skills and self-esteem. *Elementary School Guidance & Counseling, 22*(3), 199–205.

Moskowitz, D.S., Schwartzman, A.E., & Ledingham, J.E. (1985). Stability and change in aggression and withdrawal in middle childhood and early adolescence. *Journal of Abnormal Psychology, 94*(1), 30–41.

Offord, D.R. (1985). Child psychiatric disorders: Prevalence and perspectives. *Psychiatric Clinics of North America, 8*(4), 637–652.

Parker, J.G., & Asher, S.R. (1987). Peer acceptance and later personal adjustment: Are low-accepted children "at risk?" *Psychological Bulletin, 102*(3), 357–389.

Renkin, B., Egeland, B., Marvinney, D., Mangelsdorf, S., & Sroufe, L.A. (1989). Early childhood antecedents of aggression and passive-withdrawal in early elementary school. *Journal of Personality, 57*(2), 257–281.

Renshaw, P.D., & Brown, P.J. (1993). Loneliness in middle childhood: Concurrent and longitudinal predictors. *Child Development, 64*(4), 1271–1284.

Reynolds, W.M. (1990a). Depression in children and adolescents: Nature, diagnosis, assessment, and treatment. *School Psychology Review, 19*(2), 158–173.

Reynolds, W.M. (1990b). Introduction to the nature and study of internalizing disorders in children and adolescents. *School Psychology Review, 19*(2), 137–141.

Reynolds, W.M. (1992). The study of internalizing disorders in children and adolescents. In W.M. Reynolds (Ed.), *Internalizing disorders in children and adolescents* (pp. 1–18). New York: John Wiley & Sons.

Rice, D.P., Kelman, S., Miller, L.S., & Dunmeyer, S. (1990). *The economic costs of alcohol and drug abuse and mental illness: 1985.* (Report submitted to the Office of Financing and Coverage Policy of the Alcohol, Drug Abuse, and Mental Health Administration, U.S. Department of Health and Human Services.) San Francisco: Institute for Health & Aging, University of California.

Rubin, K.H., Hymel, S., Mills, R.S., & Rose-Krasnor, L. (1988). Conceptualizing different developmental pathways to and from social isolation in childhood. In D. Cicchetti & S.L. Toth (Eds.), *Internalizing and externalizing expressions of dysfunction* (pp. 91–122). Hillsdale, NJ: Lawrence Erlbaum Associates.

Rubin, K.H., & Mills, R.S.L. (1988). The many faces of social isolation in childhood. *Journal of Consulting and Clinical Psychology, 56*(6), 916–924.

Rubin, K.H., & Mills, R.S.L. (1991). Conceptualizing developmental pathways to internalizing disorders in childhood. *Canadian Journal of Behavioral Science, 23*(3), 300–317.

Ryan, N.D., Puig-Antich, J., Ambrosini, P., Rabinovich, H., Robinson, D., Nelson, B., Iyengar, S., & Twomey, J. (1987). The clinical picture of major depression in children and adolescents. *Archives of General Psychiatry, 44,* 854–861.

Sameroff, A., & Chandler, M. (1975). Reproductive risk and the continuum of caretaking casualty. In F.D. Horowitz, M. Hetherington, S. Scarr-Salapatek, & G. Seigel (Eds.), *Review of child development research* (Vol. 4, pp. 187–244). Chicago: University of Chicago Press.

Schemo, D.J. (1993, January 17). Katie's ordeal: Seeking friendship, finding 16 days of terror. *New York Times,* p. 29.

Shafii, J., Steltz-Lenarsky, J., Derrick, A.M., Beckner, C., & Whittinghill, J.R. (1988). Comorbidity of mental disorders in the postmortem diagnosis of completed suicide in children and adolescents. *Journal of Affective Disorders, 15*(3), 227–233.

Smith, K. (1992). Suicidal behavior in children and adolescents. In W.M. Reynolds (Ed.), *Internalizing disorders in children and adolescents* (pp. 255–282). New York: John Wiley & Sons.

Strauss, C.C., Forehand, R., Smith, K., & Frame, C.L. (1986). The association between social withdrawal and internalizing problems of children. *Journal of Abnormal Child Psychology, 14*(4), 525–535.

U.S. Bureau of the Census. (1992). *Statistical abstract of the United States: 1992* (112th ed.). Washington, DC: U.S. Government Printing Office.

Velez, C.N., Johnson, J., & Cohen, R. (1989). A longitudinal analysis of selected risk factors for childhood psychopathology. *Journal of American Academy of Child and Adolescent Psychiatry, 28*(6), 861–864.

Weissberg, R.P., Caplan, M., & Harwood, R.L. (1991). Promoting competent young people in competence-enhancing environments: A systems-based perspective on primary prevention. *Journal of Consulting and Clinical Psychology, 59*(6), 830–841.

Weissman, M.M., Gammon, D.G., John, K., Merikangas, K.R., Warner, V., Prusoff, B.A., & Sholomskas, D. (1987). Children of depressed parents: Increased psychopathology and early onset of major depression. *Archives of General Psychiatry, 44*(10), 847–853.

Weissman, M.M., Leckman, J.F., Merikangas, K.R., Gammon, G.D., & Prusoff, B.A. (1984). Depression and anxiety disorders in parents and children. *Archives of General Psychiatry, 41*(9), 845–852.

Weissman, M.M., Warner, K.R., Wickramaratne, P., & Prusoff, B.A. (1988). Early onset of major depression in parents and their children. *Journal of Affective Disorders, 15*(3), 269–277.

Welner, Z., & Rice, J. (1988). School-aged children of depressed parents: A blind and controlled study. *Journal of Affective Disorders, 15*(3), 291–302.

Wolin, S.J., & Bennett, L.A. (1984). Family rituals. *Family Process, 23*(3), 401–420.

Younger, A.J., & Boyko, K.A. (1987). Aggression and withdrawal as social schemes underlying children's peer perceptions. *Child Development, 58,* 1094–1100.

13

Sexually Transmitted Diseases
A Paradigm for Risk Taking Among Teens

Susan L. Rosenthal, Sheila S. Cohen, and Frank M. Biro

Ronald, a 17-year-old African-American, was referred to a primary care adolescent clinic for headaches. The clinic followed Ronald for 2 years. According to his history, he had been treated with medication for attention deficit hyperactivity disorder (ADHD) but he had never received school services. Psychological testing indicated that Ronald had a learning disability. He was an amateur boxer, and his headaches progressively worsened because of frequent head blows. His physician recommended that Ronald discontinue boxing; however, this was an activity from which Ronald derived pleasure and a feeling of success.

Ronald reported that, although he did not use drugs, he was selling drugs to support himself. He denied any risk involved with this behavior because he was "too smart." He briefly attempted to support himself through janitorial jobs; however, his difficulty with impulse control led to repeated dismissals. During one of the periods of Ronald's employment, he felt the need for a car to commute to work. Lacking both a driver's license and insurance, he purchased a car.

Ronald needed to earn money because his family provided minimal financial and emotional support. During a Christmas holiday, he attempted suicide when he did not receive presents from his family. Soon thereafter, Ronald became homeless. A second suicide attempt occurred approximately 1 year later, following his breakup with a girlfriend. Months later conflict with another girlfriend resulted in Ronald's calling the clinic to report that he felt "unsafe." He admitted that he had four guns in the trunk of his car, and he was planning to shoot his girlfriend.

Ronald contracted his first sexually transmitted disease (STD) approximately 6 months after his initial medical assessment. He reported that he was involved in a monogamous relationship, and when he learned that he had contracted gonorrhea, he became extremely angry with his girlfriend for giving him the disease. A few months later, during an out-of-town trip to procure drugs, he had intercourse with a casual female acquaintance. Upon learning that he had acquired another STD, Ronald joked about it, although he did show concern for his girlfriend and her unborn baby.

This case history demonstrates how risk-taking behavior during adolescence rarely exists in isolation. Ronald's exposure to STDs was related to a web of familial, societal, and individual difficulties. The needs to support himself and find housing coupled with his limited academic skills and poor impulse control led Ronald into illegal methods of supporting himself. His relationships were characterized by desires for closeness and poor interpersonal skills, leading to poor sexual decision making.

CO-MORBIDITY OF ADOLESCENT RISK BEHAVIORS

Although this chapter focuses on the acquisition of STDs among teenagers, Ronald's story clearly points to the interrelationship of risk behaviors. Risk behaviors by adolescents often co-occur, and one risk behavior may be a marker for others or associated with already established behavior patterns (Biglan et al., 1990; Donovan & Jessor, 1985; Ensminger, 1990; Irwin & Millstein, 1986; Jessor, 1991). For example, substance use during sexual activity is associated with increased STD risk behaviors among inner-city African-American male adolescents (Jemmott & Jemmott, 1993) and unmarried pregnant adolescents (Gillmore, Butler, Lohr, & Gilchrist, 1992). In a longitudinal study within a Chicago neighborhood, sexual intercourse was significantly associated with drug and alcohol use, as well as physical assault behaviors for both male and female teens (Ensminger, 1990). Adolescent prostitutes (Nightingdale, 1985), adolescent victims of sexual abuse (Keller et al., 1991; Zierler et al., 1991), adolescents exchanging sex for drugs (Fullilove, Fullilove, Bowser, & Gross, 1990), and runaways engaging in survival sex (exchanging sex for food or shelter) (Stricof, Nattell, & Novick, 1991; Sugerman, Hergenroeder, Chacko, & Parcel, 1991) are interrelated high-risk groups who engage in a number of high-risk behaviors, including substance abuse, multiple sexual partners, and nonuse of condoms. Adolescents who engaged in prostitution, or in male homosexual or bisexual behaviors, or who had a history of ulcerative STDs, were found also to consume more alcohol, use more drugs, and engage in more violent behavior than other teens (Stiffman & Earls, 1990). Incarcerated teens, when compared to same-age high school peers, are more likely to be sexually active, have initiated sexual intercourse at an earlier age, have had more sexual partners, and have been less likely to use condoms consistently (DiClemente, Lanier, Horan, & Lodico, 1991).

Adolescents who are at high risk for STDs are unlikely to engage in behaviors that might decrease their risk. Stiffman and Earls (1990), defined adolescents as having a high degree of risk for human immunodeficiency virus (HIV) infection if they engaged in prostitution, injectable drug use, male homosexual or bisexual behavior, or had a history of an STD with genital ulcers or sores. Moderate-risk youths were defined as those who had had more than six sexual partners or who had had a nonulcerative STD. Almost half of those adolescents in the highest level of risk reported never using any contraception, and only 14% reported consistent condom use. In the moderate risk group, similar low rates for contraception were found; 40% reported that they had never used contraception, and only 21% reported condom use. Those with previous STDs are unlikely to change their behavior to safer practices (Biro, Rosenthal, Wildey, & Hillard, 1991; Fullilove et al., 1990).

SEXUALLY TRANSMITTED DISEASES

Model

Table 13.1 illustrates three levels of prevention as they apply to STDs. An STD makes a significant impact upon the individual, the partner(s) through horizontal transmission, and the fetus and infant through vertical transmission. The costs to society are substantial; for example, the costs of pelvic inflammatory disease (PID) alone are estimated to be $4.2 billion annually (Washington & Katz, 1991). During adolescence, many teens establish behavior patterns that may be associated with risk or protection (Ehrhardt & Wasserheit, 1991). Consequently, prevention programs are critical to address adolescents' needs. In this chapter, we first discuss the extent of the problem of STDs and its sequelae for adolescents. We then address important aspects of tertiary, secondary, and primary prevention.

Manifestation

Two decades ago, medical care providers were largely concerned about the venereal diseases: the two major ones (syphilis and gonorrhea) and three minor (chancroid, granuloma inguinale, and lymphogranuloma venereum). Today, clinicians are faced with dozens of organisms that can be transmitted through sexual intercourse, causing a plethora of syndromes and medical sequelae including involuntary infertility, cer-

Table 13.1. Summary of primary prevention for sexually transmitted diseases (STDs): Focus and strategies

Population	Focus	Strategy
Universal (all teens)	Impact age at which adolescent initiates sexual intercourse Increase sexual decision-making strategies Increase interpersonal and social skills Increase communication with parents Impact social norms	Family support services Social skills training Appropriate media messages Age-appropriate sex education
Selected (sexually active teens)	Increase proper use of condoms Strengthen skills for negotiating condom use with partner Increase access to contraception Develop barrier methods that women can use Increase adherence to treatment Obtain prompt diagnosis of STDs Decrease number of partners	Access to health-care facilities designed for teens Research into barrier methods for women Social marketing of condoms
Indicated (at-risk teens[a])	Continue all the above approaches Decrease underlying social problems including substance use, economic support for teens, violence	Access to medical care for at-risk teens (e.g., runaway shelters, juvenile detention centers, mobile medical clinics)

[a]Homeless/runaway youth, incarcerated youth, substance-abusing youth, teen prostitutes, minority youth, pregnant youth, early maturing youth.

vical cancer, and opportunistic infections and death. The age group with the highest risk for nearly all STDs is the adolescent. The prevalence of STDs among sexually active adolescents is higher than that reported in the typical prevalence figures for STDs, given that only 45% of white and 56% of other-than-white females 15–19 years old are sexually active (Aral & Cates, 1989). Adolescents are at high risk for STDs for such behavioral reasons as the high prevalence of STDs in their partner pool (Bell, & Holmes, 1984), a greater number of partners per unit time (Aral, Soskoline, Joesoef, & O'Reilly, 1991; Forrest & Singh, 1990), and nonuse of contraceptive methods that protect against STDs (Catania et al., 1992). Biological factors include the low prevalence of protective antibodies, the greater permeability of cervical mucus in younger women, and the larger zones of cervical ectopy (Brookman, 1988; Cates, Rolfs, & Aral, 1990). In addition, risk behaviors pertinent to STDs may serve as a proxy for HIV risk factors (Stiffman & Earls, 1990). (For more information on HIV and adolescents, refer to DiClemente, 1992.) We review the prevalence or incidence rates for the following common STDs: *Chlamydia trachomatis, Neisseria gonorrhea*, syphilis, human papillomavirus (HPU), and herpes simplex virus (HSV).

Chlamydia Trachomatis

Chlamydia trachomatis urogenital infections are considered the most prevalent bacterial STD in the United States, with an estimated 4 million cases occurring annually. Prevalence rates vary with specific adolescent groups. For example, although it may be as high as 27% among pregnant females (Chacko & Lovchik, 1984), more typical rates are 5% among college students (McCormack, Rosner, McComb, Evard, & Zinner, 1985) to 11% in asymptomatic inner-city adolescents (Biro, Reising, Doughman, Kollar, & Rosenthal, 1994). The rate among asymptomatic sexually active adolescent males is 8% (Shafer et al., 1987).

Neisseria Gonorrhea

Neisseria gonorrhea is the most frequently reported communicable disease in the United States (Zenilman, 1990). Sexually active 15- to 19-year-old females have a higher rate of gonorrhea than women in all other age groups (Forrest & Singh, 1990). When adjusted for sexual activity during the previous 3 months, the rates of gonorrhea are nearly 24 cases per 1,000 women for 15- to 19-year-olds (Biro, 1992).

Syphilis

The recent increase in rates of syphilis represent the highest levels in 40 years. The overall prevalence of syphilis has doubled among adolescents 15–19 years of age during the past 5 years, from a rate of 15 cases per 100,000 population in 1985, to 30 cases per 100,000 in 1990. During that time, rates among adolescent males 15–19 years of age have risen from 15 to 21 cases per 100,000 and among adolescent females from 16 to 39 cases per 100,000 (U.S. Centers for Disease Control, 1991b).

Human Papillomavirus

It is unclear what the exact prevalence of HPV infections is among adolescents. In an urban clinic for adolescents, 16% of adolescent women had dysplastic changes noted on Pap smear (P.A. Hillard, Biro, et al., 1989). In a study of college women, 2% were noted to have anogenital warts, and an additional 11% were noted to have positive tests for HPV-DNA or antigen from HPV (Kiviat et al., 1989). In another study of adolescent women attending an urban clinic, 38% of sexually active women had HPV-DNA diagnosed on cervicovaginal lavage (Rosenfeld, Vermund, Wentz, & Burk, 1989).

Herpes Simplex Virus

The prevalence of antibody to HSV type 2 is less than 1% in subjects under 15 years of age, and 20% in subjects 30–44 years of age (Johnson et al., 1989). In a group of college students, freshmen had a seroprevalence of 37% for type 1 herpes and 0.4% for type 2 herpes. This increased by their senior year to 46% for type 1 herpes and 4% for type 2 herpes (Gibson et al., 1990).

TERTIARY PROBLEMS OF STDs

Problems at the tertiary level are the sequelae after the initial infection. Three potential sequelae that demonstrate tertiary problems are: PID-related complications, infant morbidity, and psychological reaction of the adolescent. The implications of each of these is discussed briefly.

PID-Related Complications

An estimated one third of women with untreated gonorrhea or chlamydia cervicitis develop clinical symptoms of acute PID (Cates et al., 1990). PID is a polymicrobial infection that may involve the uterus, fallopian tubes, ovaries, and surrounding peritoneal structures. One half to two thirds of cases of PID occur in women under the age of 24 years (Shafer & Sweet, 1990; Washington & Katz, 1991). Among sexually active women, nonwhite adolescents ages 15–19 years have the highest rate of PID, with 2,000–3,000 cases per 100,000 (Shafer & Sweet, 1990).

The acute sequelae of PID include perihepatitis and tubo-ovarian abscess. The long-term sequelae include involuntary infertility, ectopic pregnancy, and chronic abdominal pain. Perihepatitis (Fitz-Hugh-Curtis syndrome) involves inflammation of the capsule of the liver, presenting as right-upper quadrant pain, and it may be seen in 15%–30% of patients. Tubo-ovarian abscess occurs less frequently. The risk of involuntary infertility increases with the number of previous PID episodes, as well as with the severity of any particular episode. After one infection of PID, 11% of women developed infertility; 54% of those women with three or more episodes developed infertility. There is a 7- to 10-fold increased risk of ectopic pregnancy after a previous diagnosis of PID (Westrom, 1980).

Infant Morbidity

Bacterial or viral infections can be transmitted to the fetus in utero or can be acquired as the neonate passes through the birth canal (Peloquin & Davidson, 1988). Sequelae of transmission of the herpes simplex virus, chlamydia, and syphilis to the fetus and neonate are summarized as examples of complications related to STDs acquisition.

Both HSV type 1 and type 2 can produce infection in the newborn. Vertical transmission of HSV from mother to infant can occur in utero or during birth. The impact on the fetus of intrauterine infection may depend on gestational age at the time of infection. If infection occurs early in pregnancy, the result may be spontaneous abortion, whereas later infection usually produces developmental anomalies evident at birth (Stanberry, 1993). The majority (70%–85%) of fetal or neonatal herpes infections occur during contact with maternal genital lesions at delivery. Possible sequelae of HSV contracted during delivery include skin, eye, or mouth lesions (the most common), infection to the central nervous system (second most frequent manifestation), or evidence of widely disseminated infection. Although disseminated disease is the least common, it carries the worst prognosis and can involve the liver, lungs, brain, skin, and/or adrenal glands (Prober, 1993; Stanberry, 1993). Mortality of herpetic infection in the newborn period is significantly greater among premature infants (Whitley et al., 1991). Transmission rates to the newborn are higher with maternal primary (first episode) genital HSV infection than with the more common recurrent genital herpes. However, shedding of HSV from the genital tract may occur asymptomatically, thus recurrent disease may go undetected (Prober, 1993; Stanberry, 1993).

Neonatal morbidity has also been associated with intrauterine infection with chlamydia. Mothers successfully treated for intrapartum chlamydial infections have significantly lower rates of premature ruptured membranes, premature contractions, and small-for-gestational-age infants, than those who are treated unsuccessfully (Cohen, Veille, & Calkins, 1990). Postnatally, chlamydia can cause conjunctivitis, and, in 5%–20% of infants born to infected mothers, pneumonitis (Frau & Alexander, 1985).

Congenital syphilis rarely is transmitted to the neonate from active lesions during delivery; most commonly congenital syphilis is transmitted to the fetus across the placenta. The risk to the infant is related to the time of gestation when the mother contracts the infection. Spontaneous abortion and stillbirth are a common result of infections acquired before 16–20 weeks. Prematurity and low birth weight are common with later infection. At birth, the sequelae in the infant may manifest in the form of central nervous disease, including seizures, hypotonia, and increased intracranial pressure. Because syphilis is a progressive disease, many sequelae may not appear until later in life. For example, joint involvement and general paresis may not occur until the child reaches 10–15 years of age (Peloquin & Davidson, 1988).

Congenital HSV, chlamydia, and syphilis were used as examples to illustrate the complications that can arise for the next generation. All of these STDs can be transmitted to the neonate, resulting in a range of complications. Not only are there short-term and long-term medical implications for the infant, there are the psychological implications for the family. The impact of infants with developmental disabilities and at-risk infants on the family has been described elsewhere in the literature (Simeonsson, 1991).

Adolescents' Psychological Reaction

The psychological sequelae of STDs are not well understood; they often go unrecognized and are managed inadequately, despite their prevalence among those with STDs (Ross, 1990). Most of the literature has focused on adults and on coping with such viral conditions as HSV or cervical dysplasia (e.g., Campion et al., 1988; Drob, Loemer, & Lifshutz, 1985; Goldmeier, Johnson, Byrne, & Barton, 1988; J.R. Hillard, Hillard et al., 1989; Luby & Klinge, 1985). However, it is clear that STDs, both viral and bacterial, have an impact on the adolescent. For example, 82% of adolescent females with a history of STDs, reported that the anticipated feeling associated with acquiring an STD would be "a major upset" or "the worst thing that could happen" (Rosenthal & Biro, 1991). The majority (89%) of adolescents with cervical dysplasia (Biro, Rosenthal, et al., 1991) reported that they had concerns about the diagnosis of cervical dysplasia; the most common concern (71%) was about their future health. Subsequent changes in their behaviors that would reduce their risk of STDs, particularly discontinuing intercourse or consistently using condoms, were reported by 78% of the sample. However, these reported changes in behavior were not substantiated by decreased rates of STDs on subsequent clinic visits, suggesting that their responses may reflect intentions rather than actions. Another study (Rosenthal & Biro, 1991) contrasted the impact of acquiring cervical dysplasia with the impact of acquiring acute gonococcal or chlamydial infections. Diagnosis did not make a difference in terms of the impact, although across diagnostic categories, those with other psychological symptoms reported more avoidant thoughts. In general, patients in this study tended to report more avoidant rather than intrusive thoughts related to the impact of the STD diagnosis. This finding is consistent with another study (S.L. Rosenthal, Biro, Cohen, Succop, & Stanberry, in press), which found that the most common form of coping reported was wishful thinking (96%), a strategy that 28% did not find helpful. Social support and problem solving are two strategies generally believed to be productive, and most adolescents found them helpful. However, less than half used social support "a lot" or "most of the time." Although they did report the use of problem-solving strategies, others (Spirito, Stark, & Williams, 1988) have suggested that when wishful thinking is combined with problem solving, the effectiveness of the problem solving may be impaired.

LEVELS OF PREVENTION

Tertiary Prevention

When the condition of STD is manifested in adolescents, a major goal of tertiary prevention is to prevent medical and psychological sequelae. Prompt diagnosis and treatment are key aspects of prevention of the first two complications (PID-related complications and infant morbidity). Recommendations for the appropriate treatment of PID and prevention of its complications have been reviewed recently (Peterson et al., 1991; Washington, Cates, & Wasserheit, 1991). Routine screening of adolescents for all STDs during pregnancy could reduce birth complications and the transmission to neonates; however, because teenagers may continue to have unprotected intercourse throughout their pregnancies, acquisition of an STD may occur at any time. If the neonate does acquire an STD, it is important not only to implement early medical treatment but to provide early intervention strategies known to be effective with high-risk infants and families. Some of these are described elsewhere in this volume by Simeonsson and Gray (chap. 5), Zins, Garcia, Tuchfarber, Clark, and Laurence (chap. 10), and Short and Brokaw (chap. 11), as well as in previous publications (Simeonsson, 1991).

Understanding the psychological sequelae of STDs is important because it may provide the knowledge necessary for developing programs to reduce psychological morbidity and additional episodes of STDs in adolescents. However, little is known about preventing psychological sequelae in adolescents with STDs. There is some intervention literature on adults with HSV. Group psychotherapy that used cognitive restructuring decreased the recurrence rates of HSV over a 3-month follow-up period (McLarnon & Kaloupek, 1988). In addition, persons with higher levels of social support (Manne & Sandler, 1984), particularly herpes-specific social support (VanderPlate, Aral, & Magder, 1988), have lower recurrence rates of HSV.

Secondary Prevention

Secondary prevention of STDs in adolescents focuses on management of current infections and prevention of further transmission. This chapter does not address the appropriate medical management of the various STDs. (Interested readers are referred to Biro [1992] for a complete discussion of medical management.) Other important aspects include prompt diagnosis and improving adherence to treatment.

Prompt diagnosis includes routinely screening both adolescent women and men, because infections may be asymptomatic. Encouraging adolescents to notify their partners is also an important aspect of reducing transmission. Adolescents may be reluctant to discuss STDs with their partners, and many may lack the necessary communication skills. The health care provider can play an instrumental role in facilitating communication between partners by assessing the teen's fears and reviewing ways of talking to the teen's partner. Role playing may be very beneficial in allowing the adolescent to rehearse the interaction in a safe environment.

Barriers to following through on treatment, such as the cost of medicine or difficulty attending future appointments, should be considered. The literature on compliance with test-of-cure appointments has focused predominantly on adults and adolescents from STD clinics. In general, intervention studies have shown little success in improving compliance (Chacko, Cromer, Phillips, & Glasser, 1987; Cromer, Chacko, & Phillips, 1987), and the correlates of good compliance have not been well defined. Physicians, despite their level of training, are poor estimators of who is likely to comply, with their estimates being no better than chance (Litt & Cuskey, 1980). One study found that compliance appeared to be related to owning a telephone (Cromer et al., 1987), whereas other studies suggested that compliance was related to gender (Chacko, Cromer, et al., 1987; Chacko, Wells, & Phillips, 1987), with female adolescents being more likely to comply.

Primary Prevention

Effective prevention of initial acquisition of STDs among adolescents involves making an impact on the age when the adolescent initiates sexual intercourse and encouraging the adolescent to engage in risk-reducing behaviors (e.g., use of barrier methods, and healthy sexual behavioral decision making). To determine the important variables in prevention programs, a model of behavior change is required that incorporates the specific developmental needs of adolescents. Social-psychological models have been most useful in highlighting the key variables. An overview of these models is provided through outlines of four constructs. Application of primary prevention to the groups described (universal: all teens; selected: sexually active teens; and indicated: high-risk teens) is presented.

Social-Psychological Constructs The theory of reasoned action emphasizes the link between specific attitudes and behavior that results from definite intentions. A behavioral intention is determined by attitudes toward that behavior and the perceived subjective norms of important others toward performing that behavior. For example, using a condom is a function of one's attitude toward condoms and one's perception of the norms regarding condom use (Fishbein & Middlestadt, 1989; L.S. Jemmott & Jemmott, 1991).

The protection motivation theory (Prentice-Dunn & Rogers, 1986; Rogers, 1983) emphasizes cognitive processes that mediate attitude and behavior changes. Enactment of a behavior is composed of two cognitive processes: threat appraisal and coping appraisal. Threat appraisal consists of rewards (variables that increase the likelihood of the response) in the form of intrinsic and extrinsic (social approval) reinforcers, the perceived severity of the threat, and one's perceived vulnerability to the threat. The individual also makes a coping appraisal that consists of response costs, response efficacy, and self-efficacy evaluations. In the case of protecting oneself from an STD, response costs may consist of inconvenience, expense, unpleasantness, disruption of spontaneity, or nonsupport/displeasure from a partner. Efficacy factors consist of judgments about what personal responses will avert the perceived threat successfully, as well as the person's capability to implement the adaptive response successfully. Thus, the existence of a successful, effective alternative response is not sufficient; the individual must also have a sense of personal mastery or a belief that he or she is capable of implementing the preventive regimen. The threat and coping appraisals, in combination, form protection motivation that acts as an intervening variable to initiate, direct, and sustain behavior.

The health belief model (Kirscht, 1988; Rosenstock, Strecher, & Becker, 1988) is similar to the protection motivation theory. However, it evolved in an attempt to explain medically oriented preventive behaviors (e.g., heart disease, cigarette smoking, safety belt use) and also sick role behaviors (e.g., compliance with medical regimes for diabetes, hypertension). It hypothesizes that preventive health action is influenced by a person's belief that he or she is vulnerable or susceptible to disease, and that the occurrence of the disease will have some moderate-to-severe negative effect on his or her life. In addition, a person must maintain the belief that the advocated health program is effective in reducing the susceptibility and severity of the disease; that is, the recommended action is of some value when weighted against perceptions of barriers (physical and psychological) or costs of the action. Therefore, an individual's positive health behavior, according to this theory, is based on the value an individual places on a positive state of health relative to the perceptions of difficulties associated with maintaining the positive health action. The health belief model postulates that for behavioral change to occur, modifications in an individual's beliefs are critical. The belief elements produce some degree of psychological readiness motivating an individual to act despite the barriers or cost. For example, the belief that condoms provide effective protection from STDs motivates an individual to use condoms, even if they are viewed as interrupting the spontaneity of sex.

Bandura (1977, 1982, 1989) proposed a model of behavior that extends other psychosocial theories by incorporating and expanding the role of self-efficacy as a key component. Behaviors are determined by expectancies and incentives. Expectancies include environmental cues (i.e., beliefs about how events are connected), consequences of an individual's own actions (i.e., opinions about how individual behavior is likely to influence outcomes), and beliefs about an individual's own competence to perform the behavior (i.e., evaluation of self-efficacy). Incentives or reinforcements are the values placed on a particular outcome. Perceived self-efficacy is concerned with judgments of how effectively an individual can execute behaviors required to secure certain outcomes. Efficacy in affecting an individual's environment is a dynamic process involving an interaction of cognitive, social, and behavioral skills organized into integrated courses of action. In any given activity, successful functioning requires skills and the individual's self-belief in his or her capability to use those skills adeptly. There is a difference between the possession of coping skills and the ability to implement them effectively and consistently to obtain desired outcomes. Although a person may believe that a certain course of action will produce particular outcomes, he or she may be unsure whether he or she can perform those actions personally. The strength of a person's conviction about his or her own effectiveness to influence outcomes determines how well the person will cope with difficult situations. In managing sexual behavior, people must exercise influence over their own motivation and behavior, as well as over those of others (Bandura, 1992).

These social-psychological constructs point out the role of multiple variables, external and internal, that determine behavior. As such, they provide information about the critical components of interventions necessary to alter outcomes.

Universal: All Teens Sexual decision making and ways of self-protection are primary prevention strategies directed toward all teens, and they should be addressed throughout the adolescent years. Programs with a universal focus must consider the developmental aspects of adolescence. Messages must come from the family, must occur in schools, and must be part of media communications.

Developmental issues (e.g., cognitive factors, identity formation) are important to consider in programming for adolescents. During adolescence the transition from concrete to formal operational cognitive skills includes thinking characterized by the personal fable. The personal fable is the belief that the person is not vulnerable to the natural laws that affect others (e.g., acquisition of STDs). Thus, adolescents feel special and shielded from harm (Elkind, 1978). Clearly, an adolescent's personal fable will affect his or her ability to evaluate accurately the future risks associated with behaviors.

Bandura (1992) points out that it is easier to have control over preliminary choice behavior than it is for a person to attempt to extricate him- or herself from a difficult situation. However, adolescents may not have the cognitive skills to anticipate the implications of the situation. For example, an adolescent may be unable to determine that it may be better to avoid being alone with a person for whom there is a sexual attraction than to attempt to avoid having intercourse once the situation presents itself. As illustrated in the introductory vignette, Ronald's impulsive behavior and his lack of planning when he was out of town exposed him to a situation of having sex without a condom with someone he did not know.

Identity formation during adolescence is not a singular event, and it applies to many dimensions (e.g., religious, vocational). Sexual identity and the ability to develop intimate relationships are crucial components of identity formation in adolescence. Adolescents' attempts to define themselves sexually may include risk-taking behaviors. Risk-taking behavior, when defined from a developmental perspective, is behavior that is volitional, nonpathological, and has potentially positive as well as negative results (Irwin, 1990). Sexual risk taking may be directly related to such developmental issues as autonomy, affiliation, and identity (Irwin, 1990). Thus, when developing intervention programs for teens, behaviors must be considered in the context of adolescent development.

Community/school programs must be developed to enhance the interpersonal and social skills of all teens. Such skills as the ability to communicate openly and negotiate condom use with partners are critical for implementing safe sex behaviors (D. Rosenthal, Moore, & Flynn, 1991). Programs should also emphasize assertiveness training so adolescents have both the means and the confidence to engage in protective measures for themselves (Bandura, 1992).

Family variables, such as communication with parents, play an important role in the initiation of sexual activity (Brooks-Gunn & Furstenberg, 1989). Spoken and nonspoken messages are communicated by parents to teens, and one study (Darling & Hicks, 1982) reported that negative rather than positive messages are the most frequently given (e.g., "sex is a dangerous experience"), especially to female adolescents. For college students, their mothers' opinions about condoms played a significant role in their decision to use condoms (Strader & Beaman, 1989). Other research (Newcomer & Udry, 1984) suggests there is an association between teens engaging in sex during early adolescence and whether or not their mothers were sexually active as adolescents. Parental discipline and control, as perceived by adolescents, relates in a curvilinear fashion to adolescents' sexual behavior (Miller, McCoy, Olson, & Wallace, 1986). Adolescents who reported their parents had no rules about dating had the highest percentage of premarital sexual intercourse experience. The lowest percentage of sexual intercourse experience was reported by adolescents who perceived that their parents had a moderate number of rules, and adolescents with intermediate sexual experience reported that their parents had many rules. Among unmarried pregnant teens, a sense of family closeness was negatively associated with sexual risk-taking behaviors (Gillmore et al., 1992).

The development of sex education programs is an important component in the prevention of STDs among adolescents. The number of states that require sex education in the schools has increased from 3 in 1980 to 23 a decade later (Kenney, Guardado, & Brown, 1989; deMauro, 1990). However, no national standards for education about sex exist; the content and extent can vary from school to school (deMauro, 1990). Two recent surveys report that 54%–62% of high school students have received formal education about HIV or acquired immune deficiency syndrome (AIDS) (Anderson et al., 1990; U.S. Centers for Disease Control, 1990). In a survey of public school teachers, 93% of respondents noted that their school offered either sex education or AIDS education. Nearly all believed that sexual decision making, abstinence, and birth control methods should be taught, and 82% said that this was occurring in their school. A large percentage (80%) reported that they needed help with factual information, materials, or strategies (Forrest & Silverman, 1989).

The impact of sex education alone on changing sexual risk-taking behaviors has been somewhat limited. Many programs have determined that knowledge is necessary but insufficient to implement changes in attitude and behavior (Anderson et al., 1990; Brooks-Gunn & Furstenberg, 1989; DiClemente, 1991; Rosoff, 1989). For example, among students completing a course designed to postpone sexual involvement, those who were not sexually experienced were more likely to remain abstinent the following year; however, there was little effect on contraceptive use among those already sexually active (Howard & McCabe, 1990). Even when there is both increased knowledge and a change in attitude, a change in behavior does not necessarily occur (Hingson, Strunin, & Berlin, 1990; Overby, Lo, & Litt, 1989). Other factors, such as adolescents' perceptions of socially accepted norms, may need to be addressed in order to influence behavior change (Sussman et al., 1988). Dissemination of accurate information regarding normative sexual behaviors among youth may help influence perceptions and lead to changes in behavioral expectations (U.S. Centers for Disease Control, 1991a).

The impact of sex education programs is limited further because many programs are implemented after sexual activity has already begun or encourage abstinence when many students are already sexually active (Forrest & Silverman, 1989). Education programs must be culturally sensitive, age appropriate (DiClemente, Pies, Stoller, & Straits, 1989; Rothenberg, 1981), and based on the group's and individual's existing health belief system (Simon & Das, 1984). There are additional approaches to sex education programs in the schools. The use of school-based clinics offers another approach to the prevention and intervention of STDs among youth, and such clinics often include outreach to students, programs to delay sexual activity, and targeting of sexually active students (Kirby, Waszak, & Ziegler, 1991). Peer counseling has also been shown to help change attitudes (Rickert, Jay, & Gottlieb, 1991).

Reviews of the impact of media on adolescent sexuality have indicated that the media has become a most important source of sex education for young people (Brown, Childers, & Waszak, 1990; Strasburger, 1989). The available research indicates that although the media have become increasingly more sexually explicit, they have not necessarily provided information and views that would encourage young men and women to engage in responsible and healthful sexual decision making. Adolescents who rely heavily on television for information about sexuality may believe that premarital and extramarital intercourse with multiple partners without protection against pregnancy or disease is the norm. Moreover, heterosexual behavior is often associated with violence or displays of power, and it is rarely shown within the context of positive feelings (Franzblau, Sprafkin, & Rubinstein, 1977). More recently, public service announcements about AIDS are occasionally seen on television, but they are heavily outnumbered by ads to sell beer or exploit female sexuality (Strasburger, 1989). The media do not have to be negative influences; their content can convey positive and educational information.

Selected: Sexually Active Teens In addition to the approaches described above, primary prevention for sexually active teens must encourage adolescents to use condoms. The proper use of condoms, particularly the spermicidal condom, may be the best approach to the prevention of STDs (Stone, Grimes, & Magder, 1986; U.S. Centers for Disease Control, 1988; Werner & Biro, 1990). A recent review noted that latex condoms provide an effective barrier against most STDs and that spermicides inactivated many STDs (Werner & Biro, 1990). Condoms may be less effective in preventing infections with HPV or genital herpes, particularly when lesions occur outside the area protected by the condom (Kjaer et al., 1990). The failure of condoms to protect against STDs is usually secondary to user failure rather than product failure. Incorrect use was documented as the reason for condom failure in patients acquiring gonorrhea (Darrow, 1989).

There are many issues responsible for the mixed success of condom use among adolescents. Condoms often evoke negative feelings; they have been associated with extramarital sex, prostitution, and promiscuity (Solomon & DeJong, 1986). Introducing condoms into a relationship where they have not been used previously may lead partners to believe that sexual activity is occurring outside the relationship (Solomon & DeJong, 1986; Worth, 1989). Adolescents report that condom use may make sexual intercourse seem planned (Solomon & DeJong, 1986; Sugerman et al., 1991). They may be embarrassed to purchase condoms (MacDonald et al., 1990), and they often believe that condoms may interfere with pleasure (MacDonald et al., 1990; Solomon & DeJong, 1986). Many adolescents do not perceive their peers as supporting condom use (DiClemente, 1991). Adolescents also report that they use condoms to prevent pregnancy, not STDs. Moreover, if their partner is using hormonal contraceptives, they would be less likely to also use condoms (Weisman, Plichta, Nathanson, Ensminger, & Robinson, 1991). In one study, a belief in the preventive effects of condoms did not lead to increased use; convenience and social considerations (i.e., ease of use and popularity with peers) were more important factors (Kegeles, Adler, & Irwin, 1989).

There are several methods to help facilitate condom use. Healthcare providers must acknowledge potential disadvantages of condoms, and help the adolescent to explore ways to overcome the disadvantages as well as to weigh the costs and benefits of condom use (Solomon & DeJong, 1986). Conversations with adolescents that focus on condoms as part of the erotic experience, rather than an object for protection against disease only, may help facilitate the use of condoms (Tanner & Pollack, 1988).

Adolescent women must be encouraged to negotiate condom use with their partners. In one study, the strongest predictor of condom use was having asked a partner to use one (Weisman et al., 1991). However, for some adolescent girls, efforts to implement safer sex practices, such as asking a partner to use a condom, may result in concerns of sexual force or coercion. For example, one study interviewed adolescent girls regarding steps in negotiation of condom use with a partner. Of 186 adolescent girls, 12% spontaneously mentioned some concerns regarding physical or sexual coercion (S.L. Rosenthal & Cohen, in press). All adolescents need training in communication skills to help negotiate safer sex limits with their partners (DiClemente, 1991; Fisher, 1990). If methods were developed for which women could have exclusive control, such as a cream- or jelly-based virucide that would protect against the transmission of a virus (Ehrhardt et al., 1990; Freiberg, 1991), then adolescent women might feel less powerless in protecting themselves from STDs.

A promising approach to the development of prevention programs for STDs utilizes social marketing. A recent series of studies evaluated its impact to motivate changes in behaviors regarding STDs (Solomon & DeJong, 1986). Commercial marketing techniques were used to promote social goals through promotion of specific products rather than abstract ideas. Risk reduction strategies were implemented through establishing a social milieu in which AIDS risk reduction behavior was the norm, promoting concrete steps of action, acknowledging the disadvantages of condom use, addressing the asymptomatic nature of STDs, and emphasizing the importance of full compliance. Findings demonstrated that subjects increased their knowledge about STDs, had greater compliance for completion of antibiotic therapy and returning for test of cure, and had a more positive attitude regarding condom use (Solomon & DeJong, 1986).

Health-care providers must be comfortable discussing sexual activity in a nonmoralistic way, addressing the emotional and cognitive barriers to condom use (Fisher, 1990). A negative or moralistic approach, particularly regarding STDs or the adolescent patient, may provide a barrier to care (Solomon & DeJong, 1986). For example, nearly one fourth of family practitioners would not provide contraceptive services to minors (Orr & Forrest, 1985).

Adolescents' utilization of health care is also relevant to the prevention and treatment of STDs. Issues pertinent for teenagers include knowledge regarding resources, access to those resources, and appropriateness of treatment. When 8th- and 10th-grade students were surveyed, 38% did not know where to go for diagnosis or treatment of STDs, and 76% thought that parents must be informed regarding treatment of STDs (American School Health Association, Association for the Advancement of Health Education, & the Society for Public Health Education, Inc., 1989). When agency representatives were surveyed regarding adolescent use of health-care services, 75% felt that underutilization could be explained by poor visibility of the clinics (Taylor, Miller, & Moltz, 1991). Access to health care may be limited by financial resources; 15% of adolescents are uninsured (U.S. Congress, Office of Technology Assessment, 1991). Transportation to clinics may also be a significant barrier for many adolescents (Taylor et al., 1991).

Indicated: At-Risk Teens As described earlier, problem behaviors of adolescents do not exist in isolation. Thus, some adolescents are at increased risk by virtue of group characteristics because many of these additional risk factors often occur together. These adolescents need special attention to address their particular needs. For these youths, it is critically important that prevention efforts address problems at a societal level (Stricof, Kennedy, Nattell, Weisfuse, & Novick, 1991), such as inner-city violence and hopelessness regarding obtaining legal means of economic support. Support of families and communities is key because emotional support and supervision play such important roles in protecting adolescents from risk (Carnegie Corporation of New York, 1992). For high-risk adolescents (e.g., homeless, drug addicted, homosexual), specialized programs must be available to treat their specific risk factors (Rotheram-Borus & Koopman, 1991). For example, adequate programs to treat substance abuse are important. Many of these adolescents may feel alienated from typical health-care providers, and they may be reluctant to discuss factors that may make them more vulnerable. For example, many providers are not comfortable discussing homosexuality with youths or emerging sexual development with younger teens. Even those providers who feel comfortable discussing homosexuality often close conversations by asking questions in a gender-specific manner. Finally, the location of service delivery is important. For example, given the number of adjudicated adolescents who have STDs (Alexander-Rodriguez & Vermund, 1987; Moran & Peterman, 1989), it is important that adequate treatment and prevention programs exist in jails and detention centers. Although school-based services reach many adolescents, they are not accessible to adolescents who are not in school. Thus, services for STDs must be available for adolescents in homeless shelters, community health clinics, street outreach programs, or food pantries (Sugerman et al., 1991).

SUMMARY

It is well documented that adolescent risk behaviors do not exist in isolation. As the opening case history illustrates, familial, societal, and individual characteristics have an impact on problem behaviors for many at-risk adolescents. This chapter addresses three levels of prevention —tertiary, secondary, and primary—as they apply to STDs, a major health concern of adolescents. Complications of STDs include development of acute pelvic inflammatory disease, infant morbidity sequelae, and psychological difficulties. Routine screening, appropriate diagnosis, and prompt treatment in the management of STDs are crucial for tertiary and secondary prevention efforts. Primary prevention, drawing from social psychological models and developmental issues of adolescence, must address concerns of all adolescents (universal), sexually active teens (selected), and at-risk adolescents (indicated). Because of the complex nature of the acquisition, transmission, and management of STDs, and the diverse groups of adolescents at risk for STDs, it has become clear that effective prevention programs must be multifaceted in nature. Theory-based interventions, utilizing constructs from social marketing, social learning theory, and a health belief model, hold promise as future approaches to the prevention of STDs (Fisher, 1990; Solomon & DeJong, 1986).

REFERENCES

Alexander-Rodriguez, T., & Vermund, S.H. (1987). Gonorrhea and syphilis in incarcerated urban adolescents: Prevalence and physical signs. *Pediatrics, 80,* 561–564.

American School Health Association, Association for the Advancement of Health Education, & the Society for Public Health Education, Inc. (1989). *The National Adolescent Student Health (NASH) Survey: A report on the health of America's youth.* Oakland, CA: Third Party Publishing.

Anderson, J.E., Kann, L., Haltzman, D., Arday, S., Truman, B., & Kolbe, L. (1990). HIV/AIDS knowledge and sexual behavior among high school students. *Family Planning Perspectives, 22,* 252–255.

Aral, S.O., & Cates, W. (1989). The multiple dimensions of sexual behavior as risk factor for sexually transmitted disease: The sexually experienced are not necessarily active. *Sexually Transmitted Diseases, 16,* 173–177.

Aral, S.O., Soskoline, V., Joesoef, R.M., & O'Reilly, K.R. (1991). Sex partner recruitment as risk factor for STDs: Clustering of risky modes. *Sexually Transmitted Dieases, 18,* 10–17.

Bandura, A. (1977). Self-efficacy: Toward a unifying theory of behavioral change. *Psychological Review, 84,* 191–215.

Bandura, A. (1982). Self-efficacy mechanism in human agency. *American Psychologist, 37,* 122–147.

Bandura, A. (1989). Perceived self-efficacy in the exercise of control over AIDS infection. In V.M. Mays, G.W. Albee, & S.F. Schneider (Eds.), *Primary prevention of AIDS: Psychological approaches* (pp. 128–141). Newbury Park, CA: Sage Publications.

Bandura, A. (1992). A social cognitive approach to the exercise of control over AIDS infection. In R.J. DiClemente (Ed.), *Adolescents and AIDS: A generation in jeopardy* (pp. 89–116). Newbury Park, CA: Sage Publications.

Bell, T.A., & Holmes, K.K. (1984). Age-specific risks of syphilis, gonorrhea, and hospitalized pelvic inflammatory disease in sexually experienced U.S. women. *Sexually Transmitted Diseases, 11,* 291.

Biglan, A., Metzler, C.W., Wirt, R., Ary, D., Noell, J., Ochs, L., French, C., & Hood, D. (1990). Social and behavioral factors associated with high-risk sexual behavior among adolescents. *Journal of British Medicine, 13,* 245–261.

Biro, F.M. (1992, August). *Adolescents and sexually transmitted diseases.* (Maternal and Child Health Technical Information Bulletin.) Washington, DC: National Center for Education in Maternal and Child Health in cooperation with the Maternal and Child Health Bureau, Health Resources and Services Administration, Public Health Service; U.S. Department of Health and Human Services.

Biro, F.M., Reising, S.F., Doughman, J.A., Kollar, L.M., & Rosenthal, S.L. (1994). A comparison of diagnostic methods in adolescent girls with and without symptoms of chlamydia urogenital infection. *Pediatrics, 93,* 476–480.

Biro, F.M., Rosenthal, S.L., Wildey, L.S., & Hillard, P. (1991). Self-reported health concerns and sexual behaviors in adolescents with cervical dysplasia: A pilot study. *Journal of Adolescent Health, 12,* 391–394.

Brookman, R.R. (1988). Sexually transmitted diseases. In M.D. Levine & E.R. McAnarney (Eds.), *Early adolescent transitions* (pp. 149–165). Indianapolis, IN: Lexington Books.

Brooks-Gunn, J., & Furstenberg, F.F., Jr. (1989). Adolescent sexual behavior. *American Psychologist, 44,* 249–257.

Brown, J.D., Childers, K.W., & Waszak, C.S. (1990). Television and adolescent sexuality. *Journal of Adolescent Health Care, 11,* 62–70.

Campion, M.J., Brown, J.R., McCance, D.J., Atia, W., Edwards, R., Cuzick, J., & Singer, A. (1988). Psychosexual trauma of an abnormal cervical smear. *British Journal of Obstetrics & Gynaecology, 95,* 175–181.

Carnegie Corporation of New York. (1992). *A matter of time: Risk and opportunity in the nonschool hours.* New York: Carnegie Council on Adolescent Development.

Catania, J.A., Coates, T.J., Stall, R., Turner, H., Peterson, J., Hearst, N., Dolcini, M.M., Hudes, E., Gagnon, J., Wiley, J., & Groves, R. (1992). Prevalence of AIDS-related risk factors and condom use in the United States. *Science, 258,* 1101–1106.

Cates, W., Rolfs, R.T., & Aral, S.O. (1990). Sexually transmitted diseases, pelvic inflammatory disease, and infertility: An epidemiologic update. *Epidemiology Reviews, 12,* 199–220.

Chacko, M.R., Cromer, B., Phillips, S., & Glasser, D. (1987). Failure of a lottery incentive to increase compliance with return visit for test-of-cure culture for *Neisseria* gonorrhea. *Sexually Transmitted Diseases, 14,* 75–78.

Chacko, M.R., & Lovchik, J.C. (1984). *Chlamydia trachomatis* infection in sexually active adolescents: Prevalence and risk factors. *Pediatrics, 73,* 836–840.

Chacko, M.R., Wells, R.D., & Phillips, S. (1987). Test of cure for gonorrhea in teenagers: Who complies and does continuity of care help? *Journal of Adolescent Health Care, 8,* 261–265.

Cohen, I., Veille, J. -C., & Calkins, B.M. (1990). Improved pregnancy outcome following successful treatment of chlamydial infection. *Journal of the American Medical Association, 263,* 3160–3163.

Cromer, B., Chacko, M.R., & Phillips, S. (1987). Increasing appointment compliance through telephone reminders: Does it ring true? *Developmental and Behavioral Pediatrics: Selected Topics, 8,* 133–135.

Darling, C., & Hicks, M. (1982). Parental influence on adolescent sexuality: Implications for parents as educators. *Journal of Youth and Adolescence, 11,* 231–245.

Darrow, W.W. (1989). Condom use and use-effectiveness in high risk populations. *Sexually Transmitted Diseases, 16,* 157–160.

deMauro, D. (1990). Sexuality education 1990: A review of state sexuality and AIDs equation curricula. *SIECUS Report.*

DiClemente, R.J. (1991). Predictors of HIV-preventive sexual behavior in a high-risk adolescent population: The influence of perceived peer norms and sexual communication on incarcerated adolescents' consistent use of condoms. *Journal of Adolescent Health, 12,* 385–390.

DiClemente, R.J. (Ed.). (1992). *Adolescents and AIDS: A generation in jeopardy.* Newbury Park, CA: Sage Publications.

DiClemente, R.J., Lanier, M.M., Horan, P.F., & Lodico, M. (1991). Comparison of AIDS knowledge, attitudes, and behaviors among incarcerated adolescents and a public school sample in San Francisco. *American Journal of Public Health, 81,* 628–630.

DiClemente, R.J., Pies, C.A., Stoller, E.J., & Straits, C. (1989). Evaluation of school-based AIDS education curricula in San Francisco. *Journal of Sex Research, 26,* 188–198.

Donovan, J.E., & Jessor, R. (1985). Structure of problem behavior in adolescence and young adulthood. *Journal of Consulting and Clinical Psychology, 53*(6), 890–904.

Drob, S., Loemer, M., & Lifshutz, H. (1985). Genital herpes: The psychological consequences. *British Journal of Medical Psychology, 58,* 307–315.

Ehrhardt, A.A., Fishbein, M., Washington, E., Smith, W., Holmes, K.K., & the NIAID study group on integrated behavioral research for prevention and control of sexually transmitted diseases. (1990). Report of the NIAID study group on integrated behavioral research for prevention and control of sexually transmitted diseases. Part II: Designing behavioral interventions. *Sexually Transmitted Diseases, 17,* 204–205.

Ehrhardt, A.A., & Wasserheit, J.N. (1991). Age, gender, and sexual risk behaviors for sexually transmitted diseases in the United States. In J.N. Wasserheit, S.O. Aral, K.K. Holmes, & P.J. Hitchcock (Eds.), *Research issues in human behavior and sexually transmitted diseases in the AIDS era* (pp. 97–121). Washington, DC: American Society for Microbiology.

Elkind, D. (1978). Understanding the young adolescent. *Adolescence, 13,* 127–134.

Ensminger, M.E. (1990). Sexual activity and problem behaviors among black, urban adolescents. *Child Development, 61,* 2032–2046.

Fishbein, M., & Middlestadt, S.E. (1989). Using the theory of reasoned action as a framework for understanding and changing AIDS-related behaviors. In V.M. Mays, G.W. Albee, & S.F. Schneider (Eds.), *Primary prevention of AIDS: Psychological approaches* (pp. 93–110). Newbury Park, CA: Sage Publications.

Fisher, W.A. (1990). Understanding and preventing teenage pregnancy and sexually transmitted disease/AIDS. In J. Edwards, R.S. Tindale, L. Heath, & E.J. Posavac (Eds.), *Social influence processes and prevention* (pp. 71–101). New York: Plenum Press.

Forrest, J.D., & Silverman, J. (1989). What public school teachers teach about preventing pregnancy, AIDS, and sexually transmitted diseases. *Family Planning Perspectives, 21,* 65–72.

Forrest, J.D., & Singh, S. (1990). The sexual and reproductive behavior of American women, 1982–1988. *Family Planning Perspectives, 22,* 206–214.

Franzblau, S., Sprafkin, J.N., & Rubinstein, E.A. (1977). Sex on TV: A content analysis. *Journal of Communication, 27,* 164–170.

Frau, L.M., & Alexander, E.R. (1985). Public health implications of sexually transmitted diseases in pediatric practice. *Pediatric Infectious Diseases, 4,* 453–467.

Freiberg, P. (1991, February). Condom use: Burden shouldn't be woman's. *APA Monitor,* pp. 30–31.

Fullilove, R.E., Fullilove, M.T., Bowser, B.P., & Gross, S.A. (1990). Risk of STDs among black adolescent crack users in Oakland and San Francisco, California. *Journal of the American Medical Association, 263,* 851–855.

Gibson, J.J., Hornung, C.A., Alexander, G.R., Lee, F.K., Potts, W.A., & Nahmias, A.J. (1990). A cross-sectional study of herpes simplex virus types 1 and 2 in college students: Occurrence and determinants of infection. *Journal of Infectious Diseases, 162,* 306–312.

Gillmore, M.R., Butler, S.S., Lohr, M.J., & Gilchrist, L. (1992). Substance use and other factors associated with risky sexual behavior among pregnant adolescents. *Family Planning Perspectives, 24,* 255–261, 268.

Goldmeier, D., Johnson, A., Byrne, M., & Barton, S. (1988). Psychosocial implications of recurrent genital herpes simplex virus infection. *Genitourinary Medicine: The Journal of Sexual Health, STDs, and HIV, 64,* 327–330.

Hillard, P.A., Biro, F.M., Wildey, L.S., Bradley, J.M., Burket, R.L., & Rauh, J.L. (1989). Cervical dysplasia and human papillomavirus: Evaluation in an adolescent dysplasia clinic. *Adolescent and Pediatric Gynecology, 2,* 32–41.

Hillard, J.R., Hillard, P.A., Kitchell, C., Birch, L., Brennan, C., & Grubb, P. (1989). Natural history of psychological reaction to genital herpes. *Journal of Psychosomatic Obstetrics and Gynaecology, 10,* 147–156.

Hingson, R., Strunin, L., & Berlin, B.M. (1990). Beliefs about AIDS, use of alcohol and drugs, and unprotected sex among Massachusetts adolescents. *American Journal of Public Health, 80,* 295–299.

Howard, M., & McCabe, J.B. (1990). Helping teenagers postpone sexual involvement. *Family Planning Perspectives, 22,* 21–26.

Irwin, C.E. (1990). The theoretical concept of at-risk adolescents. *Adolescent Medicine: State of the Art Reviews, 1,* 1–14.

Irwin, C.E., & Millstein, S.G. (1986). Biopsychosocial correlates of risk-taking behaviors during adolescence: Can the physician intervene? *Journal of Adolescent Health Care, 7*(Suppl.), 82S–96S.

Jemmott, J.B., III, & Jemmott, L.S. (1993). Alcohol and drug use during sexual activity: Predicting the HIV risk-related behaviors of inner-city black male adolescents. *Journal of Adolescent Research, 8*(1), 41–57.

Jemmott, L.S., & Jemmott, J.B., III (1991). Applying the theory of reasoned action to AIDS risk behavior: Condom use among black women. *Nursing Research, 40,* 228–234.

Jessor, R. (1991). Risk behavior in adolescence: A psychosocial framework for understanding and action. *Journal of Adolescent Health, 12,* 597–605.

Johnson, R.E., Nahmias, A.J., Magder, L.S., Lee, F.K., Brooks, C.A., & Snowden, C.B. (1989). A seroepidemiologic survey of the prevalence of herpes simplex virus type 2 infection in the United States. *New England Journal of Medicine, 321,* 7–12.

Kegeles, S.M., Adler, N.E., & Irwin, C.E. (1989). Adolescents and condoms: Association of beliefs with intentions to use. *American Journal of Diseases of Children, 143*, 911–915.

Keller, S.E., Bartlett, J.A., Schleifer, S.J., Johnson, R.L., Pinner, E., & Delaney, B. (1991). HIV-relevant sexual behavior among a healthy inner-city heterosexual adolescent population in an endemic area of HIV. *Journal of Adolescent Health, 12*, 44–48.

Kenney, A.M., Guardado, S., & Brown, L. (1989). Sex education and AIDS education in the schools: What states and large school districts are doing. *Family Planning Perspectives, 21*, 56–64.

Kirby, D., Waszak, C., & Ziegler, J. (1991). Six school-based clinics: Their reproductive health services and impact on sexual behavior. *Family Planning Perspectives, 23*, 6–16.

Kirscht, J.P. (1988). The health belief model and predictions of health actions. In D.S. Gochman (Ed.), *Health behavior: Emerging research perspectives* (pp. 27–41). New York: Plenum Press.

Kiviat, N.B., Koutsky, L.A., Paavonen, J.A., Galloway, D.A., Critchlow, C.W., Beckman, A.M., McDougall, J.K., Peterson, M.L., Stevens, C.E., Lipinski, C.M., & Holmes, K.K. (1989). Prevalence of genital papillomavirus infection among women attending a college student health clinic or a sexually transmitted disease clinic. *Journal of Infectious Diseases, 159*, 293–302.

Kjaer, S.K., Engholms, G., Teisen, C., Haugaard, B.J., Lynge, E., Christensen, R.B., Moller, K.A., Jensen, H., Poll, P., Vestergaard, B.F., DeVilliers, E., & Jensen, O.M. (1990). Risk factors for cervical human papillomavirus and herpes simplex virus infections in Greenland and Denmark: A population-based study. *American Journal of Epidemiology, 131*, 669–682.

Litt, I.F., & Cuskey, W.R. (1980). Compliance with medical regimens during adolescence. *Pediatric Clinics of North America, 27*, 3–15.

Luby, E.D., & Klinge, V. (1985). Genital herpes: A pervasive psychosocial disorder. *Archives of Dermatology, 121*, 494–497.

MacDonald, N.E., Wells, G.A., Fisher, W.A., Warren, W.K., King, M.A., Doherty, J.A., & Bowie, W.R. (1990). High-risk STD/HIV behavior among college students. *Journal of the American Medical Association, 263*, 3155–3159.

Manne, S., & Sandler, I. (1984). Coping and adjustment of genital herpes. *Journal of Behavioral Medicine, 7*(4), 391–409.

McCormack, W., Rosner, B., McComb, D., Evrard, J., & Zinner, S. (1985). Infection with *Chlamydia trachomatis* in female college students. *American Journal of Epidemiology, 121*, 107–115.

McLarnon, L.D., & Kaloupek, D.G. (1988). Psychological investigation of genital herpes recurrence: Prospective assessment and cognitive–behavioral intervention for a chronic physical disorder. *Health Psychology, 7*, 231–249.

Miller, B., McCoy, J., Olson, T., & Wallace, C. (1986). Parental discipline and control attempts in relation to adolescent sexual attitudes and behavior. *Journal of Marriage and the Family, 48*, 503–512.

Moran, J.S., & Peterman, T. (1989). Sexually transmitted diseases in prisons and jails. *Prison Journal, 69*, 1–6.

Newcomer, S., & Udry, J. (1984). Mothers' influence on the sexual behavior of their teenage children. *Journal of Marriage and the Family, 46*, 477–485.

Nightingdale, R. (1985). Adolescent prostitution. *Seminars in Adolescent Medicine, 1*, 165–170.

Orr, M.T., & Forrest, J.B. (1985). The availability of reproductive health care services from U.S. private physicians. *Family Planning Perspectives, 17*, 63–69.

Overby, K.J., Lo, B., & Litt, I.F. (1989). Knowledge and concerns about AIDS and their relationship to behavior among adolescents with hemophilia. *Pediatrics, 83,* 204–210.

Peloquin, L.J., & Davidson, P.W. (1988). Psychological sequelae of pediatric infectious diseases. In D.K. Routh (Ed.), *Handbook of pediatric psychology* (pp. 222–257). New York: Guilford Press.

Peterson, H.B., Walker, C.K., Kahn, J.G., Washington, A.E., Eschenbach, D.A., & Faro, S. (1991). Pelvic inflammatory disease: Key treatment issues and options. *Journal of the American Medical Association, 266,* 2605–2611.

Prentice-Dunn, S., & Rogers, R.W. (1986). Protection motivation theory and preventive health: Beyond the health belief model. *Health Education Research, 1*(3), 153–161.

Prober, C.G. (1993). Reducing the risk of perinatal transmission of herpes simplex virus type 2. *Infections in Medicine, 10,* 21–24, 27–28, 44.

Rickert, V.I., Jay, M.S., & Gottlieb, A. (1991). Effects of a peer-counseled AIDS education program on knowledge, attitudes, and satisfaction of adolescents. *Journal of Adolescent Health, 12,* 38–43.

Rogers, R.W. (1983). Cognitive and physiological processes in fear appeals and attitude change: A revised theory of protection motivation. In J.R. Cacioppo & R.E. Petty (Eds.), *Social psychology: A sourcebook* (pp. 153–176). New York: Guilford Press.

Rosenfeld, W.D., Vermund, S.H., Wentz, S.J., & Burk, R.D. (1989). High prevalence rate of human papillomavirus infection and association with abnormal Papanicolaou smears in sexually active adolescents. *American Journal of Diseases of Children, 143,* 1443–1447.

Rosenstock, I.M., Strecher, V.J., & Becker, M.H. (1988). Social learning theory and the health belief model. *Health Education Quarterly, 15,* 175–183.

Rosenthal, D., Moore, S., & Flynn, I. (1991). Adolescent self-efficacy, self-esteem, and sexual risk-taking. *Journal of Community & Applied Social Psychology, 1,* 77–88.

Rosenthal, S.L., & Biro, F.M. (1991). A preliminary investigation of psychological impact of sexually transmitted diseases in adolescent females. *Adolescent and Pediatric Gynecology, 4,* 198–201.

Rosenthal, S.L., Biro, F.M., Cohen, S.S., Succop, P.A., & Stanberry, L.R. (in press). Strategies for coping with sexually transmitted diseases by adolescent females. *Adolescence.*

Rosenthal, S.L., & Cohen, S.S. (1994). Primary prevention of sexually transmitted disease: Self-efficacy in the context of sexual coercion. *Adolescent and Pediatric Gynecology, 7,* 63–68.

Rosoff, J.I. (1989). Sex education in the schools: Policies and practice [editorial]. *Family Planning Perspectives, 21,* 52–64.

Ross, M.W. (1990). Psychological perspectives on sexuality and sexually transmitted diseases. In K.K. Holmes, P.A. Mardh, P.F. Sparling, & P.J. Wiesner (Eds.), *Sexually transmitted diseases* (pp. 55–69). New York: McGraw-Hill.

Rothenberg, R. (1981). Groups with gonorrhea: The broader context. *Sexually Transmitted Diseases, 8,* 290–291.

Rotheram-Borus, M.J., & Koopman, C. (1991). Sexual risk behaviors, AIDS knowledge, and beliefs about AIDS among runaways. *American Journal of Public Health, 81,* 208–211.

Shafer, M.A., Prager, V., Shalwitz, J., Vaughan, E., Moscicki, B., Brown, R., Wibbelsman, C., & Schachter, J. (1987). Prevalence of urethral *Chlamydia trachomatis, Neisseria* gonorrhoeae among asymptomatic sexually active adolescent boys. *Journal of Infectious Disease, 156,* 223–224.

Shafer, M.A., & Sweet, R.L. (1990). Pelvic inflammatory disease in adolescent females. *Adolescent Medicine: State of the Art Reviews, 1,* 545–564.
Simeonsson, R.J. (1991). Primary, secondary, and tertiary prevention in early intervention. *Journal of Early Intervention, 15*(2), 124–134.
Simon, K.J., & Das, A. (1984). An application of the health belief model toward educational diagnosis for VD education. *Health Education Quarterly, 11,* 403–418.
Solomon, M.Z., & DeJong, W. (1986). Recent sexually transmitted disease prevention efforts and their implications for AIDS health education. *Health Education Quarterly, 13,* 301–316.
Spirito, A., Stark, L.J., & Williams, C. (1988). Development of a brief coping checklist for use with pediatric populations. *Journal of Pediatric Psychology, 13,* 555–574.
Stanberry, L.R. (1993). Genital and neonatal herpes simplex virus infections: Epidemiology, pathogenesis, and prospects for control. In L. Tint (Ed.), *Reviews in medical virology* (Vol. 3, pp. 37–46). New York: John Wiley & Sons.
Stiffman, A.R., & Earls, F. (1990). Behavioral risks for human immunodeficiency virus infection in adolescent medical patients. *Pediatrics, 85,* 303–310.
Stone, K.M., Grimes, D.A., & Magder, L.S. (1986). Personal protection against sexually transmitted diseases. *American Journal of Obstetrics and Gynecology, 155,* 180–188.
Strader, M.K., & Beaman, M.L. (1989). College students' knowledge about AIDS and attitudes toward condom use. *Public Health Nursing, 6,* 62–66.
Strasburger, V.C. (1989). Adolescent sexuality and the media. *Pediatric Clinics of North America, 36,* 747–775.
Stricof, R.L., Kennedy, J.T., Nattell, T.C., Weisfuse, I.B., & Novick, L.F. (1991). HIV seroprevalence in a facility for runaway and homeless adolescents. *American Journal of Public Health, 81*(Suppl.), 50–53.
Stricof, R.L., Nattell, T.C., & Novick, L.F. (1991). HIV seroprevalence in clients of sentinel family planning clinics. *American Journal of Public Health, 81*(Suppl.), 41–45.
Sugerman, S.T., Hergenroeder, A.C., Chacko, M.R., & Parcel, G.S. (1991). Acquired immunodeficiency syndrome and adolescents: Knowledge, attitudes, and behaviors of runaway and homeless youths. *American Journal of Diseases of Children, 145,* 431–436.
Sussman, S., Dent, C.W., Mestel-Rauch, J., Johnson, C.A., Hansen, W.B., & Flay, B.R. (1988). Adolescent nonsmokers, triers, and regular smokers' estimates of cigarette-smoking prevalence: Where do overestimations occur, and by whom? *Journal of Applied Social Psychology, 18,* 537–551.
Tanner, W.M., & Pollack, R.H. (1988). The effect of condom use and erotic instructions on attitudes toward condoms. *Journal of Sex Research, 25,* 537–541.
Taylor, K.D., Miller, S.S., & Moltz, K.A. (1991). Adolescent health care: An assessment of referral activities. *Adolescence, 26,* 717–725.
U.S. Centers for Disease Control. (1988). Condoms for the prevention of sexually transmitted diseases. *Morbidity and Mortality Weekly Reports, 37,* 133–137.
U.S. Centers for Disease Control. (1990). HIV-related knowledge and behaviors among high school students: Selected U.S. sites, 1989. *Morbidity and Mortality Weekly Reports, 39,* 385–389, 395–397.
U.S. Centers for Disease Control. (1991a). Perceptions about sexual behavior: Findings from a national sex knowledge survey: United States, 1989. *Morbidity and Mortality Weekly Reports, 40,* 255–258.

U.S. Centers for Disease Control. (1991b). Primary and secondary syphilis—United States, 1981–1990. *Morbidity and Mortality Weekly Reports, 40,* 314–315, 321–323.

U.S. Congress, Office of Technology Assessment. (1991). *Adolescent health: Vol. 1. Summary and policy options (OTA-H-468).* Washington, DC: U.S. Government Printing Office.

VanderPlate, C., Aral, S.O., & Magder, L. (1988). The relationship among genital herpes simplex virus, stress, and social support. *Health Psychology, 7,* 159–168.

Washington, A.E., Cates, W., & Wasserheit, J.N. (1991). Preventing pelvic inflammatory disease. *Journal of the American Medical Association, 266,* 2574–2580.

Washington, A.E., & Katz, P. (1991). Cost of and payment source for pelvic inflammatory disease. *Journal of the American Medical Association, 266,* 2565–2569.

Weisman, C.S., Plichta, S., Nathanson, C.A., Ensminger, M., & Robinson, J.C. (1991). Consistency of condom use for disease prevention among adolescent users of oral contraceptives. *Family Planning Perspectives, 23,* 71–74.

Werner, M.J., & Biro, F.M. (1990). Contraception and sexually transmitted diseases in adolescent females. *Adolescent and Pediatric Gynecology, 3,* 127–136.

Westrom, L. (1980). Incidence, prevalence, and trends of acute pelvic inflammatory disease and its consequences in industrialized countries. *American Journal of Obstetrics and Gynecology, 138,* 880–892.

Whitley, R., Arvin, A., Prober, C., Corey, L., Burchett, S., Plotkin, S., Starr, S., Jacobs, R., Powell, D., Nahmias, A., Sumaya, C., Edwards, K., Alfrod, C., Caddell, G., Soong, S., & the National Institute of Allergy and Infectious Disease Collaborative Antiviral Study Group. (1991). Predictors of morbidity and mortality in neonates with herpes simplex virus infections. *New England Journal of Medicine, 324,* 450–454.

Worth, D. (1989). Sexual decision making and AIDS: Why condom promotion among vulnerable women is likely to fail. *Studies in Family Planning, 20,* 297–307.

Zenilman, H.J. (1990). Gonococcal infections in adolescents. *Adolescent Medicine: State of the Art Reviews, 1,* 497–509.

Zierler, S., Feingold, L., Laufer, D., Velentgas, P., Kantrowitz-Gordon, I., & Mayer, K. (1991). Adult survivors of childhood sexual abuse and subsequent risk of HIV infection. *American Journal of Public Health, 81,* 572–575.

14

Promoting Literacy Development

Dixie Lee Spiegel

Billy. *Let me tell you about my 11-year old son. Billy started kindergarten age 5½, had done average work, went on to first grade. They waited till spring to tell me he was just immature; by now he was 7. I let them hold him back. I then started to watch more closely; halfway through the second year of first grade, he still couldn't read! They tested him (at my request); they said he had attention disorder. They assigned him to special education; he went through second grade with a class of seven students in his room that were disabled. Billy didn't read but I felt he didn't belong there. Our doctor said they had made a mistake and would not order Ritalin. I put him in one year of vision therapy, and three years of expensive tutors, and two more years in a Reading Study group at the University which is also expensive and wears us all out running back and forth. Now we wouldn't mind any of the above if some improvement had been made. At age 11 he's a normal all-boy child in every way; he shows a lot of common horse sense at home and play. Halfway through the 4th grade Billy does other subjects well, but he still isn't reading.*
Pinnell, Fried, and Estice, 1990, p. 282

Dante. *At the beginning of the year, Dante was typical of many of the low achieving students I had had in first grade over the years. Everything seemed difficult for him. He knew just a few of the sounds and words that were the core of the readiness program in kindergarten. The worksheets that accompanied the basal were hard for him. His journal entries consisted of a picture and a few random letters. His participation in group activities was limited; he seemed to be inexperienced and to lack the confidence that would enable him to join in.*
Pinnell et al., 1990, p. 288

Although we don't know the rest of Billy's story, what happened to Dante is recounted at the conclusion of this chapter. In many ways, the chapter describes both of their journeys. Billy's story is all too familiar. As a child experiencing difficulty in attaining literacy, he was placed in a variety of special settings, but nothing seemed to work. Billy is surely at risk of joining the millions of adult Americans who are unable to read well enough to be fully employed. In this chapter, I explore the tertiary effects of illiteracy on society, the secondary effects on schools, and the primary effects of lack of literacy on individuals themselves. Next I examine the ways literacy problems are currently addressed at the societal, school, and individual levels. A case is made for the need for prevention through early intervention, and early intervention efforts are reviewed. Then guidelines are given for effective literacy development, starting with universal guidelines appropriate for all beginning reading programs, followed by guidelines for programs for children at risk, and ending with one additional guideline for those children who have fallen behind. Last, one exemplary early intervention program, Reading Recovery, is tested against these guidelines.

EPIDEMIOLOGY

Illiteracy and incomplete literacy have effects for society as a whole, for schools that attempt to deal with children who are not developing literacy, and for the children themselves. The tertiary, secondary, and primary manifestations are discussed below.

Tertiary Manifestations

Although as a nation, the United States is more literate now than in the past, as many as 30 million adult Americans lack functional literacy, that is, they do not have "the reading and writing skills necessary to understand and use the printed material one normally encounters in work, leisure, and citizenship" (Stedman & Kaestle, 1987, p. 23). Employers report a mismatch between job demands and workers' skills. Minorities are especially vulnerable, with estimates that fully 40% of minority adults are marginally employable at best (Sticht, 1987). Madden, Slavin, Karweit, Dolan, and Wasik (1991) paint a gloomy picture wherein individuals "are caught in a downward spiral that ends in despair, delinquency, and dropping out" (p. 594).

The cost of illiteracy to the United States is staggering in terms of lost productivity, welfare payments, and marginalization of whole groups of people who live in poverty and despair. The National Center for Family Literacy (1993) has estimated that the cost of illiteracy to U.S. business is over one billion dollars annually. In 1991 there were 4.4 million families receiving Aid to Families with Dependent Children (AFDC), and 1991 overall welfare costs were $20.4 billion (National Center for Family Literacy, 1993). The direct financial costs of trying to deal with illiteracy are overwhelming. The figures for Chapter 1 expenditures (for compensatory programs funded by the U.S. government) give an economic snapshot of the extent of federal efforts to prevent illiteracy: 15% of American elementary school students are served by Chapter 1 (Cooley, 1981) in 14,000 school districts (Slavin, 1991). In other words, 90% of school districts receive Chapter 1 funds (Savage, 1987). In 1990–1991 the Chapter 1 budget was $5.4 billion; in 1992–1993 it was $6.2 billion (LeTendre, 1991).

Clearly, in economic terms, literacy problems are too costly to our nation. Perhaps an even greater concern is the cycle of illiteracy perpetuated when adults are unable to read and write. Parents who lack literacy skills and/or literacy confidence may read little to their children at home, may not model literacy for their children, and may not provide the rich literacy experiences so helpful to prepare children for school. Thus, these children come to school at risk for failure with the reading and writing tasks that make up much of the school day. Often these children do not gain full literacy. Later, as parents themselves, they lack the literacy skills to create a fully literate environment, and the cycle continues.

Secondary Manifestations

In addition to the long-term costs to society of adult literacy problems, children's failure to develop literacy results in additional costs to schools for special programs and further schooling. Children who do not develop literacy in the primary grades rarely catch up with their age peers (Juel, 1988; McGill-Franzen & Allington, 1991) because their current performance becomes more and more dependent on previous inadequate performance levels (Carter, 1984). Without early intervention, at-risk children are put at increased risk to be retained (Bryant & Ramey, 1987) and to drop out of school (Lloyd, 1978; McGill-Franzen & Allington, 1991). They are more likely to be referred to special education (Bryant & Ramey, 1987). Slavin (1991) summarizes the consequences of early school failure: "Success in the early grades does not guarantee success throughout the school years and beyond, but failure in the early grades does virtually guarantee failure in later schooling" (p. 588).

Primary Manifestations

The cost to the children themselves is great. Most children come to school full of enthusiasm and confidence, never doubting they will succeed. With early school failure and problems in literacy development, children may begin to view themselves as "stupid," to lose motivation to learn (why try, since trying doesn't seem to help?), and to think of school as punishing and demeaning (Slavin, 1991). Self-esteem is shattered, attendance declines, and these children grow to hate reading and writing. Madden et al. (1991) warn that we risk "squandering the greatest resource we have: the enthusiasm and positive self-expectations of young children themselves" (p. 593).

ADDRESSING THE PROBLEM

The problems of illiteracy can be addressed on three levels: 1) after individuals have left school; 2) while they are still in school; and 3) before they leave, or in some cases even enter, the primary grades. The degree of success with these interventions mirrors the order of the levels themselves—the least successful programs deal with those who have already left school and the most successful work at the early stages.

Tertiary Level

A variety of programs attempt to address the problem of illiteracy among adults. Adult education programs through local community services, technical schools, and community colleges are fairly common. However, adult basic education programs and high school equivalency (i.e., general equivalency diploma [GED]) programs often have limited success in raising literacy. The complexity of adults' lives, their fragile self-esteem, and the length of time needed to attain literacy undermine their chances for success. For example, Sticht (1992) reports that most adult literacy programs have trouble retaining their students for even 50 hours of instruction.

Some employers have instituted workplace literacy programs in an effort to teach their workers job-related literacy skills. Other efforts include tying unemployment or assistance payments to enrollment in literacy programs. However, despite many sound and accessible programs, adult illiteracy remains a problem.

Secondary Level

A common response to children who do not develop literacy as quickly as their peers is to refer them to remedial programs, usually either Chapter 1 or special education. In spite of such labels as "Chapter 1" and "special education," remedial programs come in all shapes and sizes. Even within the same program in a school district or within a school, wide variability exists across classrooms (Allington, Stuetzel, Shake, & Lamarche, 1986; Johnston & Allington, 1991; Rowan & Guthrie, 1989). Programs are labeled according to the source of their funding rather than their philosophy or their approach to instruction. Therefore, no description of *the* Chapter 1 program or *the* special education approach is given here.

Chapter 1 Programs Chapter 1 programs provide supplementary instruction designed to help at-risk children close the achievement gap with their peers. Thus, one expected characteristic of Chapter 1 programs would be that children served would receive substantially more instruction in literacy and math than children not served. The evidence on this issue is not clear. Vanecko, Ames, and Archambault (1980) found that Chapter 1 students did receive more reading instruction overall than children who were not served. However, Ligon and Doss (1982) found that they got less. After reviewing the available literature, Allington and McGill-Franzen (1989) concluded that Chapter 1 students receive about the same amount of instruction, neither more nor less, than nonparticipating students. Carter (1984) and Rowan and Guthrie (1989) point to an additional concern, the *Catch 22* of compensatory education: while a child receives supplementary education in one content area in a pull-out program, the rest of the class is learning something else in another area.

A second and more important issue with Chapter 1 programs is the extent to which they aid children with disadvantages in closing the achievement gap with their peers. The results from several sources clearly show that Chapter 1 has a "positive but marginal impact" (Fagan & Heid, 1991, p. 583) on achievement; that is, Chapter 1 students do achieve more than comparable children not receiving services, but these gains in achievement do little to close the gap (Bean, Cooley, Eichelberger, Lazar, & Zigmond, 1991; Fagan & Heid, 1991; Slavin, 1987). For example, for the 1987–1988 school year, the average gain in reading for Chapter 1 students was three normal curve equivalents (NCEs) (Fagan & Heid, 1991). Other findings are also somewhat discouraging. First, gains shown in spring testing almost always disappear by the following fall (Slavin, 1987). Second, although Chapter 1 (and before that, Title I) children may show gains in grades one to three, there are few gains through programs in grades four to six, and there are no lasting discernible effects by junior high school of participating in Chapter 1 (Carter, 1984; Kennedy, Birman, & Demaline, 1986). Third, the students who profit most from Chapter 1 services are those who least need it and are not very far behind in achievement to begin with (Kennedy et al., 1986). The best predictor of achievement at the end of a year with Title I services was the level of achievement at the beginning. The poorest readers gained little, if at all (Carter, 1984). The one bright spot in the research on Chapter 1 is that according to National Assessment of Education Progress, minority students seem to be beginning to close the achievement gap, and this progress is attributed to participation in Title I or Chapter 1 programs (Slavin, 1991).

Special Education Programs As with Chapter 1 programs, we might expect that special education resource rooms (in which children receive part of their education during the school day away from the mainstream classroom setting) would provide additional literacy instruction to supplement the classroom program. This prediction is not borne out by classroom observations. Allington and McGill-Franzen (1989) found that although special education students did receive more reading instruction in their special resource room settings than did Chapter 1 students in their pull-out settings, the overall amount of reading instruction for special education students was not greater. This was because special education students received less reading instruction in the regular classroom than did Chapter 1 students, and the amount of supplementary instruction from special education was not enough to compensate for the lesser amount in the regular classroom. Haynes and Jenkins (1986) found even more discouraging results. They concluded that students with "mild disabilities" received very little reading instruction in their resource rooms and that the amount of instruction scheduled had no relationship to the degree of need.

A second logical expectation regarding special education resource rooms is that children would receive individualized instruction. Generally, the teacher–student ratio is quite low, affording the teacher opportunities to prepare and deliver differential instruction based on assessed needs. However, Haynes and Jenkins (1986) found little individualization, and Ysseldyke, Christenson, Thurlow, and Bakewell (1989) found minimal differences in tasks and minimal setting differences between instruction provided for children with disabilities and children without them. In fact, although O'Sullivan, Ysseldyke, Christenson, and Thurlow (1990) found that students in resource rooms had more academic responding time and more academic engaged time than they did in mainstream settings, children with disabilities still did not have as much of either of these opportunities to learn as did children without disabilities in mainstream settings. Overall, Allington and McGill-Franzen (1989) conclude that special education placement did not "enhance either the quantity or quality of reading/language arts instruction the participants received" (p. 529). However, these same researchers found little individualization for children with reading problems in the regular classroom.

Pull-Out Versus In-Class Models The primary model for Chapter 1 services has been the pull-out model in which children go to a reading specialist outside the regular classroom for supplemental instruction. Recently the efficacy of this model has been questioned and the in-class, or "push-in," model has been suggested as a replacement. In the in-class model, the reading specialist works within the regular classroom, usually as a tutor to assist target children in tasks assigned by the regular teacher. It has been argued that the in-class model will lead to more congruence between the Chapter 1 (or special education) reading instruction and the instruction of the regular education teacher. Furthermore, theoretically, less time will be wasted in transitions because children will not be moving from one classroom to another.

Research has not supported optimism about the superiority of in-class programs. Allington and Shake (1986) found no more congruence or coordination between the classroom teacher and the reading specialist with in-class programs. Although Bean et al. (1991) found some differences between the two settings (e.g., children in pull-out programs received more direct teaching as members of a group, whereas children in in-class programs received more direct teaching in a tutorial situation), they concluded that in-class programs did not show any change in the role of the reading specialist, did not solve any of the problems of the pull-out setting, and, indeed, may have generated a new set of problems. Other researchers (Archambault, 1987; Rowan & Guthrie, 1989) also found few if any differences between the two settings.

Need for Primary Prevention

Research on the effects of Title I and Chapter 1 suggests that these programs are marginally effective, primarily for children in the early grades who least need the services. Research on special education resource rooms leads to the conclusion that the quantity and quality of reading instruction are neither sufficiently high nor individualized to meet student needs. Placing children in these two types of programs has been the major response to children who have failed to thrive in classroom developmental reading programs. These programs work to some degree, but not well enough. Other models must be explored. Fortunately, two strands of research show much promise for the development of effective assistance for children with great literacy needs. The first set of research is that of early intervention and the second focuses on effective instructional practices.

EARLY INTERVENTION

The purpose of most early intervention efforts is to prevent the development of problems. For literacy, the premise is that concerted efforts with young children will help overcome, at least to some degree, the disadvantages of literacy-poor homes, incipient health problems, and disabilities. Carter (1984) stresses prevention of cumulative deficits; that is, once a child begins to fall behind, he or she is less likely to profit from intervention even when it is available. Thus, the child falls further and further behind as deficits accumulate. Early intervention may be a way to avoid the onset of that cycle.

Preschool Programs

Reviews of research on preschool programs have concluded that such programs have a variety of positive effects. Bryant and Ramey (1987) did a massive analysis of the effectiveness of early intervention programs. Karweit (1989) reviewed Gray's Early Training Project and Weikert's Perry Preschool. Scott-Jones (1992) examined evaluations of Head Start. Overall, these reviewers found that children in early intervention preschool programs were: 1) less likely to repeat a grade (Bryant & Ramey, 1987; Karweit, 1989, for both Gray's and Weikert's programs; Scott-Jones, 1992, for Head Start); 2) less likely to be referred to or placed in special education (Bryant & Ramey, 1987; Karweit, 1989, for both Gray's and Weikert's programs; Scott-Jones, 1992, for Head Start); 3) less likely to drop out of school before graduation (Bryant & Ramey, 1987; Karweit, 1989, for both Gray's and Weikert's programs); and 4) more likely to be employed as young adults (Bryant & Ramey, 1987; Karweit, 1989, for Weikert's program). All reviewers found at least short-term gains in intelligence (as measured by IQ), although long-term effects were unclear. Bryant and Ramey concluded that the primary effect of early intervention programs was not to raise disadvantaged children's IQs to above-average levels but to prevent or at least slow the decline of IQ over the years.

Intergenerational Programs

Intergenerational literacy programs that seek to break the cycle of illiteracy have recently gained prominence. According to the National Center for Family Literacy (1993), more than 3,000 intergenerational programs are operating within the United States. In most intergenerational literacy programs, the family itself is seen as the client (Asmussen & Gaffney, 1991; Winter & Rouse, 1990). Typically in an intergenerational program, both a preschool child and a parent receive services, usually at the same time at the same site. They "go to school together." The parent is involved in an Adult Basic Education or GED program. She or he gets assistance with job training or interviewing skills and receives counseling on parent–child interactions, working with family support services, and coping with the stresses of day-to-day life. The preschooler takes part in an early childhood education program designed to mitigate the effects of a disadvantaged home environment.

Research on intergenerational literacy programs is sparse and often of questionable quality (Park, 1992; Sticht, 1992), partly because of the relative newness of the approach and to the difficulty in measuring change with adults. Park describes some of these problems: 1) difficulty in measuring adult literacy in the first place, 2) inability to make significant changes in adults' cognitive structures in relatively short times (most programs involve parent–child dyads for only 1 year), and 3) use of tests that do not measure what was taught in the programs. Other problems are the general lack of comparison groups and of careful research designs. Park calls for longitudinal research as well as for measures of immediate change.

The sparse research available on intergenerational literacy programs generally shows more gains for children in the program than for adults. Winter and Rouse (1990) found 3-year-olds in a pilot program were better than a comparison group in language, social development, and problem solving. In reviewing the results of three quite different programs, Nurss (1993) found children in programs had increased interest in reading and writing, better oral fluency in English, and enhanced vocabulary and conceptual development. In a recent report on the Toyota Families for Learning Programs (*National Center for Family Literacy Newsletter*, 1992), children made modest gains on the Peabody Picture Vocabulary Test. The pretest scores showed that only 7% of the children scored above the 25th percentile on the PPVT and over 50% scored at the 1st percentile. After 1 year in the program, post-test scores indicated that 27% scored above the 25th percentile and only 20% remained at the 1st percentile.

Results for parents in intergenerational programs include higher aspirations for their children (Kim, 1989), increased awareness of ways to encourage children's emergent literacy (Nurss, 1993), and positive changes in parent–child interaction patterns, especially in the ability of parents to modify their interactions based on the child's response (Nurss, 1993). A comparison of literacy gains by parents in Toyota programs indicated that parents in the intergenerational programs made greater gains in literacy than parents in California adult basic education programs (*National Center for Family Literacy Newsletter*, 1992). After her examination of three varied models of intergenerational literacy programs, Nurss concluded that even if parents do not make significant literacy gains, there seem to be positive effects on preschoolers' emergent literacy.

First-Grade Programs

One of the most promising approaches to preventing literacy problems is that of early intervention with at-risk first graders. Four programs are described briefly here: Reading Recovery, Success for All, First Steps, and Early Intervention in Reading. The first three are individual tutoring programs, and the last is a small group program.

These programs have several common features. First, their primary goal is preventing reading failure. In each program, children are identified as at risk for reading failure in the first grade, before they have actually experienced failure, lost confidence, and developed strong, but ineffective, literacy habits. Second, the tutors or teachers in these programs are trained, certified teachers—not aides, volunteers, or older children. Third, the programs are very intensive. Fourth, children are provided immediate reinforcement and corrective feedback, and they are taught consistently at the appropriate level (Wasik & Slavin, 1993).

Reading Recovery The most widespread first-grade intervention program is Reading Recovery, which was initiated by Marie Clay in New Zealand. The aim of the program is "to improve the in-the-head processing initiated by the child in reading and writing" (Clay, 1987, p. 49). Thus, the lessons emphasize metacognition and conscious use of strategies.

Based on teacher judgment and the results of the Reading Recovery screening measure, the Observation Survey, the lowest 20% of the children in a classroom are selected for participation in the program. Children who have been identified as needing special services are not excluded (Lyons, 1989, 1991). Children remain in the program until they can function in their classroom's middle reading group and when they have developed a "self-improving system: They learn more about reading every time they read, independent of instruction" (Clay & Cazden, 1990, p. 207). A child is discontinued from the program when these goals are reached. However, if a child does not reach the goals after approximately 60 lessons, he or she is released from the program, not discontinued.

Each daily Reading Recovery lesson lasts 30 minutes and follows a general framework. The setting is an intimate one in which the teacher and child sit side-by-side and work collaboratively (Pinnell et al., 1990). The lesson begins with the child rereading one or more familiar books. Next the child reads a new book (introduced the previous day) while the teacher makes a running record of the child's strategy use in attempting to make sense of the text. The child then writes a message (usually one or two sentences) and reads it aloud. The teacher and child use this message to talk about letters and sounds and about using letters to check on the child's reading. Last, the child reads a new book, which becomes the book for the next day's running record. Throughout the lesson the teacher responds to the child's reading and writing attempts in ways that help the child strengthen useful strategies and replace ineffective ones (Pinnell, DeFord, & Lyons, 1988).

There are several technical reports detailing Reading Recovery's success (e.g., DeFord, Pinnell, Lyons, & Young, 1988; Huck & Pinnell, 1985; Lyons, Pinnell, DeFord, McCarrier, & Schnugg, 1989). The results from the pilot year showed that children in the Reading Recovery program not only made greater gains than other at-risk children; they even made greater gains than those children identified as not needing extra help (Huck & Pinnell, 1985). Data for the first 3 years of the project (including the pilot year) show the percentage of children successfully discontinued to be 73%, 82%, and 86% (Pinnell et al., 1988). Data for the second state cohort show that more than two thirds of the successfully discontinued children had text reading scores equal to or better than the average band (defined as + or − 0.5 standard deviation of the mean score) of scores of randomly selected first graders. For the third cohort, the results were even better, 74.1% (Pinnell et al., 1988). normal curve equivalents (NCE) gains in reading comprehension were 9.6 and 7.0 for the second and third cohorts, respectively (Pinnell et al., 1988), which compares very favorably to the average NCE gain for Chapter 1 children (Fagan & Heid, 1991). Other researchers have concluded that children in the Reading Recovery program more readily attributed their success to their own abilities and efforts than did other at-risk readers (Cohen, McDonnell, & Osborn, 1989).

Longitudinal data are also encouraging. When children from the pilot study were followed through second grade, the effect size when the Reading Recovery children were compared to a control group was +0.14. For the second cohort, the effect size was +0.25 (DeFord et al., 1988; Pinnell, 1989). In summarizing the research for the first 3 years of the Ohio State Reading Recovery Project, Pinnell concluded that "two-thirds or more of children who receive a full program in Reading Recovery make accelerated progress and perform within the average range for their classes. Children retain their gains and continue to make progress at least two years after the intervention" (pp. 175–176).

Success for All The Success for All program is a comprehensive, schoolwide program devised by a team from The Johns Hopkins University. It is the only tutoring program reviewed here that is a comprehensive program or that works with children beyond the first grade. Data are available from seven schools in three districts. Most of these schools are predominantly African-American, and in all but one of them, over 83% of the children are eligible for free or reduced cost lunch.

Reading tutors work with target children for 20 minutes a day during social studies time. First graders get priority. The tutoring is supportive of the regular curriculum, but tutors also seek to diagnose individual learning problems and to teach alternate strategies. Tutors serve as additional teachers during a 90-minute reading period, thus effectively reducing reading class size to 15. For reading, the children in grades one to three are regrouped across ages and classes, providing a limited range of reading levels for each reading class, more direct instruction (because the teacher is working with the whole class), and less need for seatwork. Cooperative learning strategies are common. The reading teachers and the tutors meet on a regular basis. Children are assessed every 8 weeks. There is a family support team in each school (Madden et al., 1991).

Success for All schools are matched with comparison schools for the purposes of research. On the average, children in the Success for All program outperfomed control children on both the Durrell Oral and Silent Reading Tests and the Woodcock Letter–Word Identification and Word Attack Scales. The overall effect sizes are impressive: grade one: 0.55 effect size and 3 months grade-level difference; grade two: 0.54 and 5 months; grade three: 0.46 and 8 months. Children in the Success for All program are retained less often and are referred less often to special education. Results are especially encouraging for the lowest achieving children for whom the effect size increases from grades one to three (0.64, 0.94, and 1.13) and no tutored child was 2 years below grade level in the third grade, although 10% of the comparison children were at that level (Madden et al., 1991; Slavin, 1991; Wasik & Slavin, 1993).

First Steps First Steps has much in common with Reading Recovery in the selection of the lowest achieving first graders for services and in the tutoring sessions themselves, but it differs greatly in the training of tutors (Morris, 1993). Both Chapter 1 reading teachers and regular first-grade classroom teachers are trained and serve as tutors. Chapter 1 teachers tutor three to four children daily, and each first-grade teacher tutors one child from his or her own class while an aide works with the rest of the class. Training for tutors is abbreviated from the Reading Recovery model. Training for both testing and tutoring follows this plan: 1) the trainer explains the process, 2) tutors watch the trainer on video implementing the process, 3) tutors watch the trainer work with a child, 4) there is a debriefing session, 5) tutors implement the process while the trainer observes, and 6) a debriefing session follows immediately in which the next lesson is planned. In addition, tutors attend 15 evening inservice sessions during the year, most before the end of December, and the trainer observes teachers on a regular basis.

Preliminary results (Morris, 1993) for 30 children tutored in five classrooms are encouraging, especially because these children were identified as being at the greatest risk by their classroom teachers and by the screening measures. Low-reading first graders from the previous 2 years (who had had no intervention program) provided a comparison group. In three of the four schools in the study, children in the

First Steps program outperformed nontutored children on several measures. At the end of first grade, half of the children in First Steps were able to read 75% of the words from the basal primer, whereas only 7% of the nontutored children could do so. Of children in First Steps, 76% were able to read the basal primer with 90% accuracy at the end of first grade, and in the three successful schools, 38% of the tutored children could read at the second level of the first grade. Although these results are for only 1 year and five classrooms, First Steps does show promise.

Early Intervention in Reading   Another program that has interesting preliminary results is Taylor's Early Intervention in Reading (EIR) (Taylor, Short, Frye, & Shearer, 1992; Taylor, Strait, & Medo, 1994). EIR differs from the other programs in that it is not a one-to-one tutoring program; the first-grade classroom teacher is specially trained to work with small *groups* of five children. Teacher training is far more brief than in Reading Recovery or First Steps: a 1-day summer workshop and then ongoing training and support in after-school sessions.

First-grade teachers identify the five children they consider to be at the greatest risk in their own classrooms, and then they work with these children for 15–20 minutes per day. Sessions follow a 3-day cycle in which the teacher reads a picture book to the whole class and then reads a summary of that book from a chart to the children in EIR. Through repeated readings and other interactions with this summary, the children learn to use context, develop phonemic awareness, write and spell, and develop a sight vocabulary and working knowledge of phonics. Each child also works with a trained teacher aide 5 minutes per day one-to-one, or 10 minutes when paired with another child in EIR. Running records are used to gather data continuously.

When compared to 30 low achievers from other first-grade classes (control group) and 30 average ability children in the pilot classrooms (comparison group), the children in EIR did well (see Table 14.1). Comparable results were found in implementation of EIR in two additional classrooms (Taylor et al., 1992), and a follow-up study of the children at the end of second grade found 98% of children in EIR were able to read at the second-grade level, although the program did not extend to second grade (Taylor et al., 1994).

EFFECTIVE INSTRUCTIONAL PRACTICES

Much research has been done concerning effective instructional practices. From the research, guidelines for universal practices appropriate for all beginning reading programs, additional guidelines for at-risk

Table 14.1. Percentage of children performing at different reading levels at the end of grade 1

Reading level	Group		
	Experimental	Control	Comparison
Reading at least at preprimer level	67%	36%	85%
Reading at least at end of first-grade level	50%	20%	55%
Standardized reading test score, September	29th percentile	34th percentile	52nd percentile
Standardized reading test score, April	37th percentile	27th percentile	51st percentile

children, and for those already in trouble may be developed. Research is reviewed that shows the extent to which remedial programs generally meet these guidelines.

Guidelines for All Beginning Reading Programs: Universal Practices

Focus on Real Reading Reading instruction should focus on comprehension of connected text, not on the fragmented study of isolated skills. Research has shown that instruction for good readers and poor readers differs, especially in the kinds of text used. Gambrell, Wilson, and Gantt (1981) concluded that poor readers received much more instruction with isolated skills than did good readers. In reviewing Chapter 1 programs, Rowan and Guthrie (1989) confirmed this emphasis on fragmented skills. Allington et al. (1986) found that in remedial classrooms, over two thirds of instruction was at the word or sentence level, and when "selections" were used, they were generally of only one paragraph in length and had a single skill focus. Good readers read more during instruction than poor readers, up to three times as many words a day (Allington, 1983; Allington et al., 1986). Evidently, in traditional remedial classrooms, reading is often fragmented and skill based, and the evidence shows that these traditional programs have not been very effective.

Many literacy educators recommend moving away from isolated skill instruction that utilizes worksheets and skills sheets toward reading instruction that involves the reader with fully formed text (Allington, 1983, 1991; Morris, Shaw, & Perney, 1990; Spiegel, 1988). Clay and Cazden (1990) present a persuasive rationale: "For all children, the larger the chunks of printed language they can work with, the richer the network of information they can use, and the quicker they learn. Teaching should dwell on detail only long enough for the child to discover its existence and then encourage the use of it in isolation only when absolutely necessary" (p. 207).

Spend Time Reading "Children learn to read by reading" (Morris et al., 1990, p. 137) may seem a bit simplistic, but there is evidence that the amount of free reading children do has a significant impact on their reading achievement (Anderson, Wilson, & Fielding, 1986). There is also evidence that many remedial and resource rooms provide students few opportunities to practice learned strategies through applying them in real text (Bean et al., 1991; Haynes & Jenkins, 1986). Instead, learner time is often spent completing worksheets.

Be Aware of Instructional Goals This applies to both teachers and children. Because of the kinds of tasks poor readers are given, the goal of much reading instruction for poor readers seems to be accurate decoding, whereas for good readers the goal seems to be comprehension (Allington, 1983). Although it would be comforting to say that these perceptions of goals are mistaken, observational research shows that teachers often do not have clear goals for individual learners nor do they work from any long-term remediation plan (Allington et al., 1986). Furthermore, there is evidence that learners are also unable to express the purposes of the activities in which they are participating (Johnston, Allington, & Afflerbach, 1985). Surely, if neither teachers nor students can tell an observer the goals of a program, it is not surprising that learning in remedial settings is often minimal at best.

Ensure Opportunities to Learn Opportunity to learn involves allocated time, time actually given, and on-task behavior. Allington's (1983) review of research on instruction for good and poor readers concluded that good readers have more engaged time than poor readers. That is, good readers have more opportunity to learn to read because they spend more time engaged in the task of reading. Allington (1983) suggests that one solution is to add a second daily reading session for poor readers. Gambrell et al. (1981) conclude that one reason good readers are more engaged is that they are more often assigned reading tasks with which they can succeed. Poor readers, however, are often working with difficult materials; therefore, they are more often off-task.

Provide Appropriate Instructional Level Materials Instructional level for decoding (i.e., word identification) is customarily defined as the level at which the reader has an accuracy rate of about 95%–96%. Morris et al. (1990) describe this as the level at which the learner is challenged but not overwhelmed. It is the level at which the learner is able to keep moving forward. Cohen et al. (1989) stress the importance of success so that the child will attribute success to his or her own efforts, competence, and control of the task; therefore, the child will be more likely to engage in that task again. Forell (1985) reports a study in which low and low-middle group readers at a "comfortable placement" (97% decoding accuracy) made more progress than might have been expected. Unfortunately, Johnston and Allington's review of research (1991) concluded that children in remedial reading classes often are provided with materials that impede their success.

Teach Strategies and the Ability to Transfer Them Skills differ from strategies. Skills are used without thought, in a reflexive manner. However, strategies are complex "in-the-head" processes (Pinnell, 1989, p. 166). Furthermore, strategy use entails conscious choice of an approach to solve a problem. Effective strategy use in reading implies metacognition: 1) the child knows when he or she has a problem while reading, 2) he or she identifies the problem, and 3) he or she implements a corrective strategy to solve or bypass the problem. Clay and Cazden (1990) describe the "work" of reading as using strategies deliberately to solve problems, with the most effective problem solving starting with high-level strategies and shifting to lower-level strategies only as needed.

Strategies must be taught so that children can generalize the use of the strategy beyond the immediate context or task (Johnston et al., 1985). In order to do this, there must be a clear goal beyond the current task—a real-world use for the strategy. However, many poor readers have a limited range of strategies, and they have difficulty transferring those strategies to appropriate situations (Clay & Cazden, 1990). This is not surprising; several observational studies of remedial classrooms have found that little or no attention is given to transfer (Allington et al., 1986; Bean et al., 1991). The goal for students is to complete a worksheet or oral reading, not to develop a strategy that can be used independently elsewhere.

Incorporate Writing Although writing is, of course, of value in itself, one important reason for incorporating writing into a beginning reading program is that the segmentation required to invent spellings teaches sound awareness (Clay & Cazden, 1990). As emergent writers struggle to spell, trying *LFNT* for *elephant*, they are playing with the sounds of the language, breaking words down, isolating sounds, trying to match letters with sounds (which helps them to match sounds with letters in reading), and blending it all back together again.

Include Phonemic Awareness Adams (1990) concluded from her massive study of beginning reading that familiarity with the letters of the alphabet and phonemic awareness—"awareness of the speech sounds, or phonemes, to which [the letters] correspond"—are very strong predictors of the ease with which a child will learn to read (p. 7).

Many beginning reading programs do teach phonics, but phonemic awareness and phonics are not the same thing. Phonemic awareness is just that—*consciousness* of sounds as sounds, as entities that blend and can be taken apart and manipulated. Phonemic awareness involves the ability to *use* sounds, not know about sounds, which may be what is taught in a traditional phonics program. Thus, Clay and Cazden (1990) suggest that phonemic awareness is not a prerequisite for learning to read, but it is an outcome of learning to read and write. By using sounds, by "trying them out" in reading and writing, children develop phonemic awareness.

Guidelines for Children At Risk: Selected Interventions

Establish Intervention and Classroom Reading Program Congruence The child who is likely to have, or who already has, trouble learning one reading curriculum should not be required to learn two, often competing, programs. Allington and Broikou (1988) suggest that coherence or congruence is present "when the reading instruction offered on different days or by different teachers . . . is consistently and mutually supportive" (p. 807). This congruence should include method, materials, and focus. The dilemma the learner faces is clear. The learner generates hypotheses and strategies about reading from one instructional setting that may be unsuccessful or even discouraged in a second instructional setting (Johnston et al., 1985). Furthermore, the child in two competing instructional programs has little time to master either (Allington & Broikou, 1988). Carter's (1984) review of Title I programs supports the claim that coordination of instruction between special classrooms and regular classrooms is positively related to achievement gain.

Historically, funding patterns for Title I and Chapter 1 encouraged the development and maintenance of separate programs. Federal funds were originally designed to fund programs that differed from regular programs (Allington & Shake, 1986; Savage, 1987). Fortunately, recent federal legislation, in particular the Hawkins-Stafford School Improvement Amendments of 1988, mandate coordination between Chapter 1 and regular programs (LeTendre, 1991). The severity of the problem is attested to in research of the 1980s and early 1990s that rarely found congruence in either Chapter 1 or special education settings (Allington et al., 1986; Bean et al., 1991; Carter, 1984; Haynes & Jenkins, 1986; Johnston et al., 1985; O'Sullivan et al., 1990).

Increase Opportunities to Learn Allington (1991) states the need eloquently: We must provide all children with "access to sufficient instruction to allow them to become literate with their peers"

(p. 26). For at-risk children this means more instruction. Again, the importance of congruence is relevant. If the child has to learn two curricula, there is not an increased opportunity to learn.

Reviews of research (Hiebert, 1983; Johnston & Allington, 1991) conclude that increased opportunity to learn is not a standard feature of special programs. Allington et al. (1986) found that remedial reading classes did not provide additional instruction, and Haynes and Jenkins (1986) concluded that although the combined time devoted to reading in special education classes plus regular classes did provide additional opportunity to learn for children with special needs, the combined amount of instruction remained unequal to the amount of instruction provided children without disabilities in the regular classroom. This was because the children with mild disabilities received very little instruction in the regular program. This confirms Hiebert's review of research, which reported that in regular classrooms, teachers spend far more time with high reading ability groups than with children low reading ability. Haynes and Jenkins further found only a weak relationship between the degree of instructional need of a child and the amount of services scheduled for that child.

Include Direct Instruction   Direct instruction occurs when learners are shown explicitly what a strategy is and *how* to apply it. Instruction may involve teacher explanation, modeling, or discussion. Research has clearly indicated that many children do not discover reading strategies on their own (Adams, 1990; Ehri & Wilce, 1985), especially children from low-income families (Calfee & Piontkowski, 1981) or minority backgrounds (Delpit, 1988). Unfortunately, research also indicates that direct instruction is not a feature of all or even most remedial settings, whether they be remedial reading classes or special education classes (Allington & McGill-Franzen, 1989; Allington et al., 1986; Bean et al., 1991; Haynes & Jenkins, 1986). What is found in place of instruction often is completion of worksheets and workbooks, with little teacher input or direction.

Individualize Instruction   As discussed earlier, instruction often is not individualized, either in regular or special classes (Allington & McGill-Frantzen, 1989; Allington et al., 1986; Bean et al., 1991; Haynes & Jenkins, 1986). Both Bean et al. and Allington et al. found that remedial reading teachers tended to give all members of small groups the same assignments and to give the same assignments across groups of the same age or grade placement. When instruction did seem to be individualized, children in a group typically worked on different worksheets, with little instruction involved (McGill-Franzen & Allington, 1990).

Monitor and Reinforce Children When at-risk readers attempt to use strategies with text, they need timely reinforcement if they use appropriate strategies, and they should be given suggestions for more effective strategies to replace inappropriate ones. In this way they will develop a metacognitive sense of what does and does not work for them in reading. At-risk readers may also need to be reassured that they are doing well (Morris et al., 1990) because a backlog of failure may prevent these children from recognizing their own successes.

Given the small class size of most remedial and special education classes, we would expect the teacher would be monitoring and reinforcing children. However, research does not support that belief (Allington et al., 1986; Bean et al., 1991; Haynes & Jenkins, 1986), although Carter's (1984) review of Title I research found that these compensatory classes did offer "higher quality cognitive monitoring" than that found in regular education classrooms (p. 5). When monitoring does occur, it appears to provide feedback primarily about the accuracy of responses and not about the appropriateness of the strategies used to obtain those responses (Allington et al., 1986; Johnston & Allington, 1991).

Employ the Best Teachers The guidelines above describe an effective reading program for at-risk children. Sadly, research clearly shows that programs for at-risk children generally do not meet these criteria. Stanovich (1986) has called our attention to the Matthew effect, in which the learners who need the most and best instruction too often get the least and the worst (Allington & McGill-Franzen, 1989). The common practice of using federally funded aides, who may not be certified teachers, to work with poor readers is an example of the Matthew effect (Johnston & Allington, 1991). The trend toward students from advantaged backgrounds attending schools that are rich in resources and vice versa is another example of the Matthew effect (Carter, 1984). We must provide the best and richest resources to our children who are at risk.

Guideline for Children Who Have Fallen Behind: Primary Intervention

Provide for Accelerated Progress Children who have fallen behind need a program that helps them make accelerated progress. It is not enough for children who have fallen behind to make normal progress; they will never catch up with their peers unless they make *accelerated* progress. Current data indicate that programs for children who have fallen behind are not helping them to close the gap, whether in Chapter 1 programs (Fagan & Heid, 1991), preschool intervention programs such as Head Start (Scott-Jones, 1992), or special education (Haynes & Jenkins, 1986). Fagan and Heid suggest that the current Chapter 1 policy of targeting programs as "needing improvement" if they do not meet their gain goals will only encourage programs to set minimal goals.

Equivalence of services is not enough. Children cannot make accelerated progress if they are given only the same opportunities to learn as their peers who are on grade level (Allington, 1983). O'Sullivan et al. (1990) pose the question bluntly. "Does it make sense, at the elementary school level, that the same amount of time is spent in reading-instruction time for students who are good readers as for students who are poor readers?" (pp. 144–145). Haynes and Jenkins (1986) conclude that one reason children never "get out" of special education is that services for both children with and without disabilities are often comparable, and comparable is not enough. The answer, according to Allington (1991), is not to slow down the pace of instruction because that guarantees the children will learn less.

Fortunately, a few programs show promise for promoting accelerated progress. Most of these programs involve one-to-one tutoring by experienced teachers (DeFord et al., 1988; Madden et al., 1991; Morris et al., 1990; Pinnell et al., 1988; Slavin, 1991; Wasik & Slavin, 1993). One such program, Reading Recovery, is analyzed as an exemplary program that meets the criteria outlined for all beginning reading programs, for programs for at-risk children, and for programs for children who have fallen behind.

READING RECOVERY

In general, information about Reading Recovery given below is drawn from Clay (1985), Pinnell (1989), and Pinnell et al. (1990) unless otherwise cited.

Guidelines for Reading Recovery

Focus on Real Reading Reading instruction should focus on real reading; that is, it should focus on comprehension of connected text, not the fragmented study of isolated skills. The daily Reading Recovery lesson always begins and ends with reading short books that use natural text rather than controlled, artificial vocabularies. The lesson begins with the child rereading several familiar books. Some books are selected by the child and some are chosen by the teacher for a variety of purposes. "Easy" familiar books are chosen so that the child can experience being a successful reader, reading quickly and fluently, and focusing on comprehension, not word identification. A slightly challenging book might be chosen by the teacher so that the child must solve problems "on the run" while reading, which is what proficient readers must do (Pinnell et al., 1990).

Reading Recovery does not promote the study of isolated skills because "programs that involve drill on small segments of language may teach children that reading consists of looking at words or at letters; poor readers may fail to subsume those activities into the larger processes of constructing meaning from within text" (Pinnell, 1989, p. 170). Rather, attention to the visual and sound details of written language is taught through extended reading and writing experiences.

Spend Time Reading Children should spend time reading. A common statement in Reading Recovery literature is "children learn to read by reading," and the framework for the lessons is built around reading and writing of texts, not pieces of text. Pinnell (1989) points out that while reading familiar text, children consolidate their reading strategies, increase their reading vocabulary, and gain fluency. Moreover, through reading slightly challenging material, children engage in the independent problem solving that leads to accelerated progress (p. 169).

Be Aware of Instructional Goals Both teachers and children should be aware of the goals of the instruction. Reading Recovery is a collaboration between child and teacher. Part of that collaboration involves both parties being aware of the goal of the program, which is that children learn to use a flexible repertoire of effective strategies both to make use of what they already know and to move beyond that knowledge. Teachers often ask children such questions as, "What did you do to try to figure out that word?" "Did it work?" "What other strategy might you have tried?" Thus, children are constantly held responsible for knowing the strategies available to them and for selecting appropriate ones.

Ensure the Opportunity to Learn Children must have the opportunity to learn. Reading Recovery gives a child one-to-one attention for 30 minutes each day. The teacher is focused entirely on the child and works directly with the child throughout the whole lesson. The child has few opportunities to get off-task because he or she is not given independent tasks like worksheets.

Provide Appropriate Instructional Level Materials Children must be given reading materials at their instructional level. Teachers carefully select familiar books for rereading from a list of more than 1,000 short books identified as being appropriate at varying levels. Some books chosen for a particular child will be very easy (at the child's independent level), and some will be at an instructional level that will require the child to try various strategies and receive feedback and coaching from the teacher. That is, because the book is only somewhat difficult, the teacher has opportunities for instruction, based on how the child interacts with the text.

At the end of the lesson, depending on what has taken place in that lesson, the teacher selects a slightly challenging book (at the upper end of the child's instructional level). The child reads that book once, and on the following day, that book is the basis for a "running record." During a running record, the child rereads the challenging book (which she or he has read only once before), and the teacher makes a record of both deviations from the text (miscues) and accuracy. The accuracy check verifies that the teacher has selected a text at the child's instructional level.

Teach Strategies and the Ability to Transfer Them Children should be taught strategies and how to transfer those strategies to novel situations. Through Reading Recovery, children are to develop a self-improving system of strategy use so that their skill in reading improves whenever they read and when no one is there to monitor or coach them (Pinnell, 1989). Thus, children in Reading Recovery are helped to develop the control to "orchestrate" the simultaneous use of a flexible set of strategies, such as reading ahead, looking at the letters, and examining the pictures. The children are also taught to crosscheck. That is, they are taught to validate a guess by using multiple sources of information, not only one. All this requires children to be active, strategic seekers of meaning.

Incorporate Writing Writing should be an integral part of a beginning reading program. Reading and writing are viewed as reciprocal processes in Reading Recovery in that "each process provides cues and responses that facilitate new responding in the other area" (Pinnell, 1989, p. 169). Writing is a part of every Reading Recovery lesson. The child attempts to write a message, usually one or two sentences, and the teacher assists by prompting, helping the child analyze the sounds in a word, or by writing the word for the child. In addition to helping the child focus on written text as a form of communication, the writing activity encourages the child to pay close attention to the visual details of the written word and to develop an understanding of letter–sound relationships.

Include Phonemic Awareness A beginning reading program should have phonemic awareness as part of the curriculum. Through writing and the discussion of the sounds that must be represented through spelling, children develop phonemic awareness. During the writing segment of the lesson, the teacher may have the child manipulate magnetic letters to develop a sensitivity to sound ("If this is *hat*, make it say *bat*.") The teacher may also draw boxes for a word the child is having difficulty spelling, with each box representing a phoneme (*not* a letter) (see Figure 14.1.) The child may be asked what sound he or she hears first and to write the letter(s) for that sound in the first box. The child writes in the letters for all the sounds he or she hears, and the teacher may supply the rest. Thus, for *paint* in Figure 14.1, the child might write *p* and *t* and the teacher would give the rest (especially the vowels).

Establish Intervention and Classroom Reading Program Congruence The intervention program should be congruent with the classroom reading program. Reading Recovery teachers are encouraged to communicate regularly with the classroom teachers of their students, although there is no standard mechanism across Reading Recovery for doing so. (As is the program for the children, this is individualized also.) Several models for communication and congruence have been explored (S.E. Hundley, personal communication, June 30, 1993). In some schools, a reading teacher and a classroom teacher "share" a classroom. The reading teacher tutors four children from the classroom during the morning, while the classroom teacher instructs the rest of the class. In the afternoon, the roles are reversed. When this model is followed, congruence between Reading Recovery and the regular classroom reading program is guaranteed for all practical purposes.

Another approach is for Reading Recovery teachers to provide inservice for first-grade teachers. Such inservice is long term and is embedded within the classroom teachers' jobs. That is, they have assignments to do within their own classrooms that will aid them in furthering their understanding of the principles and strategies of Reading Recovery.

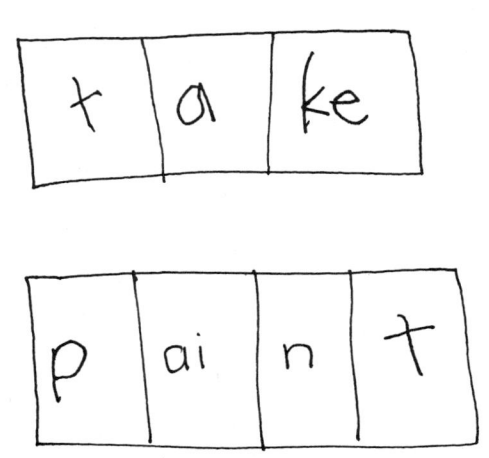

Figure 14.1. Reading Recovery writing boxes.

A third approach is to promote observation by classroom teachers of Reading Recovery lessons and by Reading Recovery teachers of regular classroom activity. Classroom teachers are invited to watch the Reading Recovery children from their classroom during a Reading Recovery lesson, with the goal that the classroom teachers will develop a new perspective on these children and be able to build on their strengths during regular classroom activities. Conversely, especially when a child is close to discontinuation, Reading Recovery teachers are encouraged to visit the regular classroom and watch the child interact with text in that setting. Special attention should be focused on whether the child was transferring strategies strengthened by Reading Recovery to daily reading and writing activities.

A fourth model simply is to arrange regular communication between the two teachers. This communication would have two goals that relate to the issue of congruence. One goal is that during these talks the Reading Recovery teacher would ascertain the classroom teacher's intended curriculum for the next month or so, looking at content themes (e.g., dinosaurs, fantasy) and strategies to be emphasized in the regular reading program. Then the Reading Recovery teacher could either take the lead by teaching these themes or strategies before the classroom teacher, thus enabling Reading Recovery children to profit more from the regular classroom instruction, or the Reading Recovery teacher could follow, reinforcing the regular classroom program. A second goal is to talk about the progress of specific children and to compare notes about children's strengths in strategy use.

Provide an Increased Opportunity to Learn   Special programs should provide children with increased opportunity to learn. Reading Recovery is based on the concept that even excellent instruction in the regular classroom is not enough for some children. Reading Recovery is designed to provide the something extra (Pinnell, 1989, p. 180) that gives at-risk children the opportunity they need to learn. The length of the program (i.e., the increased opportunity to learn) is dictated by the child's progress.

Include Direct Instruction   Direct instruction should be a part of the program. Clay (1987), the originator of Reading Recovery, does not consider Reading Recovery a program of direct instruction "because it aims to improve the in-the-head processing initiated by the child in reading and writing activities . . . and does not begin with a set of curriculum to be delivered 'directly' by the teacher" (p. 49). However, if we define direct instruction as explicit explanation, modeling, or discussion of what strategies are and how to apply them, then Reading Recovery does include direct instruction. Reading Recovery teachers seize opportunities to draw children's attention to details of print, spelling patterns, and letter−sound relationships (Pinnell et al., 1990) and "[to] intervene in sensitive and measured ways to help children take notice of sources of information they are using or neglecting in reading"(Pinnell, 1989, p. 169). Reading Recovery teachers do not allow children to fumble along in the hope that they will discover effective strategies; they guide the children toward these discoveries. Pinnell, in explaining the role of teacher intervention in Reading Recovery, points out that programs that focus primarily on stories and their content, such as some literature-based approaches, may not be sufficient to encourage at-risk children to sort out the details of print.

Individualize Instruction Instruction in special programs should be individualized. Although there is a standard framework for a Reading Recovery lesson, each child receives an individually planned lesson that focuses on his or her strengths, not weaknesses. Each daily lesson is based on the teacher's detailed notes of observations of the child's strategy use during the previous lesson. Even during the lesson, the teacher is responding to what the child is doing and adapting the lesson "on-the-fly."

Monitor and Reinforce Children Children's attempts to make meaning of text should be monitored and reinforced. Reading Recovery teachers monitor student progress in informal and formal ways. Informally, the teacher observes and responds to a child's attempts to extract meaning or to write, working alongside a child and looking for the "teachable moment" in order to take advantage of a child's discovery and extend it. Children's effective strategy use is reinforced, and when a strategy has not been successful, the child is led to consider other strategies. Formally, the Reading Recovery teacher makes a running record each day of the child's strategy use and uses this record in planning the next lesson. Teachers also keep detailed records of the number of words the child can write, and they graph the child's progress in the level of texts read.

Employ the Best Teachers Children at the greatest risk should be taught by the best teachers. Reading Recovery teachers are highly trained and only experienced, successful teachers are eligible for training. One drawback of the program is that this training must be done by an official teacher trainer. The training is intensive and involves the Reading Recovery teacher in a variety of tasks. Each trainee must tutor at least two children each day almost as soon as training starts. In addition, there is a 2½-hour seminar each week. Part of many seminars is a "behind the glass session" in which one teacher and child dyad work together in a soundproof room while the teacher trainer and trainees discuss what they observe. This discussion helps teachers rehearse the skills they need to use with children as well as to refine their understanding of Reading Recovery principles.

Ensure Accelerated Progress Children who have fallen behind need a program that helps them make accelerated progress. Reading Recovery is founded on the concept of accelerated achievement. It is expected that children will make accelerated progress, and they are not discontinued until they have caught up with their peers in the middle reading group. (The exception is the released child who has failed to make progress after 60 lessons.) Acceleration is achieved by "providing productive experiences that allow a child to move at a pace the child is ready for" (Pinnell, 1989, p. 170). The results from the first 3 years of the Ohio State Project show that over two thirds of children who receive a full Reading Recovery program do make accelerated progress (Pinnell, 1989), and we must remember that these children were selected from among the lowest achieving 20% of students in their classroom.

Reading Recovery is impressive, but of course there are some caveats. For the short term, it is a very expensive program. Teachers need released time to be trained; they work with only a small number of children; and a teacher trainer has to be hired at some point. For the long term, Reading Recovery may be expensive in some ways, too. If fewer students drop out, more teachers and classrooms will be needed at the high school level. However, the long-term benefits to society promise to be great: fewer unemployed and unemployable individuals; fewer people on welfare; and fewer disenfranchised, powerless citizens.

One last caveat concerns research. Most research on Reading Recovery is in the form of technical reports or anecdotal reports. Reading Recovery must be rigorously researched, and its results must be published in highly respected research journals in order for the program to maintain its reputation for quality.

What About Dante?

> Dante was selected for Reading Recovery and began lessons in January of first grade. After 15 weeks he was reading with the middle group in his classroom and was able to write 54 words in 10 minutes and write 36 of 37 possible sounds in a sentence dictated by the teacher. He was confident and often chose reading as a free-time activity. At the end of May he was able to read at the second-grade level with 90% accuracy. He was a solid, average student who could benefit from regular classroom instruction, without further help. At the end of second grade, Dante could read at the fourth-grade level with

97% accuracy. At the end of third grade, he could read at the sixth-grade level with 96% accuracy. In the fifth grade his teacher found him to be a strong B/C student who tested out at the eighth-grade reading level with 96% accuracy and was a strong average writer.

Because Dante made accelerated progress in the first grade, he was prepared to take advantage of the education presented to him in the regular classroom from then on, with no extra help. Dante was "recovered."

Pinnell et al., 1990

SUMMARY

In literacy education, the need for primary intervention, for prevention, seems clear. Efforts to remediate literacy problems after they have taken hold have been partially successful, at best. The research on early intervention shows much more promise for addressing illiteracy. Early intervention programs are expensive, but waiting until problems arise and failing to deal with them effectively is even more costly.

REFERENCES

Adams, M.J. (1990). *Beginning to read: Thinking and learning about print.* Cambridge, MA: MIT Press.

Allington, R.L. (1983). The reading instruction provided readers of differing reading abilities. *Elementary School Journal, 83,* 548–559.

Allington, R.L. (1991). The legacy of "slow it down and make it more concrete." In J. Zutell & S. McCormick (Eds.), *Learner factors/teacher factors: Issues in literacy research and instruction. Fortieth yearbook of the National Reading Conference* (pp. 19–29). Chicago: National Reading Conference.

Allington, R.L., & Broikou, K.A. (1988). Development of shared knowledge: A new role for classroom and specialist teachers. *The Reading Teacher, 41,* 806–811.

Allington, R.L., & McGill-Franzen, A. (1989). School response to reading failure: Instruction for Chapter 1 and special students in grades 2, 4, and 8. *Elementary School Journal, 89,* 529–542.

Allington, R.L., & Shake, M.C. (1986). Remedial reading: Achieving curricular congruence in classroom and clinic. *The Reading Teacher, 39,* 648–654.

Allington, R.L., Stuetzel, H., Shake, M., & Lamarche, S. (1986). What is remedial reading? A descriptive study. *Reading Research and Instruction, 26,* 15–30.

Anderson, R.C., Wilson, P.T., & Fielding, L.G. (1986, September). *Growth in reading and how children spend their time outside of school* [Technical Report No. 389]. Urbana: University of Illinois, Center for the Study of Reading.

Archambault, F.X. (1987, April). *Pull-out versus in-class instruction in compensatory education.* Paper presented at the annual meeting of the American Educational Research Association, Washington, DC.

Asmussen, L., & Gaffney, J.S. (1991). Reading in families: A research update. *Reading Horizons, 31,* 449–452.

Bean, R.M., Cooley, W.W., Eichelberger, R.T., Lazar, M.K., & Zigmond, N. (1991). In-class or pull-out: Effects of setting on the remedial reading program. *Journal of Reading Behavior, 23*, 445–464.

Bryant, D.M., & Ramey, C.T. (1987). An analysis of the effectiveness of early intervention programs for environmentally at-risk children. In M.J. Guralnick & F.C. Bennett (Eds.), *The effectiveness of early intervention for at-risk and handicapped children* (pp. 33–78). New York: Academic Press.

Calfee, R.C., & Piontkowski, D.C. (1981). The reading diary: Acquisition of decoding. *Reading Research Quarterly, 16*, 346–373.

Carter, L.F. (1984). The sustaining effects study of compensatory and elementary education. *Educational Researcher, 12*, 4–13.

Clay, M.M. (1985). *The early detection of reading difficulties* (3rd ed.). Portsmouth, NH: Heinemann.

Clay, M.M. (1987). Implementing Reading Recovery: Systemic adaptations to an educational innovation. *New Zealand Journal of Educational Studies, 22*, 35–58.

Clay, M.M., & Cazden, C.B. (1990). A Vygotskian interpretation of Reading Recovery. In L.C. Moll (Eds.), *Vygotsky and education: Instructional implications and applications of socio-historical psychology* (pp. 206–222). New York: Cambridge University Press.

Cohen, S.G., McDonnell, G., & Osborn, B. (1989). Self-perceptions of "at risk" and high achieving readers: Beyond Reading Recovery achievement data. In S. McCormick & J. Zutell (Eds.), *Cognitive and social perspectives for literacy research and instruction. Thirty-eighth yearbook of the National Reading Conference* (pp. 117–122). Chicago: National Reading Conference.

Cooley, W.C. (1981). Effectiveness of compensatory education. *Educational Leadership, 38*, 298–301.

DeFord, D., Pinnell, G.S., Lyons, C., & Young, P. (1988). *Reading Recovery: Vol. IX. Report of the follow-up studies*. Columbus: Ohio State University.

Delpit, L.D. (1988). The silenced dialogue: Power and pedagogy in educating other people's children. *Harvard Educational Review, 58*, 280–298.

Ehri, L.C., & Wilce, L.S. (1985). Movement into reading: Is the first stage of printed word learning visual or phonetic? *Reading Research Quarterly, 20*, 163–179.

Fagan, T.W., & Heid, C.A. (1991). Chapter 1 program improvement: Opportunity and practice. *Phi Delta Kappan, 72*, 582–585.

Forell, E.R. (1985). The case for conservative reader placement. *Reading Teacher, 38*, 857–862.

Gambrell, L.B., Wilson, R.M., & Gantt, W.N. (1981). Classroom observations of task-attending behaviors of good and poor readers. *Journal of Educational Research, 74*, 400–404.

Haynes, M.C., & Jenkins, J.R. (1986). Reading instruction in special education resource rooms. *American Educational Research Journal, 23*, 161–190.

Hiebert, E.H. (1983). An examination of ability grouping for remediation instruction. *Reading Research Quarterly, 18*, 231–255.

Huck, C.S., & Pinnell, G.S. (1985). *The Reading Recovery project in Columbus, Ohio: Pilot year 1984–1985* [Technical Report]. Columbus: Ohio State University.

Johnston, P.H., & Allington, R.L. (1991). Remediation. In R. Barr, M.L. Kamil, P.B. Mosenthal, & P.D. Pearson (Eds.), *Handbook of reading research* (Vol. II, pp. 984–1012). New York: Longman.

Johnston, P.H., Allington, R.L., & Afflerbach, P. (1985). The congruence of classroom and remedial reading instruction. *Elementary School Journal, 85,* 465–477.
Juel, C. (1988). Learning to read and write: A longitudinal study of 54 children from first through fourth grades. *Journal of Educational Psychology, 80,* 437–447.
Karweit, N.L. (1989). Effective preschool programs for students at risk. In R.E. Slavin, N.L. Karweit, & N.A. Madden (Eds.), *Effective programs for students at risk* (pp. 75–102). Newton, MA: Allyn & Bacon.
Kennedy, M.M., Birman, B.F., & Demaline, R.E. (1986). *The effectiveness of Chapter 1 services.* Washington, DC: Office of Educational Research and Improvement, U.S. Department of Education.
Kim, Y.K. (1989). *Evaluation of Kentucky's pilot adult basic educational program.* Lexington: University of Kentucky, Human Development Institute.
LeTendre, M.J. (1991). Improving Chapter 1 programs: We can do better. *Phi Delta Kappan, 72,* 577–580.
Ligon, G.D., & Doss, D.A. (1982). *Some lessons we have learned from 6,500 hours of classroom observations* (Publication No. 81.56). Austin, TX: Office of Research and Evaluation, Austin Independent School District.
Lloyd, D.N. (1978). Prediction of school failure from third-grade data. *Educational and Psychological Measurement, 38,* 1193–1200.
Lyons, C.A. (1989). Reading Recovery: A preventative for mislabeling young "at-risk" learners. *Urban Education, 24,* 125–139.
Lyons, C.A. (1991). Reading Recovery: A viable prevention for learning disability. *Reading Horizons, 31,* 384–408.
Lyons, C.A., Pinnell, G.S., DeFord, D., McCarrier, A., & Schnugg, J. (1989). *The Reading Recovery Project in Columbus Ohio. Year 3: 1988–1989.* Columbus: Ohio State University.
Madden, N.A., Slavin, R.E., Karweit, N.L., Dolan, L., & Wasik, B.A. (1991). Success For All. *Phi Delta Kappan, 72,* 593–599.
McGill-Franzen, A., & Allington, R.L. (1990). Comprehension and coherence: Neglected elements of literacy instruction in remedial and resource room services. *Journal of Reading, Writing, and Learning Disabilities International, 6,* 149–180.
McGill-Franzen, & Allington, R.L. (1991). Every child's right: Literacy. *The Reading Teacher, 45,* 86–90.
Morris, D. (1993). *First Steps, an early intervention program.* Manuscript submitted for publication.
Morris, D., Shaw, B., & Perney, J. (1990). Helping low readers in grades 2 and 3: An after-school volunteer tutoring program. *Elementary School Journal, 91,* 133–150.
National Center for Family Literacy. (1993). *Family album.* Louisville, KY: Author.
National Center for Family Literacy Newsletter. (1992). *4*(3).
Nurss, J.R. (1993, April). *Family literacy programs: Effects on young children.* Paper presented at the annual meeting of the American Educational Research Association, Atlanta, GA.
O'Sullivan, P.J., Ysseldyke, J.E., Christenson, S.L., & Thurlow, M.L. (1990). Mildly handicapped elementary students' opportunity to learn during reading instruction in mainstream and special education settings. *Reading Research Quarterly, 25,* 131–146.

Park, R.J. (1992). Commentary on three programs for the intergenerational transfer of cognition. In T.G. Sticht, M.J. Beeler, & B.A. McDonald (Eds.), *The intergenerational transfer of cognitive skills. Vol. I. Programs, policy, and research issues* (pp. 159–166). Norwood, NJ: Ablex.

Pinnell, G.S. (1989). Reading Recovery: Helping at-risk children learn to read. *Elementary School Journal, 90,* 159–181.

Pinnell, G.S., DeFord, D., & Lyons, C.A. (1988). *Reading Recovery: Early intervention for at-risk first graders.* Arlington, VA: Educational Research Service.

Pinnell, G.S., Fried, M.D., & Estice, R.M. (1990). Reading Recovery: Learning how to make a difference. *The Reading Teacher, 43,* 282–295.

Rowan, G., & Guthrie, L.F. (1989). The quality of Chapter 1 instruction: Results from a study of twenty-four schools. In R.E. Slavin, N.L. Karweit, & N.A. Madden (Eds.), *Effective programs for schools at risk* (pp. 195–219). Newton, MA: Allyn & Bacon.

Savage, D.G. (1987). Why Chapter 1 has not made much difference. *Phi Delta Kappan, 68,* 581–584.

Scott-Jones, D. (1992). Family and community interventions affecting the development of cognitive skills in children. In T.G. Sticht, M.J. Beeler, & B.A. McDonald (Eds.), *The intergenerational transfer of cognitive skills. Vol. I. Programs, policy, and research issues* (pp. 84–108). Norwood, NJ: Ablex.

Slavin, R.E. (1987). Making Chapter 1 make a difference. *Phi Delta Kappan, 69,* 110–119.

Slavin, R.E. (1991). Chapter 1: A vision for the next quarter century. *Phi Delta Kappan, 72,* 586–592.

Spiegel, D.L. (1988). What's wrong with overreliance on workbooks and skills sheets and what to do about it. *The Reading Instruction Journal, 31,* 20–24.

Stanovich, K.E. (1986). Matthew effects in reading: Some consequences of individual differences in the acquisition of literacy. *Reading Research Quarterly, 21,* 360–407.

Stedman, L.C., & Kaestle, C.F. (1987). Literacy and reading performance in the United States, from 1880 to the present. *Reading Research Quarterly, 22,* 8–46.

Sticht, T.G. (1987). *Functional context education: Workshop resource notebook.* San Diego, CA: Applied Behavioral and Cognitive Sciences, Inc.

Sticht, T.G. (1992). The intergenerational transfer of cognitive skills. In T.G. Sticht, M.J. Beeler, & B.A. McDonald (Eds.), *The intergenerational transfer of cognitive skills. Vol. I. Programs, policy, and research issues* (pp. 1–9). Norwood, NJ: Ablex.

Taylor, B.M., Short, R.A., Frye, B.J., & Shearer, B.A. (1992). Classroom teachers prevent reading failure among low-achieving first grade students. *The Reading Teacher, 45,* 592–597.

Taylor, B.M., Strait, J., & Medo, M.A. (1994). Early intervention in reading: Supplemental instruction for groups of low-achieving students provided by first grade teachers. In E.H. Hiebert & B.M. Taylor (Eds.), *Getting reading right from the start: Effective early literacy intervention* (pp. 107–121). Newton, MA: Allyn & Bacon.

Vanecko, J.J., Ames, N.L., & Archambault, F.X. (1980). *Who benefits from federal education dollars?* Cambridge, MA: ABT Books.

Wasik, B.A., & Slavin, R.E. (1993). Preventing early reading failure with one-to-one tutoring: A review of five programs. *Reading Research Quarterly, 28,* 178–200.

Winter, M., & Rouse, J. (1990). Fostering intergenerational literacy: The Missouri Parents as Teachers program. *The Reading Teacher, 43,* 382–386.

Ysseldyke, J.E., Christenson, S.L., Thurlow, M.L., & Bakewell, D. (1989). Are different kinds of instructional tasks used by different categories of students in different settings? *School Psychology Review, 18,* 98–111.

III

IMPLICATIONS

The case for a comprehensive prevention agenda was made in the first section and its relevance illustrated for an array of representative problems of children and youth. In the broadest terms, the implications of a primary prevention agenda are to remove or reduce risk factors, to capitalize on protective factors, and to promote resilience. This can be accomplished in two major ways: the provision of supportive services to child and family, and equipping them with education and skills to manage their health and behavior in competent and responsible ways. Included in such educational efforts are academics, affective education, moral education, and parenting education, among others. The goals and means of primary prevention and primary promotion are to foster healthy children, healthy families, healthy schools, and healthy communities.

The implementation of a comprehensive agenda to prevent problems of children and youth and to promote their well-being represents a significant opportunity for synergistic efforts. The task is to approach this challenge in creative and innovative ways, combining social and environmental resources. At the same time, it is important to recognize that policies, technologies, and resource deployment must be complemented by a commitment to shared principles and values that serve as the foundation for promoting human well-being. In the last two chapters of this volume, we examine the implications of such a comprehensive agenda in terms of policy and practice issues and training and research issues, respectively.

15

Policy and Practice
Implications of a Primary Prevention Agenda

Rune J. Simeonsson and Melva Covington

Coordinating services in the best interests of young people would make a fine agenda for the next decade.
Hodgkinson, 1993, p. 622

The marriage between the school and "everything else" is taking place. Like so many social innovations, it is growing out of extreme need in this case the fact that millions of young people are in jeopardy of failing to grow into productive adults.
Dryfoos, 1991, p. 636

The quotes above embody the basic premise developed in this book, namely the advancement of a primary prevention agenda for disorders of children and youth. The case has been made for conceptualizing this agenda in terms of a complementary approach of primary promotion of children's health, education, and well-being. Consistent with the World Health Organization's recommendations, total health and well-being must involve integration of services.

What are the implications of implementing such an agenda for policies, practice, training, and research? How can prevention policies be successfully advanced and maintained? Although the concept of prevention is not new and does not lack advocacy, commitment of resources, energy, and political will have not been extensive. The call for prevention from researchers, practitioners, and community leaders is growing, however, as is evidence for its efficacy. As we have noted in the previous chapters, there are programs that have demonstrated that the promotion of children's development does have significant preventive benefits. As these programs are reviewed, common themes emerge that reflect elements likely to be essential to the success of primary prevention efforts.

EXPANDING PARADIGMS AND PRIORITIES

If a comprehensive investment is to be made in primary prevention efforts, it will represent a significant paradigm shift and realignment of priorities. Increasing the investment in primary prevention does not imply corresponding decreases in secondary and tertiary prevention activities. Because prevention is an inclusive and dynamic approach, primary, secondary, and tertiary prevention represent points along a continuum. As the chapters in this volume have detailed, interventions at earlier points on the continuum are designed to be more effective and efficient than at later points.

At the present time, however, there is a strong trend to continue the formalization of disorders of children and youth and to approach treatment through curative rather than preventive means. This is evident in symptom-oriented solutions to childhood disorders and the tendency to address problems and disorders of children and youth through medical or technical ways. Examples of such medicalization and technicalization of problems and corresponding solutions are readily available in the popular media and the scientific literature. For example, excessive television viewing has been identified as a contributing factor to violence among children. The major solution proposed is the use of an electronic control device that will allow parents to regulate their child's television viewing. Although technology may be one solution, this approach seeks to substitute a technical solution for the more fundamental role of trust and responsibility in parent–child relationships. The solution to the problem of high sexual activity among teens with potential complications of teenage pregnancy and/or sexually transmitted diseases typically is defined in terms of condom use and preventive practices. If there is a breakdown in the trust, communication, and interaction between children and their parents, or children and educators, it may be more difficult to implement prevention successfully (whether primary, secondary, or tertiary). Maintaining trust and responsibility in services for adolescents can be enhanced by promoting communication, dialogue, and shared decision making.

Another example of a technical solution to children's problems is the continuing medication of school-age children for problems of hyperactivity and distractibility. Finally, the problem of prenatal exposure to drugs typically is dealt with through expensive and prolonged stays in a neonatal intensive care unit (NICU), and it may also include jail sentences for expectant mothers until they deliver. In each instance, the conceptualization of the problem and the corresponding solution is defined in medical and technical terms to the exclusion of the role of personal and social values, mores, and behavior.

Alternatively, each of these problems could be viewed in complementary nontechnical or nonmedical terms focusing on personal growth and responsibility. Technical solutions to problems are impersonal and reactive in nature. Many childhood problems can and should be approached in a proactive mode, promoting development and thereby preventing disorders. The logical representation of such a paradigm expansion toward greater emphasis on primary promotion of development and primary prevention of disorders would be to change the conceptualization of relative *risk* to one of relative *resilience*. Such a reconceptualization recognizes that protective factors and resiliency do account for favorable outcomes for most of the population, just as risk factors are associated with vulnerability and account for less favorable outcomes for a relatively small percentage. Health epidemiology, as well as developmental and behavioral epidemiology, has studied risk dimensions extensively, using such concepts as relative risk and attributable risk. Relatively little research has been devoted to the study of resilience and protective factors. There is, however, a growing recognition of the role of resilience and protective factors in explaining differential outcomes in the context of longitudinal studies (Rothman & Poole, 1988; Rutter, 1993). Illustrative of the concept of relative advantage and attributable advantage are research findings of Halsey, Collier, and Anderson (1993) on the issue of extremely low birth weight status. Comparison infant groups, 1,500–2,500 gm and over 2,500 gm, were 2½ times more likely to be characterized by favorable development at a 4-year follow up than lighter peers. Similar findings have been reported by Felhan, McGee, and Stanton (1993). Studies such as these could help to define an important research agenda on resilience and protective factors for a better understanding of variables promoting differentially favorable outcomes.

POLICY ISSUES

Remington (1990) has emphasized that policy that fails to become enacted also fails to remain policy, whereas practices implemented over time become de facto policy, even in the absence of formal policy. What are the policy issues that must be advanced for the adoption of a broad primary prevention agenda for the problems of children and youth? A number of initiatives espoused in recent years are reflective of the growing commitment to primary prevention and primary promotion efforts. The initiatives of healthy children, healthy families (*Healthy People 2000: National Health Promotion and Disease Prevention Objectives*, 1991), healthy schools (*America 2000: An Education strategy*, 1991), and healthy communities (Flynn, 1992), represent a recognition of the related importance of settings on the development and behavior of individuals, groups, and populations. These four initiatives reflect the expanding influence of the environment, from effects more proximal to the individual child to influences more distal. Not only are these initiatives characterized by positive, proactive approaches, they also reflect an increasing awareness of the significance of transactional and ecological factors in influencing child outcomes.

Several broad priority themes that have direct implications for the advancement of primary prevention policy can be extracted from the literature. The first is the consistent recognition that effective prevention programs must be *community based*. Although curative care is focused on the individual, primary prevention by definition focuses on populations, and it must be community based. In other words, strategies must be formulated at the community level, in collaboration with policy developers and/or researchers. Interventions cannot, and should not, be conceptualized in ivory towers with no grassroots input. It has been shown in this volume and elsewhere (Schorr, 1989) that programs utilizing the skills and expertise of individuals within the community are frequently better accepted, are more successful, and have the potential to last longer than do approaches designed by persons further removed from the affected communities. A second and related priority is what McKinlay (1992) has defined as the need for face-to-face decision making. He concludes that the continued erosion of face-to-face decision making has resulted in programs inappropriate for and insensitive to the populations for whom they are designed. Face-to-face decision making is essential to build a priority into programs, and most importantly to promote a sense of ownership within the community. A third theme for preventive policy is the adoption of an active strategy to advance primary prevention efforts. In an earlier chapter, Chamberlin advocates for social marketing as a timely and essential tool to implement primary prevention and promotion programs in communities (chap. 3, this volume). Stachtchenko and Jenicek (1990) has emphasized the role of advertising as a key feature of social marketing in public health strategies for health promotion. Along the same line, Walsh, Rudd, Moyekens, and Moloney (1993) have advanced social marketing as a strategy to attack many persistent problems in public health. By considering problems from new and different perspectives, it may be possible to address them more effectively.

A fourth policy priority in primary prevention is the formation of new alliances among different agencies, disciplines, and stakeholders. As established in the previous chapters, primary prevention and primary promotion efforts can not be mounted as unidisciplinary endeavors. Coordinated services in the best interest of the child require that joint efforts and new alliances be formed in the development and implementation of programs (Intriligator, 1990). The key players in these new alliances include professionals from health, education, behavioral, and social services. Moreover, such alliances may take the form of combined, complementary, or parallel services (Gensheimer, Ayers, & Rosa, 1993; Jason et al., 1993; Knitzer, 1993; Maier, 1990).

PRACTICE ISSUES

Paralleling primary prevention policies, and to some extent reflecting their application, are practices advancing primary prevention of childhood disorders and problems. Many of these practices have been described in earlier chapters; others are emerging or have been proposed as strategies that promote the development of children and prevent potential problems. We describe representative practices in the context of universal, selected, and indicated forms of primary prevention (Gordon, 1983), the framework defined in the earlier chapters of this volume.

To illustrate the application of the framework, representative target problems are described in Table 15.1 in terms of the identification of the target population, the target problem, and the nature of the primary prevention program. Although it is clear that some prevention efforts may be applicable to more than one form, it may be useful to identify the major focus of programs at each of the levels of universal, selected, and indicated prevention.

Universal

Universal primary prevention consists of programs targeted toward all children with the goal of promoting their development and adaptation. Much of the effort in this area has encompassed recommendations regarding the nature and process of schooling. Central to these recommendations have been proposals to expand the scope of school services, the role of personnel, and the nature of the relationship between school and family.

The formation of new alliances is likely to result in the need for alternative service settings. Traditionally, the clinic, school, or center has served as the central site for secondary and tertiary services. With increased focus on primary prevention, two increasingly important settings will be the home and the community. Early intervention research for young children at risk or those with disabilities has shown home visiting to be the critical factor accounting for significant outcomes (Hardy & Street, 1989). The value of home visiting is likely to rest on at

Table 15.1. Representative target problems and universal, selected, and indicated primary prevention programs

Form	Basis for identification	Target problem	Nature of program
Universal	Child populations at average risk and with average needs included without selection or screening	Poor physical fitness and health	Daily vigorous physical education (Kuntzleman, 1993)
Selected	Children identified on basis of group identity associated with increased risk and increased needs	School failure and dropout	Peer mentoring and tutoring (Srebrick & Elias, 1993)
Indicated	Children identified on basis of individual characteristics associated with high risk and high needs	Violent children and youth	Pairing as psychosocial intervention (Selman et al., 1992)

least two considerations. The first is that it is ecologically valid in that it occurs in the predominant caregiving setting of the child. The second, and perhaps more important, consideration is that it expresses the reality of an alliance between families and professionals on behalf of children. It is important to recognize, however, that home visiting alone cannot be an effective intervention; it must be paired with complementary services to address basic family needs, as Hardy and Street have shown in their study of inner-city, impoverished families.

Building on this premise, home visiting may have broader promise in primary prevention and promotion programs beyond the early childhood years. A common characteristic of services designed to address educational, health, and social problems of school-age children and adolescents is the fact that interventions not only are likely to be fragmented across disciplinary lines, but they also may not be well funded or politically supported. No matter how well intentioned, this puts interventions at risk for failure. Of greater concern, these interventions give scant attention to the involvement of parents. Given current concerns for family involvement and increased family participation in services for children, it may well be that home visiting can provide the essential component to enhance their effectiveness. A hypothesis well worth testing in this regard would be to make home visiting the central and formal component of community services for children and their families. As such, it would represent an investment in primary prevention by schools, health programs, social services, and corrective services. Consider, for example, the situation in many schools in which the teacher neither knows the parents of a student nor is aware of the student's home environment. It is interesting to speculate on the benefits that could accrue for children, families, and teachers if teachers made at least two home visits a year for every student in their classes.

However, in testing such a hypothesis, it is important to recognize that the value of home visiting must be considered in the context of the practical realities of the safety and acceptability of home visitors. Professional home visitors such as social service and health practitioners do bring needed services to hard-to-reach individuals and families, but as strangers they may be perceived as outsiders not being part of the community, they may face threats and be at increased risk for violence. Home visitors who are part of the community and who serve in a paraprofessional capacity may face a lesser threat; however, risks to their health and safety are still present. Random violence does not respect a person's address, whether child or adult. A well-designed home-visiting strategy may well be an essential element of primary prevention. The challenge is to incorporate it into a comprehensive, integrated approach of linking personal needs with community resources.

A key approach to the implementation of comprehensive primary prevention efforts is to build liaisons between the school and the community. One of the major reasons that previous efforts to address the continuing at-risk status of minority children in terms of their educational achievement have been ineffective is the fact that such efforts typically have been fragmentary (Cohen & Grant, 1993) and underfunded. Single interventions, such as tutoring or parental support, were provided rather than the combined services needed to ensure effective and sustainable improvement. These services and skills include job training, educational opportunity mentoring, police protection, and other neighborhood watch efforts that enhance supports. In this context, it is constructive to consider the lesson that history can provide. In a poignant qualitative study, Walker (1993) identified the dimensions that defined a "good" school for African-American children in the preintegration era. Walker emphasizes that what distinguished this school in a southern county was its support of the community and the community's support of the school. An important feature of this relationship was that "parents and school were united in their expectation of the students" (p. 171). The contemporary challenge for education is to build on these findings and act on the fact that the "community–schools relationship is a two-way process and that involvement should not be defined simply as how to bring the parents into the school, but also how the school can be in the community"

(p. 179). Beyond the historical example, Walker's analysis points to the value of identifying protective factors in school and in child outcome.

Nowhere is the formation of new alliances likely to be greater than between schools and everything else (Dryfoos, 1991). As Curtis (1992) notes, schools represent the ideal site for intervention because it is the universal setting where children engage in the work of childhood. Building on this premise, how would such alliances take form to advance the goals of primary prevention and primary promotion of children's development? Two examples can be drawn from the literature as illustrations, one from the preschool environment and the other from the public school setting.

Addressing the issue of supplementary care as a needed component in services for young children and their families, Caldwell (1991) proposed that early childhood education and child care have evolved historically into contemporary forms that have become artificially differentiated. Separately, each fails to provide the comprehensive services children and families need.

> By focusing on certain aspects (e.g., protection from harm versus promotion of developmental opportunities) of what actually happens, and by choosing a label exclusively on one or another set of program components, we have prevented the emergence of a concept broad enough to cover the full range of common services. With a devotion to labels that exclude rather than include, we have, quite literally diminished ourselves conceptually, thereby fostering the endorsement of a false dichotomy. (p. 201)

To redress this problem, Caldwell advocates for a unique term, EDU-CARE, to reflect a new form of child service that builds upon and integrates essential health components with high-quality educational offerings.

Prescriptions for improvement of the educational environment for school-age children have also appeared. Exemplifying the inclusive nature of comprehensive prevention programs is the Healthy For Life program described by Piper, King, and Moberg (1993). This program, designed for middle school students, builds on the assumption that the behavior of the young adolescent is significantly influenced by four key network elements: peers, family, school, and community. With this in mind, the program seeks to promote responsible behavior and prevent problems in the areas of nutrition, sexual activity, and substance abuse. There have been a variety of proposals emerging for schools providing full service in a one-stop-shopping approach (Marshall, 1993). The premise for the full-service school concept is that the use of the school building as a site to meet health, psychological, and social needs of students is both practical and effective. It appears that such school-based programs are gaining increased acceptance as a vehicle to provide comprehensive services. As Jee (1993) notes, the number of school-based clinics has expanded from a mere handful a decade ago to an estimate exceeding 500.

In a related recommendation, Ziegler (1993) argues for the provision of social services at the school site as an essential resource for low-income families. As Marshall (1993) points out, however, a crucial caveat in providing a spectrum of services in the schools is to recognize that such services are only a means to an end: The central purpose of school is to promote students learning to acquire the skills for productive roles in society.

Selected

As we defined in the framework developed earlier in this book, selected primary prevention is focused on children in the population who have increased needs and are at increased risk by virtue of group identity. Individual children may or may not be at risk, but their group identity is associated with increased need and risk. In contemporary society, there are many group identities that raise the risk of unfavorable outcomes for children. One case might be a single group identity such as migrant status; however, in most cases, it is likely that children share several group identities that synergistically raise their risk status. In any case, however, primary prevention should be provided for these groups of children selected on the basis of increased risk and increased need associated with a group identity. The fact that their selection for primary prevention is based on group identity precludes the need for individual screening. Representative groups for whom primary prevention can be provided on a selected basis include group identities reflecting residential situations (e.g., homeless [Rivlin, 1993]), geographical contexts (rural, reservation), school transition (Jason et al., 1993), and home contexts (alcoholic and/or abusive families).

One of the more common group identities by which to identify children for selected primary prevention is that of age. In the context of developmental stages, some children are differentially at increased risk at some stages and not at others. Relationships with parents, peer pressure, school transitions, and response to academic demands may differ substantially from age to age with unfavorable outcomes being much more likely at some ages. On the basis of risk modeling, it is possible to identify groups for prevention initiatives at target ages.

The problem of substance use has been identified as an important priority for primary prevention (Jack, 1992; Rohrbach, Graham, & Hansen, 1993). The risk factors for substance abuse that could be used to identify groups for selected primary prevention may vary along a number of dimensions. A social development model has been proposed by Hawkins, Lishner, Catalano, and Howard (1986), which identifies risk factors on a developmental continuum. This model posits that the major factors of family, school, and peers have differential influence in early and middle childhood and adolescence, respectively. Addressing the problem of substance abuse, Graham, Johnson, Hansen, Flay, and Gee (1990) targeted three cohorts of seventh graders with a primary prevention program on the basis of a social psychology approach. For each of the three cohorts, the emphasis was on assisting students to develop skills for resisting pressures to use drugs involving social skills, affect management, or some combination of these strategies. Overall prevention effects were gender specific with girls benefitting more than boys. While the most marked effects were found for cigarettes and alcohol, significant gender-by-program effects were also obtained for marijuana use. A data trend also suggested differential effectiveness as a function of ethnicity, with Asian-American students showing the most favorable response. Studies of this nature are supportive of the value of primary prevention designed to benefit children at increased risk on the basis of group identity.

Indicated

Whereas the basis for providing selected primary prevention is identification of subgroups sharing a common group identity, indicated primary prevention is provided for children based on individual rather than group characteristics. For the youngest of children, primary prevention may be indicated for infants defined by such risk factors as low birth weight, prematurity, prenatal drug exposure, and failure to thrive. Through early and middle childhood, primary prevention may be indicated for children characterized by developmental delay, disturbed peer relationships, depressed mood, or academic failure. In adolescence, primary prevention may be indicated for teens who are at high risk because of drug experimentation, grade retention, or school absenteeism. In each of the examples above, elevated risk is based on characteristics identified or identifiable in the individual child. In contrast to universal and selected primary prevention, screening and Child-Find activities are necessary components to identify children for whom indicated primary prevention should be provided. To complement descriptions of primary prevention for the children at high risk described in earlier chapters of this volume, such as internalizing and externalizing problems and school dropout, it may be useful to illustrate further indicated primary prevention for children presenting with other individual risk factors.

One such group is children who are overweight. As Serdula et al. (1993) note, obese children are two to six and one half times at greater risk for becoming obese adults than are nonobese children. The number of children who are becoming overweight is increasing at an alarming rate. Findings from national survey data indicate that in recent years the increase in prevalence of obesity was 54% for 6- to 11-year-old children and 39% for 12- to 17-year-old adolescents. The corresponding values for superobesity were a staggering 98% increase for 6- to 11-year-old children and 64% for 12- to 17-year-old adolescents (Kuntzleman, 1993). The nature of elevated individual risk for obesity often interacts with minority status. The risk for children with Mexican and Puerto Rican heritage is two to three times higher than that for nonminority children, and African-American females are disproportionately at risk (Williams & Wynder, 1993).

Childhood obesity and corresponding lack of fitness is clearly a significant, but preventable, problem among U.S. children. That problem is exacerbated by the fact that obese children are at increased risk for medical and psychological sequelae. The decline in fitness may be both a result of, and a contributor to, inactive lifestyles. The evidence in this regard is telling: On the basis of a study of family activity patterns, Kuntzleman (1993) reports that 78% the time spent by an average child was in sedentary activity, as compared to 1% in vigorous physical activity. A major reason for inactivity, declining fitness, and increased weight can be traced to the fact that physical education is not mandated in many states. In those states where it is required, it is of very limited duration and active exercise accounts for only about one fourth of the time spent in physical education classes (Kuntzleman, 1993). This is in sharp contrast to the sedentary activity of television watching, which accounts for 25–27 hours of the average child's week. The net result is that children "in the United States are fatter, slower and weaker than their counterparts in other developed countries" (DiNubilie, 1993, p. 589).

What are the implications for indicated primary prevention for overweight children? Recommendations have recognized the interdependence of nutrition and activity in defining fitness. With regard to nutrition, Williams and Wynder (1993) recommend lowering the dietary and saturated fat intake of all children over 2 years and reducing the frequency of eating and the proportion of caloric intake from snacks. Complementing nutritional goals, increased physical activity is seen as a national priority because "fitness should be a major corrective of any national preventive effort in terms of health promotion and disease prevention. Fitness may actually be one of the 'magic bullets' that we are looking for" (DiNubile, 1993, p. 589). The essential components of a comprehensive prevention effort call for schools and families to promote rigorous physical activity on a daily basis. Such physical activity should be reflected in mandatory physical education in the schools across all grade levels, consisting of at least 30 minutes of activity with at least 50% of that time committed to active movement (Kuntzleman, 1993). A national commitment of this kind would not only have immediate physical benefits and reduce risks for illness and disease, but it would also yield synergistic benefits of psychological growth and school achievement. Such a linkage of health and educational priorities is consistent with McGinnis's (1993) statement that "a child needs to be healthy in order to learn, and a child needs to be well-educated to stay healthy" (p. 493). In this context, a healthy outcome is defined not only in physical terms, but it also encompasses psychological, social, and academic growth.

SYNTHESIS OF EFFECTIVE ELEMENTS IN PRIMARY PREVENTION

While an integrated, comprehensive, and sustained commitment to primary prevention still awaits emergence on the national level, this book has documented the fact that there is a wealth of ideas and working models for the prevention of childhood problems. The coverage provided in each of the chapters in this book and the literature cited in this and the following chapter suggest eight recurrent themes that cut across specific conditions and populations relevant for universal, selected, and indicated prevention efforts. These prevention themes address the well-being of children through emphasis on early intervention, provision of structure, family support, relationship building, community schools, home visitation, new service alliances, and providing services in context. The consistency with which these broad themes appear in concept papers and program descriptions endorse their relevance for future prevention priorities and efforts. To that end, it would seem useful to consider them as frames for conceptualizing, designing, and implementing programs to address preventable childhood problems.

The context of the prevention literature in recent years has been one focused on health promotion in the broadest sense of individual and community wellness. Formally or informally, prevention initiatives have been defined to promote healthy children, healthy families, healthy schools, and healthy communities. Ordered in this fashion, the progressive focus from healthy children, healthy families, healthy schools, and healthy communities reflects Bronfenbrenner's (1977) ecological model of successive levels of embeddedness and complexity. At each ecological level, there are complementary rights and responsibilities defining the relationship between person and environment. For the purpose of this discussion, they may productively serve as a backdrop for the eight themes shown in Table 15.2.

Table 15.2. Ecological contexts, major themes, and representative initiatives to reduce risk and promote resilience among children

Ecological context	Themes	Reducing risk	Promoting resilience
Healthy children	Modeling and structure Early intervention	Significant adult in the life of each child (Dryfoos, 1991)	Task accomplishment and responsibility (Rutter, 1987)
Healthy families	Family support and education Relationship building	Parenting education (Weinman, Schreiber, & Robinson, 1992) Personal, face-to-face encounters (Danielson, Hamel-Bissell, & Winstead-Fry, 1993)	Family literacy (Winter & Rouse, 1990)
Healthy schools	Community schools Home visitation	Improving schools as work sites (Rudd & Walsh, 1993)	School health education (Kolbe, 1993) Schooling choice and family involvement (Fliegel & MacGuire, 1993)
Healthy communities	New alliances Contextual approaches	Technology and injury prevention as community initiative (Cowart, 1993)	Schools as integrating unit for community services (Marshall, 1993)

Healthy Children

Two themes are central to the promotion of healthy children—the provision of structure and early intervention. The importance of providing structure in the lives of children has been emphasized across a variety of topical areas. The embodiment of such structure for the child is the presence of a responsible, predictable, and caring adult. To fulfill this role, the adult must be engaged in productive work because employment fosters pride, responsibility, and respect. This may be a particularly challenging task in inner cities where the unemployment rate of adult role models is very high. Here again we emphasize the critical role of primary prevention to interrupt the vicious circle or cycle Chamberlin discusses in Chapter 3 of this volume. Addressing the need to prevent alcohol and drug abuse among youth, Cahalan (1991) insists that "every child should have or be assigned one or more adults who will be responsible for his or her welfare and behavior" (p. 241). Along a similar vein, Dryfoos (1991) has proposed that a system be established to "guarantee that every child is attached to a responsible adult—if not the mother and father, then someone else" (p. 634). In the more focused context of alternate schools for at-risk youths, Franklin (1992) emphasizes the crucial role of well-defined rules and standards. Such rules and standards may be particularly evident in physical education, a vehicle that Garber (1993) believes would be effective for physical health and fitness as well as personal skills, a position also advocated by Williams and Wynder (1993).

The second theme directed toward the promotion of healthy children is early intervention. "Early" in this case refers not only to intervention provided to infants and very young children, but also to intervention that seeks to prevent a problem at an earlier rather than later point in a causal or risk chain (as noted in Simeonsson, chap. 2, this volume). The success of preschool and Head Start programs for young children has been identified by Dryfoos (1991) and others as representative of effective programs. Price, Cowen, Lorin, and Ramos-McKay (1989) have also identified programs for individuals at later points in the life span, although programs for adults and elderly are disproportionately fewer.

Healthy Families

The themes involving healthy families can be defined in terms of efforts to promote family education and alliances with the family. In a recognition of the contextual role of the family in nurturing the development of the child, various recommendations have been made for parental education (Jones & Herndon, 1993), family literacy (Winter & Rouse, 1990), and anticipatory guidance (Hardy & Streett, 1989). The limited parenting knowledge and skills of adolescent parents has been identified as a critical target for parent education (Weinman, Schreiber, & Robinson, 1992). Anastasiow (1988) has proposed that parenting classes beginning in late elementary school should be a national policy to prevent poor child outcomes and to promote skills of future parents.

Closely related to the theme of parent education is the promotion of alliances between families and service providers. A major factor accounting for the pervasive problems of children and families at risk is the sense of alienation and distancing they experience from services and supports in the community. Coulton, Pandey, and Chow (1990) describe the growing social isolation of inner-city communities because of the drain of resources (businesses, jobs, urban flight), more pathological behavior, and increasing violence. These factors have resulted in many center cities that are now poorer and more dangerous. This scenario has been coupled with fewer resources from state, local, and federal governments for training and infrastructure. The combination of such neglect has placed a tremendous strain on local school districts, service agencies, and families. The growing social isolation of these communities from social services and individuals in mainstream society has been devastating. This situation endorses the urgency for coordinated and comprehensive approaches that are sensitive to the unique needs of vulnerable populations.

McKinlay (1992) has defined the current problem as one in which face-to-face relationships have increasingly been eroded and replaced by impersonal contacts. The need to re-establish personal encounters is a necessary base on which to build prevention programs (Gebbie, 1993; Cahalan, 1991). Danielson, Hamel-Bissell, and Winstead-Fry (1993) have poignantly spoken to this issue by calling for a change in identity so that professionals move from a "we" and "they" orientation to thinking of "us."

Healthy Schools

The goals defined in *America 2000* (1991) reflect the commitment to improve the health of schools. Calls for the reform, restructuring, and reinvention of schools have appeared in a variety of forums and have been advanced by a variety of disciplines. In its most inclusive form, the healthy school is defined in terms of the full-service school or community school. The essence of such "complete" schools is that they encompass an array of educational, health, and social services in the setting where children spend much of the first 2 decades of their lives (Bower, 1985; Curtis, 1992; Finn-Stevenson, Linkins, & Beacom, 1992; Marshall, 1993). Perhaps Dryfoos (1991) has summed up best the inclusive nature of such schools as places where

> . . . children are able to receive high-quality education and where they and their families can obtain access to a wide range of other services, such as health care, infant and child care, after school recreation, cultural events, mental health services, family planning services, adult education, and job preparation. (p. 634)

Although the establishment of such schools may seem a daunting task, acceptance of the concept is increasing, and states such as Florida have had full-service schools in place for several years. Results have shown that such schools can provide comprehensive services productively and efficiently.

Alternative schools can be seen as another variant for educational settings healthy for children. Although the designation *alternative schools* can cover a variety of settings, key features include small size, more support and individual attention, and increased choice and involvement for child and family (Franklin, 1992). Alternative schools may take the form of indicated prevention by targeting particular at-risk children (Franklin, 1992), or they may practice universal prevention through service to all children. A dramatic example of the effectiveness of alternative schools as selected prevention is given in *Miracle in East Harlem* (Fliegel & Macguire, 1993). The miracle in this case is the transformation of an inner-city school, defined by years of frustration and failure, to one of confidence and achievement. An essential feature of this transformation was the opportunity for children and families to experience and exercise choice.

A further theme defining healthy schools is that of home visiting. While home visiting has often been associated with prevention programs geared to infants and preschoolers, its value is increasingly being recognized across the developmental range and for a variety of services. In various forms, the benefits of home visiting have been documented for high-risk infants and their families (Hardy & Street, 1993), abusive or neglectful parents (Garbarino, 1986), and programs serving high-risk adolescents (Dryfoos, 1991). As noted by Olds, Henderson, and Kitzman (1994), infants in homes receiving regular nurse visitation were exposed to fewer hazards, had fewer health and behavioral problems, and made fewer visits to the emergency room. Furthermore, although home visiting may seem specific to such traditional disciplines as social work and nursing, its recognized value is growing in other disciplines such as medicine (Steinkuller, 1990). Where they have been tried, home contact and visiting appear to emerge as crucial, if not essential, elements of any successful alliance between parents and teachers. As national school reform priorities are considered, incorporating regular home contact and visitation as standard activity at all grade levels might well be an effective component of the full service school. Given current contexts in which contacts between teacher and parent are increasingly being eroded, an efficient universal primary prevention effort worth testing would be two scheduled parent contacts for every child in a teacher's class. While many contacts would take place in the home, providing teachers with a more comprehensive sense of the student's ecology outside the school, contacts could also be scheduled at other convenient places (e.g., parent's place of work, community centers, fast-food restaurants). The critical aspect is to bring the key players in the student's life together to ensure common perspectives and reinforce mutual goals. Incorporating regular home contact and visiting as an established feature of public education at all grade levels might well be one of the most important reforms of schooling, consistent with the philosophy of the full-service school.

Healthy Communities

The two themes associated with healthy communities complement the themes identified for healthy schools. Stated succinctly, these themes endorse the view of communities as schools and schools as communities. One of these themes encompasses the call for integration of agencies and services in the community to effect a comprehensive system for children and families. The Children's Defense Fund (1992) has schematized such an integrated and comprehensive approach as a pyramid with successive levels of increasingly specialized services and supports.

The second theme pertaining to the role of healthy communities in primary prevention is a recognition of environmental risk and the ecological context of prevention. Although the environment may constitute a source of risk for all children, it is clear that risk may be distributed disproportionately among some children. Environmental risk of lead exposure, infectious disease, and violence, for example, are much more likely to be experienced by children living in impoverished settings than their nondisadvantaged peers.

IMPLEMENTATION ISSUES

As we have shown in the preceding section, there is no shortage of themes defining agendas for the prevention of childhood problems and the promotion of children's well-being. Although much remains to be done, it is also clear that not everything can be done at once. Implementation of a comprehensive agenda requires prioritizing efforts and adhering to a systematic approach with consumer- and community-based decision making a central feature. There are limited resources and significant competition for prevention programs, as is true for any policy initiative. Therefore, it is important that priorities are identified to guide the development and implementation of prevention programs. Although couched in prevention terms but not addressing children's issues, Schaapveld, van deWater, and Bergsma (1992) and Remington (1990) have outlined steps that may be useful in the advancement of prevention policies and prevention practices.

Success of the primary prevention initiative is contingent upon careful planning and implementation. In regard to the problem of cardiac disease, Remington (1990) has identified 10 points he felt were essential to the success of the translation of prevention policy to preventive practice. These points were as follows: 1) a flexible mechanism for policy formation, 2) science as part of the process, 3) a practice component, 4) proactive community engagement, 5) consensus building in the community, 6) promoting coalitions and ownership, 7) informing community policy makers, 8) serendipity and the unexpected, 9) research success and its correlates, and 10) incorporating evaluation as an essential component of practice.

Although these are broad proposals, they can be useful in the identification of implementation steps for primary prevention programs. The themes developed in this chapter and Remington's proposals can be merged productively into three broad recommendations. The first recommendation emphasizes the critical role of a proactive community engagement focusing on building consensus and coalitions and ensuring that all information is fed back to the community. A central premise of this recommendation is that engagement of the community requires the provision of resources so that the sense of ownership has a basis in reality.

The importance of taking a scientific approach to planning, implementing, and evaluating primary prevention programs is a second major recommendation. As noted in Chapter 2, a prerequisite for comprehensive primary prevention is an epidemiology of childhood problems and risk factors. Two points made by Remington (1990) are particularly important to highlight here. One is to make sure that evaluation is a key component of prevention practices. The second is to carry out empirical studies of primary prevention. These two steps are essential because they can provide evidence for the benefits of primary prevention. Although the benefits of universal primary prevention may be anonymous, its successes should not be invisible.

The final recommendation may seem to be at odds with the previous recommendation for a scientific approach. The majority of current theory and research in primary prevention is likely to present a complex and multivariate picture of childhood problems and the need for correspondingly complex prevention methods. Although the role of science cannot be minimized, it is important to be open to approaches that may be novel, simple, or both.

Given the clinical orientation typical of most human services professions, approaches to prevention are more likely to focus on person-centered psychological, social, or educational interventions rather than alterations in environments or situations. For many, if not most, childhood problems, it is clear that preventive strategies must incorporate both clinical and environmental variables. For some problems, however, an environmental alteration may be more effective and efficient, if not essential (Olden, 1993). In the area of unintentional injuries of childhood, for example, specific educational materials can be provided for parents to promote safety and prevent injuries. For childhood poisoning and window falls, the use of child-resistant closures on medication packages and window guards constitute effective primary prevention strategies, respectively. In other situations, safety promotion and injury prevention may take the form of technology and regulations at the community level. Addressing the problem of unintentional scalding of children for example, former Surgeon General C. Everett Koop (Cowart, 1993) described a community's solution of a thermostatically controlled safety valve as a form of universal primary prevention. Straightforward solutions to a variety of other childhood problems may not always be as obvious; however, it is important to actively explore a variety of options. Serendipitously, unlikely but perfectly logical strategies or approaches may emerge with significant preventive potential to reduce risk and to promote resilience. Improving the future well-being of America's children will clearly require "innovative and comprehensive approaches that include health education, health services, and family support" (Williams & Wynder, 1993, p. 624). To accomplish a prevention agenda we must move beyond advocacy to the commitment of our political will, resources, energy, and creativity.

REFERENCES

America 2000: An education strategy. (1991). Washington, DC: U.S. Department of Education.

Anastasiow, N. (1988). Should parenting education be mandatory? *Topics in Early Childhood Education, 8*(1), 60–72.

Bower, E.M. (1987). Prevention: A word whose time has come. *American Journal of Orthopsychiatry, 57*(1), 4–5.

Bronfenbrenner, V. (1977). Toward an experimental psychology of human development. *American Psychologist, 32*, 513–531.

Cahalan, D. (1991). *An ounce of prevention*. San Francisco: Jossey-Bass.

Caldwell, B. (1991). Educare: New product, new future. *Journal of Developmental Behavior Pediatrician, 12*(3), 199–205.

Children's Defense Fund. (1992). *The state of America's children*. Washington, DC: Author.

Cohen, D.K., & Grant, S.G. (1993). America's children and their elementary schools. *Daedalus, 122*(1), 177–207.

Coulton, C., Pandey, S., & Chow, J. (1990). Concentration of poverty and the changing ecology of low-income, urban neighborhoods: An analysis of the Cleveland area. *Social Work Research and Abstracts, 26*(4), 5–16.

Cowart, M.E. (1993). Interview: C. Everett Koop, M.D. *Family & Community Health, 6*(2), 77–80.

Curtis, S. (1992). Promoting health through a developmental analysis of adolescent risk behavior. *Journal of School Health, 62*(9), 417–419.

Danielson, C.B., Hamel-Bissell, B., & Winstead-Fry, P. (1993). *Families, health and illness: Perspectives on coping and intervention.* St. Louis: C.V. Mosby.

DiNubile, N.A. (1993). Youth fitness—Problems and solutions. *Preventive Medicine, 22*(4), 589–594.

Dryfoos, J.G. (1991). Adolescents at risk: A summation of works in the field—programs and policies. *Journal of Adolescent Health, 12*(8), 630–637.

Elias, M.J., Gara, M.A., Schuyler, T.F., Branden-Muller, L.R., & Sayette, M.A. (1991). The promotion of social competence: Longitudinal study of a preventive school-based program. *American Journal of Orthopsychiatry, 61*(3), 409–417.

Felhan, M., McGee, R., & Stanton, W.R. (1993). Helping agency contact for emotional problems in childhood and early adolescence and the risk of later disorder. *Australian and New Zealand Journal of Psychiatry, 27*(2), 270–274.

Finn-Stevenson, M., Linkins, K., & Beacom, E. (1992). The school of the 21st century: Creating opportunities for school-based child care. *Child & Youth Care Forum, 21*(5), 335–345.

Fliegel, S., & MacGuire, J. (1993). *Miracle in East Harlem.* New York: Times Books.

Flynn, B.C. (1992). Healthy cities: A model of community change. *Family and Community Health, 15*(1), 13–23.

Franklin, C. (1992). Alternative school programs for at-risk youths. *Social Work in Education, 14*(4), 239–251.

Garbarino, J. (1986). Can we measure success in preventing child abuse? Issues in policy, programming and research. *Child Abuse & Neglect, 10*(2), 143–156.

Garber, P. (1993). Never too young: Children and heart disease prevention. *Endeavors, 10*(3), 16–17. (Office of Research Services; University of North Carolina at Chapel Hill)

Gebbie, K. (1993). You, me, or us: Prevention and health promotion. *American Journal of Preventive Medicine, 9*(5), 321–323.

Gensheimer, L.K., Ayers, T.S., & Rosa, M.W. (1993). School-based preventive interventions for at-risk populations: Practical and ethical issues. *Evaluation and Program Planning, 16*(2), 159–167.

Gordon, R.S. (1983). An operational classification of disease prevention. *Public Health Reports, 98*(2), 107–109.

Graham, J.W., Johnson, C.A., Hansen, W.B., Flay, B.R., & Gee, M. (1990). Drug use prevention programs, gender, and ethnicity: Evaluation of three seventh-grade project SMART cohorts. *Preventive Medicine, 19*(3), 305–313.

Halsey, C.L., Collier, M.F., & Anderson, C.L. (1993). Extremely low birth weight children and their peers: A comparison of preschool performance. *Pediatrics, 91*(4), 807–811.

Hardy, J.B., & Street, R. (1989). Family support and parenting education in the home: An effective extension of clinic-based preventive health care services for poor children. *Journal of Pediatrics, 115,* 927–931.

Hawkins, J.D., Lishner, D.M., Catalano, R.F., & Howard, M.O. (1986). Childhood predictors of adolescent substance abuse: Toward an empirically

grounded theory. *Journal of Children in Contemporary Society, 8*(1), 11–48.
Healthy people 2000: National health promotion and disease prevention objectives. (1991). Washington, DC: Public Health Service, U.S. Department of Health and Human Services.
Hodgkinson, H. (1993). American education: The good, the bad and the task. *Phi Delta Kappan, 74*(8), 619–623.
Intriligator, B.A. (1990). *Factors that enhance collaboration among education, health and social service agencies.* Paper presented at the 1990 annual meeting of the American Education Research Association, Boston. (ERIC Document Reproduction Service, No. EA 921 744).
Jack, L.W. (1992). Primary prevention of alcohol and other drug use. *Journal of School Nursing, 8*(2), 25–35.
Jason, L.A., Weine, A.M., Johnson, J.H., Danner, K.E., Kurasaki, K.S., & Warren-Sohlberg, L. (1993). The schools' transition project: A comprehensive preventive intervention. *Journal of Emotional Behavior Disorders, 1*(1), 65–70.
Jee, M. (1993). School-based health clinics now seen as key health site. *Journal of American Health Policy, 3*(3), 53–54.
Jones, R.T., & Herndon, C. (1991). The status of black children and adolescents in the academic setting: Assessment and treatment issues. In C.E. Walker & M.C. Roberts (Eds.), *Handbook of clinical child psychology* (2nd ed., pp. 901–917). New York: John Wiley & Sons.
Knitzer, J. (1993). Children's mental health policy: Challenging the future. *Journal of Emotional Behavior Disorders, 1*(1), 8–16.
Kolbe, L.J. (1993). An essential strategy to improve the health and education of Americans. *Preventive Medicine, 22*(4), 544–560.
Kuntzleman, C.T. (1993). Childhood fitness: What is happening? What needs to be done? *Preventive Medicine, 22*(4), 520–532.
Maier, H.W. (1990). A developmental perspective for child and youth care work. *Child & Youth Services, 13*(1), 7–24.
Marshall, K. (1993). Teachers and schools—what makes a difference: A principal's perspective. *Daedalus, 122*(1), 209–242.
McCluskey-Faucett, K.A., Meck, N., & Harris, M. (1986). Prevention during prenatal and infant development. In B.A. Edelstein & L. Michelson (Eds.), *Handbook of prevention* (pp. 43–69). New York: Plenum.
McGinnis, J.M. (1993). The year 2000 initiative: Implications for comprehensive school health. *Preventive Medicine, 22*(4), 493–498.
McKinlay, J.B. (1992). Health promotion through healthy public policy: The contribution of complementary research methods. *Canadian Journal of Public Health* (Suppl. 1), 83.
Olden, K. (1993). Environmental risks to the health of American children. *Preventive Medicine, 22*(5), 576–578.
Olds, D.L., Henderson, C.R., & Kitzman, H. (1994). Does neonatal and infancy nurse home visitation have enduring effects on qualities of parental caregiving and child health at 25 to 50 months of life? *Pediatrics, 93*(1), 89–98.
Piper, D.L., King, M.J., & Moberg, D.P. (1993). Implementing a middle school health promotion research project. *Evaluation and Program Planning, 16*(3), 171–180.
Price, R.H., Cowen, E.L., Lorin, R.P., & Ramos-McKay, J. (1989). The search for effective prevention programs: What we learned along the way. *American Journal of Orthopsychiatry, 59*(1), 49–58.
Remington, R.P. (1990). From preventive policy to preventive practice. *Preven-*

tive Medicine, 19(1), 105–113.

Rivlin, L.A. (1993). Home and homelessness in the lives of children. *Child & Youth Services, 14*(1), 5–18.

Rohrbach, L.A., Graham, J.W., & Hansen, W.B. (1993). Diffusion of school-based substance abuse prevention program: Predictors of program implementation. *Preventive Medicine, 22*(2), 237–260.

Rothman, K.J., & Pool, C. (1988). A strengthening programme for weak associations. *International Journal of Epidemiology, 17*(4), 955–959.

Rudd, R.E., & Walsh, D.C. (1993). Schools as healthful environments: Prerequisite to comprehensive school health. *Preventive Medicine, 22*(4), 499–506.

Rutter, M. (1993). Resilience: Some conceptual considerations. *Journal of Adolescent Health, 14*(8), 626–631.

Schaapveld, K., van deWater, H.P.A., & Bergsma, E.W. (1992). Setting priorities in prevention. *Health Policy, 20*(3), 277–287.

Schorr, L.B. (1989). *Within our reach: Breaking the cycle of disadvantage.* New York: Anchor Books.

Selman, R.L., Schultz, L.H., Nakkula, M., Barr, D., Watts, C., & Richmond, J.B. (1992). Friendship and fighting: A developmental approach to the study of risk and prevention of violence. *Development and Psychopathology, 4*(4), 529–558.

Serdula, M.K., Ivery, D., Coates, R.J., Freedman, D.S., Williamson, D.F., & Byers, T. (1993). Do obese children become obese adults? A review of the literature. *Preventive Medicine, 22*(2), 167–177.

Srebrick, D.S., & Elias, M.J. (1993). An ecological, interpersonal skills approach to drop-out prevention. *American Journal of Orthopsychiatry, 63*(4), 526–535.

Stachtchenko, S., & Jenicek, M. (1990). Conceptual differences between prevention and health promotion: Research implications for community health programs. *Canadian Journal of Public Health, 81*(1), 53–59.

Steinkuller, J.S. (1992). Home visits by pediatric residents. *American Journal of Diseases of Children, 146*(9), 1064–1067.

Walker, E.V.S. (1993). Caswell County Training School, 1933–1969: Relationships between community and school. *Harvard Education Review, 63*(2), 161–182.

Walsh, D.C., Rudd, R.E., Moyekens, B.A., & Moloney, T.W. (1993). Social marketing for public health. *Health Affairs, 12*(2), 104–119.

Weinman, M.L., Schreiber, N.B., & Robinson, M. (1992). Adolescent mothers: Were there any gains in a parent education program? *Family and Community Health, 15*(3), 1–10.

Williams, C.L., & Wynder, E.L. (1993). A child health report card. *Preventive Medicine 22*(4), 604–628.

Winter, M., & Rouse, J. (1990). Fostering intergenerational literacy: The Missouri Parents as Teachers Program. *The Reading Teacher, 43*, 382–386.

Ziegler, J.M. (1993). Education: Crucial variable for children? *Daedalus, 122*(1), 243–258.

16

Promoting Children's Well-Being
Priorities and Principles

**Rune J. Simeonsson
and Daphne Thomas**

A more balanced and integrated research agenda is needed in which child and family welfare is examined with a longitudinal perspective that incorporates those concepts and findings from fields spanning the biological and social sciences.
                                                  Earls and Carlson, 1993, p. 116

Much of what needs to be done on behalf of children involves nothing spectacularly new. Instead, we need to build on and tie together proven ideas.
                                                  Minow and Weissbourd, 1992, p. 17

As the end of one century nears and a new one is on the horizon, it is imperative that we enact a comprehensive prevention agenda. National as well as international demographic trends make it clear that preventable problems of childhood are increasing at an alarming rate. The challenge is to address these problems effectively. Few would debate the logic of adopting a primary prevention approach and no one would question the importance of promoting children's development. There are timely opportunities to take advantage of, and unique technological resources to draw upon, to promote the development of children's health, education, and well-being. Preventive policies are being espoused with increasing frequency in a variety of forums. Model primary prevention programs have been implemented, and their success has been demonstrated, as many of the previous chapters illustrate. As we and many others have noted repeatedly, however, relative to curative, corrective, and rehabilitative services, the primary prevention effort is still comparatively small. How can the implementation of a comprehensive prevention agenda be increased and accelerated?

In the preceding chapter, we identify the ways in which preventive policies and practices can contribute to such an agenda. In this chapter, we emphasize the importance of a parallel agenda in training and research as key mechanisms whereby the primary promotion of children's health, education, and well-being can be advanced. Essential to such an agenda is the identification of universally endorsable principles that can define and validate prevention efforts.

TRAINING ISSUES

A substantive shift toward a comprehensive prevention agenda to address childhood problems will not occur unless there is a corresponding shift in the preparation of those who are involved in the provision of services for children. With the exception of education and public health, the helping professions prepare individuals within a curative, treatment-oriented framework. Within such a framework, emphasis is placed on assessment, diagnosis, prescription, and treatment of one client or patient at a time. The focus is typically on restoring an individual's delayed or disordered function, rather than on preventing the occurrence of dysfunction. A primary prevention agenda, on the contrary, emphasizes approaches wherein efforts are directed at a population level to promote development and adaptation. Such an agenda calls for professionals who have the preparation to assume new roles, to apply new skills, to work in new settings, and to bring new disciplinary perspectives to bear on existing, and often seemingly intractable, problems. The implications of this agenda for training are summarized in Table 16.1 and are discussed in the following section.

Roles

What are some of the new roles needed in primary prevention? One key defining feature of such new roles is that they are likely to call for indirect rather than direct provision of services. A good example of an indirect approach is Cowen and Lorion's (1976) identification of school psychologists as mental health "quarterbacks," coordinating the activities of others who are providing direct services to children at risk. Another defining feature is that roles will call for interdisciplinary collaboration of effort. In a listing of future psychosocial issues in children's health care, Tucker and Roberts (1990) identified training for such a collaboration as an important priority with similar recommendations made by Bearinger and Gephart (1993) for interdisciplinary education in adolescent health. Closely related is the indirect role of a linking agent, a role described by Rohrback, Graham, and Hansen (1993) in a study on the diffusion of a substance abuse prevention program in high schools. Linking agents could be organizations as well as individ-

Table 16.1. Implications of a primary prevention agenda for professional training

Training issue	Implications
Roles	• Interdisciplinary collaboration • Coordinating responsibilities • Linking agents
Skills	• Consultation • Marketing • Epidemiological skills
Settings	• Comprehensive school-based clinics • School malls • School–community partnerships
Disciplines	• Expanded expertise of current disciplines • Add systems and population-oriented disciplines • Hybrid disciplines

uals outside the school (e.g., health professionals, agencies) that promote prevention initiatives.

Pulling together the above ideas, it is clear that there will be growing emphasis on indirect, interdisciplinary roles for professionals to join their efforts on behalf of families. Given the broader prevention agenda with related expectations for linking roles, social marketing skills, and conceptualizing risk chains, professionals in the schools will need additional preparation. Drawing on the model of school-based, interdisciplinary student support teams (Marshall, 1993), teachers, counselors, administrators, nurses, school social workers, psychologists, and physical education specialists will require new areas of training to prepare for such roles.

Skills

The skills required in primary prevention will differ from skills required in secondary and tertiary prevention. This difference is reflected in a shift from clinical skills focusing on individuals to new skills of planning and effecting change at the level of groups and populations. This distinction is exemplified in the difference between the activities involved in counseling and consultation. The former involves direct service to a student or client, whereas the latter is indirect. A representative example of an indirect approach in prevention is training others to be change agents. In this regard, DiClemente (1993) has described the value of peer-assisted interventions in the public school setting to prevent drug use and its potential as a HIV/AIDS prevention program.

Another major indirect skill crucial for primary prevention is that of social marketing. As noted by Chamberlin in an Chapter 3 of this volume, social marketing should serve as an essential method to advance the agenda to prevent childhood problems and promote healthy practices and behaviors among children. Advocacy for using social marketing techniques and tools in health promotion is increasing (Segal, 1993). In a recent review, Walsh et al. (1993) described social marketing as a disciplined and strategic approach to effect social change. Drawing on their review and generalizations, we can identify a number of skills requiring training. In the context of the three phases of research and planning, strategy design, and implementation and evaluation, the following skills seem particularly relevant to primary prevention efforts: 1) specification of the target audience, 2) understanding target audiences, 3) using incentives to foster motivation, 4) teaching skills to consumers, 5) developing a recognizable "product," and 6) fostering community participation and ownership. The application of social marketing in primary prevention programs with "the disciplined up-front technology of market analysis and formative research could help . . . to isolate those approaches that really do enable individuals and communities to gain greater control over their health and the quality of their lives" (Walsh, Rudd, Moeykens, & Moliney, 1993, p. 118).

An important aspect to emphasize in the application of social marketing strategy is to influence such constituencies as societal policy makers and community leaders. Current concerns about the detrimental effects of excessive television viewing on children's behaviors are synthesized in the title of Condry's (1993) article, *Thief of Time, Unfaithful Servant*. Social marketing needs to be directed toward networks responsible for programming for children shows. It is equally important, however, to remember that marketing can also be applied directly to effect a to change children's behaviors. Thus, strategies to foster responsible viewing by children would constitute a significant effort that could encompass a prevention agenda directed at school failure, poor fitness, and violence.

In addition to the skills of planning and implementing prevention programs, training must be directed at preparing professionals in the epidemiological skills. Such skills are needed in generating risk chains, identifying populations at selected and indicated risk, and designing and implementing programs to reduce risk factors and promote resiliency. Illustrative of new training priorities are the changing roles and skills for social workers needed to staff alternative schools (Franklin, 1992).

Settings

A major reason to provide training for new roles and skills is that primary prevention will be carried out in new school and community settings. Even if existing settings were used, they would likely take new forms. Sparsely populated areas present a special challenge for primary prevention because resources are limited and difficult to coordinate. Schroeder and Wilkerson (1993) have described the importance of community involvement in planning and implementation as key features in a successful program to prevent prenatal substance abuse.

Perhaps the most frequently identified site for primary prevention is the school with various recommendations made to enhance its role in prevention efforts. Although the specific form might vary from one setting to another, the school-based clinic concept has grown rapidly in the last decade, with current estimates exceeding 500 such clinics across the country (Jee, 1993). The underlying concept of the school-based clinic is to capitalize not only on the school setting as a place where both education and health concerns can be addressed, but the opportunity to provide services in an effective and efficient manner. As Jee has noted, there is evidence that school-based clinics can achieve primary prevention objectives effectively. Furthermore, such school-based clinics frequently have expanded into a one-stop array of programs for teens with various health and health-related services. It is not unreasonable to envision schools of the future as "malls" in which educational services are complemented by social, health, and related support services relevant to children and their families. The importance of an interdisciplinary team has been stressed by Harold and Harold (1993) in order to bring complementary perspectives to bear on overlapping health and education problems of children, including mental health. Harold and Harold see the school as a "health promoting environment" and suggest that among the professionals on the interdisciplinary team, social workers possess the skills and experience that may be well suited to develop prevention programs. School–community partnerships will also need to expand in the future. In such expansions, school environments, particularly at the secondary level, will likely be in the commercial sector. A central goal of any combined community and school-based effort is to prepare professionals to break vicious cycles contributing to underachievement, teen pregnancy, school failure, delinquency, and unemployment.

Disciplines

Although the need for interdisciplinary teams has been advocated in secondary and tertiary prevention, they are at least of equal importance in primary prevention. "Prevention is an essentially multidisciplinary area requiring the participation of many professions and disciplines" (Remington, 1990, p. 105). A major distinction between primary prevention and secondary and tertiary prevention however, may lie not only in the composition of the team, but perhaps more importantly in the skills of the team members. The interdisciplinary team with secondary and tertiary prevention responsibilities typically brings clinical expertise around issues of diagnosis, prescription, and intervention. Team members currently represent the diagnostic and therapeutic disciplines of physical, occupational, and speech therapy, social work, psychology, and various health specialities. Interdisciplinary efforts focusing on primary prevention and promotion efforts on the other hand, are likely to require disciplinary expertise in conceptualizing parameters of vulnerability, resilience, risk models, and community factors at the level of populations. Such disciplinary expertise might well be developed through expanded roles for existing professionals in school and community as well as roles to be filled by disciplines new to the field. Beginning with the classroom teacher, each of the professionals in the schools could incorporate an expanded prevention perspective in their roles and responsibilities. Primary prevention and primary promotion priorities need to be made a part of the overall school curriculum and supportive activities. The nature of those priorities would be determined on the basis of an epidemiological approach to the individual school or community as proposed in Chapter 2 of this volume. The roles of school counselors and school psychologists (Zins, Coyne, & Ponti, 1988), in particular, could be expanded substantially from a reactive to a preventive focus. Included among such roles would be assessment of risk factors, systems and environments, and the delivery of prevention services to children in school settings. Acknowledging the increasing shortage of primary health care for children and families, Redman (1993) recommends an expanded role for advanced practice nurses in community schools. Because schools are grassroots institutions in the community, Redman argues that ". . . schools are an excellent site for family-focused primary health centers, interlinked with other components of a community health care system" (p. 43). Along a similar line, Rae-Grant (1988) describes a significant shift from the clinical role of the child psychiatrist to one of prevention activities in schools and communities.

The broader view of communities and populations in primary prevention will also call for the broader involvement of sociologists, anthropologists, and economists (Earls & Carlson, 1993), as well as epidemiologists (Oleske, 1993), professionals who previously have not been part of applied programs for children. In addition, with goals of promoting wellness and lifestyle changes, Remington (1990) identifies the need for specialists in health education, behavioral science, and public information and communication. Finally, there is no doubt that the interdisciplinary collaboration expressed in major spheres of inquiry will also emerge in response to the unique challenges of primary prevention. Of particular interest in this regard are hybrid forms needed to link relevant expertise of parent disciplines. Clinical sociology is one such hybrid advanced by Garbarino (1991), focusing on the study of ecologies of risk. A second hybrid discipline is that of developmental epidemiology (Kellam & Werthamer-Larsson, 1986), bringing the conceptual and methodological elements of epidemiology to bear on the distribution, causes, and correlates of childhood disorders. Along this line, it is not difficult to envision such future hybrid disciplines as school–community planning, population psychology, educational epidemiology, and ecological engineering to tackle interdisciplinary challenges of integrated community services, population behavior change, and designed ecologies, respectively.

RESEARCH ISSUES

One of the significant deterrents to the enactment of a comprehensive primary prevention agenda for children and youth may be what Remington (1990) has identified as its anonymity. In secondary and tertiary prevention services, the client, patient, offender, or victim are not anonymous; they are identified, referred, assessed, diagnosed, and treated. In primary prevention, particularly when universal and indicated prevention programs are implemented, it is not easy to determine specifically for whom prevention will be effective. The success of primary prevention is measured not in terms of cases and statistical summaries of treatment successes, but in changing population rates of incidence and prevalence. A key research and policy agenda item might be to address the problem of anonymity and seek better ways in which to increase the visibility of primary prevention. The issue is not simply that of presenting a compelling logic for primary prevention, such a logic is generally accepted. What is needed is creativity in presenting a strong case for its benefits. Primary prevention is an underutilized but powerful strategy that can be used. Segal (1993) describes the relevance of a comprehensive application of marketing in the related area of child welfare. As mentioned previously, there is a need to formulate and test risk models and to document the extent to which primary prevention of childhood disorders is in fact achieved. Social marketing can be a powerful tool in this regard.

Perhaps the most compelling national priority for prevention research is the epidemic of violence affecting children, youth, and adults (Butcher, 1993; Rosenberg, 1993). In many ways violence epitomizes the vicious cycle and the distillation of many of the preventable problems reviewed in this volume. In public outcry as well as professional reaction, we are outraged and at a loss to comprehend its disproportionate expression among youth both as victims and perpetrators. The statistical facts are staggering: In the decade of the 1980s the arrests of those under 18 years of age for violent crimes and manslaughter increased by 60%, accompanied by increases of 56% and 28% for other violent acts such as assault and rape (Yoshikawa, 1994). Intentional injury and homicide are increasingly commonplace experiences among children and youth, particularly in environments defined by poverty, minority status, and disenfranchisement. Illustrative are findings on drive-by shootings in Los Angeles in 1991 showing that of those involved, 38% were under the age of 18 (Hutson, Anglin, & Pratts, 1993). Minority boys were disportionately likely to account for the 63% who were injured and the 5.4% who died.

The scope of the problem of violence is repeated in statistics across the country. The disproportionate manifestation of violence among minority males, particularly those in late adolescence, does not occur in a void but is defined by a number of contextual factors. Central to these factors is a climate comparable to experiencing life in a war zone (Prothrow-Stith, 1992). In such a climate, most children have witnessed assaults first hand and a fourth to a third have seen murders and the violent use of weapons. These overt expressions are embedded in a societal preoccupation with violence in which the media portrays it as a glamorous and appropriate behavior that is usually rewarded (Prothrow-Stith, 1990). It is therefore not surprising that adolescents perceive violence as a pervasive part of their lives. Results of a survey of 9th- to 12th-grade students in New York City revealed that more than one third had experienced threats and about 25% had been involved in a physical fight (Ginsberg & Loffredo, 1993). Those who had fought were less likely than their peers to view apologizing and walking away as effective conflict avoidance approaches. These attitudes in turn are exacerbated by a number of interactive risk factors identifiable for the child, the family, and the environment. The strongest among these for the child is antisocial behavior and, for the family, inadequate and ineffective parenting practices (Buka & Earls, 1993). The fact that much of the violence occurs in the summer and at night (Hutson, Anglin, & Pratts, 1994) is a further expression of the lack of adult supervision and role models. All of these risk factors reflect the cumulative consequences of racism, unemployment, poverty, and the ensuing deterioration of family and community life (Prothrow-Stith, 1992).

If these viscious cycles are to prevented, comprehensive and coordinated efforts are necessary. Such coordination includes not only responsive mental health services, school-based programs and support from the community but underscores the centrality of efforts focused on fostering parenting (Prothrow-Stith, 1992). Recognizing the multigenerational nature of risk, the two-generation programs of family support and preschool education (Yoshikawa, 1994) may well need to be extended to multigenerational programs to reinforce the significant role of parenting and grandparenting (Neergaard, 1990). Complementing these efforts should be educational programs designed to promote conflict resolution skills for at-risk children and youth (Jaffe, Sudermann, Reilzel, & Killip, 1992). Such programs can and should be integrated into the fabric of the social, health, recreational, and religious components of the community (Prothrow-Stith, 1992; Spivak, Hausman, & Prothrow-Smith, 1989).

In the search for elements of an effective agenda to prevent the development and expression of violent behavior, we can draw on creative model programs that already exist, ranging in focus from dress codes to peer counselors for conflict resolution. We must also continue to build preventive programs on a solid base of research. Included among the things we know are risk and protective factors and their contexts. Illustrative in this regard are findings by Resnick, Harris, and Blum (1993) that caring and connectedness repeatedly emerged as protective factors. From these we can identify the focus and priority of primary prevention with strategies appropriate to the needs and characteristics of local community settings. To this end it is clear that

> The confluence of biological, behavioral and emotional development is so crucial during early child development that environments created to promote the well-being of children and to decrease the risks of delinquency require broad-based services that combine physical and mental health care and early education. (Buka & Earls, 1992, p. 60)

An agenda for research on the prevention of violence must encompass a reciprocal agenda for the promotion of moral, ethical, and prosocial development of the child, family, community, and society. One necessary element of such a research agenda is the establishment of a developmental and behavioral epidemiology. Of critical importance here is the need for longitudinal studies to document the processes involved in the "escape from risk" (Rutter, 1993a) and the dimensions of resilience (Rutter, 1993b). Defining resilience is not an easy task, but it can be operationalized relative to the goals of research and to intended applications (Kaufman, Cook, Arny, Jones, & Pittinsky, 1994).

If we are to draw on the preventive paradigm of public health, then we need to have a corresponding frame of reference. It might thus be productive to operationalize the concepts of relative resilience and attributable resilience as positive counterparts to relative and attributable risk. Encompassed under resilience are a variety of protective factors, including supportive relationships with family and peers as well as identification with adult role models (Raphael, 1993). Complementing the risk calculations in Chapter 2, relative resilience as a function of role model presence can be calculated for a prospective cohort and, in a case control study, as suggested in Figure 16.1. The derived ratios for these hypothetical data provide documentation of the relative advantage afforded by this protective factor. A parallel research agenda can then be developed to evaluate prevention outcomes in terms of "well-being and competence of children and families with a view toward the long-term potential for social sustainability" (Earls & Carlson, 1993, p. 117).

In this regard, it is important to realize and act on at least two considerations. First, as Earls and Carlson (1993) have noted, there is nothing particularly novel or new about primary prevention; elements of what is needed are often already in place. The key is to reduce fragmentation of effort, to achieve efficiency through coordination of efforts. In short, a comprehensive agenda must be conceptualized and put into place as a template for integration and continuity of services. A second, and related point is that primary prevention cannot be based on the assumption of unlimited fiscal resources. The press for funding clearly has been identified as a key factor for the implementation of meaningful prevention efforts. It is important to note, however, that funding is not the sole limiting factor to a preventive solution. A number of other factors are contributing to, and exacerbating, the problems and disorders of childhood. These factors are largely in the realm of human experience, encompassing for many children and families loss of future orientation and initiative, a sense of hopelessness and alienation from community and society, and fear. We do not know how much of a role these phenomenological factors play in degrading the developmental potential of children and their families, but it is likely to be very significant.

Despite the growing recognition that social and psychological variables play a significant role in preventing disorders and promoting well-being among children (Noddings, 1984; Schorr, 1991), current solutions continue to be defined almost exclusively in fiscal or technical rather than phenomenological terms. The recognition and fostering of motivation, mastery, drive, will, trust, and initiative, however, can have a profound effect on the success of individual and group efforts. Consider, for example, the phenomenal success of a school dropout prevention program for at-risk middle school students. This program's incentive was simply a philanthropist's promise to pay the college tuition of any student willing to persist and complete high school. A second example is the inspiring success of the Habitat for Humanity program to provide housing for families with limited incomes. It stands in sharp contrast to bureaucratic and depersonalized governmental

A Secondary School Outcome Status

Dropout	High School Graduate	Dropout	
Grade Retention: Presence of Role Model	(a) 217	(b) 93	310
Grade Retention: No Role Model	(c) 130	(d) 310	440
	347	403	750

$$Ie = \frac{\text{Cumulative Incidence}}{\text{Exposure}} = \frac{a}{a+b} = \frac{217}{310} = .700 \quad Ie = 700 \text{ per } 1000$$

$$Io = \frac{\text{Cumulative Incidence}}{\text{Nonexposure}} = \frac{c}{c+d} = \frac{130}{440} = .295 \quad Io = 295 \text{ per } 1000$$

$$It = \frac{\text{Overall Cumulative Incidence}}{\text{Total Population}} = \frac{a+c}{a+b+c+d} = \frac{347}{750} = .463 \quad It = 463 \text{ per } 1000$$

$$\text{Relative Resilience} = \frac{Ie}{Io} = \frac{.70}{.295} = 2.37$$

$$\text{Attributable Resilience} = Ie - Io = \frac{700}{1000} - \frac{295}{1000} = \frac{405}{1000}$$

$$\text{Population Attributable Resilience Percent} = \frac{It - Io}{It} = \frac{.463 - .295}{.463} = 36\%$$

B Secondary School Outcome Status

Exposure/ Experience	Graduate	Dropout	
Grade Retention: Presence of Role Model	(a) 65	(b) 35	100
Grade Retention: No Role Model	(c) 40	(d) 60	100
	105	95	200

$$\text{Odds Ratio} = \frac{a/c}{b/d} = \frac{ad}{cb} = \frac{3900}{1400} = 2.79$$

Figure 16.1. A) Relative resilience: hypothetical data for association of grade retention, role model, and secondary school outcome for prospective cohort of 750 seventh graders retained for one grade; B) Odds ratio: hypothetical data for relationships of grade retention and secondary school outcome for high school students with role model as protective factor.

efforts in that not only is the former successful in cost-effectiveness terms, but, more importantly, it fosters a sense of shared values and community spirit. Both of these examples illustrate the all-important contribution of the human dimension to the success of prevention efforts. In short, these and other programs succeed because they place value on the individual, and they recognize the importance of personal involvement, thus promoting a sense of shared investment.

As we have advocated throughout this volume, the school can and should assume a focal role in primary prevention efforts on behalf of children. To achieve this, we must press for changes in attitudes and policies, for increased deployment of fiscal resources in some cases, and for redeployment of priorities and resources in others. Equally important, however, we must recognize that the prevention of childhood problems and the promotion of children's potential cannot rely on solutions solely in fiscal, legislative, technological, or programmatic terms. The challenge for those committed to primary prevention is to identify principles reflective of shared and shareable ideals to enhance the well-being of children, families, and communities. Such principles can serve as the basis for action, guiding efforts to plan, prioritize, and implement prevention programs in schools and communities.

GUIDING PRINCIPLES

Returning to the opening statement of this book, it is the best of times in terms of the exponential progress made in science and technology. This progress is exemplified by advances in unraveling the mysteries of the human gene at the microlevel and the universe at the macrolevel. Simultaneously, it is the worst of times in that unpredictable (e.g., mutation) and predictable (e.g., pollution) events continue to confound our efforts to understand, much less control, physical as well as societal phenomena. The best and the worst of times is no less relevant a consideration for the major theme considered of this book; reducing the risk and promoting the resilience of children and youth associated with their well-being.

A strategic response to variability, complexity, and unpredictability in any area of inquiry is to seek concepts and principles that facilitate explanation, provide hypotheses for testing, and serve as guides for action. In the area of human functioning, complexity is increasingly reflected in corresponding levels of explanation. In regard to the general concept of health, Antonovsky (1993), for example, has advanced Sense of Coherence as a central construct in understanding the "... human being, functioning in a highly complex and ever dynamic material–social supersystem. Complexity refers to the level of organization of a system. This level both sets the problems and provides the potential, interacting with sub and supersystem . . . " (p. 969).

The search for levels of explanation also finds it parallel in the arena of primary prevention. Addressing the specific issue of child abuse prevention, Gough (1988) traces explanations from the microlevel of the biological system through five increasingly broader and more social levels, culminating in cultural and societal variables. In another approach to the same issue, Kaufman and Ziegler (1992) build on Belsky's (1980) ecological model in the identification of risk and protective factors at the ontogenetic, microsystem, ecosystem, and macrosystem levels.

Inherent in these specific conceptions of child abuse prevention as well as in Antonovsky's (1993) broader conceptualization of health is the influential role of values and beliefs in defining well-being for the individual, community, and society. As noted earlier, an important priority in advancing a primary prevention agenda is to identify principles that define the promotion of children's adaptation and well-being. To be of value in this context, such principles should: 1) be compatible with conceptualizations of prevention and promotion, 2) reflect findings that have emerged from existing prevention efforts, and 3) express ideals likely to be universally endorsed.

The search for guiding principles can be framed in terms of attempts to define what makes some children and families relatively vulnerable and others relatively resilient. A key concept that may be associated with increased vulnerability of children and families is the depersonalization of the community, a shift ". . . from a human context ruled by face-to-face interactions and the weight of public opinion to an anonymous social context ruled by abstract laws and institutional rules" (Csikszentmihalyi, 1993, p. 49). Such depersonalization not only removes the role of communal involvement and responsibility but also contributes to isolation of the individual and a sense of alienation. This conclusion is consistent with the Manning Theory of ecological psychology (Schoggen, 1981) and the psychological sequelae of *overmanned* environments. In an overmanned environment, the ratio of opportunities and roles to persons is low, resulting in psychological situations wherein individuals have less tolerance for individual differences and feel less valued and less responsible. In undermanned environments, on the other hand, wherein the ratio of opportunities to persons is relatively high, individuals feel more valued, more responsible, and are more tolerant of individual differences. A synthesis of these ideas is that an undermanned community is also one characterized by greater face-to-face interactions with implications for increased communal exchange, support, and responsibility. As we search for protective factors with potential to prevent problems and promote development, one dimension of resilience may well be the extent to which the environment is undermanned, providing meaningful opportunities for involvement and responsibility.

A second source of ideas for guiding principles come from recent contributions defining social and educational programs for children. Writing on the topic of reform in the children's movement, Minow and Weissbourd (1993) identified several features that should characterize initiatives for children. The first two, support and sustainability, imply that programs with demonstrated or probable success should be supported and sustained. Related to these recommendations is the importance of securing a substantial constituency base. Finally, it is recommended that a larger investment be made in prevention relative to intervention, and that an active experimental approach be taken in new program development. An experimental mindset is essential in order to ensure that a potentially successful initiative is not terminated because there is a lack of immediate effects.

From the educational domain, Marshall (1993) has identified elements of effective schools that have clear implications for defining guiding principles for primary prevention. Central to a positive school climate is the student's recognition of learning as the major purpose of schooling. Complementing this recognition is the student's need to feel safe, to feel membership in a community, and to experience a sense of caring. As Marshall puts it, there must be a positive, "prosocial curriculum" beginning in kindergarten that fosters acceptance and respect for individual differences, identification and connectedness with the larger group, and a sense of personal efficacy. The essential ingredient of an effective school is the opportunity for students to emulate models. "Schools should be about the business of building character as well as competence; the best way to do this is to model ethical, tolerant, problem-solving behavior" (Marshall, p. 229). In a related view, Ruby (1993) concludes that "charismatic leaders who can connect with teenagers should be identified and brought into play on a regular basis, not as drive-by volunteers (p. 112.)" The call to build character represents a significant challenge in an era when all too often the priorities of education have been disproportionately placed on building competence.

Perhaps the most obvious, but often overlooked, source of guiding principles are values, beliefs, and ideals about human well-being that enjoy universal support. Although they are often implicitly endorsed, they are not made explicit as elements on which to base programs. Thus, for example, it is taken for granted that children are valued, parenting is respected, and communities sustain families. However, not only are these assumptions likely to remain poorly defined, scientific interest in their explication has also been limited (Earls & Carlson, 1993).

It seems ironic in this regard that the value of children is more likely to be systematically researched in the study of fertility regulation (Hoffman & Manis, 1979) than in the analysis of child neglect and abuse. This irony speaks to the limited and idiosyncratic focus of discipline-specific inquiry, and it reinforces the need for new and broader perspectives in interdisciplinary research. It also speaks to the fact that variables that are less abstract, more ecologically valid, and thus more practical in nature may constitute important topics for investigation. For example, a major theme permeating recent practice and research has been a call to celebrate cultural diversity and analyze its role in accounting for differential child and family outcomes. This important step has contributed to a clearer analysis of intercultural variability. A productive endeavor would be a corresponding analysis of within-culture variability and commonality across cultures to define more fully program policies and priorities.

In recent years, we have witnessed dramatic changes in the demographic, economic and social profile of our nation (Banks & Banks, 1993; Nieto, 1992). Our service delivery systems must now prepare for a new clientele reflective of the changes that have occurred in our society. Children and families are distinguished by both the educational, health, and social phenomena that are parts of their lives and the labels that they have assigned to them. Additionally, they are a composite of the ethnic, racial, social class, and gender groups they represent. Recent immigration to the United States, the language first spoken in the home, and the language currently spoken in the home are also critical factors. Most important in this regard is a consideration of the personal and religious beliefs they hold and the traditions, practices, and customs they value. How we respond to the diverse nature of different client groups will inform the designs of our prevention agendas and affect many generations to come.

Children from ethnically and culturally diverse populations are disproportionately represented in our juvenile justice system, special education classrooms, and emergency health care systems (Harry, 1992). Many of these children and their families are homeless and live in varying degrees of poverty (Klerman, 1991). Some grow up in one-parent households, while others share domiciles with a network of extended family members. Both of these arrangements challenge our traditional notions of family life. Migration patterns have separated some families from their natural support systems. Their lack of familiarity with the service delivery system contributes to their further isolation.

Many of these families rely heavily on their own unique internal support systems as well as their family's traditions of care and self-help. A prevention agenda encompassing the diversity of family life must reflect and celebrate the multiple ways of "being a family," while simultaneously helping families to share in the enormous network of help available to them as members of our common culture. This can be accomplished by fostering interventions that help families to develop coping mechanisms that will work within their traditions and customs of care, while helping them to gain familiarity with external support systems that can foster the resiliency necessary to survive hard times (Harry, 1993).

Hill (1972, 1993) identified these five factors that historically have sustained African-American families: strong kinship bonds, strong work orientation, adaptability of family roles, strong achievement orientation, and strong religious orientation. Garbarino (1994) echoed the belief that successful families originated from parents with "strong political and/or religious beliefs, and who avail themselves to social support strongly, believe in their ability to control their lives, and actively try to change traumatic situations.

Policy makers should examine the underutilization patterns of such preventive services as parent-training programs, school-based health clinics, and other full-service centers to determine how accurately we have combined our program development with our knowledge of the multiply ways of "being family."

Examination of culture and family life with a focus on dimensions of roles (e.g., parent, sibling), experiences (e.g., ceremony, rituals), and identities (e.g., neighbor, friend) could yield important contributions to understanding the significance of what is unique as well as what is common among families.

Bringing together these various themes, we conclude this volume with a list of principles that embody enduring ideals and may serve as a framework for initiatives to promote the well-being of children and families. Principles of this nature have been advanced by Martin (1992) as the basis for promoting change in programs and policies for children. These principles are based on two related premises. The first is that "the family is potentially the most effective social institution for rearing healthy children. From this it follows that the defense of the family is the first line of defense of the child" (Eisenberg, 1975, p. 801). The second premise endorses the centrality of the community in the lives of children and families. This centrality recognizes that

> the family is dependent on other institutions for its endurance. As a society we need a proclamation that states that 'no family is an island.' The school, church, businesses, parks, recreational facilities, and transportation links that constitute the components of community are all essential supports of a family unit. (Earls & Carlson, 1993, p. 116)

In translating these premises into realities, principles are needed that transcend family diversity and program specifics. Furthermore, such principles should endorse the fundamental values of nurturance, caring, and trust. Almost 30 years ago, Hobbs (1966) advanced a set of principles to guide intervention with children. They are still timely today. Then, as now, the value of making guiding principles explicit was a response to a pressing concern about children. At that time, existing mental health services were inadequate to meet their needs. Drawing on these principles, we have expanded their scope to address pressing concerns for children and their families (Simeonsson & Simeonsson, 1993). They are presented here as a framework for efforts to prevent disorders of children and youth, to foster resilience and to promote their well-being and resilience (Table 16.2).

The first principle, "life is to be lived now, not in the past, and lived in the future only as a present challenge," recognizes that primary prevention efforts, whether in a universal form for all children or in selected or indicated forms, must address the immediate contexts and realities of children. A second and corollary principle is the importance of capitalizing on the dynamics of development both of the child and the family. Primary prevention is by definition based on the premise that time is an ally to be used when seeking to promote expectable life experiences and to reduce or remove physical, social, and psychological threats.

The media and the empirical literature have provided extensive documentation of the alienation and deterioration of trust experi-

Table 16.2. Guiding principles: Promoting the well-being of children and families

1. Life is to be lived now, not in the past, and lived in the future only as a present challenge. . . .
2. Time is an ally, facilitating the development of child and family in a life phase of significant forward thrust. . . .
3. Trust between child and family and between children, their families, and helper is essential, the base on which all other relationships rest. . . .
4. Needs and concerns can and should be addressed directly. . . .
5. Competence makes a difference; children and families should be assisted to be good at something. . . .
6. Skills can be acquired and children and families assisted to be in control. . . .
7. "Family" is of primary importance. . . .
8. "Community" is important for children and families, offering resources and support. . . .
9. Values, beliefs, ceremony, and ritual give order, stability, and confidence to children and families. . . .
10. Physical well-being is the foundation of psychological well-being. . . .
11. Feelings should be nurtured and respected. . . .
12. Children and families should know joy. . . .

Adapted from Hobbs (1966).

enced by many families in contact with helping professions. Building trust through communication, support, and genuine caring (Noddings, 1984) must be a fundamental priority in any primary prevention effort and defines a third guiding principle.

The fourth, fifth, and sixth guiding principles provide a framework for defining the nature and scope of prevention and promotion activities. The recommendation that needs and problems of children and families be addressed directly reflects the belief that a functional, rather than inferential, approach should be the basis for the identification of intervention priorities. Thus, the operationalization of universal, selected, and indicated prevention is clear and practical, directed toward the promotion of well-being. An important dimension of well-being is a sense of competence, acknowledging personal capability. The promotion of a child's sense of competence has been identified by Marshall (1993) as one of the central responsibilities of the school. Similarly, Ziegler (1993) has described the way in which the parent's sense of competence can be fostered in the context of a supportive school environment. To this end, children and families can be supported in skill building, promoting their senses of self, and of control over their lives.

The seventh, eighth, and ninth principles recognize the embeddedness of children in the ecology of the family, which in turn are both embedded in the context of community. Demographic and sociological trends in the past decades have documented marked changes in the definition and composition of the family with significant increases in the proportion of single-parent families and blended families. Although family structure and family form may vary widely, every family has a definition of itself and attaches importance to its definition of the family as the primary source of identity and support. Given the centrality of families in any primary prevention effort, it is important to recognize and take into account family diversity. In the implementation of selected and indicated prevention programs, effectiveness may be contingent upon the involvement of crucial family members as identified by the family itself. Working within a specific frame of the family concept, Neergaard (1990) described an interesting proposal wherein foster grandmothers were to serve as role models for mothers at risk for abusing or neglecting their children. This primary prevention program was targeted for an indicated group of mothers and children at risk. As such, it was designed to involve trained foster grandmothers to provide support and to model appropriate parenting skills to the mothers.

Although the significance of the community in the child's and family's life is widely acknowledged, the definition of community, as the definition of family, may vary considerably. However a community is defined, it provides the physical and psychological context for support and identity. For both children and families, community contributes to a sense of belonging and connectedness. Marshall (1993) underscores the importance of community by stating that effective schools are those that foster a sense of community among students. That sense of community no doubt reflects the elements of responsibility, shared effort, tolerance, and valuing of the individual found to characterize undermanned environments (Schoggen, 1981). In the context of schools, this takes the form of opportunities for students to participate meaningfully not only in academic and extracurricular programs but also in the management, decision making and operation of school life. Synergistic effects can be achieved when the philosophy of schooling is changed from that of an institution to that of a community in which students, teachers, and staff work toward common learning goals. In the context of the larger community, neighborhoods, religious bodies and, civic and social agencies may, in a similar way, serve as important resource in primary prevention efforts.

Although community and culture are not synonymous, they often overlap in significant ways. In some instances, a community may be reflected by a culture, in another, the community encompasses a diversity of cultures. A family's sense of identity is often framed by the values, customs, and practices a culture defines. In many instances, religious beliefs also frame the family's identity, with ceremony, rituals, and celebrations contributing stability and meaning to life. The importance families place on values and beliefs is essential to consider because they are likely to play key roles in mediating responsiveness to prevention initiatives. Thus, the religious community can and should be involved in the design and implementation of prevention programs. Illustrative of the important mediating role played by a church is a smoking-cessation program for African-American men involving the collaboration of pastor and volunteers (Stillman, Bone, Rand, Levine, & Becker, 1993). Houses of worship, synagogues, temples, and mosques and their congregations are a special community resource that can be drawn upon increasingly, not only in disease prevention efforts but more importantly, in the promotion of well-being among children and families.

The final three guiding principles confirm the place of physical and psychological well-being of children and families as a priority in developing primary prevention programs. Given that many of the disorders of children have psychological manifestations, prevention efforts may focus directly on promoting psychological functioning. Such efforts, however, must be put into context, recognizing the dependency of psychological well-being on physical well-being. The health of many children is compromised by inadequate nutrition and preventable childhood illnesses, placing them at significant psychological risk. Investment in nutritional programs, immunization, and expanded physical education programs would constitute a comprehensive primary prevention agenda for all children. Building on a foundation of physical well-being, the environments for children also must foster personal well-being through an ethic of caring (Noddings, 1984) wherein feelings are nurtured and respected. The need for the cultural environment to promote a sense of meaning, purpose, and well-being of youth has been eloquently summarized by Eckersley (1993). "Having fostered the excessive emphasis on the individual and the material, science is now leading us back to a world view that pays more attention to the communal and the spiritual by revealing the extent of our interrelationship and interdependence with the world around us" (p. 518). In homes, schools, and communities that lack a sense of caring and nurturing, it is unlikely that children will experience much joy (Cottle, 1993). In homes, schools, and communities in which children are prized and their feelings nurtured, the joys of childhood can be realized. There are many childhood joys; the joy of accomplishment, the joy of creativity, the joy of discovery, the joy of acceptance, the joy of responsibility, the joy of trust, and the joy of innocence. Promoting these childhood joys would constitute a noble agenda for the futures of children.

REFERENCES

Antonovsky, A. (1993). Complexity, conflict, chaos, coherence, and civility. *Social Science Medicine, 37*(8), 969–81.
Banks, J.A., & Banks, C.A. (1993). *Multicultural education: Issues and perspectives.* Boston: Allyn & Bacon.
Bearinger, L.H., & Gephart, J. (1993). Interdisciplinary education in adolescent health. *Journal of Paediatric Child Health, 29*(Suppl.)(1), S10–S15.
Belsky, J. (1980). Child maltreatment: An ecological integration. *American Psychologist, 35,* 320–335.
Buka, S., & Earls, F. (1993). Early determinants of delinquency and violence. *Health Affairs, 12*(4), 46–64.
Butcher, R.O. (1993). Managed care now and forever. *JAMA: Journal of the National Medical Association, 85*(7), 505–587.
Condry, J. (1993). Thief of time, unfaithful servant, television and the American child. *Daedalus, 122*(1), 259–278.
Cowen, E.L., & Lorion, R.P. (1976). Changing roles for the school mental health program. *Journal of School Psychology, 14*(2), 131–138.
Cottle, T.J. (1993). Witness of joy. *Daedalus, 122*(1), 123–150.
Csikszentmihalyi, M. (1993). Context of optimal growth in childhood. *Daedalus, 122*(1), 31–55.

DiClemente, R.J. (1993). Preventing HIV/AIDS among adolescents: Schools as agents of behavior change. *JAMA: Journal of the American Medical Association, 270*(6), 760–762.

Earls, F., & Carlson, M. (1993). Towards sustainable development for American families. *Daedalus, 122*(1), 93–121.

Eckersley, R. (1993). Failing a generation: The impact of culture on the health and well-being of youth. *Journal of Paediatric Child Health, 29*(Suppl.)(1), S16–S19.

Eisenberg, L. (1975). The ethics of intervention: Acting amidst and ambiguity. *Journal of Child Psychology and Psychiatry, 16*, 93–104.

Franklin, C. (1992). Alternative school programs for at-risk youths. *Social Work in Education, 14*(4), 239–251.

Garbarino, J. (1991). The human ecology of early risk. In S.J. Meisels & J. Shankoff (Eds.), *Handbook of early childhood intervention* (pp. 78–96). New York: Cambridge University Press.

Garbarino, J. (1994). Parenting in violent environments. *Zero to Three, 14*, 11.

Ginsberg, C., & Loffredo, L. (1993). Violence-Related attitudes and behaviors of high school students—New York City, 1992. *Journal of School Health, 63*(10), 438–440.

Gough, D. (1988). Approaches to child abuse prevention. In K. Browne, C. Davies & P. Stratton (Eds.), *Early prediction and prevention of child abuse* (pp. 107–120). New York: John Wiley & Sons.

Harold, R.D., & Harold, N.B. (1993). School-based clinics: A response to the physical and mental health needs of adolescents. *Health and Social Work, 18*(1), 65–74.

Harry, B. (1992). *Cultural diversity, family and the special education system: Communication and empowerment.* New York: Teachers College Press.

Hill, R. (1972). *The strength of black families.* New York: Emerson Hall.

Hill, R. (1993). *Research on the African American family: A holistic perspective.* Westport, CT: Auburn House.

Hobbs, N. (1966). Helping disturbed children: Psychological and ecological strategies. *American Psychologist, 21*, 1105–1115.

Hoffman, L.W., & Manis, J.D. (1979). The value of children in the United States: A new approach to the study of fertility. *Journal of Marriage and the Family, 41*(3), 583–596.

Hutson, H.R., Anglin, D., & Pratts, M.J. (1994). Adolescents and children injured or killed in drive-by shootings in Los Angeles. *New England Journal of Medicine, 330*(5), 324–327.

Jaffe, P.G., Sudermann, M., Reilzel, D., & Killip, S.M. (1992). An evaluation of a secondary school primary prevention program on violence and intimate relationships. *Violence and Victims, 7*(2), 129–146.

Jee, M. (1993). School-based health clinics now seen as key health site. *Journal of American Health Policy, 3*(3), 53–54.

Kaufman, J., Cook, A., Arny, L., Jones, B., & Pittinsky, T. (1994). Problems defining resiliency: Illustrations from the study of maltreated children. *Development & Psychopathology, 6*(1), 215–229.

Kaufman, J., & Ziegler, E. (1992). The prevention of child maltreatment: Programming research and policy. In D.J. Willis, E.W. Holden, & M. Rosenberg (Eds.), *Prevention of child maltreatment: Developmental and ecological perspectives* (269–295). New York: John Wiley & Sons.

Kellam, S.G., & Werthamer-Larsson, L. (1986). Developmental epidemiology: A basis for prevention. In M. Kessler & S.E. Goldston (Eds.), *A decade of prog-*

ress in *primary prevention* (pp. 154–180). Hanover, NH: University Press of New England.

Klerman, L. (1991). *Alive and well: A research and policy review of health programs for poor young children.* New York: National Center for Children in Poverty.

Marshall, K. (1993). Teachers and schools—What makes a difference: A principal's perspective. *Daedalus, 122*(1), 209–241.

Martin, D.A. (1992). Children in peril: A mandate for change in health and policies for low-income children. *Family and Community Health, 15*(1), 75–90.

Minow, M., & Weissbourd, R. (1993). Social movements for children. *Daedalus, 122*(1), 1–29.

Neergaard, J.A. (1990). A proposal for a foster grandmother intervention program to prevent child abuse. *Public Health Reports, 105*(1), 89–93.

Nieto, S. (1992). *Affirming diversity: The socio-political context of multi-cultural education.* White Plains, NY: Longman Publishing.

Noddings, N. (1984). *A feminine approach to ethics and moral education.* Berkeley: University of California Press.

Prothrow-Stith, D. (1990). The epidemic of violence and its impact on the health care system. *Henry Ford Hospital Medical Journal, 38*(283), 175–178.

Prothrow-Stith, D. (1992). Can physicians help curb adolescent violence? *Hospital Practice, 27*(6), 193–207.

Rae-Grant, N. (1988). Primary prevention: Implications for the child psychiatrist. *Canadian Journal of Psychiatry, 33*(6), 433–442.

Raphael, B. (1993). Adolescent resilience: The potential impact of personal development in schools. *Journal of Paediatric Child Health, 29*(Suppl.)(1), S31–S36.

Redman, B.K. (1993). How to bring primary care back to patients. *Journal of American Health Policy, 3*(3), 42–45.

Remington, R.D. (1990). From preventive policy to preventive practice. *Preventive Medicine, 19,* 105–113.

Resnick, M.D., Harris, L.J., & Blum, R.W. (1993). The impact of caring and connectedness on adolescent health and well-being. *Journal of Paediatric Child Health, 29*(Suppl.)(1), S3–S9.

Rohrbach, L.A., Graham, J.W., & Hansen, W.B. (1993). Diffusion of a school-based substance abuse prevention program: Prediction of program implementation. *Preventive Medicine, 22*(2), 237–260.

Rosenberg, M.L. (1993). Academic medical centers have a major role in preventing violence. *Academic Medicine, 68*(4), 268–269.

Ruby, M. (1993). The children's crusade. *U.S. News & World Reports, 115*(23), 112.

Rutter, M. (1993a). Cause and course of psychopathology: Some lessons from longitudinal data. *Paediatric and Perinatal Epidemiology, 7,* 105–120.

Rutter, M. (1993b). Resilience: Some conceptual considerations. *Journal of Adolescent Health, 14*(8), 626–631.

Schoggen, P. (1978). Ecological psychology and mental retardation. In G.P. Sackett (Ed.), (pp. 33–62). *Observing behavior.* Baltimore: University Park Press.

Schorr, L. (1991). Children, families and the cycle of disadvantage. *Canadian Journal of Psychiatry, 36*(6), 437–441.

Schroeder, C.A., & Wilkerson, N.N. (1993). A multidisciplinary model for prenatal substance abuse prevention in rural Wyoming. *Family and Community Health, 16*(2), 20–29.

Segal, V.A. (1993). The relevance of marketing for child welfare agencies. *Children and Youth Services, 15*(5), 421–440.

Simeonsson, R.J., & Simeonsson, N.E. (1993). Children, families, and disability: Psychological dimensions. In J.L. Paul & R.J. Simeonsson (Eds.), *Children with special needs: Family culture of society* (pp. 25–50). Fort Worth, TX: HBJ Brace Jovanovich College Publishers.

Spivak, H. Hausman, A.J., & Prothrow-Stith, D. (1989). Practitioner's forum: Public health and the primary prevention of adolescent violence—the violence prevention project. *Violence and Victims, 4*(3), 203–212.

Stillman, F.A., Bone, L.R., Rand, C., Levine, D.M., & Becker, D.M. (1993). Heart, body, and soul: A church-based smoking-cessation program for urban African Americans. *Preventive Medicine, 22*, 335–349.

Tucker, H.S., & Roberts, M.C. (1990). Future issues in children's health care: Addressing psychosocial concerns. *Children's Health Care Journal, 19*(4), 199–208.

Walsh, D.C., Rudd, R.E., Moeykens, B.A., & Moliney, T.W. (1993). Social marketing for public health. *Health Affairs, 12*(2), 104–119.

Yoshikawa, H. (1994). Prevention as cumulative protection: Effects of early family support and education on chronic delinquency and its risks. *Psychological Bulletin, 115*(1), 28–54.

Ziegler, J.M. (1993). Education: The crucial variable for children? *Daedalus, 122*(1), 243–257.

Zins, J.E., Coyne, R.K., & Ponti, C.R. (1988). Primary prevention: Expanding the impact of psychological services in schools. *Schools Psychology Review, 17*(4), 542–549.

Index

Page numbers followed by *f* denote figures; those followed by *t* denote tables.

Abruptio placentae, 157
Access to care, 63–66, 80, 256
  medical home, 64–65
  secondary prevention, 65
  tertiary prevention, 65–66
Acquired immunodeficiency syndrome, 125, 139, 252, 323
ADHD, *see* Attention deficit hyperactivity disorder
Adolescent health
  co-morbidity of risk behaviors, 240–241
  motor vehicle–related deaths, 186
  pregnancy, 125–146
    see also Pregnancy in adolescence
  school-based clinics, 94–98, 306–307
  sexual behavior, 125–126, 136–138, 300
    demographic factors and, 137–138
    developmental factors and, 136
    family factors and, 137
    knowledge and attitudes about, 137
    psychosocial factors and, 136–137
    religious beliefs and, 138
  sexually transmitted diseases, 239–257
  suicide, 226–227
  use of birth control, 136
Advocacy group formation, 48
Affective disorders, *see* Internalizing disorders
Aid to Families with Dependent Children, 266
Alcohol use in pregnancy, 154–155

America 2000, 6, 313
American Alliance for Health, Physical Education, Recreation, and Dance, 90*t*
American Dental Association, 90*t*
American Heart Association, 91*t*
American Society of Dentistry for Children, 91*t*
Anxiety disorders, 223–224
Atherosclerosis, 84
At-risk status, 5
Attention deficit hyperactivity disorder (ADHD), 204–205
Autism, 17
Avoidant disorder, 223–224

Behavior disorders, 15, 62
  adolescent pregnancy and, 128–129
  externalizing, 203–213
    see also Externalizing disorders
  internalizing, 219–234
    see also Internalizing disorders
  prevalence of, 203–204, 220
  school dropout and, 22, 226
Behavior rating scales, 220
Bicycle helmets, 187, 189
Bicycle-related injuries, 187
Bienvenidos Family Services, 176–179
Birth cohort studies, 39
Birth control, 136, 139, 142
  condoms, 249, 254–255
Brookline Early Education Program, 42–43
Buddle Lane Family Center, 43–44
Burns, 188, 190, 316

345

Cardiovascular disease, 83–85, 315
  diet and, 83–85, 85t
  prevention of, 84–85, 85t, 99t, 315
  resource list on, 91t
  risk factors for, 79, 83
Catchment area identification, 45
Centers for Disease Control, 93t
Chancroid, 241
Chapter 1 programs, 33, 267–269, 276
Child abuse, 169–180
  Bienvenidos Family Services for prevention of, 176–179
    beliefs about family, 177
    challenges of model, 179
    family plans, 177
    family support, 179
    home-based services, 178
    model and program design, 178–179
    overview of community, 176–177
    program components, 177–178
  case example of, 169–170
  causes of, 171
  challenges to prevention approach for, 173
  drug use in pregnancy related to, 158
  ecological theory of, 170–171
  history of prevention efforts for, 172–173
  need for prevention perspective for, 171–172
  past efforts at secondary prevention of, 173–174
  poverty and, 169, 174
  prevalence of, 169
  primary prevention of, 180, 332–333
    need for, 174–176
  reasons for increase in, 169
Child Behavior Checklist, 220
Child Development Program of New Hampshire, 37–38
Child-Find, 308
Child Health Assistance Projects, 68
Child Health Report Card, 5
Child safety seats, 193–198, 196t
Children of Divorce Intervention Program, 231–232
Children with Special Health Care Needs, 55, 67

Children's Bureau, 172
Chlamydia trachomatis, 243, 245
Cholesterol, 84
Cincinnati Children's Hospital Medical Center Child Occupant Safety Program, 194–198, 196t
Coalition building, 45
Cocaine use in pregnancy, 156–157
Collaboration and coordination of services, 302–303
  for injury prevention, 193–194
  in maternal and child health, 57–58, 66–68
    among public and private health providers, 66–67
    between families and professionals, 67
    between health and education, 68
  at state and local levels, 48, 49
Community Integrated Services System, 60, 68
Community-based programs, 41–48, 302, 338–339
  Addison County, VT, Parent–Child Center, 41
  Brookline Early Education Program, 42–43
  Buddle Lane Family Center, 43–44
  for disease prevention, 92–94
  implementation of, 44–48
    building database, 45
    defining geographic catchment area, 45
    developing broad-based coalition, 45
    developing social marketing skills, 47–48
    establishing overall framework, 45–46, 46t–47t
    forming local advocacy group, 48
    providing array of programs of proved value, 46–47
  Lawrence-Weston Community Center, 44
  for maternal and child health, 57, 68–70
Co-morbidity
  of adolescent risk behaviors, 240–241

of externalizing disorders, 206
of internalizing disorders,
    224–225
Condom use, 249, 254–255
Conduct disorder, 205
Contextualism, 21
Contraception, 136, 139, 142
Coronary heart disease, 83–84
Counseling, for adolescent mothers,
    133–134
Culturally competent services, 58
Culture, 336, 339

Database development, 45
Demand for services, 4–5
Dental health, 77–78, 86–88, 87*t*,
    99*t*
  resource list for, 90*t*–91*t*
Depersonalization of community,
    333
Depression, 222–223
  co-morbidity with, 225
  hospitalization for, 226
  suicide and, 226–227
Developing Understanding of Self
    and Others, 231
Developmental disabilities, 17, 62
Diet, *see* Nutrition
Discovery School, 120
Disease prevention, 77–100, 339
  agenda for 21st century, 98–100,
    99*t*
  cardiovascular disease, 83–85, 85*t*
  case examples, 77–78
  constraints to preventive health
    care, 81
  new morbidity and, 80–83, 82*t*
  nutrition and, 91–92
  obesity, 88–90, 308–310
  oral health, 86–88, 87*t*
  resource lists for, 90*t*–91*t*, 93*t*
  school/community-oriented
    framework for, 92–94
  schools and, 78–80
  successful models for, 94–98
    Baltimore school-based health
      clinics, 94–95
    Chicago Ounce of Prevention
      Fund Toward Teen Health
      Centers, 95–96
    health and education partner-
      ship, 96–98

New Jersey School-Based Youth
    Services Program, 96
Divorce, 231–232
Down syndrome, 38
Drowning, 187–188
"Dual developmental crisis," 128
Dysthymia, 222–223

Early Intervention in Reading, 277,
    278*t*
Early intervention programs, 33,
    37–38, 312
  definition of, 60
  for literacy development, 271–277
  role of maternal and child health
    in, 62–70
Early Start, 175
Ecological psychology, 333
EDUCARE, 306
Education and training, 70–71
  for adolescent mothers, 132
  collaboration between health and
    education, 68
  health education, 61
    for school teachers, 79
  for injury prevention, 190
  of parents, *see* Parent training
    programs
  to prevent adolescent pregnancy,
    140–144
  to prevent obesity, 89
  to promote literacy development,
    268–291
  of service providers in primary
    prevention, 322–327, 323*t*
    disciplines, 71, 325–327
    roles, 322–323
    settings, 324–325
    skills, 323–324
  sex education, 252–254
  see also School issues
Education for All Handicapped
    Children Act (PL 94-142), 33,
    114
Education of the Handicapped Act
    Amendments (PL 99-457), 33,
    114
El Puente, 138, 142
Employability skills, 116
Environment
  child's transactions with, 24–26,
    25

Environment—*continued*
  modification of, 27
  overmanned, 333
Epidemiological approach, 16–19
Epidemiology, 13–29, 324
Excellence in Education movement, 111
Externalizing disorders, 203–213
  attention deficit hyperactivity disorder, 204–205
  case example of, 203
  classification and epidemiology of, 204–206
  cognitive factors and, 207
  co-morbidity of, 206
  conduct disorder, 205
  oppositional defiant disorder, 205
  parental and familial factors and, 208
  peer factors and, 209
  personal characteristics and, 206–207
  primary prevention of, 9*f*, 209–210, 211*t*
  rationale for, 212–213
  psychosocial framework for understanding of, 206
  school factors and, 22, 208–209
  secondary prevention of, 9*f*, 210, 211*t*
  tertiary prevention of, 9*f*, 210–212, 211*t*

Falls, 185, 192
Family, 312
  adolescent sexual behavior and, 137, 252
  of child with externalizing behavior disorder, 208
  of child with internalizing problems, 230
  collaboration with professionals, 67, 304, 312–313, 337–338
  coping mechanisms of, 335–336
  culture and, 336, 339
  individualized service plan for, 114–115
"Family Voices," 67
Family-centered care, 56–57
Fat, dietary, 83–84
Fetal alcohol effects, 155
Fetal alcohol syndrome, 155
Fires, 188, 190
First Steps, 276–277
Fitness, 79, 90*t*–91*t*, 99*t*, 309
Fitz-Hugh-Curtis syndrome, 244
Fluoridated water, 86
Food and Drug Administration, 93*t*
Food and Nutrition Information Center, 91*t*, 93*t*
Foster care, 158
Framework development, 45–46, 46*t*–47*t*
Frequency of problems, 16–18, 17*f*

Gonorrhea, 241, 243
Granuloma inguinale, 241

Head Start, 33, 37, 50, 272, 312
Health belief model, 249–250
Health care reform, 98–100
Health education, 61
  for school teachers, 79
Health insurance, 80
Health profile of children, 80–82
Health-education collaboration, 68
Healthy children, 310–312
Healthy Cities, 6
Healthy communities, 314–315
Healthy Communities 2000, 6
Healthy families, 312–313
Healthy For Life, 306
Healthy People 2000, 6, 60, 67, 78, 80, 83, 87, 89, 97, 98, 184
Healthy schools, 313–314
Healthy Start, 62
Herpes simplex virus, 244, 245
High School and Beyond Database, 107, 110
Home visiting, 66, 178, 303–305, 314
Homebuilders, 171
Homicide, 186, 329
Hospitalization, psychiatric, 226
Human immunodeficiency virus, 139, 252, 323
Human papillomavirus, 244

Identity formation, 251
Immunization, 62, 63, 80
Individualized family service plan, 114–115
Individuals with Disabilities Education Act (PL 101-476), 33, 39, 50, 64, 68, 70, 220
   relationship of maternal and child health to, 54–55
Infant mortality, 33–35, 60, 62
Infertility, 241, 244
Injuries, pediatric, 183–199
   case examples of, 183–184
   common mechanisms of, 185–188, 186t–187t
      bicycle-related injuries, 187
      drowning, 187–188
      fires and burns, 188
      homicide and suicide, 186
      motor vehicle–related injuries, 186, 186t
      pedestrian injuries, 186–187
   cost of, 185
   deaths from, 185
   epidemiology of, 185
   overview of, 184–185
   prevalence of, 184
Injury prevention, 10f, 188–199, 316
   Cincinnati Children's Hospital Medical Center Child Occupant Safety Program, 194–198
      interventions and preliminary outcomes, 195–198, 196t
      problem identification, 194–195
   evaluating programs for, 192–193
   media campaigns for, 195, 197–198
   methods of, 190
      educational, 190
      mandated, 190
      passive versus active, 190
   multidisciplinary collaborative programs for, 193–194
   selecting strategies for, 191–194
   tactics for, 190–191
      indicated, 191
      selected, 191
      universal, 191
   targets for, 188–190
Intensity of problems, 16–18, 17f
Intergenerational literacy programs, 272–273
Internalizing disorders, 219–234
   case examples of, 219
   complications of, 225–227
      psychiatric hospitalization, 226
      school dropout, 226
      suicide, 226–227
   conceptualization of, 220
   focus of future research on, 233–234
   primary prevention of, 230–233
      indicated, 232–233
      selected, 231–232
      universal, 231
   research bias related to, 233
   risk chains of, 220–227, 221
      anxiety disorders, 223–224
      co-morbidity, 224–225
      depressive disorders, 222–223
      loneliness, 221–222
      secondary level, 221–225
      social withdrawal, 222
      tertiary level, 225–227
   risk factors for, 227, 228t–229t
   transactional model for prevention of, 229–230
International statistics, 33–35
Intervention and treatment services, *see also* Primary prevention
   demand for, 4–5
   determining crucial times for, 26–27
   eligibility for, 14, 35
   emphasis on, 13–14
   peer-assisted, 323
   priorities for, 6
   for substance-abusing pregnant women, 159–160

Job Training Partnership Act, 113
Joy, 340
Juvenile delinquency, *see* Externalizing disorders

Kauai Study, 39

Lawrence-Weston Community Center, 44, 48
Learning disabilities, 22, 62, 130

Literacy development, 265–291
　addressing problem of illiteracy, 268–271
　case examples of, 265, 290–291
　cost of illiteracy, 266–267
　early intervention for, 271–277
　　Early Intervention in Reading, 277, 278*t*
　　First Steps, 276–277
　　first-grade programs, 273–277
　　intergenerational programs, 272–273
　　preschool programs, 272
　　Reading Recovery, 274–275, 284–290
　　Success for All, 275–276
　effective instructional practices for, 277–284
　epidemiology of illiteracy, 266–268
　guidelines for children who have fallen behind, 283–284
　　providing for accelerated progress, 283–284, 290
　manifestations of illiteracy, 266–268
　　primary, 267–268
　　secondary, 267
　　tertiary, 266–267
　primary prevention for, 271
　at secondary level, 268–271
　　Chapter 1 programs, 33, 268–269, 276
　　pull-out versus in-class models, 270–271
　　special education programs, 269–270
　selected interventions for children at risk, 281–283
　　employing best teachers, 283, 289–290
　　establishing intervention and classroom reading program congruence, 281, 287–288
　　including direct instruction, 282, 288–289
　　increasing opportunities to learn, 281–282, 288
　　individualizing instruction, 282, 289
　　monitoring and reinforcing children, 283, 289
　at tertiary level, 268
　　universal practices for all beginning programs, 278–281
　　being aware of instructional goals, 279, 285
　　ensuring opportunities to learn, 279, 285
　　focusing on real reading, 278–279, 284–285
　　including phonemic awareness, 280–281, 286–287, 287*f*
　　incorporating writing, 280, 286
　　providing appropriate instructional level materials, 279–280, 285–286
　　spending time reading, 279, 285
　　teaching strategies and ability to transfer them, 280, 286
Loneliness, 221–222
Low birth weight infants, 33, 34, 62, 128, 301
　due to maternal cocaine use, 157
　due to maternal tobacco use, 156
Lymphogranuloma venereum, 241

Marijuana use in pregnancy, 156
Maternal and child health, 53–71
　characteristics of service system for, 55–59
　　community-based services, 57
　　coordinated services, 57–58
　　culturally competent care, 58
　　family-centered care, 56–57
　　inclusive primary care, 58–59
　legislation on, 53–55
　relationship to Part H of Individuals with Disabilities Education Act, 54–55
　role in early intervention, 63–70
　　creating partnerships among providers, 66–68
　　ensuring access to health and medical services, 64–66
　　facilitating development of community-based care, 68–70
　role in prevention and intervention, 59–63
　　health education, 61
　　infant and young child care, 62–63
　　prenatal care, 61–62
　sources of support for, 59–60
　training professionals for new

roles and responsibilities in, 70–71
Maternal and Child Health Services Programs, 54
Media exposure, 4
Medicaid, 58–59, 66–68, 159
Medical home, 64–65
Mental retardation, 155
Minorities, 335
  adolescent sexual behavior among, 137–138
  culturally competent system of care for, 58
  obesity among, 309
  response to drug abuse prevention programs, 308
  school dropout among, 22, 107–109
  substance abuse among women, 152
  violence among males, 329
Miracle in East Harlem, 314
Mother–child relationship, 130, 133
Motor vehicle–related injuries, 183–184, 186, 186t

National Agricultural Library, 91t, 93t
National Center for Chronic Disease Prevention and Health Promotion, 93t
National Center for Health Statistics, 93t
National Center on Child Abuse and Neglect, 172
National Health Interview Survey, 59
National Household Survey on Drug Abuse, 152–153
National Institutes of Health, 93t
National Maternal and Child Health Clearinghouse, 91t
Natural history of disease, 20–21
Neisseria gonorrhea, 243
Neonatal Behavioral Assessment Scale, 133
Norplant, 139
Nutrition, 77–78
  cardiovascular disease and, 83–85, 85t
  dental disease and, 87
  obesity and, 88–90

primacy in child health, 91–92
resource list for, 93t

Obesity, 78, 79, 88–90, 308–310
  cause of, 88
  definition of, 88
  diet and, 89
  medical consequences of, 90
  prevalence of, 88, 308–309
  prevention of, 89, 99t, 309–310
  resource list on, 91t
Odds ratios, 21
  for relationships of grade retention and secondary school outcome, 331f
Office of Special Education and Rehabilitative Services, 68
Omnibus Budget Reconciliation Act of 1989 (PL 101-239), 54, 59
Operationalizing target conditions, 19–20, 20f
Oppositional defiant disorder, 205
Oral health, 77–78, 86–88, 87t, 99t
  resource list for, 90t–91t
Orthopedic impairments, 17
Ounce of Prevention Fund, 95
Outcome evaluation, 28–29
Overanxious disorder, 223–224

Parent training programs, 312, 336
  for adolescent mothers, 133
  for child abuse prevention, 175
  for injury prevention, 196
Parent–Child Center of Addison County, VT, 41
Parent–child interactions, 300
Part H programs, 33, 39, 50, 64, 68, 70
  relationship of maternal and child health to, 54–55
Passive smoking, 156
Peabody Picture Vocabulary Test, 273
Pedestrian injuries, 186–187
Pediatrics, preventive, 81
Peer relations, 307
  externalizing behavior disorders and, 209
  internalizing problems and, 221–222, 229–230

Pelvic inflammatory disease, 241, 244–245
Perihepatitis, 244
Phonemic awareness, 280–281, 286–287, 287f
Physical education, 79, 309
Policy, 301–303
    based on deficit model, 35–37, 36f
    examples of, 37–38
    influence of social marketing on, 324
    of U.S. compared with other countries, 33–35
Population screening, 19
Poverty, 4, 62, 97
    adolescent sexual behavior and, 137
    child abuse and, 169, 174
    school dropout and, 104, 117
Pregnancy and drug use, 151–166
    case example of, 151
    child abuse and, 158
    complexity of, 152, 158
    complications of, 154–158
        alcohol, 154–155
        cocaine, 156–157
        marijuana, 156
        tobacco, 156
    cost estimates for, 158–159
    effect of discontinuing drugs during pregnancy, 159
    primary prevention of, 160t, 160–166
        at indicated level, 164–166, 165t
        models for, 160t, 160–161, 161f
        multidisciplinary approach for, 165
        at selected level, 163–164, 164t
        at universal level, 162–163, 163t
    secondary prevention of, 161f, 161–162
    substance abuse in women, 152–154
        characteristics of, 153–154
        prevalence of, 152–153, 153f
        risk factors for, 155t
    tertiary prevention of, 161f, 162
    treatment options for, 159–160
Pregnancy in adolescence, 125–146
    case example of, 125
    consequences for child, 129–130
        emotional, 129
        intellectual and school, 129–130
        physical, 129
    consequences for mother, 128–129
        economic, 128
        physical, 128
        social and emotional, 128–129
    consequences for mother–child relationship, 130
    cost of, 134
    international rates of, 34
    primary prevention of, 127, 134–146
        accessibility of contraception for, 142
        active adolescent participation in programs for, 144
        age of participants for, 142–143
        barriers to, 140t, 144–146
        by changing attitudes, 141
        community involvement for, 142
        context of program for, 143–144
        educational programs for, 140–141
        facilitating factors for, 140t
        for indicated groups, 138–139
        levels of, 134–136, 135f
        by promoting future orientation, 141–142
        by providing structured after-school activities, 143–144
        for selected groups, 136–138
        systems-level considerations for, 142–144
        universal programs for, 139–142
    recurrent, 128
    school programs for, 116
    scope of problem, 126–127
    secondary prevention strategies for, 127, 130–134, 132t
        counseling support, 133–134
        education and training opportunities, 132
        parent training, 133
    tertiary prevention strategies for, 127, 130, 131t
Prenatal care, 61–62
    for substance-abusing women, 154
President's Council on Physical Fitness and Sports, 79, 90t

Prevalence data, 15
Prevention, *see* Primary prevention; Secondary prevention; Tertiary prevention
Primary care services, 58–59
Primary prevention, 1
  of adolescent pregnancy, 127, 134–146
  anonymity of, 327
  assumptions for, 7–9
  of child abuse, 174–176
  definition of, 7
  of disease, 77–100
  of drug use in pregnancy, 160–166, 163*t*–165*t*
  of externalizing behavior disorders, 209–210, 211*t*, 212–213
  goal of, 28
  of illiteracy, 271
  of internalizing disorders, 230–233
  lack of emphasis on, 13–14
  in maternal and child health programs, 60–63
  population-based, 14, 28, 302
    collaboration at state and local levels, 48, 49*f*
    communitywide programs, 41–48
    rationale for, 40, 40
    statewide programs, 48–50
  primary promotion and, 7, 7*f*
  of school dropout, 106, 112–120
  service settings for, 303, 324–325
  of sexually transmitted diseases, 242*t*, 248–256
  value of, 1
  of violence, 327–330
Primary prevention agenda, 6–7, 299–317
  advocacy for, 1
  ecological model for, 310, 311*t*
  effective elements of, 9–11, 310–317, 311*t*
  expanding paradigms and priorities for, 300–301
  indicated programs, 308–310
  policy and, 301–303
  practices for advancement of, 303, 304*t*
  prioritizing targets for, 16–18, 17*f*, 303, 304*t*
  problems in implementation of, 14–15
  scientific approach to, 316
  selected programs, 307–308
  universal programs, 303–307
Primary prevention initiative development, 19–29
  defining nature of risk in child and environmental transactions, 24–26, 25*f*
  differentiating characteristics of universal, selected, and indicated prevention, 26
  generating risk models and causal, sequential, or risk chains, 20–24, 21*f*, 23*f*, 24*t*
  monitoring and evaluating outcomes, 28–29
  operationalizing target conditions and risk factors, 19–20, 20*f*
  prioritizing form and nature of efforts, 27
  proposing temporal frames for implementation, 26–27
Project Health P.A.C.T., 90*t*
Promoting children's well-being, 3–11, 13, 299, 310, 321–340
  by early intervention, 312
  effective elements of programs for, 9–11, 310–317, 311*t*
  guiding principles for, 332–340, 337*t*
  by providing structure, 310–312
  research on, 327–332
  training for, 322–327, 323*t*
    disciplines, 325–327
    roles, 322–323
    settings, 324–325
    skills, 323–324
Protection motivation theory, 249
Protective factors, 1, 301
Public Law 94-142, *see* Education for All Handicapped Act
Public Law 99-457, *see* Education of the Handicapped Act Amendments
Public Law 101-239, *see* Omnibus Budget Reconciliation Act of 1989
Public Law 101-476, *see* Individuals with Disabilities Education Act

Reading, *see* Literacy development
Reading Recovery, 274–275, 284–290
  awareness of instructional goals, 285
  benefits of, 290
  employing best teachers, 289–290
  ensuring accelerated progress, 290
  ensuring opportunity to learn, 285
  establishing intervention and classroom reading program congruence, 287–288
  focus on real reading, 284–285
  including direct instruction, 288–289
  incorporating writing, 286
  individualizing instruction, 289
  monitoring and reinforcing children, 289
  phonemic awareness, 286–287, 287*f*
  providing appropriate instructional level materials, 285–286
  providing increased opportunity to learn, 288
  research on, 290
  spending time reading, 285
  teaching strategies and ability to transfer them, 286
Reality Therapy, 231
Regular education initiative, 112
Relative risk, 18–19, 21–22, 23*f*
Relative resilience, 329–330, 331*f*
Religious beliefs, 138
Research issues, 327–332
  internalizing problems, 233–234
  Reading Recovery, 290
  school dropout, 121
Resilience, 1, 27, 301, 333
Resource lists, 90*t*–91*t*, 93*t*
Risk chains, 9, 15
  generation of, 20–24, 21*f*
  for internalizing problems, 220–227, 221*f*
Risk factors, 1, 16–19
  accumulation over time, 39
  for cardiovascular disease, 79, 83
  child–environmental transactions and, 24–26, 25*f*
  early risk scores as predictors of future developmental status, 39
  identification of, 21
  for internalizing disorders, 227, 228*t*–229*t*
  predisposing and precipitating, 25–26
  for school dropout, 22–24, 24*t*, 106–109, 108*t*
  for substance abuse, 155*t*
Robert Wood Johnson Foundation, 95, 97

Safe Kids Campaign, 16
School dropout, 34, 103–121
  among minority students, 22, 107–109
  behavior disorders and, 22, 226
  case examples of, 103–104
  epidemiology of, 104–106, 105*f*–106*f*
  failure and, 110–112
  future research on, 121
  poverty and, 104, 117
  prediction of, 107
  prevention of, 106, 112–120, 331
    dimensions of, 114
    focus on relationships, 117
    individualized programs for, 114–116
    Orange County, FL, plan for, 119–120, 120*t*
    steps toward agenda for, 117–119
    by targeting at-risk groups, 116
  reasons for, 109–110
  relative risk for, 22, 23*f*
  risk factors for, 22–24, 24*t*, 106–109, 108*t*
  societal losses from, 105
School issues, 6, 11, 328
  academic achievement, 6, 39
  alternative schools, 116, 313–314
  barriers to high school graduation, 110–111
  children's health, 78–80
  community–school relationship, 305–306
  disease prevention, 92–94
  drug abuse prevention programs, 307–308
  elements of effective schools, 334

externalizing behavior disorders, 208–209
improving health of schools, 313–314
interdisciplinary teams, 326
literacy development, 265–291
problems in children of adolescent mothers, 129–130
school failure, 110–112
social service provision, 307
special education services, 33, 62–63
    for reading instruction, 269–271
vocational-technical schools, 116
School-based clinics, 94–98, 306–307, 325, 336
    Baltimore model, 94–95
    Chicago Toward Teen Health Centers, 95–96
    model for establishment of, 97–98
    New Jersey School-Based Youth Services Program, 96
Schools Without Failure, 231
School-Within-A-School program, 116
Secondary prevention, 7
    of adolescent pregnancy, 127, 130–134, 132*t*
    of child abuse, 173–174
    of drug use in pregnancy, 161*f*, 161–162
    of externalizing behavior disorders, 210, 211*t*
    of illiteracy, 268–271
    of injuries, 10*f*
    of juvenile delinquency, 9*f*
    in maternal and child health, 65
    of sexually transmitted diseases, 248
Self-efficacy, 250
Sensory impairments, 17
Separation anxiety disorder, 223–224
Service delivery systems, 80–81, 335
Settings for services, 303, 324–325
Sex education, 252–254
Sexual behavior, adolescent, 125–126, 136–138, 252, 300
    see also Pregnancy in adolescence
Sexually transmitted diseases, 125, 139, 239–257
    case example of, 239–240

co-morbidity of adolescent risk behaviors, 240–241
costs of, 241
manifestations of, 241–243
prevalence in adolescents, 242–243
    Chlamydia trachomatis, 243
    gonorrhea, 243
    herpes simplex virus, 244
    human papillomavirus, 244
    syphilis, 243
primary prevention of, 242*t*, 248–256
    indicated, 256
    selected, 254–256
    social-psychological constructs, 249–251
    universal, 251–254
secondary prevention of, 248
tertiary prevention of, 247–248
tertiary problems of, 244–247
    infant morbidity, 245–246
    pelvic inflammatory disease–related complications, 244–245
    psychological reactions, 246–247
Silver Spring Neighborhood Center, Milwaukee, 93–94
Social marketing, 47–48, 302, 323–324
Social Security Act, 53–54
Social withdrawal, 222
Societal goals, 6
Special Projects of Regional and National Significance, 59
Sports-related injuries, 185
Stanford Heart Disease Prevention Program, 45
State Systems Development Initiative, 59, 60
Statewide programs, 48–50
    Children with Special Health Care Needs, 55
Structure, 310–312
Substance abuse
    among women, 152–154, 153*f*
    during pregnancy, 151–166
    prevention efforts in schools, 307–308
    risk factors for, 155*t*
Success for All, 275–276
Sudden infant death syndrome, 127*f*

Sugar consumption, 87
Suicide, 186, 219, 226–227
Symptom-oriented problem solving, 300
Syphilis, 241, 243, 245–246

Technology, 3–4, 300–301
Teen Outreach Project, 140, 142
Television viewing, 300, 309, 324
Television violence, 189
Tertiary prevention, 7
 of adolescent pregnancy, 127, 130, 131t
 of drug use in pregnancy, 161f, 162
 of externalizing behavior disorders, 210–212, 211t
 of illiteracy, 268
 of injuries, 10f
 of juvenile delinquency, 9f
 in maternal and child health, 65
 of sexually transmitted diseases, 247–248
Thumb sucking, 86
Title I programs, 269, 271
Title V, 53–54, 67
Title V Block Grants, 59, 61
Tobacco use in pregnancy, 156
Tooth decay, 86–88, 87t

Tooth eruption, 86
Toward Teen Health Centers, 95–96
Toyota Families for Learning Programs, 273
Tubo-ovarian abscess, 244
"21st-Century School," 48

U.S. Army Exceptional Family Member Program in Germany, 37–38
U.S. Maternal and Child Health Bureau, 59, 63, 68
U.S. Perinatal Collaborative Study, 39

Values, 334
Vicious circle, 5, 34f
Violence, 4, 186, 327–330
 seen on television, 189
Vulnerability, 1, 27

Water fluoridation, 86
Workforce 2000, 105
World Health Organization Healthy Cities Project, 45
Writing skills, 280, 286